UNION OF THE

SOVIET SOCIALIST

REPUBLICS

AN

FINLAND

Helsinki

Leningrad

holm

ESTONIA

BALTIC

Z.A.T. RigaVIA

DERATION

LITHUANIA

Kaunas

Königsberg

ENTRAL

Warsaw

UROPEAN

OLAND

ATION

ARIA

west

NGARY

LKAN

ROUMANIA

Bucharest

Sebastopol

lgrade

AVIA

DERATION

BLACK SEA

Sofia

ALBANIA

BULGARIA

Istanbul

TURKEY

GREECE

Moscow

CASPIAN SEA

TURKEY

Athens

C.W.B

Crete

Cyprus

THE NEW EUROPE

G. B.

THE MACMILLAN COMPANY
NEW YORK · BOSTON · CHICAGO
DALLAS · ATLANTA · SAN FRANCISCO

THE NEW EUROPE

BY

BERNARD NEWMAN

With Maps

NEW YORK

THE MACMILLAN COMPANY

1943

SET UP BY BROWN BROTHERS LINOTYPERS
PRINTED IN THE UNITED STATES OF AMERICA
BY THE FERRIS PRINTING COMPANY

CONTENTS

The opinions expressed in the book are purely personal, and bear no relation to the author's present official appointment.

LIST OF ILLUSTRATIONS

vii

CHAPTER ONE

APPROACH TO THE PROBLEM

I

SOME of the primary causes of the present war are to be found in the treaties of peace which finished the last. We must be very careful that this does not happen again.

Mr. Lloyd George confessed in Parliament on a famous occasion that he had never heard of Teschen. Few of the members who taunted him had ever heard of it either. An ancient but obscure duchy, only 850 square miles in extent, but in older days disputed by Bohemian and Polish princes because of its rich mineral deposits—and in 1919 Poles and Czechs were quarrelling over it again. The British Prime Minister had never heard of it. Could he be expected to know all about such trifles?

Yet Teschen was one of the brooks which make the flowing river. The present war can be traced directly to the duchy of which Mr. Lloyd George had never heard. Because of the tension over Teschen, relations between Poland and Czechoslovakia were strained. Here were two nations of the same racial stock, whose main interests were identical, who were so obviously intended as the first victims of the Nazi menace; yet instead of collaborating, they quarrelled over Teschen.

At the height of the Sudeten crisis, Poland pressed an ultimatum on Prague: the Czechs, apparently abandoned by their allies, could scarcely resist: Polish troops marched into Teschen. Had the Poles stood by the Czechs, there might have been no Munich. Had there been no German seizure of Czechoslovakia, there might have been no Polish war—for the German occupation of Slovakia exposed the Polish southern

flank and made disaster inevitable. Many of the present misfortunes of Poland and Czechoslovakia can thus be traced
directly to the quarrel over this insignificant little duchy of
which Mr. Lloyd George had never heard.

These two countries have already plainly shown that they
realise their tragic error, and that it shall not happen again.
But there are many other Teschens scattered over Europe.

The time has come when their problems should be closely
examined: indeed, it is overdue. It is a common complaint
that in 1918 we won the war, and that in 1919 the politicians
lost the peace. Even if the jibe were true, the blame would not
rest solely on the politicians, but on the people, who were
singularly uninterested in European affairs. We shall lose the
peace again unless we take at least as much trouble over the
post-war settlement as is done over the World Series.

(H. G. Wells argues that the post-war indifference of the
British to world politics was due to their preoccupation with
economic troubles and disillusion over the 'land fit for heroes'
theme. It is true that a man who is unemployed or engaged in
a fierce competitive struggle for a livelihood can scarcely be
expected to be vitally interested in the troubles of Balkan peoples. With better conditions the outlook should change: already there are welcome signs of a wide extension of what has
been called the 'Trade Union outlook.' An extra nickel an hour
is important to a man on a small wage: but a Balkan squabble
which may lead to a European war is even more important.)

A surprising number of British and American people re-
sponded to German propaganda claims that the majority of the
ills of Europe were due to the Peace Treaties which concluded
the first World War. (Incidentally, how many people who
echoed the German parrot cry ever read the Treaty of Versailles? Today we are agreed that the Atlantic Charter shall be
the basis of the new peace. The readers of a book like this will
be among the more intelligent and better-informed sections of
the British and American communities; this is no flattery—it is
unfortunately true that they would not be reading the book if

they were not. But how many of them could quote the clauses of the Atlantic Charter?)

The impression was created that the men who gathered in Paris in 1919 to make the peace were either a pack of incompetent fools or a gang of revengeful jingos, or both. This idea is utterly absurd. It is perfectly true that some of the statesmen of the day were Nationalists, and were too old to become Internationalists, but of their intelligence or good intentions there was never any doubt; and among the others were men like Masaryk and Smuts, outstanding statesmen of their generation. Further, behind them, for consultation and advice, they had a remarkable collection of experts. The American delegation was particularly impressive: because of the mixed origin of its people, the United States has always been interested in the ethnic problems of Europe, and could, and did, produce a remarkable array of men of surprising knowledge; nor for that matter did we have cause to be ashamed of the intelligence and knowledge of the British delegation.

The greatest difficulty confronting the Allied leaders in 1919 was not the attitude of the defeated enemy, but that of their own publics at home. In all the victorious countries there was complete confusion of public opinion; millions of people seemed to imagine that a clean cut could be made between the state of war and the state of peace; now that victory had been won, they demanded immediately the promised blessings and advantages. The leaders might be well advised, but public opinion generally was shockingly ill-informed of the questions at issue.

It is true that political and nationalist opinion affected the peace negotiations. The Americans, having entered the war with natural reluctance, were anxious to get out of it quickly, rapidly ridding themselves of any lingering effects. Thus President Wilson in his idealistic schemes found himself moving without the backing of his people. In Great Britain, a 'khaki' election had been held, with the inevitable result that the British statesmen were pledged to make the most exacting demands on their defeated enemy. Fortunately, most of them had the common sense to realise that many of these demands were simply ridiculous. The French leaders had one natural dominating idea—that never again should the provinces of France be despoiled by German invaders.

There were two possible approaches to the problem of relations with Germany. We had proclaimed that our main objective was the destruction of German militarism: now, apparently, we had destroyed it, and a democratic government had assumed office. One policy would have been to sustain and support that democratic government, enabling it to suppress the strong element of militarism which still survived in Germany. The alternative policy was that favoured by France— to hold the Germans down militarily so that there should never be any question of German aggression again. If either of these policies had been followed, Europe would not have been at war today; instead, however, we wobbled in confusion from one to another. The power of the democratic German government was never very pronounced, and was weakened by the continuance of the blockade: further, it had perforce to accept conditions of peace which appeared to the Germans as harsh— any conditions appear as harsh to a sullen, defeated nation. At the right moment, therefore, it was possible for the militarists to blame the democratic government for the peace treaty it had signed: actually it had no option.

It is good to note that one lesson at least has been learned from our policy in 1919: there will be no food blockade at the end of this war.[1] Indeed, we have already organised, in conjunction with the United States, the provision of food supplies to the occupied countries and Germany immediately on the conclusion of hostilities. Generosity is likely to be a more effective weapon than hunger.

One difficulty, however, is very likely to arise again—many

---

[1] Actually, the food blockade was raised soon after the Armistice of 1918, but the confusion in Germany and the disorganisation of transport all over the world were so great that few supplies reached the enemy countries for some time.

of the decisions of the statesmen in Paris were hasty improvisations because of the insistent demand from all corners that the armies should be demobilised and the troops allowed to return to their homes. Indeed, this demand reached such proportions and yielded such results that had the Germans been able to attain any degree of unity, even in spite of the weapons they had given up, they might have been able to resume the fight in 1919!

It seems certain that the same sentimental cry will arise at the end of the present war. Most of our troops are civilians in uniform, and once the war is over they will want to get home. Actually, the situation this time need not be as serious as it was in 1919. If every form of military aircraft is taken from defeated Germany, then the Allied Air Force alone would be able to hold the balance of power necessary to ensure that no German army could ever take the field again.

At the same time a considerable land force will necessarily be required for the policing of Germany. It may prove that regular armies and the air corps of the United Nations, together with units from the occupied countries, will be sufficient for this purpose. For the maintenance of local order German units under Allied direction might usefully be employed.

(One interesting suggestion might be considered. There is some inevitable discontent amongst the troops because some of their fellows in war work have been earning high wages during the war, whilst the soldiers exist on their very limited pay. Further, the men already in jobs stand a better chance of retaining them when the war is over. It is argued that, since it is possible to train men for internal police duties in a few weeks, why should not munition workers, who have had the better end of the deal, be sent as an army of occupation into Germany, whilst the fighting men are allowed to return home?)

The statesmen at Versailles made their mistakes in ample profusion, but their peoples can scarcely claim exemption from responsibility. True, in those days the study of foreign affairs was not officially encouraged among ordinary folk. (Some of the British *Cabinet Ministers* in 1914 did not know—had not been allowed to know—the extent of their country's commitments to France and Belgium!) Now the situation has changed.

Another consideration impels early study of the principles of frontier re-settlement. Many of the decisions at Versailles were merely confirmations of conditions actually existing: when Austria-Hungary collapsed, the newly freed subject races seized the territory they considered to be their natural right. In only minor instances did decisions at Versailles affect the resultant frontier situation.

Almost certainly we shall have to face a situation potentially similar. When victory is won, Poles, Czechs and Serbs will rush to secure their frontiers—not necessarily those of 1938, but those they think they ought to have. Such a course might lead to endless complications: it would be much better to settle in advance with the responsible governments the provisional outline of the post-war settlement. A first principle of a lasting peace is that the Allies should agree among themselves: this did not happen in 1919, and we must not delude ourselves today—there are many points of difficulty which will not resolve themselves merely because we have fought side by side against a common enemy.

It can be argued that the initiative should come from us. The small, occupied nations are in a difficult position. They might incur suspicion from short-sighted people if, while fighting for their very existence, they were to do so much as mention possible claims after victory: yet these claims may be perfectly legitimate.

There are potential difficulties and dangers on every hand. It is noteworthy that a dozen men will agree unanimously on the absolute necessity of destroying the Nazi menace, but will quarrel violently about what is to happen when the Nazi menace is destroyed. Yet unity of purpose will be as vital in the post-war years as it is today. Even if it is too early to settle the shape of Europe to come, it is not too early to understand the problems which will have to be solved.

They are many, intricate and difficult. This book is concerned primarily with the frontiers of Europe. The peace conference will probably find that economic considerations are at least of equal importance, but on this complicated subject I have no more authority to speak than the next man. To the frontier problems I can at least offer a personal approach: for twelve years before the war I spent every spare moment astride the disputed frontiers, studying their difficulties on the spot. The more I saw, the more I was dismayed by their intricacies: yet they are not insoluble, if they can be approached free from the passion of propaganda or nationalist bias.

One sincere school of thought tends to belittle the importance of frontiers in its advocacy of a European Federation. My own opinion agrees that such a federation is not merely possible, but inevitable. Yet I do not believe it will be attained yet: nor, perhaps, is it wise that it should. Nationalism breeds wars, but wars also breed nationalism. Patriotic spirit was never so high as it is in Europe today. Poles and Czechs risk terror and murder day and night in a great fight for freedom—freedom for Poland and Czechoslovakia.

After the last war many countries acclaimed the League of Nations. Alas, they did it, not because they understood or accepted the implications of the League, but because they were tired of war. It would be a tragedy if this happened again: a second failure might retard political progress for a hundred years.

Before federal or any other communal system can hope for lasting success, the idea must have been firmly accepted on its own merits by the mass of the people. It cannot be claimed that this situation exists today. The bulk of the British public is woefully ignorant of the elementary implications of federalism. Many American ideas seem to be theoretic rather than practical: in Europe, the idea has only just begun to take root. Years of ardent work are necessary before it is firmly planted.

In the meantime—and even *after* federation—there must be frontiers in Europe, and their determination will be one of the first and most difficult tasks of the post-war months. This book is planned as a sort of elementary hand-book to the Peace Conference; a plain statement of the problems which have to be solved: a primer, to encourage the study in more detail and from more authoritative specialised books on the intricacies of the problems involved. It makes no pretence of offering final solutions: its main aim is to present the problems fairly and dispassionately.

Certainly it is not too early for the problems of the peace to be considered. As the months of war pass, and the strain intensifies, passion may replace reason. From day to day we hear accounts, only too firmly substantiated, of appalling cruelty in the occupied countries. The people of these lands must not be expected to view problems dispassionately. The Pole who has seen his family murdered cannot weigh questions of right or wrong impartially: the call for revenge is human. Already we are faced with the prospect of wide demands from the tortured peoples: demands based on righteous wrath rather than equity. As our own sufferings are increased, so also will our own judgment inevitably become warped. Already there are people who clamour for the complete destruction of Germany. Indirectly and unintentionally they help to lengthen the war: their outbursts are gratefully seized by German propaganda and used to stimulate German resistance. For there is no more forceful prompting to battle to the death than the knowledge that surrender means destruction.

At least we can agree on the essential feature of the new peace terms: they must secure what the last failed to do—that this sort of thing can never happen again. Acceptance of this principle involves a further argument—that we must never assume that Germany must or can be destroyed. A famous judge once proclaimed that it was not only essential that justice should be done, but that it should manifestly be seen to be done. We have not merely to plan peace terms which are fair, but which are manifestly seen to be fair by the peoples of Europe: including, eventually, the people of Germany.

I have heard it argued that this Peace Conference will be simpler than the last because there will be fewer voices to be heard. In 1919 it is true that the victorious powers quarrelled hopelessly among themselves; now, it is stated, Britain, the United States, and Russia will be able to dictate terms for everybody. I think this is a dangerous idea: it is indeed far away from the principles of the Atlantic Charter; further, it could never produce a lasting peace. No settlement of Europe is likely to be permanent unless it is agreed to by a very substantial majority of its people. No peace will ever be permanent unless, with the passing of time, it is recognised even by the defeated peoples as a reasonable peace.

As this book will at least demonstrate, the task of re-drawing the frontiers of Europe is alone of immense difficulty: all the more reason why it should be approached with courage and patient study. It is certain that if we throw up our hands in despair, and claim that the task is impossible, then there is no prospect of peace in Europe.

II

On every hand are heard lamentations for our policy during the inter-war years of 1919–39. Our principal fault was short-sighted lack of interest in foreign affairs. It can be claimed that successive governments could scarcely be blamed, since they could depend on only the slightest of backing from the general public. It is even more regrettable that few of our governments attempted to give a lead to people with a woeful and apparently hereditary ignorance of European affairs. No more cruel confession of failure was ever made than when Mr. Chamberlain referred to Czechoslovakia as 'that remote land, of which we know so little.' True, millions of people agreed with him; but his outlook should have been wider than theirs. Our failing in the twenty years was not that our foreign policy was wrong, but that for long periods we had no foreign policy: or, in others, that we were not prepared to back our ideals, since we held firmly to few principles. Such confusion of mind was bound to aggravate the unsolved problems with which Europe abounded. A good many of them owed much of their importance to the fact that they were ignored (though it is true that others became dangerous because they were exaggerated, and the necessary correctives were not applied). Many a festering sore on the body of Europe could have been cured permanently had it been treated when it was a skin rash. Some were legacies of older maladies: others were artificially stimulated.

It was unfortunate but inevitable that European problems should be directly concerned with the principle of Treaty Revision. I shall argue that on the whole the Peace Treaties were very fair, but there were some details of them which obviously were not—and were seized by the defeated powers for propaganda purposes as if they were typical of the whole. On the issue of Treaty Revision, political parties in Britain were split in two—or more. It was not a question of Conservatives holding one view and Socialists another—each party was divided within itself on this vital issue. Presumably because of this, successive governments refused to face the resultant problems, and many of these became intensified by neglect. If our governments had said firmly (it would not have represented my own view, but I present it as a possible policy), 'These treaties are sacred: not a yard of the frontiers shall be altered, not a comma of the clauses deleted, except at the expense of war with Britain'—if this had been our consistent policy, then the condition of Europe would have been vastly different today. But such was *not* our policy. We accepted or condoned breaches of the treaties by default or by force, and even negotiated amendments. That is to say, we indicated plainly that we did *not* consider the treaties as sacred. Consequently we could scarcely be surprised when the defeated powers proposed to carry further amendments.

It is important to emphasise that a purely negative policy is not enough. Take the case of the mandated German colonies.

They are scarcely mentioned in the Nazi bible, Hitler's *Mein Kampf*—to Hitler they were obviously unimportant either from the point of view of economics or of national pride. Not until long after his emergence did he make the first hesitant suggestion that the colonies ought to be returned to Germany. Up to that time millions of Germans had almost forgotten about their lost colonies—the Germans were never colonial-minded. A forceful group, true—consisting mainly of ex-officials of the colonies—kept up an enthusiastic propaganda, but it would be absurd to contend that there was any over-whelming enthusiasm.

Hitler's first pronouncement about colonies was restrained enough; he was evidently feeling his way—flying a kite, if you will. For the results of his demand he watched London, not Berlin—it would be easy to whip up a demand in Germany at the appropriate moment. The reaction of London appeared favourable enough. A member of Parliament asked the inevitable question, and received the diplomatically accurate reply that the government was not considering the transfer of any of its mandates.

Now one of the weaknesses of diplomatic language is that it is used universally, irrespective of the mentality of the people concerned. A brusque reply to a French communiqué would be taken as a deadly insult by the French people, who appreciate the delicacy of language. The Germans have never claimed such a national trait: they understand only plain speaking. My own opinion is that, assuming that British policy was definitely to decline the return of the colonies, it would have been better to have said so then in plain, unmistakable terms. I am convinced that we should then have heard little more of colonial demands—war with Britain was the last thing the Nazis wanted, and there were plenty of more urgent problems nearer home. A creed based on energy cannot survive failures, and does not care to risk them. If its kite meets a strong head-wind, it is promptly hauled down and flown some-where else.

There was no need to haul down the colonial kite. It was

not stated categorically that at no time and under no circumstances would Britain consider return of the lost colonies.
Therefore, argued Berlin, at some time and in certain circumstances Britain might—would—consider their return. Thus the
national appetite was stimulated, since the first obvious circum-
stance was a unanimous German demand. Today there can be
no doubt about it—ninety per cent of the Germans firmly
believe that they were cheated of their colonies, and that it is
no more than their just right that they should be returned.

It will be understood that my argument has nothing to do
with the rights or wrongs of the case, but it does show that
postponement can aggravate a problem rather than solve it.

It is admittedly difficult for some people in Britain, particularly those who have never left their native shores, to appreciate the character of the frontier problems of Europe. Our
ancestors a thousand years ago might have understood some
of their characteristics more clearly than we do. When the
human swarm pressed from the east, when tribes settled and
emigrated, then men lived for the day. Nationalism was almost
unknown, or at most its force was small: the family, the tribe,
the feudal clan represented common limits of loyalty. The
development and intensity of modern nationalism, which have
only developed since the time of, say, Joan of Arc, have bred
problems for which the haphazard settlements of previous
centuries were the worst possible preparation. Five hundred
years ago it was looked upon as proper and ordinary for
Czechs and Germans to share the same life, the same towns:
today, apparently, it is a crime. To our cost, we have to deal
with things as they are today, not as they were five centuries
ago.

Then our task would have been easier. Nationalism is a
potent force. It brings to the fore many of the best qualities
of man: in its finest forms it is an inspiration, a guide to life.
But in a world where a man in London can speak to the world,
or can fly to America in half a day, then it is obvious that
mental outlooks can no longer halt at national frontiers. There

were people in Britain as well as in America who preached isolationism—that we had no concern in the intricate problems of Europe. They ignored the fact that we had helped to create these problems, and that it is hardly British to leave other people in the confusion we had helped to create. American opinion and responsibility were very similar.

Further, isolationism is simply impossible: it resembles the attitude of a man in the top floor of a burning building who claims that the fire has nothing to do with him. Nevertheless, isolationists will arise in the first days of peace, when disillusion can so easily stalk the world. If it gains headway, then the prospect is gloomy. The present war resulted largely from the fact that we took insufficient interest in Europe. We did not entirely ignore the flames on the floors below, but hoped that they would be satiated before they reached us—or that somebody else would put them out.

As the conflict ends, the greater part of Europe will look to Great Britain and the United States for leadership. In 1919 the tragedy was that France and Britain disagreed between themselves. Now the United States shall have a new opportunity, a grander chance. If we seize it, collaborating with others in the rebuilding of Europe, then the prospect is good. If we fail, through indolence or ignorance, then we condemn Europe and ourselves to further misery.

This book is modest in its scope. I am not sufficiently skilled to submit plans of the new European edifice: I can only suggest the shape of the bricks to be used.

III

If Britain was comparatively uninterested in European frontier problems during the inter-war years, violent word battles were fought from Paris to the Pripet Marshes. The British and American reader, plunged haphazard into such arguments, found himself assailed by 'facts' and 'principles' which turned out to be ideas and opinions. Above all he was confused by discussions of frontiers. His outlook was limited because he has the fortune to enjoy the protection of the only complete and realistic frontier in Europe—the English Channel. No land frontier can ever be fully satisfactory. A European frontier is supposed, speaking generally, to mark out a line where one race ends and another begins. It is impossible to point to a single possible frontier which would satisfy this condition.

There are three types of frontier line. There is the *historic* boundary, which came into being after age-old turmoils in which neither science nor reason played any part. A suitable example is the frontier between France and Belgium—which was that of France and the Spanish Netherlands. How many British soldiers knew when they stepped from France into Belgium? The boundary is purely artificial, running across cornfields and through the middle of villages. It was determined centuries ago, on the basis of the land holdings of border nobles, and is no more than a political division.

Then there is the *natural* frontier, which every country claims: all satiated countries proclaim that their present boundaries are 'natural.' A range of mountains, a mighty river—here, we are told, is the perfect geographical division, a real separation of races. The most potent example, invariably quoted, is that of the Pyrenees. Certainly, on the map, here is the perfect 'natural' frontier stretching obligingly from Atlantic to Mediterranean, separating Frenchmen from Spaniards. This is a complete fallacy. It is not even true that every dweller to the north of the Pyrenean watershed is even politically a Frenchman, and he to the south a Spaniard, for the frontier zigzags haphazardly along the range. At Roncesvalles, Spain reaches down into the French valleys, and in the Cerdagne a great area of physical Spain is under French rule. But this is by no means all. So far from separating men, the Pyrenees form the backbone of two races which are neither French nor Spanish. For thirty miles to the north and a hundred miles to the south of the Western and Eastern Pyrenees respectively stretch the lands of the Basque and the Catalan—vigorous races, each with its own language and culture. So far from being a 'natural' division, therefore, the Pyrenees act as a binder of racial interests and development.

A river is even less complete as a frontier. When the settling tribes of old found green pastures on one side of a river valley, they did not halt—they occupied the other side of the valley as well. Rivers never were real frontiers, but rather veins around which racial bodies grew. You will not find a solitary river of Europe which has the slightest claim to be called a boundary between races.

The importance of natural physical features as frontiers has always been stressed from *strategic* points of view. This is likely to change in the light of modern war conditions. No river in Europe, however wide, has been able to arrest the march of a stronger opponent: no range of mountains can shut out bombing aeroplanes. One of the bases of ancient frontiers has already lost much of its meaning, and if we are wise we shall bear the implications in mind when planning the detailed shape of the new Europe. We shall, of course, accept it as axiomatic that the military power of Germany is destroyed, and that so far as it is humanly possible she shall be prevented from future aggression. But the building up of 'strategic frontiers' alone will never secure this necessary state.

Nor is *language* a decisive factor in frontier determination. It does not follow automatically that a country has a right to claim as its citizens those who speak its language. If so, Switzerland would be immediately divided between France, Germany and Italy. Germany would also occupy Holland and part of Belgium, Spain would demand the greater part of South America, and Britain would claim to rule the United States! (Or, of course, the United States might claim to rule Britain!) A common language may be meaningless as an ethnic guide— there are countless cases of the forced change of language of subject peoples. H. G. Wells once said that a common language was not evidence of a common past, but of a common future— but there are millions of people in Europe who would never agree.

Historic, as well as geographic, ethnic and economic considerations must be given full weight in determining a frontier; the wishes of a people, as developed through history, provide an important—almost overwhelming—factor. The language frontiers of Europe often differ very considerably from political lines, but it does not follow for a moment that they are advisable; in fact, their adoption would lead to hopeless confusion, even assuming that the peoples in question could even be induced to the experiment.

Yet, although the 'natural' frontier does not and cannot exist, we must have boundaries—at present, at all events. In a few centuries' time our descendants may laugh at our comic maps of Europe—just as some Europeans laugh at the long straight frontier between the United States and Canada, a line which is considerably more settled than Europe's twisting curves! Since we must have frontiers, therefore, we must do the best we can.

No war can ever settle a frontier. For a frontier is a compromise—it has to be a compromise. When the many tribes of Europe settled down, they did so indiscriminately—they had no thought for modern political conditions. They intermarried and raided freely among neighbouring tribes. Consequently, on any land frontier you inevitably find a mixed race—mixed in two senses. Along both sides of the French-Italian frontier, for example, you will find thousands of people of mixed French-Italian parentage; you will also find thousands of Italians living inside France, and thousands of Frenchmen living inside Italy. Sometimes these families have been there for so many generations that the French have forgotten they ever were French.

In Eastern Europe the medley of races is more pronounced. And here we approach an important axiom: *it is quite impossible, however hard you try, to draw a line and say (for example)*: 'All the people to the west of this line are Germans, all those to the east are Poles.' It is utterly impossible, although your frontier may have ten thousand wobbles. You must compromise, must arrange a frontier that will inflict the least possible hardship and injustice.

Nor, of course, are ethnic considerations the only concern in determining a frontier. The accidents of history, the vagaries of geography, the demands of economics—all these have played a part in the demarcation of frontiers which have successfully endured for many generations, although they may not follow an ethnic line. As Renan says, 'Nations have always settled their boundaries in the rough.'

In approaching European frontier problems, we shall find that our difficulty is not to decide between a right and a wrong, but between two wrongs—or, more usually, two rights. In 1919 the statesmen at Paris set themselves to redress the wrongs of peoples who had suffered repression or oppression for many generations. In general, they accomplished their task: but such was the complicated ethnic medley in Europe that each act of justice was bound to leave minor injustices behind.

The result of their labours, moreover, represented the best ethnic division of territory Europe has ever known in its history—not perfect, but much nearer to ethnic perfection than that of 1914. *More people lived under the rule of their own kin in 1919–1938 than ever did before*. The Treaties, in fact, were an honest attempt to re-draw the map of Europe on lines of justice and freedom—an attempt which, in spite of the many difficulties and mistakes, achieved considerable success. Versailles was, in fact, the culmination of the eastward advance of self-determination which had been in process for a hundred years. Many of its decisions were inevitable—the release of peoples whose liberty had been hitherto suppressed by force.

It might be useful if we considered a few sample problems before plunging into the ethnic medley of Europe.

Take the case of Monmouth, even today a subject of discussion as to whether it belongs to England or Wales. If England and Wales had been two separate states, the county would have formed the cause of a dozen wars, and would have changed hands many times. Let us consider some possibilities:

assume for the moment that England and Wales *are* separate sovereign states.

(*a*) Suppose by the accidents of conquest and settlement Newport were largely British and the rural districts largely Welsh. Should the county, which is one economic whole, go to England or Wales?

(*b*) Suppose the *eastern* half of the county were populated by Welsh, the *western* half by English: *i.e.* each race were separated from its kinsmen. Which county has the stronger ethnic claim?

(*c*) Suppose the wealthy and cultured classes of Monmouth were English, the labourers Welsh. (Readers in the Principality will naturally put this supposition the other way round!) The English have developed the province, and govern it, but are heavily outnumbered. Should they retain it?

(*d*) Many of the people of Pembroke are of English stock. Suppose the whole county were largely populated by English, although separated from England by large tracts of Welsh territory. Would England have a just claim to Pembroke?

(*e*) More difficult still: suppose Worcester, an inland county, were populated by Welsh—separated from Wales by Hereford. Would Wales be able to claim Worcester? And Hereford?

(*f*) Wales, in older days, was continually attacked by England. As a strategic frontier for protective purposes, suppose she seized the line of the river Severn, though this involved placing English population under Welsh rule? Is this just?

(Fervent nationalists should pose to themselves parallel problems the other way round!)

These are samples of the frontier problems of Europe in their simplest form. It is quite common to find three or four of the supposititious cases rolled into one intricate practical example. American readers can pose the same question to themselves by supposing that Nevada and Oregon were very largely peopled by Mexicans, and were claimed by Mexico. Yet it will be understood that in a new, growing and rapidly developing continent frontiers have never had quite the same meaning as they have in a Europe of ancient and confused settlement.

In the case of England and Wales, no problem arises, because the two countries have a common government: thus the national status of Monmouth is only of sentimental interest. Even if England and Wales were separate states, Monmouth under any of our hypothetical conditions need not be a serious problem. Englishmen could live in Wales, and Welshmen in England, so long as mutual tolerance exists. Unfortunately, in Europe the word tolerance is scarcely known, and in any case has lost its meaning. When subject races regained their freedom, it was too much to expect them to show much tolerance to their ex-masters, who had never exhibited such an attitude to them. What is to be expected at the close of the present conflict, when revenge and hatred will be the most common feelings in the hearts of millions of men?

It is perfectly true that in the long run the only things which can give Europe uninterrupted peace are toleration, confidence, mutual trust, co-operation. Yet, unhappily, these admirable things were losing ground well before the war began: today they are overshadowed by a vast pall of hate, and years must elapse before the smoke of suspicion clears away. There are, of course, many sincere people who believe that permanent peace will only come with the world-wide adoption of Christianity, or Socialism or some other belief. The argument may be sound, but at the best is unlikely to be accomplished for a long, long time. We have to make a start from where we are—and it is a bad start. In planning for the week after next we should not forget tomorrow. I do not believe in the much-quoted axiom that 'you can't change human nature.' You can: at least, you can change human behaviour, but it takes a long time. But I am not content to sit down and wait for a miracle. The conditions under which my grandchildren will live are of some importance to me, but much more important are those under which I may live the remaining portion of my life.

IV

Two ideas ought to be considered before we plunge into the implications of European frontiers. In my *Danger Spots of Europe* I suggested serious consideration of a scheme which has been much in the news—transference of populations. If Monmouth were a bone of contention because Welsh occupied the eastern half and English the west, why not let the people change over and divide the county in two? This is one of the simplest possible cases: most others are far more intricate, yet the potential solution is so final and certain that the method must be most carefully pondered. The very nationalism which has fostered racial ideas in its exiled members must be held responsible for their present predicament. Yet one principle is clear: the inconvenience of the few cannot be allowed to prejudice the safety of the many.

For a hundred years Greece and Turkey glared at each other across the Aegean, and half a dozen times they were locked in combat. In the World War the Greeks were on the winning side, and as their principal share of the spoils were awarded a huge area in Asia Minor. The contention was that Smyrna was a Greek city, and that its natural hinterland—containing large numbers of Greeks—must go with it.

But the broken Turkish power revived miraculously, and the Greek army in Asia Minor was hopelessly defeated. Tempers were primitive. Smyrna a Greek city? Very well, argued the Turks—burn it down, then it was no longer a Greek city. A million Greeks in Asia Minor? Very well—bundle them back to Greece: then there could be no question of a Greek claim.

There was no discussion. The ancestors of the Greeks of Asia Minor had lived there for dozens of generations, but they were ruthlessly uprooted and shipped to Greece. The Greeks naturally retaliated, and all Turks in Greek territory were immediately turned out of Greece. This did not solve the problem of making room for the Asia Minor refugees, for there were only 200,000 Turks in Greece. But Greece housed many thousands of Roumanians. These—more politely—were returned to Roumania. The Roumanian government, to make room for them, evicted thousands of Bulgars.

I saw something of the terrible scenes of those days—thousands of weeping, starving refugees, arriving in an unprepared land, suffering incredible hardships, decimated by disease. I never thought that I could even do so much as to suggest consideration of such a method. But the point is this: the Greeks and Turks, enemies for hundreds of years, are now friends and allies. During the Greek domestic crisis of 1935 it appeared as if Bulgaria might take advantage of the confusion to invade Greece. Without prompting, Turkey immediately warned Bulgaria off! Any Victorian statesmen, could they return to the European scene today, would stare in amazement at the sight of Greece and Turkey standing side by side as friends and allies.

Whether we like the idea or not, the system of transference of population has become a matter for European politics. And, of course, there is a vast difference between the sudden upheaval of a population under appalling war conditions, and the transfer of that population under friendly and prepared conditions of peace. So far back as 1919 Greece and Bulgaria exchanged thousands of families by mutual arrangement and without hardship or distress. This is perhaps a better example than the other, for the Greeks of Asia Minor were mostly traders, much easier to transplant than peasants almost rooted to their native soil.

In some quarters there is a prejudice against transference of population because Hitler had adopted it as part of the policy of his only partly defined 'New Order' in Europe. Yet Hitler did not invent the method—it has been used throughout centuries. It was deliberately developed only a few generations ago in the form of mass emigration.

Those who consider that such a forced emigration as is suggested is an intolerable tyranny should remember that emigrations are no less forced when the compelling agent is economic

—when the emigrant is driven off his land by unemployment, poverty, or by a foreclosed mortgage. Such circumstances may produce heart-rending results, families broken up, folk driven from the homes of their fathers and regions full of dear associations—and in them there is no compensating gain in easing international frictions. In British history, consider what tragedies were produced by the dissolution of the monasteries and the enclosure of the commons. A planned scheme for transference of population, carried out with due regard for the people who were being forced, in a novel sense of the phrase, to 'leave their country for their country's good,' should involve much less injustice and suffering.

Migrations of people have been universal since the world began. Most of them were impelled by the search for food. In those days men were not tillers of the soil, but hunters or collectors of food. The game frequently migrated in search of fresh feeding grounds: sometimes the move was seasonal, sometimes permanent. In either case the hunter had to follow his quarry.

Even when man became an agriculturist, migration was frequently forced by changes in climatic conditions. As tribal and racial ties developed, whole populations moved—either in search of rich fields or plunder, or to escape the attentions of other plunderers.

The discovery of new continents altered the scope of mass migrations; these did not, however, reach their peak until the development of the industrial age. In the years about the turn of the last century, many millions of people crossed the seas. Emigration was unrestricted and almost unorganised: most of the emigrants had to make their own arrangements and pay their own expenses, and conditions were not always of the best: but they survived and made good: only a comparatively small percentage returned to their original habitations. In 1907 over 1,285,000 immigrants entered the United States alone: in addition, the countries of the British Empire received 125,000 from the British Isles alone. Parallel with this was a considerable emigration from Southern Europe to Latin America. It would scarcely be an overestimate to say that in each of the early years of this century about 2 million people left their homes in Europe to begin a new life over the seas. Two million people transferred themselves, with little official assistance, and with the minimum of organisation.

(Incidentally, many of the European problems of today are directly traceable to the practical cessation of emigration in 1914, and the subsequent legislation introduced by the United States, by which only a small number of emigrants can enter the United States annually, in strongly defined quotas for each country. States like Italy were especially hard hit. The land is not rich, and the natural increase of population amounts to 500,000 a year. In pre-1914 years, over 200,000 people emigrated annually. The sudden stoppage caused great distress. For some years France was able to absorb many Italian workers—in the early nineteen-twenties the figure actually reached 250,000 a year, but subsequently declined greatly. The pressure of population inside Italy may account for some of her violent adventures at home and abroad.

On the other hand, some countries—like Czechoslovakia and Lithuania—have deliberately restricted emigration, believing it to be a danger to their national strength. This is a common outlook in countries with minority populations, where battles of ethnic statistics continually rage.)

If millions of people can be transferred to the other side of the Atlantic, or even to the other side of the world, without serious hardship and certainly to the eventual benefit of themselves and the recipient countries,[1] then it ought not to be

[1] The short-sighted view looks upon a foreign immigrant as a man who will do a native out of a job: the long-sighted view, as a present of an asset by another country. For the capital value of a skilled man, in feeding and training alone, is many thousands of dollars. The United States owes a good deal of her prosperity to her reception of immigrants: in a little over a century she received more than 37 million—all of whom had been reared at the expense of other countries! The Huguenots proved to be a great asset to Britain: in more recent years we have gained by the skill and initiative of Czech and Austrian refugees.

impossible to work out similar schemes in Europe. Such is the jumble of nationalities that it is calculated that from 5 to 7 million people would need to be moved in order to tidy up the frontiers of Europe: the figure might prove to be as high as 10 millions. Yet, considering the emigration figures quoted, the task is not too frightening. It would be expensive, of course— but it is surely worth the cost of a week's war to take a step which would go far towards the permanence of European peace.

The problem varies in its degree of complexity. In the Balkans there are Bulgarian peasants in Roumania and Roumanian peasants in Bulgaria. It demands no impossible organisation or hardship to let one peasant exchange farms with another, probably only a few miles away. The simpler the form of civilisation, the easier the exchange.

Further, it is important to remember in all our considerations that in Eastern and Southeastern Europe nationalities are more fluid than in the west. An Englishman and a Frenchman are very conscious of their nationality, but a man who calls himself a Bulgar may be merely a Greek who speaks Bulgarian. That is to say, while it might take generations for an Englishman to be assimilated in France, this Bulgar could revert to Greek in a very short time.

The peasant outlook in these areas is usually purely local. The peasant belongs to his farm, his village; he finds it difficult to appreciate larger loyalties. Sometimes he would rather change his nationality than his farm. Give him a good piece of ground, and he can be happy, even if the yardstick of nationality is not used in too stereotyped a fashion.

The resettlement of Eastern Europe would have been easier a generation ago. Now national feelings exist where they were unknown a comparatively short time ago.

In Western Europe the difficulties of transference of population increase. You cannot make a clean and sudden exchange of German mechanics and Czech farmers. Already Hitler is experiencing difficulties in his German settlements in Western

Poland, where he has settled on the land German professional
and commercial men withdrawn from the Baltic states: they
are not happy; nor are they good farmers.

The higher the degree of civilisation, too, the greater the
reluctance to leave familiar haunts, friends and facilities. Yet
this difficulty is not insuperable. In normal years in Britain
tens of thousands of men change their jobs, and tens of thousands more change their homes. There are even signs that men
brought up in urban surroundings can be taught to appreciate
the advantages of the countryside, where cultural and recrea-
tional opportunities are rapidly extending. Although exchanges
of population in Western Europe are more difficult, they are
by no means impossible. Fortunately, the largest numbers involved lie further east.

In 1939 there were three-quarters of a million Germans in
Poland, and over a million Poles in Germany. There is no
logical reason why their exchange should not be considered.
Spread over a period of years, with detailed preparation and
friendly and efficient supervision, the exchange of a couple of
million people is not a great problem. Our forefathers would
have thought little of it two thousand years ago. Life today is
more complicated, and there are hundreds of difficulties—but
none of them are insuperable. The cost would be that of one
or two battleships.

It is understood that vehement protests would come from
the uprooted families: this is only natural. Yet it is far more
important that hundreds of millions of people should not suffer
or die, than that thousands of families should be temporarily
inconvenienced. Any member of a civilised state has to do
many things he does not want to do, in the interests of the
community. Further, the change is not violent. This is no
sudden transition of a European to the Gold Coast or South
Sea Islands. In many cases it would involve a move of only ten
or twenty miles—scarcely a change of scene.

One problem will certainly demand immediate post-war
consideration—that of the German settlers scattered over

Europe. As we shall see, most of them have resisted local assimilation and have remained German.

The Germans scattered over Europe vary from the descendants of settlers planted centuries ago to ordinary commercial representatives. They are not likely to be very welcome in any European country after the war. Unfortunately, German residents, settlers, agents and 'tourists' have become synonymous with spies and 'Fifth Columnists.' Of the 44,000 Germans normally resident in Holland, for example, it is known that a fair proportion were engaged in clandestine or open activity directed at the downfall of the country which gave them hospitality and a livelihood. The Dutch can scarcely be blamed if they are not quite so ready to welcome German residents after the war: and they will certainly want to get rid of the present German population. This problem applies to greater or less degree to practically every country in Europe.

Hitler gave the figure of German 'exiles' in Europe as 10 millions. This is probably an exaggeration. It includes over 3 million people of German stock in Czechoslovakia, many of them in areas adjacent to the German frontier. As we shall see, Hitler has already removed some hundreds of thousands of these 'exiles' from the Baltic states, Northern Italy and the Balkans, planting them in areas seized from Poland. His plan has been freely applauded in Germany—except by the returned exiles, most of whom did not want to leave the homes where their ancestors had lived for generations. The Germans can scarcely complain, therefore, if other countries decide to continue the policy they have themselves adopted.

One serious problem immediately presents itself. If millions of exiled Germans are to be returned to the fatherland, there must be some place for them to go. This involves either an extension of Germany's frontiers or an increased industrialisation to support a larger population. On the other hand, it is argued that by the end of the war Germany's casualties are likely to be so large that she ought to be able to receive large numbers of immigrants, to her own advantage.

Two problems are therefore involved in the transference of populations: (*a*) the exchange of people who by the confusion of history are bound to be found on the wrong side of any frontier; (*b*) the repatriation of Germans who are not included in (*a*). I agree that the prospect of forced migration will be abhorrent to my readers of liberal opinions. They will, however, agree with my premise that our first objective is to make certain that the circumstances of 1939 can never be repeated. In that case, I can only suggest that they withhold their objections and opinion until we have completed our outline of the problem; it will then become apparent, I think, that no other solution is possible.

V

I have mentioned Federalism as one of the possible keys to European peace: indeed, have suggested its ultimate inevitability in some form or other, while insisting that even with the possibility of Federation we have still to determine frontiers. I have expressed misgivings lest we should move too rapidly, beyond the ideas of ordinary men.

The tragedy of the League of Nations can never be overlooked. A grand conception failed because men were not ready for it: most were ready to receive its benefits, but not to give. Men who were weary of war expected too much of it: its geography was too vast for human comprehension. Who could expect Ecuador to be intensely interested in Siam? Its biggest failures arose not from lack of goodwill, but from sheer limitation of human outlook. The Japanese invasion of Manchuria was a clear case of aggression, defying all the League's principles, yet few nations of the world were directly interested, and popular response was amazingly limited. Only in Britain and America was the national pulse moderately stirred: and America was not in the League, and Britain could not move without France.

The case of Abyssinia was even more blatant. This time British public opinion was almost unanimous. A world-wide empire encourages a wide view, and to Britain a threat in Africa is just as important as a threat in Europe—often more so, in fact, for although they are interested in world affairs, they were not nearly so interested in European affairs—until recently. The French, on the other hand, have a very restricted world view, but are intensely interested in Europe. The blame for the Abyssinian fiasco is today heaped on Laval, but a substantial part of France was behind him. What did Abyssinia matter to France? it was argued. It was much more important to keep Italy on the side of France for the potential struggle against Germany.

It is natural that the man in the street should now be suspicious of everything connected with the League of Nations, or anything like another League of Nations. He considers that the League let him down: it will take time to convince him that he let the League down. The nations failed, not the League. They failed because its ideas were only imperfectly understood—or, in some countries, not understood at all. In the Balkans I met peasants who had never even heard of the League!

It was too much to ask. Human outlook had been so limited: it could not suddenly change its character in a night. We should have learned by now that you cannot rush these things. The grandiose conceptions of the League would have been decades nearer attainment had they evolved from more modest beginnings. A beneficent ideal can only be established so far as the minds of men are prepared to receive it.

Now we cannot even start from the same place. Disappointment and disillusion are bound to have wide effects: there will be loud demands for older and more primitive 'guarantees' of security. These have to be countered, and the process will take time. We should be able to adopt it as axiomatic that no form of international control is likely to be successful unless it is backed by considerable majorities in all the countries concerned.

To satisfy the elementary urge of national patriotism we must have frontiers. These must be as fair as human brains can

devise. That is our consideration in this book. I have emphasised that the fashioning of frontiers is only a modest contribution to the peace of Europe, but it is primary and vital: it is
the base of the world edifice.

Once fair frontiers are firmly established, our next task is to
effect a gradual diminution of the importance of these lines on
the map. This seems paradoxical, but is actually quite logical.
A man secure in his ownership can be generous, and often
is: the real miser is the man who has not an over-sound claim
to his possessions, or who has grabbed far beyond his deserts.
The man who has been robbed naturally has small confidence
in the generosity of others.

I believe that the approach to the commonwealth of peoples
should be gradual; it cannot be rushed, for it has to overcome
traditions and prejudices which have been inculcated in a thousand years of history. It would be best to approach the problem
step by step, as confidence returns to the world: an edifice
built on confidence is worth a hundred rushed up in moments
of fear.

The geographic approach will probably prove to be the
best. Federal apologists are fond of comparing the order of the
United States of America and the confusion of the disunited
states of Europe. The comparison is strained. The states of
America started off with the advantage of housing people
largely of common stock and with a common language. Yet
for some time after they had won their independence they
found it impossible to unite; so hopeless did the prospect
seem that they even thought of obtaining a king—from Germany! Only when instead of regarding themselves as the
'people of Maryland' or the 'people of Delaware' and so on,
they thought of themselves as the 'people of the United States'
did unity become possible. Even then it was precarious: it
nearly collapsed over an economic question, that of slavery.
And the bloodiest civil war in history had to be fought before
the states became finally united. A firmer argument can be
based on the Pan-American Congress, one of the first steps

towards a regional federation. I believe that its power and influence will expand.

An association of European nations would make a more immediate appeal to the peoples of Europe, generally of limited vision, than another world-wide League of Nations. Even a European federation is scarcely possible in the present limited state of mental advancement. It might be usefully prefaced by a series of regional federations: in my own opinion, this should be our immediate goal.

There are some obvious possibilities. Britain and France might form the basic partners in a Western European Federation in which Holland, Belgium and the Scandinavian states would be valuable members. The Balkan Entente was a germ of potential value: it failed to stand up to the force which threatened it, but a Balkan Federation is already overdue. The German states provide a ready-made regional federation, and Poland and Czechoslovakia have already laid the practical foundations of a fourth: it might later be joined by adjacent countries like Hungary and the Baltic states.

We must have no illusions. Great difficulties confront us even in common-sense moves like these—we shall consider in some detail those of the projected Polish-Czech federation. Yet they are not insuperable.

Such a series of commonwealths would only be a beginning. They would remove the fear of a future crocodile state gobbling up the small fry one by one: but they would not remove the possibility of bigger and better wars between more powerful opponents. That is, regional federations are a beginning, not an end. Other means will be necessary to ensure that period of peace during which the regional federations can be established and developed. Their success would engender the confidence which is essential to the operation of wider schemes. These might first be economic. When nations can co-operate in economic fields, then friendship and federation follow close behind.

I repeat that even modest regional federations will present

tremendous difficulties in their making. In the course of our examination we shall see, for example, that the Serbs and Bulgars are of cousin races. Yet they have been at war three times since 1913; three ruthless Balkan wars, whose effects cannot be forgotten in a day. Serbs and Croats are own brothers, yet the story of their federalisation has been long and stormy. After far sight, the greatest attribute in international affairs is unlimited patience.

Details of world associations are beyond the scope of this book, which is limited to considerations of European frontiers. Yet, even if we cannot yet visualise the final edifice, we must never lose sight of the fact that we are planning to build, even when we are engaged on such mundane tasks as making the bricks.

VI

Before attempting to adjudge our own ideas for the resettlement of Europe, we should first cast a glance at Hitler's plan. This has not yet been announced in detail, but it is possible to build up a synthetic picture from fragments of official pronouncements.

Berlin is to be the capital of a new United States of Europe. Germany itself will be the workshop of Europe, and all other countries will devote themselves to the supply of agricultural products, raw materials and cheap labour.

The Reich itself will consist of the Germany of 1919 plus territories already annexed—Austria, Sudetenland, Memel, Eupen and Malmedy, Western Poland and Northern Slovenia: to these are to be added, immediately after victory, Alsace-Lorraine and Luxembourg. Further, Bohemia-Moravia and the rump Poland (now enlarged by the addition of Eastern Galicia) are to continue as German Protectorates.

So much is already clear. Other German intentions in Western Europe are obscure only as to form. It is their intention to bring Holland, Belgium and northeastern France under German rule. This might be done by annexation outright, or

by establishing 'protectorates' over them. 'Economic fusion'
was one phrase used. Rotterdam has been plainly marked down
for German sovereignty. Holland was told by her German
gauleiter, the notorious Seyss-Inquart, that 'the idyllic life she
has lived for centuries in a quiet, sheltered home is a vanished
dream.' Her place in Europe 'would depend on how far she
could arouse herself to a creative attitude towards Germany.'

The intended permanent occupation of the Low Countries
is not merely economic. The position is envisaged when Britain
will be so weakened as to accept a negotiated peace, even if she
cannot be forcibly knocked out. In such case the Germans
want suitable strategic advantages for a resumption of the
attack at the earliest propitious moment.

Denmark has been informed that 'her inclusion in the German sphere of interest is not a passing phase,' and the same
fate awaits Norway. These two countries will probably become additional 'protectorates,' with local autonomy but German garrisons—and a German economy.

Yugoslavia has already been divided, and we shall see that
the fertile Banat is designated as a German state from which
the whole of the Balkans can be dominated. The present
frontiers of the Balkan states are to be regarded as permanent.

The puppet states of Slovakia and Croatia will be trans-
formed into the lower class of 'protectorates' when victory is
won. They are largely agricultural, so fit in very well with the
new economic plan. The outlook of the satellite states is envisaged along similar lines. 'The independence of the Finnish
nation as well as of the Balkan states and other countries is
conceivable only on condition that Germany protects them,'
ran an official German dictum. The term 'other countries' presumably includes Italy!

Hitler's ideas in respect of Russia have not yet been clarified. The Ukraine is already designated as under German
domination, however: indeed, to date the Nationalists who
played into Nazi hands have been given singularly little power.
Further north, a new province has been formed: 'Ostland.'

It includes Latvia, Lithuania, the Vilna province of Poland, and a large part of the White Russian Republic of the Soviet Union—the greater portion of the provinces of Tver, Smolensk, Mogilev, Minsk and Chernigov. This is an old conception: it was freely used prior to 1939 as propaganda among the German Balts, to encourage them as missionaries of the Nazi creed. (These gentry, having been transferred to Western Poland, are to go back after victory, for a strong German frontier is to be established.)

The position of Estonia is still obscure. It may be included in Ostland: on the other hand, there is a suggestion that a Finno-Ugrian state shall be formed, consisting of Finland, Estonia, Soviet Carelia and the territory around Leningrad. The new country would of course be under German protection.

None can be more apprehensive than the remaining states of Europe. Hitler does not recognise neutrality, of course. In the official Nazi newspapers, France and the neutrals are classed with the puppet or satellite states, as nations 'whose fate is bound to the Axis Powers.' Switzerland, neutral of neutrals, was warned that the German origin of most of her people was noted. 'From this fact derives an obligation for the Swiss to take the necessary measures which will enable them to fulfil their task in a reorganised Europe. The Swiss Confederation has reached a venerable age, but the Reich is older.'

No plan has been detailed for France, after the German annexation of the north-eastern provinces. It has been made clear, however, that she will be completely dependent upon Germany.

Nor is there any real indication of Hitler's plans for the rest of Russia. Having seized Ukraine, it is doubtful if he would miss the chance of getting the oil of the Caucasus. The remainder of Russia, impoverished by the loss of its richest provinces, might be permitted to exist as another dependency.

The picture in general is thus quite clear: the doctrine of the *Herrenvolk* and their *Lebensraum* is to be implemented. The

Germans are to be the administrators and soldiers of Europe, and its skilled and highly paid workers. The rest of the Continent shall serve the master race: the people who are of lower quality than the Germans will have a much lower standard of living. They will be subjected to intense Germanisation,[1] and their local cultures will rapidly disappear. In a couple of generations Europe will be no more than a much Greater Germany.

Such is the outline of Hitler's Europe. It has two disadvantages: (*a*) it would be vigorously opposed by the entire population of the Continent except 80 million Germans and half a million quislings: (*b*) this 'permanent' plan disappears in a night on the defeat of Germany.

Our task is to plan a New Europe which is much better than Hitler's 'New Order.' It ought not to be difficult.

VII

In our attempts at drawing the post-war frontiers of Europe we shall need some general guide. Fortunately there is one at hand: the declaration of policy popularly known as the 'Atlantic Charter.' There is an objection in some quarters that it is far too general, but it went as far as responsible statesmen could be expected to go—especially for the leader of a nation which was not at war. Most important feature of the Charter is that today it is not merely a declaration of Anglo-American policy: its principles have been adopted by all the Allied countries, including Russia. Thus it is a real guide to our considerations.

Before examining its potentialities, however, we must not overlook its predecessor. In 1918, when the tide of war turned against the Central Powers, President Wilson by tacit consent acted as spokesman for the Allies. He had formulated his

---

[1] There is one serious German plan whereby alien men shall be sterilised, German sires be provided for suitable women, the resultant children being brought up as Germans. In this way the character of a country could be completely changed in half a century. This is one of the plans intended to be used in Britain!

famous Fourteen Points: he did not invent them, for many of them had been bulwarks of democratic policy for generations. Their importance can scarcely be over-estimated. Clever propagandists used them as a bait for the peoples of the Central Powers. Since that time German and other defeated statesmen have complained that they were promised treaties of peace on the basis of the Fourteen Points. Their disillusionment was rapid, but it is one of their major complaints today that they were cheated—that the Peace Treaties were a travesty of the spirit underlying the Fourteen Points.

We must, therefore, accept as a guide to equity not only the Atlantic Charter, but the Fourteen Points. In some respects the latter are more important than the former. Germany has not accepted the Atlantic Charter, and is unlikely to do so: she *did* accept the Fourteen Points. Since her principal complaint after 1918 was that she surrendered on the basis of the Fourteen Points, but that the Peace Treaties were nothing like the Fourteen Points, it ought to follow that if the Peace Treaties could have been revised so that they followed the spirit of the Fourteen Points, then Germany ought to have been satisfied.

The German contention that they were cheated by the Peace Treaties is sound enough on paper. On October 5th, 1918, the German Government requested President Wilson to 'take into his hands the task of establishing peace on the basis of the Fourteen Points.' Later they asked him to inquire if the Allied Governments also agreed to them. A memorandum to Wilson was sent by Britain, France, Italy and Belgium in identical terms. 'Subject to the considerations which follow, they declare their willingness to make peace with the Government of Germany on the terms of peace laid down in the President's address to Congress of January 8th, 1918 (*i.e.* the Fourteen Points), and the principles of settlement enunciated in his subsequent addresses. They must point out, however, that what is usually described as the Freedom of the Seas is open to various interpretations, some of which they could not accept. They must therefore reserve to themselves complete freedom on this subject when they enter the Peace Conference.' One other qualification stated that by the 'restoration' of invaded territories the Allies understood that 'compensation would be made by Germany for all damage done to the civilian population of the Allies and their property by the aggression of Germany by land, by sea, and from the air.'

Thus the Fourteen Points *did* become the basis of the peace negotiations. The German leaders surrendered because their armies were beaten and their home front had crumbled, but the German people believed that the Fourteen Points were to be the basis of the peace: so did President Wilson. (It is, of course, quite pertinent to remark that Wilson formulated his Fourteen Points on January 8th, 1918. At that time the Germans showed no disposition to accept them—on the contrary! Not until they were on the point of collapse were the Fourteen Points adopted.)

What the Germans should have realised was that the Fourteen Points were foreign to the atmosphere of the hour. For four years the world had been full of hate, and they themselves had been among the best haters. Could they credit that the minds of men would change in a moment—the moment of victory?

(The younger of my readers—and I hope there are many of them—will probably find it hard to credit the violent hatreds of those days. I advise them to turn up the files of any popular newspaper. The French press was worse: there was a coldly scientific series of articles in *Le Matin* discussing the exact dose of famine necessary in order to create the maximum of individual suffering and public weakness in Germany. Politicians spoke in the same vein—the famous phrase about squeezing Germany 'till the pips squeak' was coined by a responsible statesman. Yet press and politicians alike but reflected the atmosphere and ideas of those retrogressive days.)

It is worth while reading through the Fourteen Points very carefully.

1. *Open covenants of peace openly arrived at, after which there shall be no private international understandings of any kind, but diplomacy shall proceed always frankly and in public view.*

The implication of the first seven words is a negotiated peace: the basis was agreed—the Fourteen Points—and it was assumed by the defeated powers that the actual treaty would be a matter of discussion and negotiation. Nevertheless, at the last moment the President had referred the Germans, very correctly, to the Allied Commander-in-Chief, who had demanded what was in effect the complete surrender of Germany: with Germany at their mercy, the Allies decided that peace terms should be imposed, not negotiated. As Professor J. M. Keynes has shown, this decision had a profound effect on the treaties: the original draft was drawn up as a basis of bargaining, the Allies demanding a little more than they were ultimately prepared to accept. Then the entire draft was imposed.

Actually this Point in its entirety is frankly impossible in the present stage of mental evolution. It was clearly unworkable, as Wilson himself had to admit when, on the first day of the Peace Conference, representatives of fifty-three nations turned up!

Since that time, the principle of open diplomacy has been frankly abandoned. Even in the League of Nations the open sessions were little more than show-pieces—the real work was done behind the scenes. The proposed abolition of 'private international understandings' never won any firm adherence. At first treaties were camouflaged as being 'within the framework of the League,' but later even this pretence was dropped. The unfortunate fact is that man and his governments have not yet reached the ideal stage visualised by the first Point. Nor are there many signs that he is likely to reach it in the near future. Indeed, recently there has been an alarming lapse in international morality. There is scarcely a state in Europe which has not blatantly failed in its foreign obligations—not merely those inherent in the League charter, but direct alliances with friendly powers. The German attitude to treaties has been to use them as temporary palliatives or as deliberate strategic moves. It is certain that many uneasy years must pass before men will put their trust in treaties, whether they are negotiated in private or in public. The shock to the morals of the world is not likely to be rapidly repaired.

> 2. *Absolute freedom of navigation upon the seas outside territorial waters alike in peace and in war, except as the seas may be closed in whole or in part by international action for the enforcement of international covenants.*

As this was definitely excluded by the Allied Powers, it need not concern us here. Had Britain adhered to it in 1914–19 she would have lost the War. It is as meaningless now as it was then. In times of war, what belligerent is likely to be restricted by an imaginary line across the seas? By the Neutrality Act, the United States admitted the impossibility of the Point. There is no such thing as Freedom of the Seas—at the moment. Power of passage depends upon force. This is all wrong, but it is a condition likely to endure as long as war. No peace-time regulations are likely to be respected unless they can be enforced by the overwhelming weight of world opinion *and power.*

> 3. *The removal, so far as is possible, of all economic barriers, and the establishment of an equality of trade conditions among all the nations consenting to the peace and associating themselves for its maintenance.*

This is an excellent principle: if adopted, it would solve many of the world's problems. Unfortunately it has lost ground rather than gained since it was formulated, and the new doctrine of 'self-sufficiency' is not likely to aid its revival. Nevertheless it has to be tackled firmly, and was wisely included in the Atlantic Charter. Its discussion does not come within the scope of this book, but I need no persuasion of its overwhelming importance.

4. *Adequate guarantees given and taken that national armaments will be reduced to the lowest point consistent with domestic safety.*

One of the German complaints is that her army was forcibly reduced to 100,000 men, but it was promised that her neighbours would also disarm. The French persistently refused to do so: there were no doubt adequate reasons for their action, but the fact remains that the spirit of this Point was ignored.

The argument today can be worked both ways. If France had disarmed, her condition would have been even worse than it proved. Or if France had disarmed, then Germany would not have rearmed.

The tragedy was that France, refusing disarmament, did not maintain a stronger army. If you are going to have arms at all, let them be first-class. By maintaining a large numerical army, France invited German rearmament: by allowing it to fall into a poorly equipped state, she invited her own defeat.

There is much that is sound in the argument. On the other hand, if France *had* disarmed, how many people can believe that Germany would have resisted the open temptation to revenge?

5. *A free, open-minded and absolutely impartial adjustment of all colonial claims based upon a strict observance of the principle that in determining all such questions of sovereignty the interests of the populations concerned must have equal weight with the equitable claims of the Government whose title is to be determined.*

No pretence was made of implementing this. Colonial territories were allocated on an older principle—that of conquest.

There are at least signs that the spirit of this Point means more today.

6. *The evacuation of all Russian territory, and such a set-tlement of all questions affecting Russia as will secure the best and freest co-operation of the other nations of the world in obtaining for her an unhampered and un-embarrassed opportunity for the independent deter-mination of her own political development and national policy, and assure her of a sincere welcome into the society of free nations under institutions of her own choosing, and more than a welcome, assistance also of every kind that she may need and may herself desire. The treatment accorded Russia by her sister nations in the months to come will be the acid test of their good-will, of their comprehension of her needs as distin-guished from their own interests, and of their intelligent and unselfish sympathy.*

In some respects this Point was the most tragic of the whole fourteen. So far from receiving co-operation and welcome, Russia was opposed and shunned. True, her own policies made matters worse. Thus there arose that shadow of suspicion between Russia and the Western Powers which has been so largely responsible for the unhappy fate of Europe. If this Point had been implemented, there would probably have been no Nazi Germany today: certainly no Nazi war. Blame should be equally accorded to both parties. Once suspicion develops, it is more dangerous than open enmity.

One good thing likely to emerge from the evil of war is a new understanding with Russia. Our position today is quite clear. There is a wide gap between our ideas of government and theirs—and, among our own people, those who would dislike the Soviet system most intensely are those of the Left. The system of government adopted by Russia can scarcely be claimed as our business: conversely, our internal affairs are no concern of Russia. Yet Russian suspicion was mainly directed against British groups thought to be planning the overthrow of the Soviet; and British suspicion was prompted by the thought that 'international communism' was merely an agency of Russian foreign policy: both suspicions had a very real basis of fact.

Soviet foreign policy has made little pretence to be anything else but Russian. (When the country was attacked, Stalin did not appeal to his people to defend Communism, but the Russian Fatherland—his appeal was national, not international.) A Foreign Office is a Foreign Office, even if it calls itself a People's Commissariat for Foreign Affairs.

The influence of Russia in post-war Europe is bound to be profound. The gallant resistance of her people has properly evoked widespread admiration, and has done a great deal to banish the lingering prejudice and distrust in many British and American minds. This is all to the good. Yet sentiment is a poor guide in European frontier problems. We admired the Russian resistance—but we also admired the Finnish resistance in the winter of 1939. Sentiment must not cloud our judgment when we approach those problems in which Russia is especially concerned: the Russians would not ask it, for they are realists in affairs. Problems in which Russia is concerned must not be judged by Russian gallantry, but by reason and justice. But at least we can affirm that there is a far better chance of the Sixth Point being implemented after this war than after the last!

7. *Belgium, the whole world will agree, must be evacuated and restored without any attempt to limit the sovereignty which she enjoys in common with all other free nations. No other single act will serve as this will serve to restore confidence among the nations in the laws which they have themselves set and determined for the government of their relations with one another. Without this healing act the whole structure and validity of international law is for ever impaired.*

The whole world did agree, including Germany. But Belgium was again invaded in 1940: and, unless we learn from the mistakes of 1919, there is no guarantee that she will not be invaded again.

> 8. *All French territory should be freed, and the invaded portions restored, and the wrong done to France by Prussia in 1871 in the matter of Alsace-Lorraine, which has unsettled the peace of the world for nearly fifty years, should be righted in order that peace may once more be made secure in the interest of all.*

The point was accepted by Germany without question. Leaders of a military machine realise that if you fight a war and lose, you have to pay: you are very lucky if you get off with the loss of the booty you secured in the previous war. It is already obvious, at a moment when the Germans are convinced that they are winning that they have earmarked Alsace-Lorraine once again for annexation to the Reich.

> 9. *A readjustment of the frontiers of Italy should be effected along clearly recognisable lines of nationality.*

Before the war over a million Italians were subjects of Austria-Hungary. As we shall see, however, the readjustment of the frontiers was carried out too generously, and 500,000 Yugoslavs and 250,000 Germans became Italian subjects.

> 10. *The peoples of Austria-Hungary, whose place among the nations we wish to see safeguarded and assured, should be accorded the freest opportunity of autonomous development.*

This was done: but, although this Point was tackled sincerely, it has left more problems than perhaps any other. We shall consider these in some detail. When we come to talk of the demarcation of frontiers, readers will perhaps recall the phrase 'readjustment of frontiers should be effected along clearly recognisable lines of nationality' from the previous

Point, and the phrase 'along historically established lines of allegiance and nationality' from the one following. These principles are obviously intended to apply to all new frontiers, and sometimes one cancels out the other.

11. *Roumania, Serbia and Montenegro should be evacuated, occupied territories restored; Serbia accorded free and secure access to the sea; and the relations of the several Balkan States to one another determined by friendly counsel along historically established lines of allegiance and nationality; and international guarantees of the political and economic independence and territorial integrity of the several Balkan States should be entered into.*

We shall find to our cost that frontier lines determined by nationality and history are not necessarily the same thing. This Point was honestly attempted, but there are plenty of problems in the Balkans still.

12. *The Turkish portions of the present Ottoman Empire should be assured a secure sovereignty, but the other nationalities which are now under Turkish rule should be assured an undoubted security of life and an absolutely unmolested opportunity of autonomous development, and the Dardanelles should be permanently opened as a free passage to the ships and commerce of all nations under international guarantees.*

The problems arising from this Point are closely related to those of the two previous.

13. *An independent Polish State should be erected which should include the territories inhabited by indisputably Polish populations, which should be assured a free and secure access to the sea, and whose political and economic independence and territorial integrity should be guaranteed by international covenant.*

This is the most discussed Point, as we shall see. Even its phrasing is the source of vigorous argument.

14. *A general association of nations must be formed under specific covenants for the purpose of affording mutual guarantees of political independence and territorial integrity to great and small States alike.*

The Point which raised the greatest hopes: had it succeeded, it might have covered any failure in the other thirteen. We have argued that its principles were in advance of the world's thought: they appealed to men's hearts, but not to their minds. The idea was presented too suddenly to counter the inherent prejudices of generations of nationalism, and followed too closely on a conflict which had been fed on patriotic slogans.

When eventually an association of nations is formed—as it must, if civilisation is to survive—then it would follow better from an educational campaign which would convince people of its essential value, rather than as an expression of war-weariness after a terrible conflict, when men will grasp at anything—for the moment. This Point is discussed in another section: it remains the most important of the fourteen.

It is essential to realise that the outlook on war in Europe is not the same as in Britain or the United States. We are satiated states—in no circumstances could we gain by war. We talk about the 'futility of war,' and mean it. Yet when I used the phrase in Eastern Europe men stared at me in amazement. How could the Balkan countries have obtained their freedom except by war? How else could Poland have been re-born— can you imagine Russia, Austria and Germany voluntarily liberating their Polish subjects and handing back freely the historic Polish territories? It is true that you may wander over Europe and find few people who want war, but it is equally true that you will find few people who believe that war is futile. War has persisted throughout the ages for lack of any alternative. So long as there are international problems to be solved, war will persist until an alternative *is* found.

While we are on the subject, we must glance at the 'Four Principles' on which the Fourteen Points were based.

1. *Each part of the final settlement must be based upon the essential justice of that particular case.*

2. *Peoples and provinces must not be bartered about from sovereignty to sovereignty as if they were pawns in a game.*

3. *Every territorial settlement must be in the interest of the populations concerned, and not as a part of any mere adjustment or compromise of claims among rival States.*

4. *All well-defined national aspirations shall be accorded the utmost satisfaction that can be accorded them without introducing new or perpetuating old elements of discord and antagonism.*

Few people will have any quarrel with these Points or Principles—except that some of them contradict each other!

We must now pass to the enumeration of the principles of the 'Atlantic Charter.'

The President of the United States and the Prime Minister, Mr. Churchill, representing His Majesty's Government in the United Kingdom, being met together, deem it right to make known certain common principles in the national policies of their respective countries on which they base their hopes for a better future for the world.

1. *Their countries seek no aggrandisement, territorial or other.*

This means that there are to be no new 'mandates' or 'protectorates.' It implies that Italy will be allowed to keep her original colonies—but *not*, of course, Abyssinia, Albania and her 'conquests' in Yugoslavia. The subsequent adoption of the Charter by Russia has had big effects in Eastern Europe, as we shall see.

2. *They desire to see no territorial changes that do not accord with the freely expressed wishes of the people concerned.*

No one will doubt the justice of this clause. It coincides exactly with the principles of the Fourteen Points. Nevertheless, even our superficial examination will reveal that it is more difficult to apply than to state. The ethnic medley in some parts of Europe is such that we have argued transference of population as the only equitable solution. It is safe to anticipate that this will seldom be effected 'with the freely expressed wishes of the people concerned.'

The clause implies local plebiscites, which will almost certainly play a considerable part in the determination of the new frontiers. Yet even under the fairest possible method of freely expressed wishes there are bound to be immense difficulties. In Transylvania, for example, the Roumanians outnumber the Hungarians by more than two to one. A plebiscite would certainly result in such a vote. Then the Hungarians could claim that their fate was not being decided by their freely expressed wish!

However, it will be better to consider these difficulties as they arise: and to recall that ethnic considerations, though of great importance, are not the sole determinants of a frontier.

We have at least one advantage over the statesmen of 1919. While adhering to the spirit of peoples being ruled by leaders of their own kin, they found it impossible to follow their own principles because of treaties arranged before Wilson propounded his Fourteen Points. For example, in order to bribe Italy into the war, the Allies promised her territory which went considerably beyond her ethnic frontiers. Thus, very dangerous precedents were created when we implemented some of our promises. This time we are not handicapped by such bargains. Our biggest difficulties in applying the ethnic principle are likely to be (*a*) the understandable clamour for a revengeful peace on the part of those countries which have suffered the most; (*b*) a sentimental assumption that the countries which fought best on our side have necessarily the strongest claims. As we shall see, in 1919 the benefit of any doubt was always given to the victors: it is only human that this should happen again. It is our task first to reduce the cases of doubt to a minimum.

> 3. *They respect the right of all peoples to choose the form of government under which they will live, and they wish to see sovereign rights and self-government restored to those who have been forcibly deprived of them.*

There are two important problems outlined in this liberal clause. The first confirms our comment under Wilson's Sixth Point: Russia, Britain, Switzerland, Italy, Greece—and Germany—may have the form of government considered by their people best suited to their needs.

One query immediately arises—Is Germany to be allowed to retain a Nazi government? Or any other form of militarist government? Surely it clashes with the oft-stated principle that one of our main objects is the overthrow of such things. Actually, this query is answered by the eighth clause of the Charter, which deals with disarmament. If this is firmly applied, there is little danger of a further spate of militarism in Germany.

The second part of this clause is one of elementary justice. The British government has repeatedly stated that it will not recognise territorial changes made by force during the war: the United States has taken the same logical and reasonable line. There may be adjustments of frontiers, but at least we shall return to the 1938 position before debating them.

> 4. *They will endeavour, with due respect for their existing obligations, to further enjoyment by all States, great or small, victor or vanquished, of access on equal terms to the trade and to the raw materials of the world which are needed for their economic prosperity.*

5. *They desire to bring about fullest collaboration between all nations in economic fields, with the object of securing for all improved labour standards, economic advancement and social security.*

These clauses represent a definite advance from Wilson's Second Point. The phrase 'with due respect for their existing obligations' struck chill on many eager hearts. It shouted of the phraseology of the Old Diplomacy. To some men it killed the whole spirit of the Charter. At the same time the insertion of the phrase 'victor *and vanquished*' ought to restore a warm glow.

These clauses are recognised as the essence of common sense. Yet there was some disappointment because no detail was given. Many times previously statesmen have agreed on the principle of equal access to raw materials, but to date no satisfactory economic method has been found. A successful solution would alter the whole course of human conflict: prosperity is the best antidote to totalitarianism; dictatorships are born of despair. Hitler himself was a product of economic despair. Following the French march into the Ruhr in 1923, Germany suffered agonies from hopeless inflation. In the world crisis of 1930 it seemed likely that this appalling fate was likely to be repeated. It is reputed that drowning men catch at straws. Certainly men rush to extreme palliatives when threatened with economic distress.

6. *After the final destruction of Nazi tyranny, they hope to see established a peace which will afford to all nations the means of dwelling in safety within their own boundaries and which will afford assurance that all men in all lands may live out their lives in freedom from fear and want.*

If we can translate this from a pious hope into a practical policy, then we shall have made a vast advance. It obviously envisages some super-national organisation, but wisely does not discuss its form. One of the first desirabilities of the post-war New Order is that the United States should play in it a prominent part. Isolationism and nationalism are even more strongly entrenched there than in Europe, and big educational strides are necessary before the perfect world organisation emerges.

Nations have always formed the components of international society, and always will. We must build from the bottom, not the top. In 1919 we visualised our edifice without sufficient consideration of the building materials. In this book we shall examine their possibilities and their deficiencies. A good architect does not plan his building until he knows what constructional materials are available.

7. *Such a peace should enable all men to traverse the high seas and oceans without hindrance.*

The Freedom of the Seas again. In view of the character of the two men who made and signed the Charter, it would seem that their benevolent and excellent idea crystallises around the existence of British and American fleets strong enough to drive pirates from all seaways.

8. *They believe all of the nations of the world, for realistic as well as spiritual reasons, must come to the abandonment of the use of force.*

Since no future peace can be maintained if land, sea, or air armaments continue to be employed by nations which threaten or may threaten aggression outside of their frontiers, they believe, pending the establishment of a wider and permanent system of general security, that the disarmament of such nations is essential.

They will likewise aid and encourage all practicable other measures which will lighten for peace-loving peoples the crushing burden of armaments.

This clause is at least more realistic than the disarmament phrases of the Fourteen Points. Total disarmament must rank high among the aspirations of thinking men: nations have always claimed arms because their neighbours have them. It is obvious that the beginning of the attainment of the ideal must be the disarmament of those nations which have used their arms for aggressive purposes. There could be no confidence in Europe while Germany continued to exercise predominant military force.

The aggressor nations must remain disarmed until their outlook is reorientated. This may be a long and difficult process. However, even if we cannot convert the younger Nazis, we can at least convince them that force does not pay. The first phrase of this clause is important—'for realistic as well as spiritual reasons.' Hitler and Goebbels frequently urge on the German population by claiming that never in all history have German arms been so successful, never has Germany had such a chance of achieving world power. This is perfectly true, and is one of the main incentives behind the German onslaught. But the Germans are intelligent people: when they see that force fails, in spite of all the advantages they hold today and are never likely to hold again, then they will surely appreciate the 'realistic reasons' in favour of the abandonment of force. Further, this war is being brought home to Germany more intimately than any previous conflict: this will have wide effects. Moreover, in our re-education of the German people we must not overlook the spiritual appeal. To us the Nazi creed in theory and practice is a disgusting thing; it is difficult for us to credit that it has a spiritual basis: unfortunately, millions of Germans believe that it has. The human mind is malleable, the German mind particularly so: its inherent spirituality may be directed in more worth-while directions.

We shall find, in the course of our study, that the clauses of the Atlantic Charter are not merely a collection of pious aspirations. They do offer a real guide towards the solution of many of Europe's pressing problems. Their possibilities depend to no small extent upon the co-operation of Britain, the United States and U.S.S.R. after the war. Hitler has achieved one miracle in uniting these three diverse communities in a common aim. In Britain the greatest danger is a post-war demand for relapse into a life of isolated ease: in the United States by the fact that policies are fleeting and tend to follow the personalities of presidents—if the tragedy of Wilson in 1919 were to be repeated, the cause of international peace would receive a deadly blow: fortunately, Roosevelt is of a vastly different type. From the east the most comforting feature lies in the fact that Soviet Russia has adopted the Atlantic Charter as the basis of its own peace aims.

VIII

We can now summarise the argument in this introduction: it is understood that any suggestion I may make is intended as a basis of discussion rather than as a conclusive decision.

(a) The Treaty of Versailles, and the other treaties of 1919, were not deliberate instruments of venomous revenge. Generally speaking, the territorial clauses were very moderate; the economic clauses were unreasonably harsh—and were abandoned one by one, so that in the outset Germany escaped very lightly.

(b) The Atlantic Charter provides a fair and workable basis of the settlement of European problems.

(c) It is important that territorial difficulties shall be resolved in principle, so far as is humanly possible, *before* the end of the war. Otherwise the resultant scramble for frontiers will add enormously to the inevitable confusion which will follow the termination of hostilities.

(d) Even if a minor or major degree of federalism is introduced into Europe, frontiers will still be necessary. It would be unwise to rush through any major scheme until the minds of Europeans have been educated and matured to the idea. Any organisation which is set up merely as an aftermath of war weariness is scarcely likely to survive.

There is no sign that the necessary maturity of outlook exists today. In the last days of France Mr. Churchill made a dramatic gesture, and offered a full and solemn union between France and Britain: the scope envisaged went far beyond many federal schemes. The offer attracted attention only because of its drama: it was widely interpreted as a desperate last-minute bribe to keep a weak and collapsing France in the war. How often is it referred to today? It is probable that most British people have forgotten that the offer was ever made, and it is certain that lengthy missionary work is necessary before such and similar ideas would be completely acceptable to them, much less to races whose nationalist and patriotic sentiment runs even higher.

(e) The task of re-drawing the frontiers of Europe is not easy. Nevertheless, the resultant boundaries are not likely to differ widely from those of 1938.

(f) While it is only human that we should regard our allies with more friendly eyes than we do our foes, peace after victory must not be based on sentiment or revenge, but on reason and justice. No settlement will appear fair to the Germans immediately after defeat, but the principles of a just peace can be represented over an adequate period of time so that they are accepted as fair. No settlement will endure unless it commands the confidence of the large majority of the people of Europe.

(g) The ethnic complications of Europe are so vast that it is impossible to give justice to large numbers of people without injuring others. Democratic principles must apply—the minority must accept the decision of the majority. At the same time, the lot of the minority should be alleviated to every possible degree.

(h) Since races in frontier regions are so tangled, an organised programme of transfers of populations will probably be necessary. Inevitable hardships can be reduced to a minimum by careful planning and financial generosity. The sorting-out of a few million people may avert another world war.

(i) The economic consequences of the peace will probably be as important as, or more important than, racial and boundary questions. Economic affairs are, however, beyond the scope of this book, which is concerned with one aspect of European re-settlement—the new frontiers. Further, the economic aspects must not be unduly stressed at the expense of nationalist outlook. There will probably be a resurgence of nationalism after the war, which is being fought in nearly all countries on patriotic grounds. In a contest between economics and nationalism the latter nearly always wins: maybe it ought not to be so, but it is. Even in our own country, where nationalism has probably passed its peak of intensity, its influence is profound. At the height of our unemployment crisis many thousands of jobs were available abroad: the call of country was so strong that few men could be found to fill them.

In many countries of Europe nationalism is still a growing force: this applies especially to those which have only recently been released from bondage—like Poland or the Balkan states: or have only recently been formed—like Germany. In those countries there is no comparison between the powers of nationalism and economics. Perhaps it is rightly so: a man's mind is of more importance than the potatoes he grows in his ground.

(*j*) The duration of world peace is likely to depend to no small degree on the nature and extent of collaboration between Britain, the United States and Russia. One good result emerging from the evil of war has been the gradual diminution of the fog of suspicion between Russia and the Western Powers. If this can be completed and the atmosphere cleared, then the outlook becomes measurably brighter.

(*k*) No democratic government can ever act firmly in its peace objectives unless it is soundly backed by public opinion in its own country. Foreign affairs are no longer the sacrosanct property of a few specialists. Our greatest need is a foreign policy which will be backed consistently by all political parties: let us argue at will on means tests and nationalisation of railways, but if we quarrel on the great issues of war and peace, then we are giving an open invitation for future strife in Europe.

(*l*) It is certainly the greatest error to assume that the night of war will pass directly into the light of day: in between there must inevitably be a period of grey dawn. In that period problems will be urgent and desperate; conditions in the occupied countries are so terrible that uprisings and massacres can scarcely be avoided unless previous preparation on a vast scale has been made. There will be endless clashes between the opposing powers—even between those which have fought on the same side—unless we are ready at short notice to outline provisional arrangements: for example, we can reasonably assume that Roumania and Hungary will be at one another's throats on the question of Transylvania the moment Germany is defeated, unless we are ready with some scheme that will at any rate gain time for a more mature settlement.

Thus it is highly desirable that the Allies should agree on major issues before the moment of victory—and not, as in 1919, keep a devastated Europe waiting while they quarrel among themselves. The argument that frontiers cannot be discussed until we know the character of the victory implies that decisions are to be made in accordance with the verdict of battle: this is contrary to the spirit and letter of the Atlantic Charter.

At the same time, the frontiers which we should be ready to fix immediately after the war should be declared liable to review in detail after, say, five years. No hastily drawn frontiers can be perfect, and transfers of populations may involve later adjustments of frontiers.

(*m*) Although it is very true that the influence of America will be vastly important, even vital, during peace negotiations, the internal problems of Europe have still to be solved primarily by Europeans. If America were to overthrow Isolationism completely, and enter into World affairs, then the prospects of peace would be very bright. American backing of the League of Nations, and American guarantees of European frontiers after the last war, might have ensured peace without costing the United States another dollar.

It is improbable that American policy after the present war will be similar to that of 1919. Nevertheless, isolationist sentiment there is of long standing. There is so little that is traditional in American outlook—and those things which are traditional favour Isolationism rather than participation in World affairs. While Europe hopes that America will be interested in European problems, for her detached outlook upon them is invaluable, she must prepare, if the worst comes to the worst, to solve them herself.

After America, the British outlook on European questions is the most detached. It is of no importance or economic interest to us whether the Roumanian frontier is moved ten miles one way or the other; thus our opinion can be sounder and more reasoned and judicial than that of a closer neighbour with a direct interest in the question. But before we can attempt judgment we have to know far more about the problems of Europe than we did in 1919—or than we do today.

It will be useless to send our statesmen to any Peace Conference unless they are backed up by a soundly informed public opinion; otherwise the treaties they sign are not likely to be more permanent than those signed in 1919. Our objective is a peace that will endure: this can never be founded on vengeance.

(*n*) Every idea for the betterment of Europe is dependent upon victory; I should really print this at the end of every chapter. We need a total victory—a compromise would be a defeat. Not for an hour must we relax our efforts; but even in the battle there are moments when it is possible to think—when it is a relief and a stimulation to think. What better subject for thought than the cause for which we struggle? However hazy we may be about war aims, we can at least agree on one—that this sort of thing must never happen again.

CHAPTER TWO

POLAND

I

PADEREWSKI, the famous pianist who became first Prime Minister of Poland, used to tell a story of a professor at a cosmopolitan university. One day, setting a thesis for his class, he selected as a general subject: 'The Elephant.' The Englishman produced an essay on 'The Elephant, and how to hunt him.' The Frenchman submitted a sparkling disquisition on 'The Love Life of the Elephant.' The German considered: 'Gastronomical Possibilities of the Elephant.' The Russian, after smoking several hundred cigarettes, produced the startling caption: 'The Elephant—does it exist?' And the Pole headed his thesis: 'The Elephant and the Polish Question.'

There always has been a Polish question: today there are many. They are vital not merely to the well-being of Poland but to the peace of Europe. There is more potential trouble to the mile along Poland's frontiers than anywhere else in Europe. After the war the reconstruction of Poland will be one of Europe's major tasks. It has been well said that we shall know whether we have won by what happens to Poland.

Poland is geographically one of the most important states of Europe. Ethnically its situation is even more vital, since it joins—or separates—the contrasted cultures of Germany and Russia. Politically Poland has been much under-estimated in Britain, and our lack of interest in Polish affairs was remarkable. Our grandfathers knew much more about Poland than we do, and Polish struggles for freedom from Russian and Prussian tyranny were sympathetically followed in Britain. After Poland obtained her freedom, however, our cordiality declined. Maybe a Polish friend of mine struck a psychological

ruth when he explained this: 'The British are the friends of
he under-dog, and have been throughout history. But, once
the under-dog has got up, the British are no longer interested.'

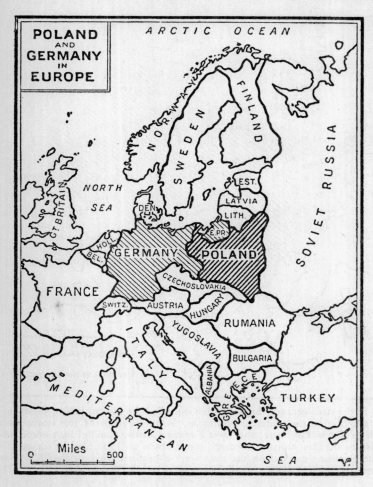

British outlook tends to ignore Eastern Europe—yet Warsaw is a *Central* European capital, and does not belong to the
east. Take a map of Europe and draw a few lines from one
extremity to the other—from the Shetland Islands to the

Crimea, from North Cape to Cape Matapan, from Gibraltar to the easternmost point in the Urals—you may be surprised to find that they intersect near Warsaw.

In the sixth century the Slav tribes occupied the eastern half of Germany in addition to their present territories. Many survivals of this occupation still persist in Germany, and most Eastern German families have some admixture of Slav blood. (Bismarck himself was an Elbe Slav by descent!) The Prussians marked on the map were a heathen tribe, neither Slav nor Teutonic, which was eventually conquered by the Teutonic Knights.

The Poles are, of course, a branch of the great Slav race, akin to Russians, Ukrainians, Serbs, Bulgars, Czechs and Slovaks. The Polish Empire was founded towards the end of the tenth century but it was at first no more than a loose authority over innumerable petty princes. Even the kingship was by election—which gave the country the disadvantages of a kingdom and a republic, with the advantages of neither.

The social structure was peculiar. As so common at that time, the great landowners were the most powerful men in the land. Next in importance were the *Szlachta*, the gentry. The Polish system of inheritance was responsible for the existence of this class. A Polish knight would be rewarded for his valour in battle by a grant of land: at his death, this would be divided among his sons: and so on, until after a few generations men of noble birth would find themselves the owners of no more than peasants' holdings: but they themselves still belonged to the *Szlachta* class.

The peasants themselves were virtually serfs. Only one son of a family might emigrate to a town: the rest were tied to their lords' land. The system may not have been quite so bad as it sounds, for the noble usually took a patriarchal interest in his flock, but conditions of life were generally low. To ensure an adequate supply of cheap labour, peasants were forbidden to engage in trade. Polish tradition—one of the strongest forces in the land—forbade the gentry and nobility to soil their fingers with commerce: thus Poland never formed that stabilising influence, a middle class: traders had to be imported from abroad—they were mostly Germans or Jews.

At this time Poland was regarded as a haven of liberty: so it was, at least for the enfranchised classes. Certainly the history of Poland is clear of those religious and racial persecutions which have disfigured the records of so many European states. 'I am not king of your conscience,' declared a Polish monarch. 'Nobody shall be imprisoned until he is legally convicted,' another king ruled—two hundred and fifty years before the passing of the Habeas Corpus Act in England.

There was at least an attempt at democracy in Poland before the word was ever heard of in Western Europe. True, its benefits were confined to the gentry class, but they were large. Ten per cent of the people of Poland had the right to vote—

at a time when the proportion was only 5 per cent in England. Any man of the *Szlachta*, even if he owned but a tiny farm, had rights as secure as those of a great landowner. Yet democracy was reduced to a farce by the *liberum veto*—the free vote: if one member of the Polish Parliament voted against a measure, then automatically it was not merely defeated but completely dropped—and on the motion of one member the whole Parliament was adjourned. Consequently, progress was almost impossible. It is interesting to note that the League of Nations also required a unanimous vote on all major questions!

It was fortunate that Poland was free from the internecine religious wars of the middle centuries, for she had enemies enough on her borders. For generations she was the outpost of Christendom against marauding barbarians. Tartars and Turks alike were repelled by Polish arms.

More pertinent to our study is the conflict between Poland and the Teutonic Knights. In the thirteenth century the Baltic shores were peopled with pagan races—Prussians, Lithuanians and their neighbours. With the blessing of the Pope, a great military order had been formed among the German kingdoms, the Teutonic Knights of the Cross. Formed originally for service in the Crusades, these knights perceived more profitable battlegrounds nearer home. They began to organise expeditions to the north-east: capturing a village by virtue of their superior armaments, they would summon the people to accept the Cross. Those who refused and clung to their old gods were massacred: those who accepted Christianity became the serfs of the Teutonic Knights. Such was the terror of their methods that for generations the Lithuanian peasants used to shudder at the sign of the Cross.

(There is a deep similarity between the Teutonic Knights and the Nazis. Both started off with high-sounding ideals which were almost a religion: both degenerated into bands of unscrupulous opportunists intent on their own aggrandisement.)

Along the Baltic shores the Teutonic Knights built strong

castles from which they dominated the countryside. Under their 'protection' trading cities developed. They ruled over what are now called Estonia, Latvia and Lithuania. They almost exterminated the heathen Prussians, taking from them all their possessions—even their name. By the accidents of history the Knights failed to occupy a narrow strip of territory to the west of the Vistula, which remained in the hands of its Polish inhabitants. Thus the problem of the Polish 'Corridor' was born.

Weak Polish rulers invited the Knights to protect them against pagan tribes raiding from the north and east. The Teutonic Knights did this—and more: they seized not only heathen lands but Poland's Baltic coast. The time came when the reality of the danger could no longer be ignored. By this time the power of Poland had increased, for in 1386 a royal marriage had resulted in union with Lithuania. The Teutonic Knights, too, had vastly increased their influence, and their Prussian kingdom was a menace to Poland. The Polish king was a man of peace: like Hitler, the Knights interpreted his distaste for war as weakness: they discovered their mistake.

At Tannenburg in 1410, the Teutonic Knights were hopelessly defeated. Their Grand Master bore a proud name, Albert of Hohenzollern, but he had to pay homage to the king of Poland. This is one of the indignities of history which Hitler finds so irritating.

Thence, for three hundred years, Poland continued as a considerable empire; its boundaries stretched from the Baltic to the Black Sea, and included a considerable portion of the Ukraine. On the outskirts of Poland were vassal kingdoms—including Prussia.

Gradually the power of Poland declined. The system of electing the kings was bound to be unsatisfactory—the nobles who elected them chose weak men they could dominate, not strong men who would rule. The *liberum veto* killed social and political advancement. Poland, which had been in the van of progress, rapidly fell behind.

Her difficulties were immense at the best. Kingdoms and empires were now taking shape in Europe. Poland stood at a European cross-roads, without natural defences, exposed to the inroads of grasping neighbours, the battleground between Teutonic, Russian and Turkish ambitions. Nevertheless, the country was large, rich and fertile; her knights were famous,

and her peasants sturdy men-at-arms. Yet it is difficult for any country to fight a war on two fronts, as history has shown: Poland was to suffer onslaughts on three.

Russia, Prussia and Austria combined to attack Poland in 1772. The king at that time was an elected puppet: the country was disunited. True, the aggressors were rivals, but they made

an infamous bargain at Poland's expense. Russia seized the
eastern province, Austria the south-western corner: Prussia
annexed Pomorze, better known today as the 'Polish Corridor.'

A rump Poland remained: the Poles, appalled by their fate,
rallied. The revolutionary flame spread from France—with
which country Poland had always had strong cultural ties.
A new Constitution was agreed upon in 1791: all privileges of
nobility were voluntarily renounced—Poland was about to
enter on a period of genuine democracy.

But ideas of liberty and freedom were anathema to the three
autocratic states bordering Poland's frontier. They set themselves to suppress such dangerous theories as those that men
had the right to think for themselves, and to govern themselves: otherwise this unholy leaven might spread to their own
dominions. Obviously such ideas must be exterminated at once.
So Russia, Austria and Prussia proceeded with the final partition of Poland in 1793. Napoleon re-established a portion of
the ancient kingdom for a brief period, but on his fall Poland
again became no more than a name.

For a hundred and fifty years Poland was no more than a
name, an almost forgotten name—except in Poland. There
patriots schemed and fought for freedom against hopeless
odds. It says something for the tenacity of race that in spite of
appalling repression from the Russians—who occupied two-
thirds of the old Poland—the language and culture of Poland
survived. The Poles faithfully followed the advice of Rous-
seau: 'Poles, if you cannot prevent your neighbours from
swallowing you, you can at least secure that they will not
succeed in digesting you.'

In Austrian Poland the hand of authority was not too harsh
—Poles even enjoyed some local rights of self-government:
the Prussian yoke, on the other hand, was stern. For the
whole period of Russian domination Eastern Poland was
administered as a subject province by Russians. The Poles had
no rights and little liberty. The extraordinary feature was that
if a Pole cared to emigrate to Russia proper, any career was

open to him. As he was more virile, energetic and intelligent than the average Russian, he usually did very well, and before 1914 a big proportion of Russian professional men—engineers, architects, doctors and the like—were actually Poles. Similarly the higher ranks of the Russian army were freely recruited

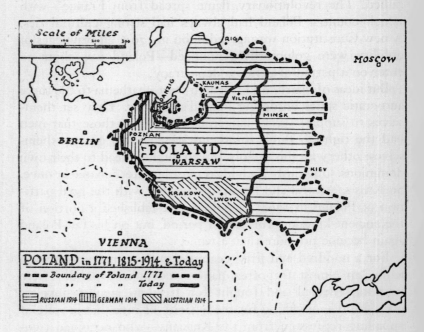

Scale of Miles

POLAND in 1771, 1815-1914, & Today
- - - Boundary of Poland 1771
,, ,, ,, Today
RUSSIAN 1914   GERMAN 1914   AUSTRIAN 1914

from Germans of the Baltic states—descendants of the Teutonic Knights.

Then came the World War, and with it a miracle. Poland's prospects were not bright. If Russia won, the Poles could only look forward to a greater Poland under the tyranny of the Czars. If the Central Powers won, there would still be no reborn Poland. The impossible had to happen—first the defeat of Russia, and then the defeat of Austria and Germany. For the people of Poland the war was agony, for Poles fought on both sides: Pilsudski's legions fought beside the Austrians, while Poles were conscripted into Russian and German armies.

Yet the miracle happened, and in the last days of 1918 the name Poland again appeared on the map of Europe.

The early days of the new-born state were precarious. In the south-east were millions of Ukrainians and Poles engaged in a confused civil war. There followed open conflict between Poland and the new Russian Bolshevik state. At first the Poles were successful, but then they were beaten back to the gates of Warsaw. Here Pilsudski launched a counter-attack with devastating results, and the Russian retreat resembled a rout. A peace was hastily patched up: and, as we shall see, the agreed frontier was ethnically unsound, for millions of Ukrainians were left inside Poland.

We have agreed that there is no such thing as a 'natural' frontier, but Poland's boundaries are purely artificial, and a source of endless irritation. Only in the south, where the frontier follows the watershed of the Carpathians, is there anything resembling a 'natural' division. East and west—and especially east—the line of demarcation was settled arbitrarily, and we shall have to consider some of its principal complications.

Many of the internal difficulties of Poland can scarcely be blamed on the Poles. It must be remembered that for a hundred and fifty years the country lay under foreign yokes— a hundred and fifty critical and formative years, which saw the development of modern civilisation and the birth of modern economic progress. The Prussians ruled their subject races efficiently but firmly. The Poles were given little share even in local responsibility, and their own culture was vigorously submerged. Nevertheless their standard of living was comparatively high.

The Austrians were far more tolerant; Galicia, the Austrian share of Poland, was almost a self-governing province. Here at least Polish culture could thrive, and statesmen and administrators be trained against the day when Poland would live again. The lot of the millions of Poles who lived under the corrupt and inefficient Russian rule, on the other hand, was miserable. They were reduced almost to the level of serfs, and all reminders of their race were brutally suppressed.

Thus the new Poland of 1918 comprised people who had been brought up under three very different codes of conduct and law. Even twenty years later the codification of Polish law was still incomplete, and the three previous codes still survived—so that what was lawful in Cracow might be illegal in Warsaw. I did not need to look at a map as I crossed from Prussian Poland into Russian Poland. Communications deteriorated at once, peasants were miserably housed, education was backward—in the old Russian Poland not more than 25 per cent of the people could read or write. The first task of the Polish government, still incomplete, was to level up the standard of life among the three divisions. Polish language and culture, by the way, survived with remarkable firmness, and Polish is freer from dialects than any language in Europe.

Gradually domestic difficulties were being overcome, and there was every indication that the time was near when Poland would be a powerful state again. Indeed, the dignity of recognition as a Great Power loomed brightly on the horizon. The population of Poland in 1938 was 34 millions and her birth-rate was high. By 1950 her population was likely to be 50 millions—and by that time Great Britain and France would count little more than 40 millions each. Further, Poland was a young country. During the World War, apart from ordinary casualties, over 1 million Poles died of privation. Naturally, most of these were old people, so that the normal age balance of population was disturbed. Thus in 1938 50 per cent of the people of Poland were under twenty-five years of age—66 per cent under thirty!

These were remarkable figures. They meant that Poland, with a population of only 34 millions, could mobilise an army larger than France with 41 millions. The conscript classes being called up in the immediate pre-war years were nearly as large in Poland as in Germany.

Consider the situation in the immediate post-1918 years— a defeated Germany in the trough of despair, bankrupt and without hope, and a resurrected Poland charged with enthusiastic and optimistic virility. Thus in the years 1920–25 the average number of boys born in Poland was 515,000. In Germany, with double the population, it was only 675,000.

More recent figures are even more striking. Although free from government stimulus, the Poles are naturally more prolific than the Germans, and in the last ten years the average number of boys born in Poland was 511,000, while in Germany it was 595,000. In young man-power, therefore, Poland was only slightly inferior to Germany.

When the clash came in 1939, the defeat of the Poles was not due to their lack of men, but to their lack of arms.

A few statistics of the reborn Poland will be interesting. The country comprised 388,634 square kilometres—three times the size of the British Isles. The density of population was 89 per square kilometre as compared with 193 for the United Kingdom and 76 for France. These figures could be misleading: Poland is an overwhelmingly rural country. Only 27 per cent of the population live in towns (only eleven towns have a population of more than 100,000): the density of its rural population is two and a half times as high as that of France. The limits of economic land settlement were reached long ago. Due to the cessation of emigration, the Polish countryside was grossly overcrowded: large families attempted to drag a living from a small plot of land, and in many parts of the country—especially the eastern districts—the standard of life was low.

Only 19,000 land holdings exceeded the moderate area of 250 acres—which disputes the common taunt that Poland was still a feudal country. (There *are* still some large landowners in Poland, as in England, but a new share-out of peasant holdings is inevitable.) 3,200,000 farms were of less than 50 acres, and of these 1,110,000 were less than 5 acres. The principal crops included wheat, rye, oats, potatoes and sugar beet.

Wages were not high by our standards, but ordinary items of food could be purchased more cheaply. A farm labourer earned about $2.75 a week: a miner or factory hand $4.20. A policeman received $7.00 a week, a colonel in the army $2,000 a year, and a judge of the High Court $2,700.

The Pole is noted in Europe and America as a good worker. I was not surprised at this reputation when I saw the peasant in

RACES IN POLAND

his fields. Statistics prove that his industrial brother is just as effective. The British miner, who is no slacker, raises an average of 1116 kilograms per shift: the Polish miner raises

1410. (No wonder Poles have been used freely to exploit the mines of France and Germany.) Hence the severity of Polish competition in Scandinavian markets. Polish wages, however, were already tending to rise. In a new democracy, conditions of labour are likely to draw more closely to those of Western Europe.

As might be expected in a country which has occupied the centre of the European stage for so many centuries, Poland housed large numbers of minority races. Of the total population, 68.9 per cent spoke Polish as their first language, 10.1 Ukrainian, 3.8 Ruthenian (an Ukrainian dialect), 3.1 White Russian, 0.4 Russian, 2.3 German, 8.6 Yiddish or Hebrew and 2.8 a variety of oddments. In the different religions—and, as we shall see in the Russian chapter, a man's religion is often a good guide to his racial origin—64.8 per cent were Roman Catholics, 10.4 Uniat,[1] 11.8 Orthodox, 2.8 Protestant, 0.5 other Christian sects and 9.8 Jewish.

Of the Jews, only 1 per cent were engaged in agriculture, 21 per cent in industry, 7 per cent in communications, 12 per cent in various trades and professions, and 59 per cent in commerce. Of the whole population, 60.6 per cent were engaged in agriculture and only 19.4 in industry.

The difficulties confronting the reborn state were appalling. Economic conditions were fantastic—Poland inherited three currencies all sliding towards bankruptcy. The land had been impoverished and desolated by war—over half a million houses had been destroyed. Livestock had been killed off: farm implements and industrial machines stolen. It says much for the spirit of the Poles that they advanced with courage from the first moment of their freedom.

The governments of the new Poland were, however, seldom worthy of their people. The first thought was for a democratic Constitution on most liberal lines. It is easier to talk about democracy than to apply it. External difficulties aggravated internal dissensions. I once compared the Poland of 1919

[1] The Uniat Church follows the forms and doctrines of the Greek Orthodox Church, but accepts the authority of the Pope of Rome.

to a baby suffering from a poisoned appendix, with an abscess pressing on its windpipe, with every sign of malnutrition, with disfiguring excrescences of irritating boils and pimples, and with two wicked and unscrupulous uncles hovering in the background disputing its inheritance. True, the infant had some friendly aunts, but they lived a long way off. However, it is often the weakly child which survives to become great.

A succession of governments failed to grapple successfully with the innumerable problems of the new state. Despairing of their democratic debates, declaring that they always talked and never acted, Pilsudski seized power and exercised a virtual dictatorship until his death in 1935. His methods were the exact antithesis of those of Hitler and Mussolini. His dictatorship was exercised from the background; his intentions were benevolent enough, but some of his methods were crude. I met him in 1935 and appreciated his character if not his manners. He insisted that he was not a dictator. 'We have a legacy of confusing legislation from three states. While we argue about them, the world goes by. It won't do. I know neither the Right nor the Left—I know only Poland.' No one would quarrel with that last phrase at least.

His successors in power, Marshal Smigly-Rydz and Colonel Beck, had neither his genius, his courage nor his single track of mind. Pilsudski might swear at you, but at least you knew where you were. His first alliance was an obvious one—with France, anxious to find a partner to replace Russia and to supply the essential 'second front' in case of a new war with Germany. Gradually the alliance lost its force, as French governments followed one another in and out of office. On the rise of Hitler, the realistic Pilsudski wanted to march at once: France refused—and then was staggered when Hitler and Pilsudski signed a Ten-Year Pact of Friendship. Pilsudski's outlook was simple. If you can't knock down your enemy, make friends with him.

Both Hitler and Pilsudski gained invaluable time. After the Polish leader's death, the position rapidly deteriorated. Hitler was now gathering strength. The Poles were uncertain of France's fixity of purpose. When Hitler marched into the Rhineland, Poland proposed a march into Germany to rid the world of the Nazi menace. France refused. Thereafter Polish leaders thought only of the safety of their own country, not of their alliance. For a while it seemed that they wobbled between the Axis and the democracies. But, as the German threat developed, it was soon obvious what Poland's role must be: a role of suffering unequalled in her own unhappy history.

And at this stage, obviously, we must turn to the problems which provided the occasion for the second World War—but not its cause. It will be as well to consider first the difficulties as they existed up to August 1939; then trace briefly the course of the war, examine the German 'solutions' which are now being applied, and finally suggest a post-war settlement.

II

The difficulty about the Polish Corridor is that it is Polish.

If, without previous education or propaganda, a plebiscite could have been taken in Britain ten years ago on the subject of the Polish Corridor, the result would certainly have been heavily in favour of Germany. The emergence of Hitler meant that many people would vote against him automatically, irrespective of the merits of the case, but even a year before the war it is probable that Poland would have lost. Our knowledge of Polish history is remarkably slight, but the map spoke for itself. Here, argued the man in the street who could forget Hitler, is a province of Germany cut off from the mainland by an artificial corridor solely designed to give Poland an outlet to the sea. Of course Germany is not satisfied, he argued; of course there is a clamour for the rejoining of East Prussia to the Fatherland. But the problem was not quite so simple as that. If the Polish Corridor *were* merely an artificial creation, then it would have disappeared from the map long before.

The Germans claim that they were cheated by the Treaty of Versailles. They surrendered, they say, on the understand-

Density of Polish Population
in the Polish "Corridor" in 1913

Under 25%

25% to 50%

50% to 75%

Over 75%

.... 1920 frontiers

BALTIC SEA

GERMANY

EAST PRUSSIA

Danzig

Bydgoszcz
(Bromberg)

R. Netze

R. Vicula

Poznan (Posen)

POLAND

R. Warthe

Kalisz

R. Oder

Breslau

ewb

THE 'CORRIDOR'—BY PRE-1914 GERMAN FIGURES

ing that peace would be made on the basis of President Wilson's Fourteen Points. If for the moment we accept the German contention in full, we are logically forced to the conclusion that Germany ought to be prepared to accept such clauses of the Treaty of Versailles as do not conflict with the Fourteen Points. Point Thirteen of the latter read: 'An independent Polish State shall be erected, which shall include all territory with an indisputably Polish population, to which a free and safe access to the sea shall be given, and whose economic and territorial integrity will be assured by international treaties.'

The phrase 'to which a free and safe access to the sea shall be given' was very unfortunate—it can be read to imply an artificial creation. The first important consideration in the Corridor problem is this—that, had the boundaries of Poland been determined purely on the first phrase of the Thirteenth Point ('All territory with an undisputably Polish population'), the Polish frontiers, including those of the Corridor, would have been substantially the same as they were.

In our thumb-nail sketch of Polish history we have seen the ancient kingdom of Poland ruthlessly divided among her three neighbours between 1772 and 1795. The bulk of Polish territory went to Russia, the southern provinces to Austria, and the north-western corner (including the area now known as the 'Corridor'), to Prussia. Thus, until 1772, the Corridor was Polish territory, as it had been for hundreds of years. The Teutonic Knights who colonised East Prussia stepped lightly over Pomorze, as the Poles called the Corridor area. Prior to 1772, it is undisputed, Pomorze was overwhelmingly Polish.

Once German territory, however, Germans began to settle in Pomorze: naturally, they came as the landowner and trading class. The Poles were not seriously ill-treated, but were definitely a subject race, and many thousands of families emigrated, as opportunity offered, to America and France. Germans replaced them, so that by 1910 (according to German figures) there were 440,000 Germans in Pomorze to 550,000 Poles. It is necessary to comment on these figures—battles of statistics have been waged furiously since 1919. The Poles claim that the German figure is grossly exaggerated: it included soldiers, police and officials—that is, people quite foreign to the province—and their families, and the real figure for Germans in Pomorze was not more than 200,000. On the other hand, the Germans counter-claim that the figure for Poles included 110,000 Kashubians, who are not true Poles at all.

These Kashubians inhabit the northern section of the Corridor—that is, the most important part of it, adjoining the sea. Are they Poles or are they not? They are certainly not Germans—I was soon convinced of that. They speak a Slav dialect akin to Polish—the difference is a matter of accent rather than language. A Kashubian in Warsaw is equivalent to a Northumbrian in London, no more. In ethnic details they are definitely Slav and not Teuton. They are Catholics, while the Germans about them are Protestant. They themselves say that they are Poles, and historically they have always been classed as a Polish tribe. The Germans themselves classed the Kashubians as Poles until 1918. It was not until the Corridor arguments began that it was discovered that the Kashubians were really Germans after all. A more moderate opinion in Germany classes the Kashubians as Slavs, but as a non-Polish tribe. It is claimed, too, that although the Kashubians are certainly Slavs, they received all their culture and civilisation from German sources, and at heart are nearer to Germany than Poland.

Another German grievance—and a weighty one—is that the Corridor was handed over to the Poles without plebiscite. Germany would have been prepared to give up the Poznan province—which, apart from the towns, was overwhelmingly Polish—but did not class Pomorze as an 'indisputably Polish' area. Had a plebiscite been held, it is claimed the vote would have been in Germany's favour. Nor is this a fantastic statement, urged as propaganda since it can never be proved or disproved. Certain similar areas *were* submitted to a plebiscite, and the results were startling—especially to the Poles.

To the south of East Prussia is a district known as Masuria. It is inhabited by Germans, Poles and a Slav tribe called the Masurians—a people not unlike the Kashubians. The Poles claimed that the Masurians were their blood-brothers—which was ethnically true. The Germans claimed that the Masurians, like the Kashubians, had been German so long that culturally they were Germans. This is not a strained argument—the descendants of French Huguenots or the Flemish weavers are just as English as descendants of warriors who came over with William the Conqueror or those who fought against them. The powers at Paris, since the principle of access to the sea was not involved, decided to hold a plebiscite. It was known from German figures that the Polish and Masurian minorities were considerable. The Poles claimed that (counting the Masurians as Poles) the Germans were easily outnumbered, and there is reason to believe that their claim was well founded. Yet in the plebiscite 95 per cent of the voters declared in favour of Germany!

Now this result is certainly surprising. It implies not only that all the Masurians voted German, *but that large numbers of Poles voted German as well*—since even German figures showed a minority of Poles considerably larger than 5 per cent. Why should Poles vote against incorporation in Poland? Is it true that they had become Germanised by long subjection to German rule and by association with German culture? A more likely reason is this: Poles, certainly Germanised, had to choose between their present settled life under just if strict German rule, and life in a new Poland of unknown size, potentialities and capacity: a Poland engaged in a precarious war with Russia, and with a currency in confusion; they had to choose between comparative security and a risk, and their latent nationalism was not strong enough to induce them to chance the risk.

Thus the German argument about the Kashubians must be given serious consideration, since it is quite possible that the Kashubians would have voted the same way as the Masurians.

This is purely a matter of conjecture, but I am confident of one thing—that if the plebiscite had been held shortly before the present war the Kashubians would have decided heavily in

A German map for school use, published in 1909. The shaded areas represent territory inhabited by absolute Slav majorities. A thick black line has been added to show the 1919–39 frontiers of Poland. It is interesting to note not only the Slav nature of the Corridor population, but that of the southern portion of East Prussia, and of Upper Silesia.

favour of Poland. Poland justified its new existence; the risk which scared the Masurians faded; Polish trade passing through the Corridor brought a new prosperity to the Kashubians, and Pomorze was one of the most settled districts in Poland.

Even if we deduct the 110,000 Kashubians from the Polish figure for the Corridor, however, it still leaves 440,000 Poles —exactly equivalent to the German population, which cer-

Polish Speaking
Population
of Pomorze
Census of 1931

Over 90%
80 to 90%
Under 80%
The whole Province 89·9%

tainly included over 200,000 soldiers, officials and their families. Indeed, the immediate reduction in the German population after the war tends to prove the Polish point, for when soldiers, officials and their families had been withdrawn the German population of Pomorze fell from 40 per cent to 12 per cent. It can be claimed that the people who were left after the soldiers and officials had gone were the 'natural' pre-war population.

Thus we can agree without effort that the natural population of Pomorze before 1914 had a Polish majority. Actually this majority was considerable, for events have shown that the claims to regard the Kashubians as Poles were justified.

By 1939, naturally, the population figures were vastly different. The latest census figures show about 110,000 Germans to 860,000 Poles. The changes are easily explained. The German troops and officials were of course withdrawn; further, more than 100,000 Germans decided that they might not be happy in Poland, and emigrated to Germany. This considerable exodus was compensated by an approximately corresponding influx of Poles from Germany, who decided to return to their reborn mother country. The ethnic change in Pomorze, therefore, is the result of an exchange of population, to a large extent on a voluntary basis.

It is interesting to note, by the way, that the Germans are still a powerful landowning class in the Pomorze. Although forming only 12 per cent of the population, they own more than 40 per cent of the land area.

It is equally interesting to note that actually the Corridor area was the most Polish corner of Poland! There the Poles form almost 90 per cent of the population—and this figure is reached in no other corner of Poland. The explanation is that there are practically no Jews in the Corridor, whereas over the rest of Poland they average more than 10 per cent of the population; as we shall see, there are other considerable minorities, especially in the east. This point is so interesting that it is worth repeating—that the Corridor area comes nearer to being purely Polish than any other province of Poland.

Immediately to the south of Pomorze, and in British and American eyes part of the Corridor problem, is the province of Poznan. Here, before the war, the balance of population was even more in favour of the Poles. The problem was more complicated, however: there were in the province three cities —Poznan, Bydgoszcz and Torun (the old Posen, Bromberg and Thorn); here the Germans had a considerable majority. We have, in fact, the elements of a common problem in Eastern Europe—the towns largely German and the country districts overwhelmingly Polish. Again, however, the withdrawal of troops and officials and the departure of emigrants effected a vast change in the proportions. In pre-war German Bromberg, for example, the Germans formed 84 per cent of the population. In post-war Polish Bydgoszcz there were no more than 8 per cent. Based on the undoubted pre-war German character of these towns, at one time a fantastic suggestion of a 'German Corridor' through them was advanced, connecting East Prussia with Germany, but isolating a Polish Pomorze. Even if it were practicable at all, this solution would create more problems than it solved.

In considering all these figures, it should be remembered that Pomorze and Poznan formed German frontier provinces adjoining the potential Russian enemy. Consequently, considerable bodies of troops—over 100,000—were stationed there and were naturally and legitimately included in German census figures—which were compiled for domestic use, with no thought of a future Poland. The withdrawal of these troops, with civil servants and their families, explains the complete change in the composition of the towns.

The policy of Germanisation of the region was thoroughly applied. All young men had to serve in the German army or navy; all children were taught German—often in German; young men who wanted further education passed to German universities and imbibed German culture; the administration of the province was purely German. A study of local tombstones reveals that after the fall of Napoleon, when Poland seemed doomed for ever, many Poles succumbed to Germanisation and adopted German names. Further, German immigrants were invited into the province. The responsible organ-

isation was the Ostmarkenverein, which supplied German settlers with loans and marketed their products. The Poles re-
sponded: poverty-stricken peasants pooled their pennies in
attempts to keep land out of German hands. So late as 1913
the Germans had to admit failure. In spite of all their efforts—
repression of Poles and bribery of German immigrants—the
Ostmarkenverein published an ethnic map of the Corridor
area. It was intended to stimulate Germans to settle in a vital
area which was still not German: actually, it conclusively
proved the Polish claim to the territory. It provided the best
evidence for the Peace Conference—its importance was proved
by the feverish attempts of the German government to call in
copies of the map.

Summarised, therefore, the position in the Corridor area is:
the land was Polish for seven hundred years until 1772, when
it was seized by Prussia. At that time it was overwhelmingly
Polish, but by 1914 German immigration and Polish emigration had led to a settlement of Germans amounting to something between about one-third and one-half of the population;
this proportion consisted to a considerable extent of military
and governing classes, plus the landowners and the traders of
the towns. There is no complicating history of cruelty and
real oppression, as we shall find in some Balkan problems, and
the German rule was firm but just. In 1939, as was not questioned even in Germany, the district was again overwhelmingly Polish.

Here, then, is a Polish province: with a break of foreign
occupation, it has always been Polish. It adjoins Poland, and
is part of Poland. The question is, should it remain part of
Poland?

This seems a fairly simple question to answer. Yet it does
not dispose of the problem by any means. Although historic
and ethnic considerations were against her, Germany's point
of view was unchanged and was perfectly comprehensible.
Here was a famous German province, breeding-ground of
many of the military heroes of Prussia, cut off from Germany
by a strip of foreign territory.

The real issue was one of national pride; the practical difficulties were greatly exaggerated. The negotiations which followed the Treaty of Versailles made ample provision for trade between East Prussia and Germany. Twenty-four direct trains a day crossed the Corridor, and more could be had for the asking. The difficulties arising out of Corridor transport in 1938 were due to the fact that Germany, desperately short of foreign exchange, neglected to pay the Polish bills for the haulage of German trains across the Corridor.

Much capital was made, in Germany and elsewhere, of the legend of the 'sealed' trains across the Corridor. The implication was that a sanitary cordon of suspicion guarded the German trains on their journey—the expression is used in precisely the same way as that describing the famous 'sealed' train in which Lenin was transported from Switzerland to Russia during the war. Actually, the 'sealing' of the train at the frontier was purely a customs precaution. Arrived at the Polish frontier, a Polish engine took over the German train, Polish customs officers came aboard, and carriage windows were closed. There was no examination of baggage, but the customs officers remained on the train to see that you did not dump contraband stuff in Poland during the train's run across Polish territory. This was reasonable enough. There was nothing insulting or degrading in the procedure. On one occasion I happened to be asleep during the crossing of the Corridor, and I never knew that I had left German territory.

Ample railway transport and unlimited sea communications were thus available between East Prussia and the rest of Germany. The trade between the two was not large, and was only one-twelfth of the trade passing the other way—from Poland to the sea. On economic grounds, therefore, Poland's claim to the Corridor is as strong as on historic or ethnic grounds.

The fact that the Corridor area is Polish does not mean that its frontiers were perfect. They were drawn to follow the approximate ethnic line of division, which is naturally confused, and the very haste of their drawing made errors inevitable. There have been hundreds of irritating incidents, of which full propaganda value has been made by whichever country felt aggrieved. In a dozen places minor modifications of the frontier were possible and advisable.

Actually, I believe that Poland would have been ready to consider these, except for the overwhelming fear that Germany might interpret her action as weakness, and, having received a little, demand more. Nor were their apprehensions groundless. When we withdrew our garrisons from the Rhineland long before the date named in the treaty, our action was not interpreted as a gesture of goodwill, but as an admission that we were wrong to go there at all; alternatively, by the German militarists, that we were weakening, as they had expected— they would never have done such a thing themselves. We are going to find ourselves continuously up against this difficulty in our tour of European problems. In an atmosphere of confidence, there would be little difficulty in arranging the necessary modifications. But let there be no misunderstanding; the minor adjustments I have suggested would have removed many sources of friction, but would not have solved the problem of the Corridor.

And before we make up our minds about the Corridor, let us consider the problem of Danzig, which is so closely related.

III

Danzig is today a German city. During the years preceding the outbreak of war in 1939, indeed, it was the most Nazi city of Europe. And yet Danzig's association with Germany has never been remarkably solid.

The port was founded by the Poles, who, though not a seafaring people, naturally gravitated to the mouth of the Vistula, the main artery of their country. We have seen that the peculiar social structure of the country led to the invitation of Germans and Jews to carry on the trade of Poland. So Danzig changed its character: though a Polish town, most of its trade passed through German hands. The nobles and the labourers were Polish, the traders German.

Then, in 1308, it passed into the hands of the Teutonic

POLAND'S MAIN ARTERY—THE VISTULA

Knights. In succeeding generations Danzig and East Prussia became thoroughly Teutonised. In the country districts the knights were the local squires and the local Slavs their serfs, but Danzig was different. German merchants settled there in large numbers; its situation at the mouth of the Vistula made it a vital centre of trade—it was one of the chief cities of the Hanseatic League. When, as was inevitable, the Teutonic Knights rotted in their own corruption, the trading community of Danzig refused to be associated with a religious 'order' which was an open scandal. *Danzig, a German city, offered itself to the kingdom of Poland.* This was in 1455.

The Polish kings gave Danzig their protection, but allowed the wide privileges of a free city. Nevertheless, legally it was Polish and was duly represented in the Polish Parliament. Practically the whole of Poland's maritime trade passed over its wharves. This condition prevailed until the unhappy partitions of Poland, when it was seized by Prussia. For a brief space under Napoleon it was a free city once more, but returned to Prussia in 1814.

In President Wilson's Thirteenth Point Poland was promised an access to the sea. Automatically she demanded Danzig. She claimed, with reason, that Danzig was the natural port for Poland—the only natural port. Agreeing that Danzig was largely German, Poland claimed that this fact could not stand against her own obvious geographical rights—the Vistula was Poland's river, the main trade artery of the country: was a foreign power to control its mouth? With Danzig left in German hands, Poland's export trade would be impossible; the narrow strip of coastline allotted to the Corridor was merely a mud-bank, utterly unsuited for a deep-sea port.

The 'Big Three' at Paris—Wilson, Clemenceau and Lloyd George—considered these and many other arguments more forcibly advanced. Clemenceau would cheerfully have allocated Danzig to Poland—anything to despoil Germany. But Lloyd George was reluctant. He was a believer in the principle of ethnic frontiers, and could not get away from the fact that Danzig was not Polish. To award a German city to Poland could only lead to disaster. So a compromise was arranged.

Danzig with a hinterland of nearly eight hundred square miles and a population of 400,000, became a free city under the protection of the League of Nations. Poland's rights in

Danzig were exclusively economic. The railways and docks of the port were administered by a commission of Poles and Danzigers, with a neutral chairman. Foreign affairs and customs were within the Polish orbit, but the Free City had its own currency, and its Council was responsible for all other services—education, posts and telegraph, police and so on. The official language was German. A League of Nations High Commissioner was appointed to co-ordinate affairs and to keep the peace between the two parties.

There were many potential difficulties to such an arrangement, but they were by no means insuperable. A little goodwill on either side, a frank acceptance of the situation and Danzig might have settled down to a friendly prosperity. But the Danzigers had no goodwill; we must not blame them too hardly—torn from their fatherland in the bitterness of defeat, they could scarcely regard Poland with immediate smiles. Almost at once there was friction. It came to a head in 1920. Then Poland was fighting for her infant life against Bolshevik Russia. England and France were too war-weary to send men, but both had ample spare stocks of unwanted munitions, which were shipped to Danzig. And the dockers of Danzig refused to handle them!

Poland's reply to this action greatly complicated the whole problem of Danzig and the Corridor. Yet it was but natural. Such a position, it was argued, was intolerable—Poland's *only* port, and it refused to handle vital supplies at a moment of life or death! There must never be a chance of a repetition—Poland must have a Polish port.

There was little choice in Poland's tiny coast-line. Eventually Gdynia, a fishing village, was selected. The construction of the port was a colossal task, for the site was utterly devoid of natural advantages. Every basin had to be dug out of peat bogs, and all approaches had to be dredged. But in twelve years a tiny fishing village became a modern city of 100,000 inhabitants, with a harbour handling 8 million tons of merchandise a year, and capable of handling almost double. Not even America could beat the rapid transformation of Gdynia to a well-planned town of most modern construction. The Poles are justly proud of their achievement—even if it was backed by French capital. Yet Danzig has one advantage Gdynia can never possess—the Vistula.

Now, before the World War, Danzig handled little more than the local trade of West Prussia. Its old days of glory, when it was the port of the entire Vistula basin, were over—for Russia, now controlling the greater part of that basin, insisted that Russian trade should go through Russian ports. But Danzig, as the only port of Poland, waxed prosperous immediately after the war. Its 1 million tons of trade became 10; merchants and labourers of Danzig were well paid and well fed at a time when Germans were bankrupt and starving. Had they worked in friendly fashion with Poland their unlimited prosperity might have continued indefinitely. Gdynia, of course, made a big difference.

In the immediate pre-war years, Polish trade was shared almost equally between the two ports. Danzig still handled 7 million tons—a great increase on the pre-1918 figure, but less than ten years earlier. So Danzig grumbled at Poland. You must make some allowance, too, for the jealousy of the veteran of a new and successful rival. As Danzig's trade fell and that of Gdynia mounted, political action resulted.

No one could mistake the German character of Danzig—particularly after the rise of Hitler. There was an insistent demand for return to Germany—though sober people realised that this step might mean the bankruptcy of the city. Because this was so obvious, the Nazis received severe set-backs in their early attempts at the Nazification of Danzig. Their opponents were not only Poles, but Germans: they would have welcomed re-union with their fatherland, but were not prepared to condemn their city (and themselves) to ruin in the process.

(I ought to emphasise that the word 'German,' in spite of all that Hitler may claim, does not mean a man of any particular birth or racial descent, but of German speech and culture. At the time of the First Partition, the population of Danzig was more than 50 per cent Polish, and remained so for several generations. After the fall of Napoleon, it was obvious that the future of Danzig lay with Prussia, and the Poles rapidly lost their language—if they wanted to prosper, they had to speak German. Soon Germans and Poles were hopelessly mixed: their descendants, German-speaking, are all classed as German. Of the first two Germans I met in Danzig —both Nazis—one admitted to four Polish grandparents, the other to three. It is amusing to inspect family vaults, and to notice how Polish names became Germanised early in the nineteenth century. There is something in the Polish argument that if Danzig had been handed over to them completely in 1919, these people would rapidly have become Polonised, and in a couple of generations the city would have been largely Polish again.)

I suggested in 1935 the return of Danzig to the Reich, with the erection of a Port of Danzig Authority, which would have complete control over all docks and harbours: Germans and Poles would have equal representation. The wharves would be in the nature of a Customs Bonded Warehouse. Incoming goods destined for Germany would pay duties as they passed from the wharves; goods for Poland would pay duties as they crossed the Polish frontier—or, if more convenient, on leaving the wharves, the duties of course being paid to the Polish customs. The Authority would act as a clearing-house for all financial transactions. Poland would pay her due share of harbour costs, and no more. She would have the unlimited use of railways from Danzig to the frontier at agreed rates. Many foreign countries use London as a Bonded Warehouse for many commodities. The scheme would not have been impossible had Poland and Germany acted together with mutual confidence. It must be abandoned today, for there is likely to be little confidence between Poland and Germany for a generation to come.

At the same time, I suggested an approach to the problem of

the Corridor which, though it scarcely touched German economy, did touch German pride. 'There being no natural solution, we have to manufacture an artificial one. Consider such a scheme as this: with Danzig returned to Germany, and Polish harbour rights suitably safeguarded along the lines I have previously suggested, the northern part of the Corridor becomes little more than twenty miles wide. It is a pleasant district of low hills and green valleys: is it too much to expect of the human intelligence which plans regular Atlantic flights, tunnels the Mersey and bridges Sydney Harbour, to suggest that German ingenuity should plan and build a combined railway and motor road entirely on high viaducts or enclosed in tunnels through the Kashubian hills? Far more fantastic things than this are likely to happen within the next twenty years.' This idea may possibly be revived after the war: I doubt it, for it, too, depends for its success on mutual trust, which can scarcely be forthcoming for some time.

In the autumn of 1938 I was in Danzig again, and found the tension heightened. The Nazification of the city was complete: Poles and Jews were beaten up, and all German opponents of the Nazi 'ideology' had disappeared. Many of the Danzig leaders were not Danzigers at all, but Hitler's nominees, imported from Germany.

The trading classes were frankly apprehensive. It seemed to be only a matter of time before Hitler seized the Free City. How would he take it—by force, maybe involving a European war? Even if he did it by peaceful methods, ruin lay ahead for Danzig. I found even fervent Nazis (who were also merchants) quite content that things should remain as they were: and ordinary people, who had heard of the shortage of food in Germany, and contrasted it with their own plenty.

It was quite apparent that no one in Danzig wanted war. Yet considerations of reasonable solutions must be temporarily postponed. In March 1939 Germany made a formal demand for the return of Danzig, promising that Poland should retain ample port rights. The moment was unfortunate. A few weeks earlier Memel had been seized; precisely similar promises being made to the Lithuanians—and immediately broken. Assuredly our pre-requisite of confidence was not present! The seizure of Czechoslovakia quite naturally destroyed confidence in Hitler's word, and Poland was not disposed to make a settlement which might have been possible a year earlier. Memel was immediately converted into a naval port: Danzig as a naval port would be a stranglehold on the throat of Poland.

Colonel Beck's reply to Hitler was dignified but firm. Poland would never allow herself to be barred from the Baltic, he declared. Two conditions were necessary for negotiations, he pointed out—'peaceful intentions and peaceful methods of action'; and he was ready at all times to discuss the problem under such conditions. A solution by force or bluster he barred, making it quite plain that Poland would fight for her rights.

He also outlined Poland's own solution to the Danzig problem—that the League of Nations Commissioner should be withdrawn, and that a common Polish-German guarantee should be given of the existence and rights of the Free City. This would satisfy German aspirations in every respect except prestige, since the administration was already purely German.

His offer—a reasonable one, admirably suited for the necessary years of gathering confidence—was received with a storm of abuse. Events followed only too reminiscent of those in the Sudetenland the previous autumn: attacks were made on Polish customs houses; Polish newspapers were held up at the frontier; thousands of storm troopers entered Danzig as 'tourists'; supplies of arms and ammunition were smuggled into the city, or even dropped by parachute from aeroplanes.

The intention was obvious—not necessarily to provoke open conflict, but to break Poland's nerve. If conflict came, Poland was to appear to be the aggressor. German troops would not be the first to enter Danzig: instead there would be a military demonstration by the people of Danzig, together with a 'vol-

untary' offer of the territory to the Reich. Yet these devices
were too obvious, and the whole parade of them have no real
bearing on the principles of the problems. They did not succeed in breaking Poland's nerve. Indeed, the seizure of Czecho-

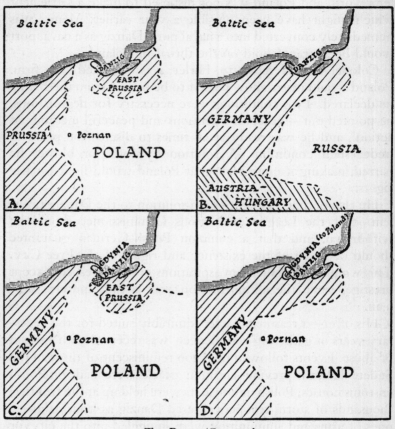

THE POLISH 'CORRIDOR'

(*a*) 1771   (*b*) 1772–1918   (*c*) 1919   (*d*) A German 'solution'

slovakia rallied the Poles to a remarkable degree. Despite their
political differences, there had never been two opinions about
Poland's right of access to the sea. Someone had to be the first
to say 'No' to Hitler, and Poland girded herself for that declar-

ation of principle which must inevitably entail immense suffering.

Before we plunge into the invasion of Poland, we must mention some of the solutions of the problems of Danzig and the Corridor put forward at different times. One was to the effect that Poland should give up Danzig and Gdynia and accept Memel in lieu. This was absurd. The whole of Poland's transport system ran towards the mouth of the Vistula: Memel as a Polish port was hopelessly situated—90 per cent of Polish exports came from her western provinces. We must never make the mistake of separating considerations of Poland from those of the Vistula. 'The problem of the Polish Corridor is not one of right against wrong,' wrote Professor L. B. Namier. 'It results from a conflict of two principles, of the unity of the sea-board *versus* the unity of the river basin. . . . The Poles are the nation of the Vistula, and their settlements extend from the sources of the river to its estuary: no other European nation is centred to that extent on one single river.'

The most reasonable German solution was not very helpful. It was argued that too much was read into the phrase 'access to the sea.' President Wilson, when he formulated the phrase, had in his mind economic access, not political—not a corridor of Polish territory, but an arrangement of Polish rights in German ports, such as Czechoslovakia once enjoyed. (This argument is somewhat weakened by the fact that President Wilson was one of the creators of the Polish Corridor. Thus, if such an arrangement was in his mind, he must have changed it.) This reading of the phrase was still possible, the Germans argued. The port of Gdynia was a new factor, but raised no great difficulty. Gdynia itself should remain Polish, together with a small hinterland—a breathing-space and market garden, so to speak. The rest of the Corridor area, as far south as the line of the river Netze, should be returned to Germany. Poland would retain the fullest possible control of the railway to Gdynia, and Poland would naturally have the fullest use of the docks of Danzig. Thus the map would be cleaned up in a manner appealing to the German tidy mind, and East Prussia could be rejoined with the fatherland: true, Gdynia would now be separated from its motherland by a German corridor, and Poland would lose a few hundred square miles of territory, but she would gain in German friendship.

The principal objection to the plan was that no Pole would ever agree with it—nor would many Germans. The men who first formulated it may have been sincere, but it became obvious that it was the same old 'sprat to catch a mackerel' which had been employed in Czechoslovakia: the Corridor was to play the part of the Sudetenland, the excuse for the first move. No one can blame the Poles because they were suspicious of German intentions: they lived next door, and knew their neighbours. If we had been a little more critical in pre-war years, then the course of history might have been changed.

Early in 1939 Hitler advanced yet a third 'solution'—which had been foreshadowed for some time. Germany and Poland should attack Russia, he argued: then, as compensation for the loss of the Corridor, Poland should take the vast and wealthy Russian Ukraine. The Poles refused, of course. The suggestion was not merely immoral: it was absurd.

IV

When Hitler wished to arouse the fury of his race to a German wrong, he had only to wave a map and to point to the Corridor. (And any future Hitler would be able to do the same.) Here was an argument which a child could understand: yet all the while the principal bone of contention between Germany and Poland never was the Corridor or Danzig. The real point at issue lay three hundred miles further south. The Corridor touched the German pride, but Silesia touched the German pocket.

In the early days of the present age, Silesia appears to have been occupied by Celtic tribes, eventually driven westward by the Slavonic horde pressing from the east. As early as A.D. 1000

Silesia was part of the loose-knit Polish kingdom, but under a series of weak rulers it disintegrated into a medley of petty states—still nominally subject to Poland, however.

Early in the fourteenth century the local nobles transferred their allegiance to Bohemia, and Silesia thus eventually became a province of the Austrian Empire. In 1742, however, Frederick II of Prussia obtained Silesia by conquest: he made no claim to any other rights. 'I take what I want,' he explained. 'Then I can always find clever lawyers to prove that it is really mine.'

At the time of its Prussian conquest, Silesia was an agricultural province inhabited mainly by people of Slav origin—not all pure Poles, by any means, but nearer in kinship to the Poles than to any of their neighbours. There had always been a considerable number of German settlers, however, and the discovery of coal and other minerals led to German immigration on a considerable scale. After the Prussian conquest, naturally, this was intensified. In the last century Silesia developed very rapidly into one of the most important coal and iron fields of Europe. New towns were built, and the old enlarged beyond recognition. The development was almost entirely the work of German engineers, backed by German capital. Thus the towns became largely German, while the agricultural peasantry remained overwhelmingly Polish or—in Lower Silesia—quasi-Polish. It should be pointed out that the immigrants into Silesia were not only Germans, but included tens of thousands of Poles from contiguous districts, attracted by the demand for labour in the mines.

During the peace negotiations, Poland put forward a claim for Silesia on the grounds that ethnically the province was largely Polish. Whatever the French attitude, Mr. Lloyd George and President Wilson declined to admit this claim without proof. It was decided (Article 88 of the Treaty of Versailles) that a plebiscite, under Allied control, should be held in Upper Silesia. The plebiscite deserves close study by those people who consider plebiscites as a panacea for all ethnic troubles. The fact is that plebiscites are only decisive arguments when held under conditions which are perfectly fair and just, *and which are recognised as fair and just by both parties*. In the case of the Saar, these conditions prevailed; in the case of Silesia they certainly did not.

Thoughtful men have aways held that it is hopeless to expect a reasonable plebiscite in the frenzied aftermath of war: it has been argued that such thorny problems should be postponed until the heated tempers of all have subsided, and reason and confidence prevail. The Silesia plebiscite offered ample argument for their case. At the same time disputed areas cannot simply be set on one side to await the slow down of confidence: their populations must live. It seems essential that decisions on the main problems should be made at the earliest moment, while it should be clear that detailed amendments would be made later in the light of experience.

Silesia at least gave useful lessons in how a plebiscite should *not* be held. The moment the decision to hold a plebiscite was announced, both Germany and Poland naturally got busy, and soon Silesia shuddered under a wave of propaganda. The Polish leader was a gentleman by the name of Korfanty. Not content with verbal propaganda, he led armed bands into Upper Silesia, attempting to seize the province by force. He believed that the powers in Paris might be influenced by the presentation of a *fait accompli*, and later events at Vilna proved that he had not misjudged his men.

The Germans, however, although willing to accept the control of the French, British and Italian Mission sent to conduct the plebiscite, were furious at this new insult—gangs of terrorists, of the despised Polish race, running amok about the country, beating up potential opponents. An irregular patriotic force was hastily organised, and Silesia experienced the miseries of guerrilla warfare. Very disturbing was the attitude of the French, who controlled the Allied Mission, and who openly favoured the Poles. A brigade of British troops was hastily sent out to assist the forces of fair play but, had the

Germans lost the poll, they would have been justly entitled to complain of the methods of their opponents and the one-sided attitude of the principal 'returning officer.'

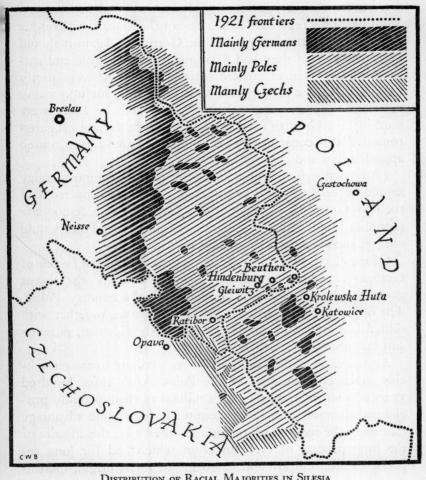

DISTRIBUTION OF RACIAL MAJORITIES IN SILESIA

Due perhaps to last-minute British and Italian influence, the actual plebiscite was carried out without major incidents. The result of the polling was a surprise to the Poles and the

French: 98 per cent of the qualified electors voted—700,000 for Germany, and 480,000 for Poland: that is, about 60 per cent for Germany and 40 per cent for Poland. Now these figures are remarkable, for even the Germans admit that there were more than 40 per cent of Poles in the plebiscite area. Thus we find a repetition of the case of the Masurian plebiscite —many Poles must have voted for Germany. Again it should be explained that they had been under German rule and surrounded by German culture so long that they were partly Germanised—the local Polish dialect naturally includes many words of German origin. Further, most of the Poles were working for German masters. And if Korfanty and his gangs roused Polish consciousness in some, they must have roused apprehension and censure in others.

(Any deductions drawn from the plebiscite figures today should be very carefully considered. In 1919 it appeared as if the new Germany were about to settle down as a democratic republic. It does not by any means follow that Poles would vote in such numbers for Nazi Germany today!)

Of the electoral districts, 614 showed a majority in favour of Germany, 597 in favour of Poland. Naturally the towns generally showed a heavy German poll, the country Polish. The official, professional and employing classes, together with skilled labourers and artisans, were mostly German; peasants and labourers were largely Polish.

Actually, the plebiscite figures were a tribute to the remarkable racial consciousness of the Poles. After three hundred years of alien rule, nearly half a million of them proudly proclaimed themselves as Poles, despite any economic advantage that might be secured by voting the other way; this in spite of the long process of Germanisation which had for long repressed Polish culture and language. In racial origin, there is no dispute; far larger numbers would be classed as Polish.

The very nature of the distribution of the population, too, affected the result. Even in our country it is not unusual for the farm labourer to vote the same way as his squire. All local

officials, including policemen, were Germans; they had been
the ruling race for generations. In spite of the apparent secrecy
of the ballot—not always observed—a man had to have courage to vote against his masters.

The most weighty of the Polish objections to the character
of the plebiscite concerned the right of emigrants to vote. An
emigrant was defined as a man who had been born in the area.
Thus thousands of men were rushed from all parts of Germany to vote because they had been born in Upper Silesia—
where their fathers may have been stationed as civil servants
or soldiers, and where they may never have been since child-
hood. This 'emigrant' vote accounted for 16.2 per cent of the
total. Poles, of course, had the same privilege, but by the
nature of the German occupation of the province the majority
of the 'emigrants' were German—94.7 per cent of their votes
were cast for Germany.

(Many of the incidents of the plebiscite which I have
recorded appear today of only trivial interest. They are worthy
of consideration, however. One type of mind, when in doubt
over a frontier, demands a plebiscite automatically, without a
just appreciation of its difficulties.)

The result of the plebiscite provided a delicate problem for
the Commission of Control. The Germans naturally rejoiced,
claiming the entire province; Korfanty, on the other hand,
again attempted a *coup d'état*, and for a time did control a big
stretch of Upper Silesia, actually ejecting the representatives
of the Allied Powers from his area. German patriots prevented
the spread of his invasion, and British reinforcements gradually obtained control.

France had wished to allocate Upper Silesia to Poland,
despite the plebiscite; Britain and Italy desired to honour the
result. A council on a broader basis, including neutrals, now
considered the problem, and in October 1921 divided Upper
Silesia into two parts.[1] It was a delicate problem—how to
divide a province where the towns were German and the rural

[1] See map, page 508.

districts Polish—complicated by the fact that many highly industrialized and German-majoritied districts adjoined the Polish frontier. Only one-third of the territory was allocated to Poland, but it included 75 per cent of the mines and foundries of Upper Silesia.

Germany scarcely needed the impetus of the dispossessed industrialists to raise a great cry of dismay. It was pointed out that Silesia had been developed as one economic sphere; its mines and communications were interdependent, and an artificial separation must spell catastrophe; it had been entirely developed by German brains and capital; the towns, surely the more important, were overwhelmingly German.

Petty sources of irritation were not wanting, as is inevitable in any re-drawn land frontier. Mines in Germany found that their administrative offices were in Poland; foundries belonging to a single German company were connected by railways which now ran through Poland; communications built at great expense were now useless; towns found their waterworks and hospitals in a foreign country; and so on—the story is not novel, and was repeated on a dozen new frontiers in Europe.

The Commission appointed by the League of Nations did its best to safeguard the interests of the region over the difficult immediate period. For fifteen years railways in Upper Silesia were to work under a joint German-Polish management; natural products should pass from one country to the other without duty—*i.e.* in effect, Germany could draw coal and iron from Poland without artificial dues; any inhabitant of the plebiscite area might hold a *permis de circulation*, permitting him to cross the frontier without formality; private rights should be respected; minorities in both countries should receive the fullest privileges (detailed in 100 printed pages); and so on. Although it sounds clumsy and makeshift, this arrangement actually worked surprisingly well.

German imports of Polish coal, however, declined—Germany naturally concentrated on the further development of mines within her own frontiers. Twenty years ago, therefore, Poland was faced with a strange situation—she was producing far more coal than she could use! For home consumption was very small; industry was not highly advanced, and domestic heating in Eastern Poland was almost entirely by wood. The problem was solved by the stoppage in the British mines in 1926; Poland invaded the Scandinavian markets. Even when Britain returned to full production Poland kept her grip, assisted by subsidies and absurd rail-rates. The rate from Silesia to Gdynia, for example, was about 87 cents per ton—a journey of over two hundred miles! Special selling prices for export were arranged, well below the figure for home sales, and British rates were scarcely competitive. Polish conditions of labour and wages were, of course, very inferior. In the end Britain had to compromise, and to make an arrangement with Poland sharing the Scandinavian markets.

Although many thousands of Germans went back to Germany after the partition, the ethnical position in Polish Upper Silesia was much the same—except that now, of course, the proportion of Poles was larger. But the towns were still German; in Katowice (the old Kattowitz) I could easily have imagined myself in Germany; directors, engineers and foremen were still German, labourers and peasants Polish.

Here, then, was a difficult situation. The Germans claimed that, having won the plebiscite, they should have been awarded the whole province. The Poles say that this is absurd—they got 40 per cent of the votes, so were entitled to 40 per cent of the province. The Germans argued that cession would never have been considered by the Allies had it not been for Korfanty's insurgents; the Poles say that the raids into Silesia were a natural patriotic outburst, with emphatic local support. The Germans point out that the partition made 350,000 Germans become Polish subjects; this is true—but there were still more than 500,000 Poles on the German side of the frontier. The Germans point to the German development of Silesian industry: the Poles claim this to be a vagary of history—if, when coal was discovered, the province had been Polish (as it ought to have been), then Poles would have done the developing. And so on, *ad infinitum*.

The Ten-Year Pact smoothed down the petty irritations which complicated the administration of Polish Silesia in its early years. Nevertheless, the district was never lacking in 'incidents.' I investigated one typical case. A German schoolmaster was dismissed, and a howl of indignation arose from the German minority. I found that the schoolmaster, a fervent patriot, was using his influential position to spread anti-Polish views among his pupils. The Poles, who paid his salary, promptly dismissed him. What would you have done? Such things were seized upon by German propaganda, and any local difficulty became a matter of hate. Police action against a rioting crowd was 'persecution,' and every incident provoked by German irredentism was grossly exaggerated and perverted.

Minor revisions of the frontier were always possible, but the problem remained: as vital a clash of principle as the Corridor, with the added interest of economic wealth—important to Germany, vital to Poland. I spent longer in Silesia than I did in the Corridor. Marshal Foch and Lord d'Abernon pointed to the Corridor as the cause of the next war. Mr. Lloyd George, who knew something of these problems, referred to Silesia as Europe's new Alsace-Lorraine.

v

The defence of Poland under the most favourable conditions was certainly difficult. Her frontiers extended for 3438 miles, and only in the south was there any suggestion of natural defences—the remaining frontiers were just artificial lines across a vast featureless plain. Anything in the nature of a Maginot Line was quite impossible.

The Polish army was strong in numbers: Poland ranked as the fifth military power of Europe. Nevertheless the gap between the first and the fifth was very, very wide. The Polish weakness lay in equipment: the average quality of the men was very good.

Light arms and machine-guns were reasonably adequate, and very well used. Tanks were deplorably deficient: the Polish army deployed less than a thousand, most of them of a light pattern. Modern Polish aircraft were good, but older types proved useless against the faster German fighters.

The Polish cavalry was the best in Europe, as it had been centuries earlier: it could live on the country, and might have been very valuable in a campaign on the eastern frontier. Against German mechanised forces it was of course helpless, though it fought with desperate courage. Near Kattowitz a Polish cavalry brigade of 3000 men charged a German tank column: less than two hundred men returned from this new and tragic Balaclava.

The Polish weakness in equipment was of course realised: the difficulties were financial and geographic. She had to import most of her supplies: this involved the expenditure of precious foreign currency—and her Baltic coastline would almost certainly be overrun in the first days of war. Further, nearly all her supplies of raw materials were situated in Upper Silesia, adjacent to the German frontier.

The problem was left until late, but then tackled with energy. In 1937 France offered a loan of £25 million for Polish rearmament, being naturally anxious to see a strong partner on Germany's eastern frontiers. The Poles used the money well. While other countries talked of five-year plans, the Polish press and Polish conversation re-echoed with the continual mention of 'C.O.P.'

The initials stand for 'Centralny Okreg Przemyslowy,' or the Central Industrial Area. In a triangle within the confluence of the rivers Vistula and San, about the town of Sandomierz, had been created a new industrial development. Existing towns and villages had increased their population by thousands per cent. One new town of 30,000 inhabitants had sprung up within a year! Soon dozens of giant factories were in produc-

tion. Considerable reserve stocks of essential commodities had
been accumulated. The mountain streams of the Carpathians
to the south yielded abundant power. There was even a
direct supply of 'earth gas' from the Polish oil-fields.

The German General Staff, of course, was not slow to
appreciate the meaning of the new and extensive schemes.
C.O.P. affected German strategy to a vital degree. Before the
attack on Poland could be mounted, Czechoslovakia must be
overrun. With German armies in Slovakia C.O.P. would be
already outflanked. It is apparent that the Polish government
did not see this quite so clearly, or their attitude to Czechoslovakia would have been very different.

While it is true that the Polish command was hopelessly
over-optimistic, they can claim with justice that they never
expected to bear the full weight of the German attack—that
at least half of it would be borne by France. The defensive
plan—rather hastily improvised, for only a few years earlier
Polish generals had considered thrusts *into* Germany when
war came—aimed at holding the Germans, while yielding territory until the weight of the attack was reduced by Allied
pressure in the west. This did not materialise.

Britain and France must carry a serious share of the blame
for the rapid Polish defeat. In April 1939 the British government offered a loan: but it was wrapped up in so many conditions that the war had begun before the Poles had gathered
much benefit. When, early in August, the danger was only too
obvious and the Poles wished to mobilise, they were deterred
—such a move might annoy Hitler!

On September 1st, 1939, therefore, Polish mobilisation was
still incomplete. It never was completed. The vastly outnumbered Polish air force was shot down from the skies in the first
days of battle, despite innumerable epics of heroism—Polish
pilots in obsolete machines deliberately charging head on
against German bombers. Thereafter the Luftwaffe wreaked
its will. Towns and villages were fired—timber is the most
common building material in Poland, and a few dozen incen-

diaries destroyed a village. Bridges and railways hundreds of miles from the battle area were wrecked. Tens of thousands of Polish reservists never even reached their depots before the war was over.

Many bombing raids were completely indiscriminate, designed to break the nerve of the civilian population. They did not succeed in their object, but they inflicted cruel losses.

'Fifth Columnists' behind the Polish lines played an effective part in the early stages of the campaign. The German minority had been effectively organised and armed, and many Polish units were attacked from the rear by local German partisans. The vast espionage system, based on German residents, yielded immediate results: not even the decisions of the Cabinet or the orders of the Polish command were unknown to the Germans.

The German armoured forces were immensely stronger than the opposition. A column of overwhelming strength plunged into the heart of Poland. The 'new tactics' were displayed—battle in depth, not width. Armoured divisions did not wait for infantry to catch up and consolidate ground gained, but plunged forward towards Warsaw. In the meantime, the strategically indefensible Corridor had been overrun and a German army was striking south from East Prussia.

The Polish Command ordered a rapid retreat to the Vistula. But this defensive line was already outflanked—by the German forces in Slovakia. The C.O.P. was threatened from the first moment of battle: the situation was hopeless.

Yet the Poles still fought on. One army, encircled near Lodz, fought its way out and regained the main force. Then, on September 17th, the Russians crossed the eastern frontier. The military situation was already hopeless; now Poland's surrender was merely a question of days: Poland was the nut between the crackers.

No one could have blamed the Poles had they flung up their hands in despair. Yet they fought on. Isolated detachments, totally surrounded, defied all attacks. Warsaw stood a siege, short in duration but almost unparalleled in its horror.

The fighters in the trenches were not all soldiers: not all men, indeed—as often in history, Polish women fought beside their men: boys and girls seized rifles and fought beside their

THE FOURTH PARTITION OF POLAND

fathers. They shared the isolated and the common graves scattered about the city's ruins.

The end was inevitable. By the end of September all but guerrilla fighting had ended. Now the spoils must be divided.

Germany seized the western part of Poland—188,000 square

kilometres, with a population of 22 millions. Russia's share was 201,000 square kilometres, with a population of 13 millions. The richest areas, naturally, went to Germany. The Russians promptly held a 'plebiscite' in their share—one of the plebiscites of the type so familiar in Europe, where a man can vote only one way. Naturally the voting was almost unanimous for incorporation in Soviet Russia. There might have been a considerable vote for such a course in any case, but this plebiscite was farcical.

Over conquered Poland a great terror reigned. In the Russian half Polish leaders and intellectuals were arrested and interned. There had been ugly incidents in moments of disillusion. So complete was the confusion that, when the Russians first crossed the frontier, some Polish units thought they had come to help in the fight against Germany—and cheered as Poles and Russians marched side by side. There was trouble when the truth emerged.

Yet repression in the east could scarcely be compared with massacre in the west. There was nothing new in the Nazi policy. 'Beat the Poles: drive them to be sick of life: they must be exterminated.' This sounds like Hitler, but the words were uttered by Bismarck.

(It is a strange commentary. Bismarck was the apostle of nationalism in Germany, but its most bitter opponent in other countries—especially Poland. Even earlier, in 1848, Bismarck had forcibly opposed the wave of national patriotism which swept over Europe—but encouraged it in Germany in 1871. Hitler was by no means the first to employ one law for the German, another for all other races.)

The German plan was at once made clear. A huge area of Poland—far beyond the 1914 frontiers—was incorporated into the Reich. It included not only the Corridor, Upper Silesia and Poznan, but the industrial area about Lodz and a large district south of East Prussia—territories which had never been German in their history. This is important. These areas were not formed into a 'protectorate,' but were annexed 'in perpetuity,' without plebiscite and without compensation. It may be necessary to remind the Germans of this action at a later date: if any Germans objected to the obvious and gross injustice of the move, they were unable or unwilling to voice their protests.

The remaining territory was divided. South of Lublin was formed a 'Jewish Reservation,' which will be described in the appropriate section. The rest of German-occupied Poland was termed a Governor-Generalship: it extended from Warsaw to Cracow, had an area of 95,540 square kilometres and a normal population of 11,484,000. This, by the Nazi scheme, was to be the rump Poland, and all surviving Poles were to be concentrated there.

The Polish territory definitely added to the Reich covered 92,160 square kilometres, with a population of 10,740,000—of whom less than 6 per cent were Germans. Immediately there began a process intended to raise this figure to as near a hundred as was practicable.

First it was necessary to get rid of the Poles. Already a campaign of murder had savagely reduced the Polish ranks. Mass executions were a daily feature of Polish life—and still are. The Germans entered Poland prepared, bringing with them portable gallows—iron structures, with room for six victims. There was no pretence of humane execution. A rope was knotted round the victim's neck, and he was hauled a few inches off the ground. Death came to him by slow strangulation. I have written 'he,' but thousands of women shared the fate of their men.

Over 10,000 people perished in a week at Bydgoszcz. Here the German timing went wrong—the local Fifth Column began its treacherous attacks too soon, and was promptly dealt with. This was presented by German propaganda as a murder of Germans, and a terrible revenge was executed.

Some months after the campaign, a young friend of mine escaped from Poland. His story was typical of those shocking days. When the Germans entered his village, they seized five hostages—the headman or mayor (my friend's father), the

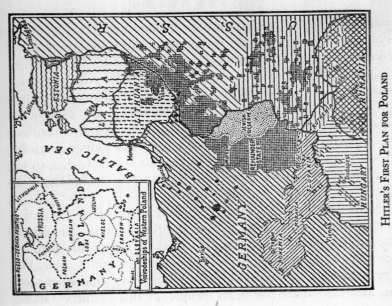

THE POLAND OF YESTERDAY

HITLER'S FIRST PLAN FOR POLAND

priest and three peasant farmers. That night an impetuous Polish youth swarmed up the flagstaff, hauled down the swastika and replaced the Polish flag.

Next morning the entire population of the village was assembled and the five hostages were shot. My friend described the scene: he had to hold his hands behind his head: his mother stood by his side. As his father was shot, his mother collapsed; he moved to support her, and a bayonet was plunged into his flesh. Then the people were forced to file by the bodies, to see at close quarters what happened to those who defiled the Nazi flag.

When my friend returned to his mother, he was scarcely surprised to find that she had lost her reason under the ordeal: mercifully, a few days later she died. After an adventurous journey he reached England and is now a fighter pilot. His age is twenty, but he looks fifty. His stare of amazement can be imagined when he hears people in this country talking about 'making a deal' with Hitler. With this scene enacted ten thousand times in Poland, can it be wondered that Poles find more difficulty in distinguishing between Nazis and Germans than we do?

In the first year of German occupation a conservative estimate is that 70,000 Poles were executed: often without trial, usually without cause. It is true that not all Germans view these mass murders with pleasure. Nor are all quite so confident of German victory as their leader. There have been cases of German officials who persuaded Poles to sign testimonials agreeing that they had behaved decently to the local population!

This orgy of murder is likely to prolong the war. Tens of thousands of Germans are not Nazis, and in their hearts abhor the horrors perpetrated on the subject races: yet they fight on as sternly as the rest. They believe that if Germany were beaten, the Poles would demand a terrible revenge, and they are afraid.

Next in horror to the mass executions was the deportation

of Poles from their homes in the occupied provinces. In the first two years nearly one and a half million Poles were driven from their homes into the Governor-Generalship, often under appalling conditions.

Gdynia was the pride of Poland, and an object of German jealousy. It was therefore singled out for the first attack. Street by street, at an hour's notice, its people were turned out of their homes: they might carry a suitcase, but all household goods had to be left behind. They were marched along a road: old men, women and children—the young men were already dead or prisoners. As sick or feeble fell by the way, they were pushed into the ditches by the guards. At night the pathetic companies lay in the open fields.

Then they were herded into cattle trucks, sixty to a truck, and locked in. Through the Polish winter trains jogged sullenly forward. In the trucks people died, women gave birth to babies, children shrieked in fear and lost their reason. Hundreds perished on this appalling journey. Even the hardened German soldiers were taken aback when from one train they removed the bodies of thirty children, frozen stiff.

The survivors found themselves dumped in the midst of a forest, somewhere in the Governor-Generalship. Now they might 'do as they liked.' The nearest village was already overcrowded, and its food supplies exhausted. They set off to march to Warsaw. Did you ever face a Polish winter? Bitterly cold winds sweep from the Russian plains, driving before them not snow, but tiny particles of ice which cut like a knife. The road to Warsaw was dotted with crude crosses to mark the last rest of those who lay down and could not rise again. And those who reached Warsaw found it a dead city of destruction and famine, where a hundredweight of potatoes cost fifty dollars, and a dog was sold for ten dollars.

These appalling cruelties have an importance far beyond their present horror. They are bound to affect the outlook at the time of victory. We cannot dictate terms: we must carry our allies with us, or the terms will be of short endurance.

And we must not expect the outlook of a Polish survivor of a campaign of cruelty and murder to be the same as that of the occupant of a club armchair in Fifth Avenue. It is essential that the New Europe shall be based on reason and justice: but it is going to be immensely difficult to procure this. People who have scarcely felt the close touch of war may soon be willing to slip into the 'kiss and be friends' mood with Germany. It is not human to expect this in Poland.

Many of my Polish friends were among the Nazi victims, and I suffered with them in spirit. Yet what was in some ways a harder blow was to follow. Pillage and murder are inevitable adjuncts of war. I have always cultivated an international outlook, and have always respected those things which are international: arts and sciences, for example. But the art treasures of Poland have been looted—by German artists. Some years ago a new Physical Institute was opened in Warsaw, one of the finest in the world. Deputations of learned men came from all countries for the ceremonial opening, among them a committee of German professors. In 1939 these professors returned to Warsaw, to select from the Institute the choicest pieces of its valuable equipment, which were at once transported to Germany: they came with a list ready prepared! How many years must pass before Germans are trusted again?

The sorry tale of German repression of Polish culture is too well known: professors arrested, teachers killed, all schools closed. Education was to be reserved for the ruling class. Why educate people of whom Hitler declared, 'We need not hesitate to call them the modern slave class'? Polish intellectuals form a heavy proportion of the 140,000 people murdered. Tens of thousands more are held in prison camps. Polish books were burned by the million; newspapers suppressed or turned into German propaganda vehicles. The Governor-General, Frank, at least lived up to his name when he announced: 'We

do not want a Polish educated class. The Reich has an abund-
ance of educated men of her own. By the will of the Führer,
you are to be a nation of peasants and workmen.'

The Germans are right in one contention: if they destroy
Polish culture, they would attain their objective—the destruction of the Polish nation. Yet it survived incredible hardships
for 150 years in the days of the Partitions: it will not be submerged now. The schools are closed, but Polish children are
taught at home. Newspapers are suppressed, but underground
journals flourish: I have already seen samples of twenty-two
of these remarkable publications, fervent apostles of liberty;
hundreds of others exist.

A deliberate policy of extermination is pursued: an impossible policy. Neither the mass murders, nor the years of semi-
starvation, nor the agonies of mind and body, can break the
spirit of this remarkable people. As I write, Hitler has ruled
over 20 million Poles for two years. All that time he has been
trying to set up a puppet Polish government in his Governor-
Generalship. But in two years, out of 20 millions, he has not
succeeded in finding a single Pole to serve under him.

Today the children of Poland play a new game. Horror and
terror are now too familiar to terrify. Thousands of children
have died: a hundred Boy Scouts were shot because they had
dared to help their country. The new game is topical, as children's play always tends to be.

One group, with wooden rifles, forms the firing squad.
Another—and there is great competition to belong to it—lines
up by a wall to be shot. As the officer gives the command to
fire, the children by the wall cry 'Long live Poland!' as they
sink to the ground.

VI

It is important to keep a careful eye on German schemes in
Western Poland. Their objective is obvious. They hope to
clear large areas of Poles and re-settle them with Germans.
Then, if things go badly and the war is lost, they could

present the world with a *fait accompli*, believing that war-weary nations would have no desire or energy for undoing the work which had been done. In this contention I believe that they are hopelessly wrong: it should be made quite clear, now and continuously, that they *are* wrong. One Nazi leader stated: 'Even if we are defeated, Hitler will win.' He was referring to schemes like the re-settlement of Poland, which he believed would persist after the war. Unless we are exceptionally blind, or are in too much of a hurry to return to our football and baseball, he has made a very great mistake. We shall know whether we have really won the war by what happens to Poland.

A German State Organisation has been set up for the colonisation of Western Poland. In addition to the million and a half Poles who have been expelled, over 800,000 have been deported to Germany for forced labour. The programme involves transfers of Poles to the Governor-Generalship on an even vaster scale. In their stead, German settlers are to find a new living-space.

It is recognised that the colonisation cannot be completed until after the war, but a big start has been made. First, by arrangement with Russia, the German Balts [1] were withdrawn from the Baltic states. A preliminary batch of 55,000 arrived from Estonia and Latvia in the first month of the war; they were followed by a further 12,000, and by more than 50,000 from Lithuania.

Most of these colonists left their ancient homes reluctantly; yet at least the change was easy. They found themselves installed on farms in going order, from which the Polish owners had only recently been driven. The household goods and farm stocks were handed over to them freely. Enough Poles were left behind to provide cheap labour. This was transference of population in the easiest conditions.

Yet there are reports of great discontent. Some of these colonists are so German that they cannot speak their mother

[1] See Chapter Four.

tongue! They complain that German neighbours look down on them. Further, in the Baltic states they were generally traders, now they are forced to become farmers. Yet their biggest grumble is the most significant. When they left their homes, they believed they were to be settled in the Reich. Instead, they find themselves on stolen ground. They are suspicious: what will happen to them if Germany loses? Their suspicions are well-grounded: no one envies their lot. The Baltic states will never want them back—and they certainly will not be permitted to stay where they are.

The next batch of colonists came from the scattered German settlements in the Governor-Generalship, 130,000. Most of these came willingly, for they could not stand the hostile atmosphere about them. The Russian occupation of Bessarabia and Northern Bukovina produced another large consignment of settlers, about 350,000 in number. These latter were very pleased with their accommodation, which was far in advance of that they had left behind: further, most of them were farmers. But they too complained of the overbearing attitude of 'real' Germans, who despised their brothers so long distant from the family fold, and admittedly on a lower standard of material civilisation.

Thus, in two years, about 600,000 German colonists have been brought in from outside areas to re-settle Western Poland. This was not good enough. These people, added to the original German population, formed only 12 per cent of the whole— a figure not likely to impress even tired statesmen at the Peace Conference.

Consequently, urgent steps are being taken to improve the percentage. First, an intense process of Germanisation is afoot. We have seen that Germans and Poles freely intermarried in the frontier areas—and that the resultant families were often Polish. The Germans are trying to reverse this. The Nuremberg racial laws [1] have been abandoned. A man who had

---

[1] These proclaimed that if *one* grandparent out of four was non-German, then the grandchild was also *non*-German.

two German grandparents is now classed as German: the fact that he speaks only Polish does not matter. His children are taught German only—all Polish schools are closed—and it is hoped in a space of years to turn the whole family into Germans. The usual bribes are forthcoming: it pays a man to be classed as a German, since his wages and rations are twice those of a Pole.

We must remember this in the post-war arguments, when we shall be confronted by all kinds of figures 'proving' the German character of Western Poland. Fortunately, to date, few Poles have been willing to be denationalised.

We have already discussed the Polish tribes known as the Kashubians and Masurians. Although classed as Poles by Germany until 1918, it is now declared that they can be accepted as Germans and given the privileges of German colonists. Whether they will it or no, we must expect these people to be included in German population arguments after the war.

In addition, a tremendous propaganda drive has been opened in Germany to attract more settlers. It has not been very successful. The German problem in the past few generations has been the same as ours—the drift from the land to the manufacturing towns of the west. There is no great enthusiasm to take an agricultural holding—especially in an area which will inevitably be lost if the war does not go well.

Consequently, a policy of bribes and privileges has been adopted. Colonists are offered lower taxes, financial grants, low rents, family allowances and agricultural subsidies. So far these bribes have only produced about 30,000 settlers. This failure led to the announcement that most of the farms in Western Poland were being reserved as rewards for gallant soldiers after the war is won. So slow has been the flow of volunteers that even Dutch Nazis are being settled in Western Poland.

The depopulation and re-settlement of Western Poland is a planned movement of high importance. It has been hailed in Germany—not merely in the Nazi press—as a wonderful achievement, a promise of bigger things to come. Often there comes a point when argument recoils on itself.

Conditions in the Governor-Generalship are appalling. The standard of living is a mere existence: every pronouncement is intended to remind the Poles of their position as serfs. The area is hopelessly overcrowded, and there is severe distress—to say nothing of the campaign of terror which has now become so familiar that a few hundred executions are scarcely news. Dr. Hans Frank, the Governor-General of Poland, made a straightforward statement at the annual meeting of the German Academy of Law at Munich on November 22nd, 1940: 'The German Governor-General in Poland represents the best example of the New Europe under the direction of Greater Germany.' The Nazis cannot grumble if we accept this as true: no more terrible indictment was ever spoken.

VII

There are over three million Jews in Poland—10 per cent of the entire population. It may seem strange to include an outline of their problem in a book designed as a commentary on frontiers, but the two are strangely entwined.

Throughout history the Polish record on the treatment of Jews is very good. In the old days of Polish glory Poland had no middle class—only aristocrats and peasants: the aristocrats were often peasants promoted for valour in battle, but they must never engage in trade. The Jews were invited by successive Polish kings to settle in the country to supply the missing link. Poland was for them a happy hunting-ground: aristocrats were forbidden to trade, and peasants never do, so the Jews flourished.

Thus the Jews, in effect, became the middle class of Poland, and as such were powerful. They enjoyed a remarkable degree of religious freedom and even of local self-government. Their numbers were greatly increased during the generations following the Partitions—indeed, one of the most difficult features of the present problem is that not all the Jews in Poland by any means can be classed as 'Polish Jews'; under the old Russian Empire, practically all Jews were compelled by a series of enactments to live in the 'Pale of Settlement'—the western provinces—and consequently Poland received as settlers hundreds of thousands of Russian Jews. The Jews in Poland have retained their race, culture and religion to a remarkable degree, and a walk through the ghettoes of Warsaw or Cracow is like a visit to a legendary world. In Western Poland their numbers are not overwhelming, but in the towns of the east they are very strong: in Lwow and Vilna they number 40 per cent of the inhabitants, and in Pinsk as much as 70 per cent!

A century ago a Polish middle class began to emerge. Naturally enough, it came into conflict at once with the Jews. It is in fact important to record that then and now the principal base of anti-Semitism in Poland was economic, not racial. The feeling developed in strength during the war, when it was claimed that the Jews, men of no nation, supported German or Russian ideas rather than Polish aspirations.

Although the official policy on the re-emergence of Poland was liberal enough, difficulties were at once apparent. The reborn Poland found the greater part of its commercial life in Jewish hands—the distributive trades almost entirely so. But the new Polish middle class was now strong, and had no snobbish views on trade: naturally enough, they wanted to control their own commerce. There was no organized persecution of the Jew, as in Germany, but of late years he has not been particularly happy. Sometimes there were local 'incidents' where peasants attacked the man who held their mortgages; there were occasional minor outbursts by irresponsible hotheads who imagined themselves to be budding Hitlers. But until recently most of the misery of the Jews had been purely economic.

Polish firms—sometimes with government backing—began to drive the Jews from the trading field: even in the rural districts the Jewish trader was being driven out of business by the new co-operative societies. The 'poor Jew' had become one of Poland's thorniest problems. I emphasise again, there was

no organised pogrom against the Jews: you would find Jews
of brilliant attainments in the highest ranks of Polish culture,
science and commerce. But in bad times it is too easy to blame
the Jew for everything; it was not difficult for a Polish trader
to incite a boycott of his Jewish competitor.

This is no simple question—there *is* a Jewish problem in
Poland. It scarcely existed in Germany, where the few hundred thousand Jews had adopted German manners, had freely
intermarried with Germans, and were in many cases indis-
tinguishable from Germans. (There were Jews among Hitler's
backers.) In Poland the Jews are a race apart, with their own
culture, religion and costume. Except for the professional
class, it is impossible to mistake a Jew for anybody else—and
he does not intend you to mistake him. He has never become
assimilated into the local population, as in Western Europe.

The problem was accentuated by the restriction of emigration. Before the 1914 war an average of 250,000 emigrants
left Poland every year. Since then the numbers became negligible—because the United States, the principal field for emigration, has been closed: on the contrary, hundreds of thousands of emigrants returned to Poland. The economic situation in Poland was severe, due to the effects of the world
'crisis.' There were no official figures, but there must have been
two million unemployed in Poland—a serious proportion of
the population. Over one million peasants lacked that strip of
land which means life to them. When there is so much to be
done, and so little money available, it is only natural (argued
the Polish government) that the Poles should have the first
choice, and the Jews must take anything that was left. It was
not entirely the fault of the Poles that there was not much left.

Even in the best of times, a million Jews in Poland—mostly
the descendants of those herded out of Russia in pitiable
circumstances—existed under appalling conditions of poverty. I saw them in the ghettoes, working long hours under
shocking conditions for a mere pittance. Nor were they free
from exploitation by men of their own race.

Gradually the power and influence of the Jew in commerce was waning. From 1921 to 1931 the proportion of Jewish holdings in the commerce of Warsaw fell from 73 to 65.9 per cent. This decline was the result of natural economic development, and its pace was quickened as anti-Semitism became a stronger force, to reinforce the inevitable economic rivalry between Jew and Pole. At the same time, the decline of Jewish trade, while it helped to solve Polish economic problems, only added tens of thousands of 'poor Jews' to the already large total.

Ideas are contagious. In 1792 Poland's neighbours were afraid of the spread of democracy to their domains. From 1933 Fascist ideas began to permeate the minds of some Polish factions—as they did in Britain. Crossing Poland again in 1937, I was appalled at the change in atmosphere. Four years earlier Poland had appeared as the champion of the Jews, standing up to Germany. The Ten-Year Pact altered that attitude; though the Polish government remained scrupulously correct in its outlook, there were many signs of economic boycott. The trouble was that people were getting out of hand. The repercussions of ruthless German propaganda were bound to have their effects in Poland. Picketing of Jewish shops was common. The younger irresponsible elements were imbibing the impression that it was 'patriotic' to beat up Jews. I saw a gang of students in Warsaw following a group of caftaned Jews to the synagogue, jeering and jibing. When one of the exasperated Jews turned on these heroes, he was roughly handled, and only the timely intervention of the police saved him from a worse fate. These incidents were for a time all too common in Poland. If they are what they appear to be—an indication of worse to come—then the outlook is not bright. I hesitate to prophesy, but I suggest that the Jewish problem is likely to be one of Europe's outstanding difficulties within the next ten years. And the Jewish problem is really a Christian problem.

In Poland it was aggravated by the Zionist campaign—the first demand on the rebirth of Poland was for a separate Jewish

Parliament—a state within a state. The Poles rightly dismissed this idea as impracticable: it is obviously impossible that one law should apply to a Jew living on one side of a street and another to the Pole who lived opposite.

Two-thirds of Poland's three million Jews were in the area occupied by Germany. If the lot of the Poles has not been pleasant, that of the Jews can be imagined.

Of the two millions, the greater part lived in the Governor-Generalship—we have seen that there were few Jews in that part of Poland which was occupied by Germany before 1918. The Germans have now vastly extended their 1918 frontiers, however, so as to include the manufacturing city of Lodz, where nearly half the population was Jewish.

While the Nazi plan for the treatment of Jews in Poland appears to fall under two main headings, it is subject to the widest variations. If the Jews can be used, they are used: if not, then their treatment is worse than that of mediaeval serfs.

The first point in the German policy was to clear all Jews from the annexed area. To receive them, a 'Reservation' was enclosed south of Lublin. It bounded the frontier fixed between Germany and Russia, and was part of the Governor-Generalship. This was to be the dumping-ground, not merely for the Jews of Western Poland, but of Austria and Germany as well.

It is a poor district, a land of peasant farms. In normal times the Jewish population was small. To make room for a new influx, the Germans have cleared out tens of thousands of Polish peasants. In the very best conditions the Reservation could not possibly support the huge numbers of Jews now being dumped there: in the worst conditions, as prevailing today, the sufferings are appalling. The Reservation is but one huge concentration camp, completely surrounded with barbed wire—but with no arrangements for feeding the prisoners.

The first part of the plan was to remove to the Reservation the Jews of Western Poland: next, those from Austria, Czecho-slovakia and Germany proper. The expulsions were carried out with the usual callousness. Jews were ordered to pack a suitcase and leave their homes at an hour's notice. The first contingents were of men only, to build camps to house their families: few of these anticipations have been fulfilled, and Eastern Europe today is filled with anxious fragments of broken family groups.

Few neutral observers have been allowed to visit the Reservation. They tell of appalling conditions: hundreds of thousands of people without work, almost without food, living in conditions at which a healthy beast would shudder; above all, without hope. The traditional Jewish capacity for enduring suffering is being sorely tried: the suicide rate is very high.

For the Jews of the Governor-Generalship a different plan is enforced, with many variations. In most Polish cities there was already a Jewish ghetto, a relic of older days. In our time it had lost much of its ancient meaning. Thousands of poor Poles lived in the ghettoes, pitiable slum horrors of filth and despair, while thousands of better-off Jews lived in the Polish quarters. Now the ancient ghetto rules have been renewed and greatly extended.

The city ghetto is today enclosed within a high wall, with much broken glass and barbed wire. In Warsaw nearly half a million Jews are imprisoned in this new form of concentration camp, cut off from the world. Limited supplies of food are passed in through hatchways, as if to lepers. The Jews are responsible for their own discipline—naturally, no respectable Nazi thug would demean himself by entering a ghetto. Any disturbance, any petty infringement of German rules, meets a terrible retribution. Jewish hostages are freely gathered, to be executed on the slightest provocation.

The Jews are being driven out of trade. Able-bodied men are enlisted in forced labour companies. Jewish girls are sent to Germany and parts of occupied territory for 'agricultural' purposes, which usually means for service in army brothels. Naturally, Jewish property was seized wholesale, and the pogrom of murder, arson and suppression exceeds any previous

Nazi records. Never in their history has this much-tried race
had to undergo such torture.

The problem of the Eastern European Jews will become
urgent immediately after the end of the war. Even at the best
there are too many Jews in Poland: a considerable proportion
are not Polish Jews in origin, but Russian Jews escaping from
pogroms in older days. We have seen that in earlier centuries
the Jews formed the Polish trading class: now their monopoly
has already disappeared, and it is certain that in succeeding
years the Jewish proportion of commerce will decline as
energetic and youthful Poles decide to conduct their own
commercial affairs. Even if there were no trace of anti-Semitic
feeling, there is but a poor future for three-quarters of the Jews
of Poland. For many generations already a million of them
have been existing under conditions of abject poverty.

What can be done with the Polish Jews? In the past years
ten thousand a year have emigrated to Palestine—the Polish
government operated a special shipping line direct to Palestine
from Roumanian ports. Tens of thousands more would be sent,
but for the maximum quota allowed by the British government.
I found in Poland a poor understanding of their position, and a
growing suggestion that Poland, as the greatest Jewish country,
should take over the Palestine mandate.

A group of members of the Seym—the Polish Parliament—
invited me to address them. I accepted, thinking that they
would be interested to hear an Englishman's casual view of the
Polish Corridor. But I found, to my concern, that they wanted
me to speak about the Palestine Mandate.

I know no more of this subject than the next man—this was
before the recent troubles enlarged our knowledge—and have
never been to Palestine, but one of two arguments were
obvious. I pointed out that the Balfour Declaration did more
than proclaim a National Home for the Jews—it confirmed
the rights of the Arabs in Palestine. There arose also the question as to which was the more binding—the Balfour Declaration or Lawrence's pledge to the Arabs on Britain's behalf.

Unconsciously I strayed into prophecy by saying that undue haste or swamping of Palestine with Jews would be certain to arouse violent resentment among the Arabs—with serious repercussions throughout the Moslem world, in which Britain was vitally and intimately interested. This solution of the Polish-Jewish problem, therefore, would only create others much vaster and more dangerous.

I added a severely practical argument—that Britain, having recently constructed a most expensive oil pipe-line from Iraq, could scarcely be expected to hand over the control of its vital coastal terminus to another power, however friendly.

I think I was able to persuade my hearers that the idea of a Polish Mandate for Palestine was out of the question, and should be abandoned. In any case, even if Palestine were cleared of Arabs, it could never support even the Polish Jewish population, much less the seven million Jews from other countries. Palestine offers only a partial solution: we must consider others.

It has been suggested that a huge colony of Jews should be planted in one of the undeveloped South American countries. The scheme is sound. Several South American states have already received block settlements of Europeans, to the profit of both. They might be persuaded to do it again. Madagascar or an area on the African mainland have also been suggested as possibilities. The principal objection raised to these schemes has been that of cost. This obstacle is not likely to appear so overwhelming in the aftermath of war.

One Polish suggestion is that a Jewish colony should be established in Libya. Already the population includes more than 20 per cent of Jews—many of them descended from those who fled from the Babylonian Captivity. The difficulty of this scheme is that the territorial area available for settlement in this desert country is small, and that any further influx of Jews would swell the Jewish-Arab antagonism.

(On the other hand, it seems certain that Arab nationality is likely to rise in stature after the war—a widespread Arab confederation is by no means impossible. In such case, the Arabs might agree to the clearance of some area like Palestine or Libya so as to accommodate the Jews. Again, it must be insisted that even a gesture like this only touches the edge of the problem.)

In some respects the solution of the Jewish problem of Poland will be easier than elsewhere. I have emphasised that anti-Semitism is a comparatively recent growth there: that Poland's record of tolerance is remarkably good. Thus there is no background of violence, so disturbing to a just consideration. And two features of the tragedy of 1939 are important: when Hitler threatened, Jews stood behind Poles almost to a man: and when disaster descended on Poland, Jews and Poles suffered side by side.

VIII

The first problem of post-war Poland will be to undo the work the Germans are doing. It would be a travesty of justice if any section of the 'settlement' so brutally imposed were to be allowed to persist.

The second problem is as important but perhaps not so difficult—the internal conduct of affairs. We have seen that Pilsudski, despairing of the vacillating democrats who did not face the stern realities of the day, established a virtual dictatorship. In many respects it was anachronistic, for the Polish people are essentially democratic; but it worked, so was accepted. The tragedy was that after Pilsudski's death the system persisted under the leadership of men who had neither his clever vision nor his strength of character. The electoral system was as farcical as that in other European states: suffrage was open, but all candidates were selected by special assemblies selected by the government! Most of the popular parties boycotted the elections completely.

Nevertheless, the growing temper of the people even before the war indicated considerable changes. A new electoral law was announced: the first election under its clauses would

change the face of Poland. It is likely to be implemented and
extended, for General Sikorski is a democrat and always has
been.

I first came into contact with him in 1935, and was struck
by his foresight and imagination. His appreciation of the
European situation was masterly: there was no peace in
Europe, he declared, but a state of permanent siege.

Sikorski was one of Pilsudski's companions in arms, and
played a leading part in the liberation of Poland. In 1926, however, he resigned his command: as a democrat, he could not
countenance the use of force in Pilsudski's political *coup
d'état*: for thirteen years he was outside public life. It was
Poland's fortune that he was available at the moment of crisis.
He is no tub-thumping orator or swaggering dictator, but a
man of affairs, inspiring confidence.

The shape of the new Poland is already foreshadowed, to be
established at the earliest possible moment after the present
all-party government has assumed control. Voting will be free
and secret. The peasants will be recognised as the basis of the
population, with a gradual development of industry. The
proposed federation with Czechoslovakia (discussed in another section) will be the basis of Poland's foreign policy,
which will closely collaborate with ours and that of the
restored France. The presence of a large Polish army in
Britain has bred ideas which may swell to amazing proportions
when the soldiers regain their own country. After I had lec-
tured to a Polish unit in Scotland, one question from an officer
was greeted with tumultuous applause. He asked on what
terms Poland would be permitted to join the British Empire!

We must revert to our primary consideration—the frontiers
of Poland. On some of the problems a reasonable judgment is
possible. (Those discussed in this chapter are not final: the
Polish frontiers had more problems to the yard than any others
in Europe. Vilna is discussed in the section on the Baltic states,
Ukraine in the Russian chapter and Teschen under Czechoslovakia.)

(*a*) We can agree that the Polish Corridor is Polish territory, always has been, and always ought to be.

(*b*) The correlated problem of Danzig must now be tackled more realistically. In 1919 the people of Danzig were offered a compromise solution in their status of a Free City. They failed to accept it: indeed, many of them never intended to accept it, and from its inception schemed against its smooth working. The compromise solution *was* fundamentally sound and practically quite workable: the Danzigers preferred national pride to toleration; they cannot grumble if they are not given a second chance.

The vital importance of Danzig to Poland is indicated merely by a glance at the map.[1] Control of the port is essential to the development of the country. We must consider whether the port should not now be handed over to Poland outright.

Of the German inhabitants, those whose intransigeance was at the root of the trouble will probably prefer to go to Germany. Some of the others—especially those of Polish ethnic origin—will choose to remain. It should be made clear in any form of decision that those who stay on in Danzig will do so as Polish subjects, subject to Polish laws. Realisation of this will do more than anything else to sort out one type from another. By the clearest possible methods it should be emphasised that Danzig is to become a Polish city, never to be returned to Germany. In 1939 the Danzigers helped to bring pain and death to millions of people: they must now be prepared to experience some personal inconvenience themselves.

(*c*) We have anticipated that in the hour of victory many extravagant claims will be preferred—one of our objects in presenting the problems of Europe for study now is to avoid the heated atmosphere of the post-war weeks, when calm judgment will be difficult if not impossible. It would only be natural if some of the widest claims should come from the people who have suffered most. From Poland, bitterly oppressed, will flow a reasonable demand that this kind of thing

[1] See page 83.

shall never happen again: coupled with it will be an instinctive craving for revenge. The two may combine, perhaps subconsciously, to produce results which do not accord with the terms or spirit of the Atlantic Charter.

There will be Poles who will claim the western half of Silesia. They will point not only to the Polish character of the rural population, but to the fact that the loss of its rich industries would seriously weaken Germany. The latter argument would certainly find appreciative echoes in some British minds.

It is quite true that, in Upper Silesia, the population on the right bank of the river Oder is largely Slav in origin—this is admitted even by the German census figures. The Nazis confirmed this by their action when they occupied Polish Silesia in 1939. German and Polish Silesia were combined into one province, with some Polish districts added; the name of the new province is Oberschlesien—and over 60 per cent of the population is Polish. German official sources have admitted the necessity for intense Germanisation—in the western as well as the eastern half of the province. The *gauleiter* of the new province was quite frank. 'I have been commissioned by the Führer to make Upper Silesia German,' he stated, so recently as May 3rd, 1941. It is certain that we shall be faced with strong Polish demands for the western half of Silesia, at least as far as Oppeln.

Other Poles, desperately anxious for the safety of their country, will go further, and demand the removal of Poland's western frontier to the river Oder *along the whole of its course*. Here, it is argued, a strong Poland could maintain herself.

I do not agree. A river is no serious strategic barrier in modern war. In any case, we have assumed the permanent disarmament of Germany as a *sine qua non* of our discussion. Further, such a move would be totally at variance with the ideas of the Atlantic Charter, which will be invoked by Poland in settling some of her other frontier problems.

There are many people who hold that the frontiers dividing
Silesia should not differ greatly from those of 1919—minor
adjustments, for economic tidying-up purposes, of course, are
quite legitimate. We cannot hold a plebiscite in any district
every quarter-century particularly in an area which is economically dependent on industry—and trade. And after the

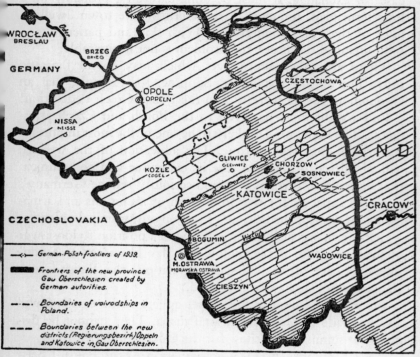

HITLER'S 'SOLUTION' FOR UPPER SILESIA

first shock of partition, both parts of Silesia were on their way
to recovery. Another generation, and the reorientation of their
economy might have been satisfactorily completed.

Instead of extending Polish frontiers to the west, therefore,
and thereby bringing in another large block of Germans in addition to the local Polish population, it has been suggested that the
1919 frontiers should be approximately maintained, and that

Silesia should be the base of an exchange of populations which might do a lot to ease the atmosphere in this part of the world, once the sting of the initial irritation was soothed. Including Danzig, there will be in Poland something like a million Germans to be transferred to the Reich. In Germany there are approximately the same number of Poles. Here is an obvious case for exchange. It must be done carefully, probably on a long-term plan, for most of the Germans are town dwellers, most of the Poles countrymen. With skill and patience, and with financial resources, the problem is not insuperable.

There are other alternatives which may sound fantastic today but normal tomorrow. Suppose, for example, that an autonomous Silesia were to join the Polish-Czech Federation!

Full weight must be given to the Polish and Czech arguments. The Federation is likely to be one of the most important features of post-war Europe. The allocation of the western half of Silesia to it would ease its economic and communication difficulties; further, it would seriously reduce Germany's potential capacity for the production of munitions and armaments. In view of the bearing of this on our principal objective —that Germany shall never again be in a position to loose war on Europe—and of the undoubted Slav character of a considerable part of the Silesian population, the Polish-Czech claims cannot be lightly dismissed.

(d) Claims which at the outset appear to be extreme will also be made in respect of East Prussia. They cannot be dismissed as summarily as those for the Oder frontier.

It has been argued that a perpetuation of the Polish Corridor will enable a future Hitler to rouse the German people by appealing to their pride, by pointing to the division of their territory. The Poles may not trust our assurance that we will never allow another Hitler to arise. We mean it now, but what in 1960? By that time we shall have slipped back into our old easy-going habits, and be so engrossed in our football (or whatever is the fashion of the day) that we can spare no attention to Hitlers and Corridors. The Poles can scarcely be blamed because they pay more attention to problems of national existence than to football.

Any peace settlement, following defeat, is going to be a severe blow to German pride. Since the Corridor is to irritate them by showing a divided Reich, why not allocate the whole

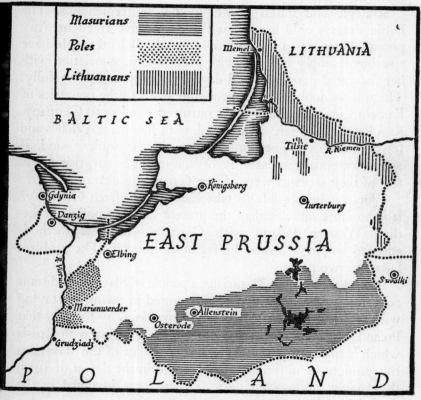

RACIAL DISTRIBUTION IN EAST PRUSSIA

of East Prussia to Poland? it is argued. Then Germany would be all in one piece. Certainly German pride would be hurt. East Prussia is the home of the Junker class, who have ruled Germany for centuries, who have provided her with military heroes. But do we need to conciliate these people? Without entering into the argument whether all Germans are good or bad, at least we can agree that the Nazis are no more than the embodiment of the Prussian spirit: that the German War Machine, not Hitler, controls Germany today—and that a vital blow could be struck at the German War Machine if we removed its base.

Strategic and moral effects would be tremendous. The Baltic states would breathe with comparative freedom. Any potential menace to Russia would recede. Poland would have a seaboard amply supplied with ports, and in association with her federated partners could develop rapidly and powerfully. There is no doubt that the economic gains to the countries of Eastern Europe would greatly outweigh the loss to Germany. East Prussia is largely agricultural, with few natural riches and fewer industries. The Junkers are still the squires—and, if search were made in parish records, it might be surprising how few of their servants were of true German stock.

Would it be possible to take East Prussia from Germany? It is no more difficult than the present German policy of settling Western Poland with Germans—and the methods adopted would of course be far more humane. The problem falls into two parts.

In the south are the Masurians, a people of Slav stock, distant relatives of the Poles. In 1920 they voted in favour of staying with Germany—influenced, as we have seen, by the fact that Poland was then an insecure state fighting a war with Russia which it appeared she might lose. The choice of the Masurians today might be different: they suffered in the defeat of 1918; they might suffer even more if they were involved in the downfall of Hitler.

The total population of East Prussia is 2,250,000 (this figure does not include Danzig). In addition to the Masurians, there are considerable numbers of Poles in the west of the province, about Marienwerder. Altogether, Masurians and Poles number about 400,000. Some have been largely or partly Germanised; on the other hand, in the rest of East Prussia there are tens of thousands of people of Slav extraction who are wholly Germanised. Further, to the east, adjoining the Memel territory, are about 60,000 Lithuanians.

The Masurians occupy the southern one-third of East Prussia, immediately adjoining the Polish frontier. There are thousands of Germans among them, of course. And although the Masurians have been thoroughly Germanised for many generations—practically all of them today speak German as their first language—the passage of a few decades might change the character of their pleasant land of gentle hills and lakes.

The northern two-thirds of East Prussia is blatantly German—though, as we have said, many of the labouring classes are of Slav origin. Here is the original Prussian home: its capital is Königsberg, the Castle of the King. At Marienburg is the palace of the Grand Master of the Order of the Teutonic Knights, and in almost every town is one of their castles, by the establishment of which they subjugated the country. Certainly the loss of this territory would be a severe blow to German pride—especially to Prussian pride!

There are less than two million Germans in East Prussia. In the strain of war years the Germans have transplanted one and a half million Poles from Pomorze and Poznan to the Governor-Generalship; is there any reason why, in the reasoned days of peace, two million Germans should not be transferred from East Prussia to the Reich? So runs the argument: and the first move was made by Germany.

Actually, it would not be necessary to transfer the entire German population of East Prussia, or anything like it. The Junkers of the countryside, and the rich merchants of the towns—these have been the essence of Prussianism, and would have to go. Of the peasants, a proportion would prefer to remain, even at the expense of becoming Polish subjects. Their outlook is purely local; their attachment is to their village or farm rather than to a nation. Many of them have Slav blood in their veins. It would need to be made quite clear to them that they would remain as Poles, not Germans; their children would be taught in Polish at school. They would be treated exactly as Poles have been treated in Germany for generations. If they remained Germans indefinitely, they would be an ever-present inducement to the next Hitler. Many even of the poorer classes in East Prussia will probably not wish to remain under such conditions; some will. The conditions should be quite clear from the beginning.

Undoubtedly there will be a serious demand for the clearance of East Prussia, with all its intransigeant dangers. It is essential to realise that such a plan would arouse violent resentment in Germany today and tomorrow: its success would depend largely on our resolution in the maintenance of Point 8 of the Atlantic Charter: the one declaring that future German aggression will be halted by threat of arms.

Yet the tremendous blow to German pride could be softened. The salient to the west of Poznan is overwhelmingly Polish: yet if the clearance of East Prussia is to be considered, I suggest a minor rectification of Poland's western frontier in Germany's favour, moving back the Polish population, or transferring it to East Prussia. This would have two advantages: (i) it would soften the blow to German pride by representing the cession of East Prussia as an exchange of territory; (ii) it would provide living-space for part of the East Prussian population. The Junkers would miss their palatial manor-houses, but the peasants would be housed quite comfortably in the West Polish farmsteads. In an atmosphere of tolerance and confidence, such a vast task might be tackled quite cheerfully. We have to face the fact, however, that there is likely to be little tolerance and confidence in this area for many years after the war.

(e) A suggestion has been advanced that, if East Prussia is allocated to Poland, a district should be given to the Jews of Poland and Germany for their joint settlement. True, this would be an even heavier blow to Prussian pride—and especially to Nazi pride. To some people this is an argument in its favour.

Yet there are many objections. Western and eastern Jews do not mingle freely—those of the west generally look down on their cousins of the east, for so long accustomed to a lower standard of life. Nor is the district especially suited for Jewish settlement—they are essentially a Mediterranean people. The principal objection to the idea, in fact, is that neither Germans, Poles nor Jews have a word to say in favour of it.

Certainly the Jewish problem in Poland must be faced. It is unnecessary to be dramatic. The problem will not immediately be more serious than it was in 1939: but it was urgent then. There will never be any question of the emigration of all Poland's three million Jews. Among them are highly educated men and women, prominent in Polish arts and sciences: as usual, they are well represented among the professional classes. There will always be room for a large number of Jews in Polish commerce. But there still remains a considerable residue. It is impossible for this question to be settled finally and completely within Poland.

It will have become obvious, even from my superficial sketches of her problems, that even in victory the path of Poland is no easy one. She deserves, and will doubtless get, the utmost consideration from Britain and the United States. She will re-inherit a ruined economy, and will have to begin again. In 1919 we tended to take the view that, having assisted the young nations at their birth, we could leave them at once to make their own way. We must not make the same mistake again. After the last war Britain, France and the United States gorged Germany with money, granting loan after loan: that is, in effect, gift after gift. Meanwhile, Poland was starved. Had one-tenth of the loans granted to Germany been made to Poland, her state in 1939 would have been immensely stronger.

I am confident that the Poles will tackle their vast problems with energy and courage. Like us, they made mistakes in the past; they have learned from their misfortunes. I have said that Poland is a young country: there is no cause for despair in a land where two-thirds of the population are under thirty.

CHAPTER THREE

RUSSIA

I

DURING the winter of 1939 I went to France to lecture on European problems to units of the R.A.F. After my first talk I called for questions. A flight sergeant promptly demanded: 'When we have won and got the Germans out of the western half of Poland, how are we going to get the Russians out of the eastern half?'

The question was pertinent: yet the problem should have been solved by the German attack on Russia and subsequent events in the relations between Russia and Poland. In any case, before approaching Russian-Polish controversies of today or tomorrow, we must obviously glance at the history of Russia, so involved and so fascinating a story that I must leave it largely untold, lest it run away with me. One or two points must be mentioned, however, not so much for the light they throw on modern conditions in that country as on our own attitude towards them. It is still difficult to write about Russia without arousing ire at both ends of the political scale.

As usual, a mountain range is no natural boundary, and the Urals, though they separate Europe and Asia, mark no real break in race or culture. Certainly they formed no obstacle to the wild Tartar invaders who in the thirteenth century swept westwards under Jenghis Khan from Mongolia. They reached Russia and there many of them stayed, making themselves masters of the Slavonic peoples there: overlord of the region was a chieftain with the romantic name of the Khan of the Golden Horde.

From this sovereignty Ivan III, Grand Duke of Moscow, won free in 1480; before long he proclaimed himself Tsar

(Caesar or Emperor). His successors mastered all Russia, still largely an oriental country; under the vigorous rule of Peter the Great and Catherine the Great it became painfully and reluctantly westernised. It still remained a curious mixture, most Asiatic of all western countries, most European of all eastern.

Particularly, even in the modern Machine Age, when it began to develop industrially, it remained oriental, even barbaric, in government. Its rule was 'despotism tempered by assassination'; a corrupt nobility and an inefficient bureaucracy held down an insurgent town proletariat, a baffled and discontented intelligentsia, and an illiterate peasantry living in conditions of squalid poverty and still possessed by the traditions of virtual slavery from which they had recently escaped. The press was gagged, the Duma (Parliament) a mere committee of 'yes men' bound to endorse every imperial decree. The very religion of the country, the Orthodox Greek Church, was too often only an agent of the State machine. Protest, criticism, free speech, even expression on non-political subjects, were suppressed as ruthlessly as in modern Germany, and by much the same methods. In pre-1914 days the words 'Cossacks,' 'Siberia,' 'the knout' conveyed exactly the same horror as do 'Gestapo,' 'concentration camps' and 'rubber truncheon' at the present day.

Russia's interest in her kindred Slav tribes, to say nothing of her part in the power politics of the day, ensured that she should be violently involved in the Great War, in which she suffered more than any other belligerent. Badly led, betrayed in high places, inadequately provisioned and provided with munitions, her peasants died in millions before the efficient German Armies of the East; meanwhile its rulers—even its court—became the prey of unspeakable corruption—who, even now, does not remember the name of Rasputin?

Here was a creature who transcends in foulness even the thousands of legends gathered about his name. He was the virtual ruler of Russia for a decade. No one could hope for advancement except by his favour. The tragedy was that Russians of high principle began to withdraw from public life rather than be associated with the vile corruption surrounding the administration.

It was only natural that such a country should be the first victim of the war neurosis which afterwards overtook Germany. One of the prime causes of the first revolution was the huge casualties sustained by the Russian armies. Often whole companies were literally without arms, and more often without ammunition. Annihilation of Russian detachments was quite common—not that they were inferior in courage to their opponents, but simply because they had nothing with which to fight. There is a limit to the endurance of man. Only a tenacious race would have endured until it had sustained casualties including ten million dead before it revolted against the impossible odds—just when the moment was due when munitions should have been forthcoming from abroad in substantial quantities. (Actually, vast quantities of equipment and ammunition were already in Russia, but because of the poor communications and appalling organisation they never reached the front. Hundreds of trucks littered the Trans-Siberian railway, held in sidings because no one was available to bribe the station-masters to send them on.)

An outbreak of popular disgust swept away the Tsar's government and replaced it with that of Kerensky. He was liberal in his views, and endeavoured to carry on the war; but the Russian people had had enough of war: in a few months there were two million desertions. And now a strange new factor was introduced.

On the career of that extraordinary figure Lenin I need say little here. One episode is well known—the attempt of the German High Command to disrupt Russian unity by sending him in a 'sealed train' from Switzerland to Russia. In this they succeeded beyond their wildest expectations.

At the head of the Communist Party Lenin became ruler of Russia. He made the Treaty of Brest-Litovsk (which at least

had the merit of showing the world what would be the character of a German-dictated peace), and then proceeded to run
his country on a modification of the lines advocated by Karl
Marx. The revolution took place with extraordinary violence
—as it seemed to an age less accustomed to violence than ours
—and involved the massacre of the Tsar, his family and tens of
thousands of others.

Aghast at this slaughter, and alarmed lest Communism
should spread to their own lands, the Western Powers began
a campaign against Russia, the more bitter for being unofficial
and undeclared. They carried on an embittered propaganda,
ringed Russia off by a *cordon sanitaire* of new-formed states,
and supported the nine counter-revolutionary armies which
invaded it. Even when these armies had been repulsed and
overt hostilities had ceased, the propaganda campaign continued with undiminished vigour.

Nor was the western fear of 'Bolshevism' entirely void of
foundation. The new-born Russia aimed at spreading its
'ideology' to the rest of the world. Its armies invaded Poland
and were spectacularly defeated. Its ideas were more insidious;
they found loud-voiced advocates in every land. The fear they
produced was more far-reaching even than themselves. Con-
servative-minded people saw the 'Red hand of Moscow' everywhere, in every strike or demand for higher pay, in every
change in a changing world of which they did not approve.
Left-wing folk accused the Communist party of bringing into
English political life a method of intrigue which was completely unscrupulous, an attempt to capture or disrupt all con-
structive movements. Religious people saw only a materialist
propaganda which attacked all religious beliefs and condemned
as 'bourgeois' all the accepted canons of morality. It will of
course be understood that I am neither affirming nor denying
these accusations: I am merely pointing out that they existed.

Of this position Hitler later took full advantage, obtaining
much tacit support in the west as the arch enemy of the 'Red
menace,' Marxian Communism. This in some measure accounts

for the complacency with which his rise was in some quarters watched—for the condoning of the march into the Rhineland, of the rape of Austria, of his growing influence in Italy and Spain, and for Munich itself.

A clarification of ideas on Russia in many quarters is overdue. Today, some of Russia's sternest critics have become her most vociferous supporters—because they have been thrilled by her magnificent resistance. If she collapsed tomorrow, their enthusiasm would gradually fade.

The truth is that few people have been able to look on Russia without conscious or unconscious bias. This is as dangerous and unhealthy today as it was ten years ago. On the day of the German attack I met in turn two friends: one, a man of the Right, exclaimed 'Russia won't last a fortnight.' The other, of the Left, was convinced that Hitler would be defeated in a month. The incident is typical of the confused outlook of the times, often so absurdly sentimental. It is difficult to gauge the mentality of those who judge the internal organisation of Russia merely by the quality of her military prowess. If this were the criterion, then National Socialism would have a legitimate claim for consideration as the leading political doctrine of the day.

There is a considerable gap between the character of life in Russia and in Britain or America. This gap will not be immediately narrowed by a common victory. At the same time, it has been artificially widened for twenty years; I have suggested that one of the good things this war has done was to begin the dissolution of the fog of suspicion which separated Russia from Western Europe. Our aim must be to complete this dissolution. The mere fact that the internal political character of Russia differs from ours is no bar to close co-operation: we are both fighting for our lives against a common enemy; when he is beaten, it is to the interest of both of us to plan and maintain the peace.

It would be well to outline briefly the principal causes of that devastating suspicion. It has its origins on our side long

before 1914, when liberal thought in Britain detested the terrorism of Tsarist rule. Nevertheless Russia was our ally, and
was treated as such: there was a suggestion that more democratic methods might rule in Russia after victory.

Then came the Russian revolution and the military collapse: old treaties meant nothing to the new government,
which broke all pledges in making a separate peace with Germany. There was a feeling in Britain that 'Russia had let us
down'—for there was little knowledge or appreciation of
Russia's vast difficulties and immense casualties. The situation,
indeed, resembled that of 1940, when France collapsed.

(Incidentally, our first support of the Russian interventionists can be compared with our backing of General de Gaulle.
Later, this support had a political background, but in its first
steps it was designed to rescue what could be got from the
wreck—to establish a régime which would carry on the war.
This was quite comprehensible from our point of view—but
was the source of the greater portion of Russian resentment
and suspicion.)

In the immediate post-war years there was a complete break
between Britain and Russia. All ideas were tainted: most of our
information came from the Russians we knew—now exiles:
Lenin and Trotsky were merely names to us, associated with
violence and murder. The outlook of these exiles was, naturally
enough, biased, and their information unreliable. (Hitler discovered this same failing. Russian *émigrés* in Germany assured
him that he had nothing to fear—that Russia would collapse at
the first blow. They were wrong again!)

For many years communications between Russia and Britain
were scanty. Few British newspapers maintained correspond-
ents in Russia. Even these published accounts which were
scarcely unbiased, for by this time suspicion of the political
basis of the second revolution was more acute than ever.
Difficulties abounded. A friend of mine, sent to Russia as correspondent for a Right-wing popular journal, complained: 'If
I write appreciative accounts of what the Russians are trying

to do, my paper won't print them. If I am critical, the Russians will expel me from the country.'

It is true that there could be little in common between Revolutionary Russia and Britain. A common mistake is to confuse the Russia of 1941 and that of 1921. A lot has happened in twenty years.

Communism came more easily to Russia than to any other country. The community feeling was always strong—the communal farm a feature of the northern plains. This community feeling had developed into a deep patriotism: despite the tyranny and inefficiency of the Tsarist rule, there was a fervent love for Russia—even for the Tsar.

The collapse of the régime left the Russian mind empty. The ideas of Marx filled the blank. Apart from the community feeling inherent in Russia, the wholesale confiscation of land and property did not come with such a shock as it would in Britain—there, they were already accustomed to the arbitrary confiscations of the Tsar. It was the seizure of property which so shocked many western minds: perhaps the shock would not be so great to the present generation. Our system differs only in principle. The Russian government seized a rich man's land: we take nine-tenths of a rich man's income.

Another subject of suspicion was the Soviet antipathy to religion. Now, the Russians—indeed all the Slav peoples—are essentially religious in their traditions. When the Russians adopted Marxism as the basis of their new society, they made a religion of it. No one who visited Russia could fail to be impressed at the missionary fervour of the Communist party members.

The Bolshevik onslaught was actually directed against the Church rather than Christianity. There was no small basis for their hatred. We have seen that the Church in Russia was hopelessly corrupt. Rasputin appointed all bishops. The organisation of the Church became an auxiliary of the secret police: its directing committee was actually called 'The Tsar's Eye.'

Most of the priests loathed their role, whereby they were ordered to act as spies against their parishioners.

Further, the Church in Russia was over-rich. Some of the large monasteries were landowners of vast tracts of ground, often with inefficient and corrupt administration. Such things were bound to provoke reaction. When the Bolsheviks launched their attacks on organised religion, it found but few defenders.

The actual legislation did not forbid the practice of religion. It did, however, prohibit the teaching of religion to persons under eighteen years of age in groups of more than three or four. In practice, the anti-religious campaign was more forceful. Villagers were asked to decide whether the local church should be demolished, remain as it was, or become the village club or hospital. In the hectic atmosphere of the day, many of the rural churches disappeared. In the towns the number of churches was drastically reduced. The State owned all property—and, without passing any further legislation, it sought to strangle religion by refusing to lease buildings as churches.

Yet, ten years after the Revolution, it was decided that anti-religion should be a feature of Soviet education: that is to say, the previous policy had failed. Religion cannot be exterminated in a generation.

In 1937, after twenty years of repression, I found ikons in every other peasant cottage—often side by side with portraits of Lenin. In Kiev there were six churches open—once there were a hundred and twenty: everybody might attend them— they might have to face the jeers of bystanders. Russians had tried to persuade me that only old people went to church— that this 'superstition' would die out with them: but by no means all the people I saw at worship at Kiev were old.

When the Russians marched into Eastern Poland, the churches were crowded with invading soldiers—so that the Soviet commanders had to limit drastically the hours for which the churches were open. The religious spirit of the Slav peoples can never be doubted. Whether the Christian Church will ever revive fully in Russia is another question. The Soviet government can scarcely go back on its former policy: though the security of the régime which would follow victory might compel more liberal treatment of religious institutions, as of individual liberty. The position at the moment is that the State has almost killed organised religion, but has not eradicated religion from the hearts of all its people.

Economically the difficulties of Bolshevik Russia were very great. Communist thinkers had always anticipated that the expected revolution would first come in an industrial country. Instead, it came in an agricultural community, for revolution tends to follow the line of least resistance: in Russia there were millions of people with much to gain and nothing to lose. But the methods which had been thought out for a manufacturing country did not quite fit a rural countryside. Peasants were supposed to keep a portion of their crops and give the rest to the State: the system did not work—it would not work in England. The peasants grew enough for themselves only: then came the tragedy—the State, faced with the burden of feeding the towns, seized the village stocks. Famine followed this strange internecine economic war.

Although the State won the first round, it had the sense to modify its policy. No system can succeed without the willing co-operation of the working classes: and the outlook of the average man is limited. Lenin, a very clever man, recognised these two fundamentals. He had with keen observation noted the characteristics of the British working classes during his sojourn in England. He classed the British workman as the aristocrat of world labour. He enjoyed unusual conditions: why should he share them with coolies—or members of Balkan races whose standard of life was not nearly so high?

Until 1928 the Soviet leaders pursued their 'international' policy—that is, they hoped to spread their revolution to other countries, especially industrial lands. It was at this period that the greatest suspicion of Russia was born in conservative circles, for it was true that Soviet agents were active abroad, and that in most countries the Communist party was little more than an agent of Soviet policy. In the nature of things, this suspicion was often exaggerated, but it had real foundations—and was remembered long after the abandonment of the policy which had generated it.

In Russia the 'international' era ended, and the Russian nation re-emerged. This was the culmination of the bitter quarrel between Stalin and Trotsky. Stalin, a stern realist, was Russian in outlook, scarcely interested in world revolution. More than once he emphasised that 'revolution is not for export.' 'Socialism in one country' was his motto: he declared that he was prepared 'to establish working relations with any government, even if capitalist, which is friendly to the Soviet Union.'

Trotsky was the leader of the opposite school. He had spent long years involved in foreign intrigue: his outlook was international. Stalin won—and the vast majority of Russians backed him, for they were primarily interested in Russia. Yet it was typical of the confused British thinking of the day that part of the Right-wing British press chortled with glee whenever Trotsky made a point at Stalin's expense.

While it is true that we were generally ill-informed about Russia, Russian ideas on Britain were quite fantastic. One girl I met in Russia was genuinely shocked at our housing conditions in London. I discovered that as a reward she had been given a cruise on a boat from Leningrad to London. The ship had berthed at London docks—and she had never strayed more than a few hundred yards away! I admit that housing conditions there are no advertisement, but at least they are not typical! At Kiev they showed me their standard Russian-English grammar, and wondered why I laughed aloud. The stock phrases were about British children dying of starvation in the streets, or workers in factories treated like slaves. Today, quite rightly, we are correcting our old erroneous ideas about Russia: at the same time a parallel campaign is badly needed in Russia.

Some of the economic comparisons made between Britain and Russia were equally fantastic. The usual fallacy lay in the fact that the trouble had a purely artificial value, and that prices in the Soviet were rigidly controlled. Thus food and absolute necessities were generally reasonably cheap, but luxuries impossibly dear. Among the luxuries must be included items like wireless sets and bicycles. The standard of life in Russia was not nearly so high as in Britain—but is much higher than it used to be. The standard in the towns is generally higher than in the villages—except, perhaps, in food: this seems to be an almost universal practice. Industrial workers are nearly always better off than peasants.

I remember my first visit to Russia was made at the same time as a Communist friend. I returned impressed, he bitterly disappointed. He had made two serious errors. First, he had only read one side of the subject, and believed that Russia was a little heaven—and found that it wasn't. Further, he sailed direct from London to Leningrad, and all his comparisons were made between Russia and Britain: this was unfair—we had a big start. On my journey, it so happened that I entered Russia *via* Bessarabia, which was Russian until 1918, and had scarcely changed since; thus I tried to make my comparisons between Russia and Bessarabia: and all my comparisons favoured Russia.

The failure of an industrial country to turn Communist led to the introduction of the first Five-Year Plan in Russia. Local industries were to be established—Russia must be self-supporting so far as was possible: and, with her immense resources, much *was* possible. The Plan had many setbacks in its execution, and was often too optimistically conceived, but on the whole it was remarkably successful. Here is a difference between the Russia of today and that of the last war: then she was largely dependent upon the fitful flow of foreign equipment; now she makes her own. Had it not been for the Five-Year Plan, Russia would have been knocked out of the war in a few weeks.

The Five-Year Plan was partly responsible for the present low standard of living in Russia. It was the Soviet equivalent of 'guns or butter.' If, after victory, Russia can be relieved from the overwhelming burden of armaments she has carried for twenty years, there are prospects of vast advances in the domestic field.

Russia's foreign policy was no more successful than ours. A country's foreign policy is directed primarily or exclusively to its own interests. In the first years after the revolution, we have seen, Russian ideas were of internationalist Communism, a policy which aroused the deepest suspicion abroad: this distrust scarcely abated when the ideas were dropped—once born, suspicion is immensely difficult to stifle. Yet for a long period Russia's foreign policy was without reproach: she entered the League of Nations—as Russia, not as a Communist germ-state; she endeavoured to infuse some vivid realism into the meetings of that body; she was co-operating on equal terms with other powers.

Her objective was quite clear and comprehensible—the security of Russia and the maintenance of the régime. The wars of intervention were never forgotten: nor was the rearming of Germany overlooked. The rise of Hitler occasioned anxious moments. In *Mein Kampf* the Soviet régime received special attention, and Russia was designated as a German colony. Since 1933 her policy was directed to the neutralisation of the German menace. Hence the alliance with France in 1935: it proved worthless, largely because powerful elements in France distrusted Communism as much as they did Nazi-ism.

(Incidentally, there is little which could be described as Communism in Russia—as Stalin himself admitted. There is a strongly developed form of State Socialism. Ideas change—rapidly in wartime. An economic system which appeared obnoxious and wicked in 1925 may be quite normal in 1945. Even in conservative circles it is estimated that State control of essential industries is likely to persist long after the war is over, and that State long-term planning is essential. The gap between this and some features of the Soviet economic system is not so wide as might be imagined—for the Ogpu and other undesirable elements are *not* essentials. It may happen once again that the British will have a revolution in their own way —without violence, so gently that many people will scarcely realise that it is a revolution at all. This form of progress suits them best. Many features of the Soviet system would never suit them at all. The gaps between English standards and modes of life are still very wide. It may prove, however, that when the régime has been solidified by victory, the Soviet will embark upon new ideas of personal liberty which their people so well deserve. There is much the Russians can learn from the British—and much they can learn from the Russians: this latter applies especially to educational and social service standards. The co-operation of war may lead to an exchange of ideas in peace, to the advantage of both. Nevertheless, it is the most common error in Britain today to look at Russia with sentimental eyes: the Russian outlook, on the contrary, is most realistic!).

But if Soviet foreign policy from 1934 to 1939 was realistic and firm, from that time her leaders missed some of the essentials of the situation. Not all the fault lies with them: the western democracies were wobbling one moment, firm the next, and the Russian knowledge of our character was not deep enough to appreciate our many changes. After the agreement of Munich, for example, Russia believed that her policy of collaboration had failed: she was naturally enough gravely offended because she had not even been consulted about the fate of Czechoslovakia—a country with which she had a direct alliance: she noted how frantically the maintenance of peace, however bitter the price to be paid by others, was welcomed by the people of Britain and France. When, six months later, Hitler seized the rest of Czechoslovakia, the British attitude changed completely: they were now firmly decided that this was to be the last aggression. The Russians knew little of the English: did not appreciate their absurdly casual and optimistic outlook on foreign affairs—and did not understand that when Britain stood, she stood.

Immediately after the seizure of Czechoslovakia in March, 1939, Russia proposed an immediate conference at Bucharest between Britain, France, Russia, Poland, Roumania and Turkey. Had such a conference been held, and had its results been practical, it might have stopped the present war. But Mr. Neville Chamberlain, who lived at the other end of the political world from Stalin, still distrusted Russia as much as he did Germany: maybe more. He rejected immediate collaboration and gave a guarantee to Poland. A glance at the map showed that such a guarantee could only be implemented by Russian aid. At this stage Russia was approached: but by this time most of her leaders were thoroughly antagonised and more suspicious than ever. They did not know the British business man or type represented by Mr. Chamberlain. It is not difficult to trick him once: it is very difficult to catch him twice. He had trusted Hitler, and had been grossly deceived—apparently refused to believe in the extent of the defeat for some days. When he saw the true position, he turned—and thereafter could be as firm as any man in the world. The Russians did not appreciate this characteristic.

Thus it is doubtful whether Stalin was serious in the negotiations with the British and French governments in the spring and summer of 1939: indeed, he was already negotiating secretly with Hitler. On the British side there were many difficulties—with Poland and the Baltic states, as we shall see: none of these wanted either Germans or Russians on their soil. Stalin's first objective was to keep Russia out of the now inevitable war. So he made his famous pact with Hitler.

It was argued that he wished to see Hitler exhaust himself against the Western Powers, and this may be true. Yet Stalin gave much help to the Nazi scheme. In Britain the influence of the Communist party was very small: in France it had 70 deputies and commanded a million and a half votes in the last election. Most of these people became a liability to the State.

Until August 1939 they reviled Hitler more fiercely than any other section: now they turned the other way round.

The collapse of France, and the failure of the aerial on-slaught on Britain, made it obvious to thoughtful observers that Hitler would once more look to the east. Still Russia pursued her policy of isolation: her own military preparations were active, but she could not be induced to prepare joint schemes of battle—could not be persuaded that attack was imminent. It seems that Stalin had indeed been misled by Hitler's protestations. As he exclaimed bitterly, 'Once we trusted that man!'

Certainly the Russian policy of appeasement was no more successful than the British: and Stalin had had ample warning. With Russia in the battle in 1939, the war would have been over by now. In the event, Russia had to face the German on-slaught under the worst possible conditions. Her people fought as gallantly as Russians always do: the equipment of the Red Army proved to be very different from that of Tsarist days: the Germans gained victories and territories, but the war went on. Stalin had suffered for his mistakes, but now he was ruthlessly realistic. He was fighting for the régime for which he had planned and endured: if he failed, it would fall.

The suspicion between Russia and Britain was not imme-diately cleared by a common cause. Mr. Churchill was crystal-clear from the first day, but Russian reactions were slower. The practical character of the British assistance gradually altered the outlook: as the war progresses, and as we ourselves bear an increasing share of its burdens, then the atmosphere is likely to change rapidly—to the benefit of both. There is much to do. I have said that many Russian ideas about Britain are almost comic: some of the British about Russia are almost as absurd.

The habit of reading headlines only is perhaps to blame. The crude propaganda methods of some of our newspapers arouse uneasy thoughts. More than once after a lecture I have been asked a question like this: 'Ten years ago the papers tried to persuade us that everything in Russia was bad. Today we are told that everything is good. Today we are also told that everything in Germany is bad; who can say that in ten years' time they will not try to persuade us that everything in Germany is good?'

I have suggested that the gap between Russia and Britain is not so wide as might be thought: yet it is still wide. I repeat that we must not judge a nation merely by the quality of its military prowess—otherwise there will be little chance of justice in the terms of peace. Yet, with the new stability which victory will bring to the Soviet régime, I am optimistic: sternly ruthless at times, the Russians can be amazingly generous. I can imagine that they will firmly implement Point 8 of the Atlantic Charter: but their adherence to the other seven is an event of major importance.

II

The heading of this chapter is somewhat misleading. Our primary purpose is to examine Russia's frontier problems in Europe: even then, some of them are postponed to following chapters. Foremost in importance is that of Ukraine: the name means 'the borderland.'

Very few of us had ever heard of Ukraine before the last war. We have heard a lot about it since, but still have not heard the last.

For many years Ukraine has been the principal granary of Europe. Its famous belt of black earth is two and a half times the size of France. Its natural resources in minerals are vast. Culturally the Ukrainians have usually been in advance of the other Russian tribes—their folk music is perhaps the loveliest in Europe. Nor are the people artistic dreamers—in battle they have always maintained a worthy reputation. In spite of this, Ukraine has never had an independent history—it has changed masters as often as any feudal fief in Western Europe.

In the great days of Poland and Lithuania their empires included many thousands of Ruthenes, a Slav tribe claiming near

kinship with both Poles and Russians. The Ruthenes were unhappy under the Polish and Lithuanian rule—they were treated
as little more than serfs—and many of them emigrated to the
basin of the Dnieper. Here, although still nominally under
Polish-Lithuanian rule, they were too far away from the
centre of things to be oppressed. They formed themselves
into free democratic communities, and came to be known as
Cossacks. Only the lightest of bonds connected these communities, who found a plentiful livelihood on the rich steppes
of black earth. A nominal tribute to their theoretical overlords
was paid, but the parent hold over the new colony was of the
slightest. The Ruthenes mixed freely with the sparse local
population of Russians, and with later immigrants, and eventually the whole province came under Russian rule—that part
east of the Dnieper in 1667, and the remainder in 1793, during the partitions of Poland.

The Russians considered the Ruthenes as Russians, and
accorded them the liabilities and privileges of Russians: they
were generally known as 'South Russians.' Their language
differed somewhat from Russian—but by no more than did
Great Russian from White Russian, or any of the dozens of
dialects in common use in Russia. For generations the Ruthenes
themselves had no other idea, and Russians still claim that
Ruthene is no more than a Russian dialect. Certainly a Russian can converse with a Ruthene with ease, for I have heard it
done on dozens of occasions. Russian was always the official
language of the country. Gogol, a Ukrainian, wrote in Russian.

But in the middle of the last century there arose in Ukraine
a new movement of national consciousness. As so often happens with the Slav peoples, the driving force was not a politician, but a poet. Just as Mickiewicz rallied the Poles, so
Shevchenko passionately poured out the claims of the
Ruthenes to independent nationality: Ruthene culture was
assiduously preached; the rich Ruthene folklore was revived
and embellished. The new movement went much further, however—it demanded the political union of all the Ruthenes.

Now before 1914 the Ruthene tribe was split between
Russia and Austria. When Russia seized the western half of
the Ukraine during the partitions of Poland, Austria seized
Galicia, the eastern portion of which housed some 3 million
Ruthenes—there were 25 millions of them in Ukraine. Political union at that time, however, was, to put it mildly, most
unlikely. No sane person could possibly imagine that Austria

DISTRIBUTION OF THE UKRAINIANS

would give up Eastern Galicia to the Ruthenes; still less likely
was it that Russia would give up the rich province of Ukraine.

The Austrians, with German backing, attempted to exploit
the possibilities of the situation. At this time the Ukrainian
demands generally envisaged an autonomous Ukraine within
a Russian Empire. Austrian and German agents now began to
encourage Ukrainian separatist movements, with the idea of
weakening Russia. (Germany, as we shall see later, had even
wider objectives.) Operating from Austrian Galicia, Ukrain-

ian enthusiasts began what we now term a propaganda campaign.

Nevertheless, by 1914 the separatist plans had advanced but slowly. The Austrians were disturbed because the Ukrainians in their ranks went over freely to join their brothers in the Russian armies. One important German experiment was a complete failure. Of 3 million Russian prisoners of war, nearly 700,000 were Ukrainians. Offering many practical advantages to those who would declare themselves as Ukrainian nationalists, the Germans could only persuade 15,000 to come forward. Of these, only 3100 were found to be sufficiently separatist-minded to be formed into armed regiments—a mere fraction of the number of Ukrainians who passed over from the Austrian side to the Russian.

The collapse of Russia in 1917 naturally caused the utmost confusion in her provinces. Now the Ukrainian patriots from Galicia had an open field—and armed backing. A Council, called the *Rada,* was formed, proclaiming an autonomous Ukraine. This was recognised by the Bolsheviks *and by the Germans,* and Ukraine sent a separate delegation to Brest-Litovsk, and negotiated a separate peace with Germany and Austria. This is important—the first appearance of Ukraine as a national state in history: its importance is minimised by the fact that the German recognition of an independent Ukraine was no more than a cunning device to detach the province from Russia.

The Germans attached great importance to the treaty with Ukraine—they were desperately short of foodstuffs, and Ukraine is a vast granary. When the Bolsheviks decided that Ukraine, after all, was really a part of Russia, German and Austrian troops marched into the province to keep out the Bolsheviks and to safeguard the invaluable supplies of food. For a few brief months, therefore, even if under foreign 'protection,' there did exist an independent Ukraine.

The people of Ukraine generally regarded the Germans as conquering invaders. In modern Nazi language, they 'refused to co-operate' with the occupying forces, and only a fragment of the agreed supplies ever got back to Germany. The Ukraine rulers were a series of German puppets. One of them has returned to the headlines: General Skoropadskij.

He is a descendant of a well-known Ukrainian *hetman*, or chieftain. (This gives him no claim to authority, for the office was elective, and never transmitted by inheritance.) His background was Russian rather than Ukrainian: he had always opposed and derided separatism. When eventually the end of the war compelled him to leave the country, he retired—to Berlin!

The force which drove Skoropadskij from Kiev was headed by Simon Petliura. Ukraine was in utter confusion: at the same time the Ruthenes of Eastern Galicia had taken advantage of the Austrian collapse to proclaim a republic at Lwow—the old Lemberg. Galicia, however, had been allocated to the Poles, and Petliura's attempt to march to the aid of Lwow was easily defeated.

The winter of 1918–19 was unhappy for Petliura, for in February he was driven from Kiev, the Ukraine capital, by the Bolsheviks. Petliura retired into Poland—and joined the Poles, his late enemies, against the Bolsheviks!

Several times Ukraine changed hands—successively held by Bolsheviks, Denikin's 'White' Army, Poland and Bolsheviks again. When Poland and Russia eventually made peace, *they both recognised the independence of the Ukraine*, which promptly began to manage its own affairs—including the conclusion of treaties with foreign states. But in 1923, when the form of the Union of Socialist Soviet Republics was settled, Ukraine became a founder member of the new combination. In fact, the independence recognised by Poland and Russia was one of form—Ukraine was never far away from Bolshevik Russia. Polish recognition of an independent Ukraine had indeed as its object the weakening of Russia—a copy of the policy of Austria a decade earlier.

The position in 1939 was, therefore, that Ukraine, now

housing 30 million inhabitants, mostly of Ruthene descent, was one of the Soviet Republics: Eastern Galicia, with about 3 million Ruthenes, was part of Poland; Ruthenia, with half a million Ruthenes, was now a part of Hungary—and there were an odd half-million Ruthenes in Roumania!

(Incidentally, Britain has a very real interest in the Ukrainian problem, for outside these countries the greatest group of Ukrainians—half a million—is to be found in Canada. After British and French they form the largest racial group in that dominion.)

The population of the Russian province of Ukraine is not entirely Ukrainian. After 1861, following the emancipation of the serfs, hundreds of thousands of Russians flocked to the south to find work in the newly developed mines; or, if they could achieve such a heavenly objective, to obtain a few acres of the black earth.

Theoretically there is nothing to prevent the secession of Ukraine from the U.S.S.R. Article 17 of the new constitution reads quite plainly: 'Each Union Republic reserves the right freely to secede from the U.S.S.R.' Stalin, in his famous speech in November 1936, defended this right, and refused to accept an amendment deleting the clause. He explained that the U.S.S.R. was a voluntary union, that no Union Republic ever wanted to oppress another Union Republic. Although no republic wanted to secede, he maintained that it ought to have the right to do so if it wished.

Russia is not the only country where theory differs vastly from practice. The situation is obvious. Ukraine is the richest corner of Russia—its 'black earth' has been famous throughout history. Its mines are very important—the Donetz coal mines provide 80 per cent of all the coal raised in Russia. There are also vast deposits of iron, manganese, graphite, copper, mercury and other minerals. Further, Ukraine houses the famous Dnieper dam, first major achievement of the new Russia, and as much a source of pride as is Gdynia to Poland. In short, whatever may be written on paper, it is quite inconceivable that Ukraine would be permitted to secede from the U.S.S.R., even if it wished. Its loss would spell ruin to many of the new Russian industries and would lower the standard of life over the whole Soviet territory.

Strategically an independent Ukraine would be helpless. Its long frontiers would be indefensible—artificial lines across a great plain. Its wealth would make it always an object of jealous acquisitiveness by powerful neighbours. Economically it is bound up with Russia, whose developing territories offer vast markets for Ukrainian industrial products.

There are still, however, nationalist Ukrainian organisations. The fact that some of their leaders have been backed by foreign powers is not so significant as it appears at first sight: in the course of history many patriotic revolutionaries have been backed by Britain. If a Ukrainian leader accepts German backing, it is legitimate to suspect ulterior motives in the German policy, for Germany does not hand out large sums of money for nothing: the event does not prove, nevertheless, that the Ukrainian is other than sincere, accepting this method of the advancement of his ideas because he sees no other alternative. On the other hand, it is quite certain that there are Ukrainians who have deliberately fallen in with the German plan with a view to power for themselves: the new word 'quislings' describes them exactly.

One of the movements formed with German support was the U.N.O.—Ukrainian Nationalist Organisation. Its leader, Ataman (Colonel) Melnyk, made his headquarters in Berlin. A second group operated from Paris; it comprises the successors of the Petliura régime. A third has always operated from German territory; its leader is General Skoropadskij, now seventy years old! Nor must the Ukrainians in America ever be overlooked—they include some of the most fervent nationalists of all. Living in an anti-Communist atmosphere, remembering the cultural rather than the political history of their land of origin, they can be either useful or dangerous in their enthusiasm.

The real point at issue is the opinion of the Ukrainians themselves. Here I must record my own impressions, formed in Ukraine in 1937, that I found no suggestion of any real demand for secession from the U.S.S.R. There were many groups anxious for a wider autonomy, but that is a very different thing.

At first, it is true, the Ukrainians were very unhappy in the new Soviet State. They, as the richest province, had to give the most in the levelling up of the standard of life. Further, the agricultural organisation was individual. In Russia proper there had always been rural communities which readily accepted the idea of the collectivised farm, an idea scarcely differing in principle from their original pattern. In the Ukraine individual peasants had their own holdings; possession of land means a lot to a peasant, and the Ukrainians vigorously opposed collectivisation. They suffered the more in the repressive measures adopted, and in the famine years their state was especially unhappy.

Since then, however, the rich province has recovered and developed. New industries have been established, new sources of raw materials exploited; and the rich black earth never fails to feed its people and to provide an ample surplus for the rest of Russia. There is little impetus to violent change in moments of prosperity.

The prospect of an increase of Ukrainian nationalism cannot be dismissed, but this is unlikely to be a cause of unrest. The problem is not unlike that of Scotland. At the moment we have a small group of Scottish Nationalists who demand varying measures of home rule. If these groups ever grew so powerful that they controlled the majority of the votes, then it is probable that Scotland would get some form of local autonomy.

It is much the same in Ukraine. If the demand were sufficiently strong, Russia might agree to the allocation of self-governing powers. (Not to secession: this would be too severe a blow at Russian economy—and would seriously harm that of Ukraine.) My own opinion is that the nationalist feeling in Ukraine is little stronger than it is in Scotland.

When the invading Germans in 1941 attempted to get the Ukrainians to co-operate, they dropped the nationalist appeal and descended to more elementary inducements. We have seen that the Ukrainians adopted communal systems more reluctantly than the other Russian races: there remained hundreds of thousands of peasants with the inherent longing for land of their own. The Germans have been bribing these peasants by the grant of land—or the promise of land. Nevertheless, their progress has been slow; guerrilla warfare by local 'partisans' was sustained and savage in its character.

This does not rule out the possibility of some degree of autonomy in the near future. After the Revolution, the Russians wisely centralised their power in Moscow: their first thoughts were of the defence of the régime against its many enemies. After victory, with the collapse of Germany, the fear of danger will no longer need to dominate Russian ideas. In such case, a programme of decentralisation might follow within a reasonable time: with it, I am convinced, the wilder dreams of the extreme Ukrainian separatists would fade.

III

But I imagine that some of my readers have followed with some surprise my skeleton outline of the problem of Ukraine. To them the problem is, not whether there should or should not be an independent Ukraine, but whether there shall be a German colony there. Presumably because the Germans occupied Ukraine in 1918, the question of their return has been frequently mooted.

When Hitler wrote, 'When we speak of new territory in Europe today, we must think principally of Russia and the border states subject to her,' he was expressing no new principle of German policy: he seldom did. We have revealed German interest in Ukraine in 1918; it dates back far beyond that period.

During the Russo-Turkish war of 1789–90, a Ukrainian nobleman named Kapnist appealed to Frederick William II of Prussia for help in 'the liberation of Ukraine from the Muscovite tyranny.' The German reply was significant: even then German policy was based on opportunism, on fishing in troubled waters, of dividing states within themselves. It did not offer the immediate help demanded, but it did suggest that if ever Russia and Prussia were at war 'Ukraine should do everything in her power to get Prussian help.'

Ever since that time responsible Germans have considered the idea of Ukraine as a German colony or protectorate. More than once the project came out into open politics: at the time it was scarcely practical, but a parade of Ukrainian separatist demands always irritated the Tsar and tended to weaken Russia's resistance to the plan of the day. The 'independence' of Ukraine in 1918 was of course purely a political convenience: its effectiveness depended entirely on the strength of the German garrison. Despite the constant armed clashes with the population, and the more passive resistance which reduced the flow of supplies, the Germans were delighted that at last they had set foot in the Promised Land.

After her defeat in 1918—but long before the rise of Hitler and the Nazis—Germany was again active in Ukrainian affairs. Little could be done in Russia, where opposition to the régime could count on stern repression: the Germans, however, got to work among the Ukrainians of Poland. We shall read of their results in the following section.

The Ukrainian agitation in Galicia, often with German backing, caused a lot of trouble to the Poles and the local Ukrainians, and seriously affected Polish-Russian relations. Yet the pace was too slow for a hustler like Hitler. He at least had nothing to hide; he and his lieutenants—Rosenberg in particular—had always proclaimed Ukraine as a legitimate area of German expansion. Rosenberg (who in turn had drawn freely from the ideas of Ludendorff) wrote: 'If we have now understood that the removal of the Polish state is Germany's foremost demand, an alliance between Kiev and Berlin and the creation of a common frontier becomes a national necessity for Germany's future policy.' The date of this declaration is important: 1927. Who can claim that we had not been warned?

The first move was typical of the cynicism of Nazi foreign policy—a proposal that Germany and Poland should march on Russia. Poland refused emphatically: on moral grounds, and because it was obvious what the next move would be. Hence the plan had to be temporarily shelved, but was revived with acclamation on June 22nd, 1941.

Now Germany was to reap the benefit of her expensive propaganda. The Ukrainians of that part of Polish Galicia under German rule had been suitably flattered during the occupation of September 1939–June 1941. They were classed as equals with the Germans, above the Poles. They were allotted many petty privileges, and one major one—the right of enlistment in the German army. The 'patriotic' organisations were deputed to whip up the necessary enthusiasm. They were not very successful. There had been one short burst of Ukrainian nationalist sentiment. At the dissolution of Czechoslovakia, the local Ruthene leader, Father Volosin, was allowed to set up a tiny Ruthene (i.e. Ukrainian) state in Sub-Carpathian Russia. The effect was tremendous: we shall see that Ruthenia, or Sub-Carpathian Russia—the 'toe' of Czechoslovakia—is of great sentimental interest to all Ukrainians. A few days later Volosin was promptly dropped; the Hungarians occupied the territory, and the germ-state of the new Ukraine was killed. Even fervent Ukrainians could but feel that they were cats'-paws in the grip of stronger and unprincipled powers.

The Ukrainians who were induced to enlist in the German army discovered that they held another privilege: to be used as cannon fodder. So indiscriminate was the carnage among their battalions that even Colonel Melnyk, leader of the U.N.O., was disgusted. He left Berlin—for Rome! True, there were few places where he could go.

The German territorial objective in the Russian campaign was immediately clear. They held one advantage over the Russians—superior mobility. After attacking heavily in the centre and north, and attracting Russian reserves thither, the Germans struck hard in the south. In spite of desperate resistance they overran Ukraine: even the Crimean Peninsula. With the coming of winter conditions the Russians became more mobile than the Germans, and the first tide of battle turned. In the summer of 1942, the Germans again made huge territorial advances, but the character of the fighting had changed. In the 1941 campaign the Russians stood up to the Germans in a slogging match, and took nasty punishment. Their winter gains were poor compensation, for in most cases the Germans withdrew their main forces deliberately to winter quarters, with the minimum of casualties or material loss. The following summer, however, the Russians reverted to a traditional policy—the use of ground. Holding vital points with desperate courage, they allowed the German armies to spread themselves towards the Volga and the Caucasus. The winter campaign of 1942–3 was *not* as the Germans planned. They sustained huge losses in men and material, to say nothing of prestige. The legend of the invincible German War Machine was shattered; political considerations were allowed to govern strategic decisions, and involved the loss of entire armies. Stalingrad ranks with the Battle of Britain among the decisive features of the war.

The Russian economic losses of course were very severe; and, although the policy of destruction reduced the German gains, these must have been very substantial. Especially interesting was the political scene. Behind the Germans in their march there tailed the quislings and 'patriots' who had operated with German support for years. These were to help in the restoration and pacification of the country; so far as was practicable, they were to foment anti-Russian feeling on the other side of the fighting zone.

In this latter objective they were singularly ineffective. The Ukrainians have always been among the best soldiers in the Russian army, and in this war they did not belie their reputation. After the conquest of Ukraine, however, the quislings did have successes in some areas. While in parts of Ukraine guerrilla warfare continues on a vast scale, ruthless in its form and in repression, some Ukrainian areas are reported as comparatively quiet. The approach was psychological. Peasants who co-operate with the invaders have been given or promised individual grants of land instead of shares in collective farms!

During the early weeks of the campaign, Skoropadskij and his assistants were useful to the Germans. Suddenly they were dropped. When victory appeared to be in sight, all pretence of a German backing to an 'independent' Ukraine was abandoned. The territory has been declared a 'protectorate,' of the same helpless status as Poland and Bohemia-Moravia. The quislings may be used as local officials, but they will be no more than agents of the Reich.

During the World War the Austrian Chief of Staff wrote: 'In Ukraine the Germans pursue a definite economic and political aim. They want to keep for ever the safest road to Mesopotamia and Arabia, to Baku and Persia, which the occupation of Ukraine has put into their hands . . . They will never again completely surrender the valuable Crimean Peninsula. To make full use of this road they also need the possession or control of the connecting railway here, and, as the supply of coal for this railway and for the Black Sea is impracticable from Germany, they need the most important mines of the Don Basin. Somehow or other they will secure both these objectives. Besides, the Germans wish to use Ukraine as their granary, and on the other hand open in the rich Ukraine a market for their own industries. This intention is borne out by the frank assertion of General Groener that as long as Britain bars the way to the West, Germany's main interest goes through Ukraine and Crimea towards India. . . .'

This appreciation was written in 1918; it is not out of date in 1941. On one aspect of the problem there can at least be no dispute—that Germany intends to hold Poland and Ukraine indefinitely as 'protectorates' or colonies. 'Somehow or other' they will try to secure these objectives. There will be great confusion and retaliation when they fail.

IV

No small share of the difficulties in Eastern Europe arises directly from the Russian Wars of Intervention, following the Revolution. The Bolsheviks, fighting for their régime, retained a natural suspicion of those who took part in the wars, the countries which supported the interventionists, and especially the countries where the interventionists rallied. At the same time Russia's neighbours had a point of view too: just then, the Bolshevik régime had few appearances of permanency; why should they make accommodations with a régime which might fall tomorrow?

The Poles had already had such an experience. Naturally opposed to the Tsarist government, they welcomed the fall of the autocratic régime and the establishment of a democratic government. The Polish attitude was of course dominated by aspirations to independence: on March 30th, 1917, the provisional Russian government made a declaration offering a free Poland. Then, on November 7th of the same year, the Kerensky régime was overthrown by the Bolsheviks.

The first object of the new government was peace at any price, to give time to strengthen their grip on Russia. Thus they patched up the Treaty of Brest-Litovsk which left Poland in German hands until November 1918. At the same time the Bolsheviks denounced all the Tsarist annexionist treaties—which presumably included those by which Poland had been partitioned! This attitude, naturally, was not forgotten when Poland was a nation once again.

Relations between the new Russia and the reborn Poland had the additional irritant of frontier disputes. Petliura, in Kiev, saw Eastern Galicia handed over to Poland—and Eastern Galicia housed a Ukrainian majority. True, it had never been Russian territory: up to 1918 it was part of the Austrian Empire; before 1772 it was a corner of Poland: yet it housed more Ukrainians than Poles.

Pilsudski advanced the idea of a Polish-Ukrainian federated state—had this been formed, it might have changed the history of the world. Petliura, the Ukrainian leader, refused: the two states went to war. Already Ukrainian peasants in Galicia were in arms against the Poles: Petliura preached a crusade to their 'rescue.'

He was defeated: what was worse, while he was engaged in his liberating crusade, the Bolsheviks invaded Ukraine from the north and captured Kiev. Petliura was staggered—and promptly joined hands with the Poles against the new enemy. If he had done this a year earlier, a different tale would have been told.

At first the alliance of Pilsudski and Petliura was successful: Kiev was recaptured. Then the Bolsheviks recovered their strength: by this time the White armies on Russian soil had been liquidated. Further, by no means all Poles were behind Pilsudski in his drive to the east—the majority of members of the Seym were in fact against him. The very fact that Polish armies were on Russian soil savoured of aggression; and among Polish peasants, even if the character of the Bolshevik régime was still obscure to them, there was a deep sympathy with their cousins in Russia who had suffered as deeply as they had, and for much longer.

The Bolsheviks counter-attacked, advancing into Poland, to the gates of Warsaw. Here the Poles rallied, united again in the defence of their own land. The battle of the Vistula was more than a struggle between rival states. At this time Russia was agog with revolutionary fervour. 'Our way to world-wide conflagration passes over the corpse of Poland,' declared the Russian commander.

The Poles won a decisive victory. The routed Russians

streamed to the east in a disorganised rabble. There was nothing to stop the Poles overrunning Russia—except the realism of the Bolshevik leaders.

They recognised defeat when they saw it. Time was essential for the development of their economic plan for Russia.

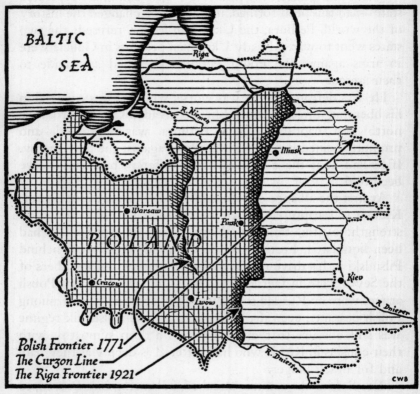

THE EASTERN FRONTIER OF POLAND AT THE TIME OF THE PARTITION IN 1772, AS SUGGESTED BY THE 'CURZON LINE,' AND AS SETTLED BY THE TREATY OF RIGA, 1921

Poland could be dealt with later. When the delegates met at Riga in March 1921, the Russians were not much interested in territorial problems. In those days they counted peace only as a truce. Joffe, the chairman of the Russian delegation, openly declared that they looked upon all the frontiers with their neighbours merely as temporary expedients, expecting the whole world to turn Communist very soon!

Now the peace treaties of 1919, while settling Poland's western frontier, fixed no boundaries for the east—except in Eastern Galicia, where Polish authority extended to the old Austrian frontier. An Allied committee, with Lord Curzon as its chairman, had indeed marked out a provisional frontier—usually called the 'Curzon Line'—but this was accepted neither by the Poles nor the Russians. The 'Curzon Line' was never intended to be the frontier between Poland and Russia. It was first suggested, in December 1919, as a temporary line within which Poland could set up a normal administration—the Allies expressly admitted Poland's right to claim territory east of the Line. Later, in July 1920, in an effort to limit the Soviet-Polish war, Lord Curzon suggested that both armies should halt 50 kilometres *east* of the Line. Both sides ignored the appeal, and the 'Curzon Line' was never even mentioned in the peace negotiations: the original Soviet offer to Poland was for frontiers on an average of 200 miles east of this Line.

Nor was the 'Curzon Line' an attempt at ethnic division. The population on both sides is very mixed. Between the Line and the Riga frontier live about 2,000,000 Poles, 1,500,000 Ukrainians, 900,000 Bielo-Russians, 550,000 Jews, 100,000 Russians, and a number of smaller groups. It broke away from the Lithuanian East Prussian frontier near Suvalki, then continued almost due south until it joined the old boundary of Eastern Galicia. The first claim of the Poles had been for the frontier of 1772, which had been seized by the Russians by force. The Allies could not agree to this: it would have involved placing ten million people of Russian races under Polish rule. In the eastern borderlands near the 1772 frontier, indeed, there were very few Poles at all. The dominant character of the masses had always been Russian or Ukrainian, and a hundred and fifty years of Tsarist rule had driven most of the Poles nearer to the centre of their own culture and hopes.

The Treaty of Riga, which ended the Russian-Polish war,

was therefore a compromise. The new frontier was approximately halfway between the Curzon Line and the 1772 boundary. Even this agreement left a sequence of problems in its wake. There were over 3 million Ukrainians in Poland, contiguous to the new frontier. But—and this is important—they were hopelessly mixed with Poles. Over the whole of Galicia there were 5 million Poles, but in the eastern half—the part under discussion—the Poles formed only 40 per cent of the population, even counting Polish Jews as Poles. Speaking generally, the Poles were preponderant in the infrequent towns, the Ukrainians in the country. This is a parallel case, in fact, to that of Vilna. The capital of Eastern Galicia, Lwow (the old Lemberg), is unquestionably a Polish city, yet it is surrounded by a peasant population of Ukrainians.

For years after the war there was discontent and distress among the Ukrainians of Eastern Galicia. There were stories of outrage and murder, and not all of them were exaggerated. Galicia under the Austrians had enjoyed a liberal measure of home rule. The Poles had promised to continue this, and all the blame for the non-fulfilment of their undertaking cannot be placed on them. It will be recalled that there was a period of non-co-operation and violent discontent, fostered from both Germany and Russia. In these disturbed years the missionary zeal of Lenin and Trotsky had not yet been replaced by the more sober realism of Stalin. The defeat of 1920 rankled. There were many men in the east, Russian as well as Ukrainian, who looked meaningly towards Polish Ukraine (or Eastern Galicia), and spoke openly of the day when it should rejoin its 'motherland.' Small wonder that the Poles were suspicious: you can scarcely admit to authority people you do not trust.

Local conditions did not help towards a settlement. The Ukrainian of Eastern Galicia at that time was of no great educational or intellectual standard. Nor was he nationality-conscious, despite the fervent claims of his champions, usually self-appointed. His outlook was purely local. More than once, when I asked a man what he was, he replied, 'I am from here.' One of the most useful methods of distinguishing a Pole from a Ukrainian is by his religion—it is the method he would usually choose himself. If he is Roman Catholic, he is a Pole; if Uniat, a Ukrainian. (Ethnically the method is unsound; it does not indicate what a man is, but what he thinks he is.)

In neighbouring lands vast policies of agrarian reform were being carried out. Russia adopted the system of collective farms—economically sound, but not so attractive to the peasant mind. In other countries adjacent to Poland the large estates were split up into peasant holdings. If this had been the Polish policy, there would have been little trouble in Galicia. There was indeed a considerable scheme of land reform in which Ukrainians shared the advantages with Poles, but if a few hundred thousand Ukrainian families had been settled on land of their own, all external propaganda would have lost its force. A satisfied man whose nationalist vision is limited to 'I am from here' is not likely to be attracted by irredentist appeals.

Probably land hunger must be ranked among the principal causes of unrest in Galicia: it certainly helped to intensify the dispute between Poles and Ukrainians. I rode a bicycle along the appalling dust-tracks of the Galician countryside. (If, as some people claim, statesmen ought to investigate problems on the spot, I can only say that we ought to breed a special race of athlete-statesmen for investigations in Eastern Europe. In this corner of Europe I wallowed for days among sand, and then sank in the mud of the Pripet Marshes.)

There is no need to report my own impressions of the troubles in Eastern Galicia—if you will recall the days of the Black and Tans in Ireland you have a picture exactly parallel —a murdered policeman, reprisals, burned cottages and so on. When German or Russian money was not forthcoming, the Ukrainian bands broke into Polish post-offices and banks and helped themselves. Then followed punitive expeditions—and the rest of the vicious circle.

In the early post-war years tempers were raw. As Poland gathered her strength, the situation was viewed more calmly. A special force of frontier police was allocated to the task of pacifying the provinces. In 1934 the administrators found their problem suddenly eased.

The date 1934 seems to crop up in the discussion of all Polish problems—the date of the Ten-Year Pact with Germany. The fact is that most Polish troubles were aggravated or instigated by Germany prior to that date, presumably to weaken Poland with a view to the recovery of the Corridor. German influence could be traced in most Polish affairs. The famous 'Ukrainian Bureau,' which fomented many of the disturbances in Eastern Galicia, was claimed by the Poles as being a German creation, and it is significant that its activities diminished abruptly in 1934.

The respite was only temporary. As Hitler proposed to advance towards his third objective, pacts of friendship were forgotten. In October 1938, following the Munich agreement, there were serious riots and disturbances in Eastern Galicia— the Polish Ukraine—fanned if not provoked by a wave of propaganda from German-controlled Ruthenia. The Ukrainians demanded the same rights of self-government as their brothers, the Ruthenes. They pointed out that the Poles had posed as the prophets of self-determination in Teschen, and what was right for Poles in Teschen was surely right for Ukrainians in Poland. This sounds reasonable enough, but the forcible expression of the claim was vigorously repressed, with much loss of life. Blood does not make a people forget its grievances, but perpetuates their memory.

Nevertheless, when in April 1939 it appeared that Poland was to be the next victim of aggression, the Ukrainians hastened to express their loyalty to Poland, offering their services in its defence: agitation for autonomy was temporarily dropped. But only temporarily. When the moment of victory comes, the problem is bound to arise again, and it would pay the Poles to take a liberal view.

My own impression was that there was no serious demand over a large part of Galicia for union with Soviet Russia. If the nervous post-war weeks can be safely surmounted, then the character of the new Polish régime should make the position easier. A liberal grant of local autonomy, and a much fuller measure of agrarian reform, and many of the troubles of the Ukrainians in Poland would lose their force.

v

The inhabitants of Galicia undergoing the greatest sufferings of the war have not been Ukrainians, but Poles.

(Western Galicia, although it houses over a million Ukrainians, is overwhelmingly Polish. In Eastern Galicia there are over three million Ukrainians to less than one and a half million Poles. I have emphasised that the Poles generally predominate in the towns, and form the greater part of the landowning class, while the majority of the peasants are Ukrainian.)

On September 17, 1939, the Russians marched into Eastern Poland. Stalin claimed that as the Polish government had lost control, and as Poland had virtually ceased to exist, he was entitled to move in to protect people of Russian stock—although they had not appealed to him to do so. By arrangement with Hitler, he eventually advanced to a boundary which in its northern portion was considerably to the west of the Curzon Line, and in the south included Eastern Galicia, which had never been Russian in its history. The population of the portion of Poland occupied by Russia consisted of about 5,250,000 Poles, 4,500,000 Ukrainians, 1,100,000 Bielo-Russians, 1,110,000 Jews, 130,000 Russians, and about 500,000 people of smaller groups of indeterminate nationality.

So confused was the situation that at some points the Polish troops marched beside the Russians, believing that these had come to help them against the Germans! When disillusion came, the moment was ugly. There were stories of persecution and execution from the occupied provinces. Tens of thousands of Poles were imprisoned: Ukrainians too. For the first battle to be fought was one of religion.

Immediately the Sovietisation of Eastern Galicia began: with it came an attack on the churches. Ukrainian as well as Polish priests were persecuted. In those days the petty feuds of earlier days were forgotten: common martyrdom is a great unifier.

Even allowing for the exaggeration of war-time news, there is no doubt that the Soviet hand was hard. It was not merely a question of revenge for the defeat of 1920, or of the resolution of the quarrels of the intervening years, or of the clash of régimes, or of personal or racial antipathies. One explanation is to be found in the basic reason for the Russian march into Poland: to be followed later by the seizure of the Baltic states, portions of Finland, and Bessarabia and Northern Bukovina. Racial idealism was not the propelling factor behind these moves; in the Baltic, indeed, it was never involved.

In diplomacy it seems to be a proper thing for a man to lie in the supposed interests of his country. In a welter of statements and counter-statements, however, one claim by Stalin stands out as fundamentally true. He stated that he was making these moves to protect himself. Certainly he did it. With his armies in Finland, Estonia, Latvia, Lithuania, Eastern Poland, Northern Bukovina and Bessarabia he had built up a remarkably complete series of buffer provinces to take the first shock of an attack. But, it was always pertinent to ask, against whom was he defending himself? If some of the British Communists had asked themselves this question, then they would not have been confronted with the pathetic necessity for a sudden reversal of their policy. For, of course, the question had only one answer. The only man who could attack Stalin was Hitler.

The erection of a protective barrier does not condone Russian conduct in Eastern Poland; it merely explains it. The Russians sought to make their defences strong—which involved a loyal population behind them. Instead of appealing to the

STALIN'S PROTECTIVE BARRIER

Poles for support, they chose instead to repress them. This wa
a mistake, for which Russians as well as Poles were eventuall
to suffer.

(Here was my answer to the sergeant pilot who wanted t
know how we should get the Russians out of Poland afte
we had beaten Hitler. I suggested that Stalin had moved int
Poland to protect himself against a German menace: onc
that menace was removed, it ought not to be difficult to pei
suade him to retire to his own frontiers.)

Eastern Galicia was the crux of the problem; particularl
the area about the Polish city of Lwow. To the north was
similar area, with a mixed population of Ukrainians and Pole:
but which differed from Eastern Galicia in that it was unde
Russian rule from 1772 to 1918. Further north still was an are
where a considerable Polish minority lived among a majorit
population of White Russians, or Bielo-Russians. (This latte
term is perhaps preferable, since 'White' Russians are asso
ciated in the popular mind with the Tsarist supporters wh
fought the Interventionist Wars.) Still further north, an
stretching to the east, was a large Polish population mixed witl
Lithuanian and Bielo-Russian minorities. The whole length o
the frontier was an ethnic medley. It should be added that oi
the Russian side of the inter-war frontier there were of cours
large numbers of Poles; nearly a million in all. In particula
there were considerable settlements in Russian Ukraine, wher
in certain areas the Poles actually form the majority.

In spite of the difficulties, it would not have been impossibl
to solve the problem of the Russian-Polish frontier in ai
atmosphere of goodwill following the disappearance of th
German menace. The German attack on Russia provided thi
atmosphere at an earlier date than had been anticipated. Nov
Russians and Poles had indeed a bond between them—a com
mon enemy.

The Poles had much to forgive. They had been averse to
full Russian guarantee in the months before the war begar
because this would have involved a Russian occupation o

'oland. (The Poles were prepared to welcome Russian air
leets and technical troops, but not armies. The Russians rea-
onably argued that they were the only people who could
letermine what assistance they should give.) The outlook of
he Poles was quite clear—they were no more anxious to have
Russians on their soil than Germans. No Pole could recall an
occasion when Russians ever evacuated an occupied territory
of their own free will: the last time they came into Poland
hey stayed for a century and a half. It is always important
to remember that, at the promptings of history, Poles have not
been anti-Soviet, but anti-Russian.

The conduct of the Russians in their half of Poland confirmed the worst fears of the Poles. Eastern Poland was evidently destined to be de-Polonised: tens of thousands of men
were sent to Siberia; hundreds were executed. Yes, the Poles
had much to forgive: but Sikorski was a statesman.

On July 30th, 1941, a pact was made between Poland and
Soviet Russia, with the blessing of the British government.
The state of war between the two countries was declared at
an end: now they would co-operate in the war 'against Hitlerite Germany.' A Polish army was to be formed from the
250,000 prisoners of war on Russian soil; it should be officered
by Poles, but would of course be subordinated in operational
questions to the Russian High Command. The Soviet government pledged itself to release all Polish citizens detained as
prisoners. Later, the re-formed Polish force was transferred to
the British command in the Near East.

From the point of view of our study, however, the most important clauses are those concerning the frontiers. The Soviet
government declared that the partition of Poland agreed on
with Germany on September 28th, 1939, was now null and
void. The British and American governments indicated that
they did not recognise any change of frontier made as a result
of force. The Russian-Polish agreement gave the impression of
the same fundamental idea: most Poles assumed automatically
that it meant a resumption of the frontiers established by the

Treaty of Riga in 1921, which persisted until the German attack.

The Russian newspaper *Izvestia*, however, commenting on the agreement, said: 'Frontiers are not eternal: we do not consider immutable the Polish-Soviet frontiers established by the Treaty of Riga in 1921, nor do we share the view that "no one dares to presume that the borders of the Polish State of 193 may be questioned," as expressed by Sikorski in his speech . . . The problem of Soviet-Polish frontiers is a matter for the future.'

The formula of the agreement, and especially the interpretation quoted above, aroused keen concern in some Polish quarters. M. Zaleski, the Polish Foreign Minister, resigned, unconvinced that Polish rights were safeguarded sufficiently. The Russians might argue after victory: 'Yes. The German-Soviet treaties have lost their validity. Russia has, however, another claim to other territories involved—the will of their people for, in an election held after the Soviet occupation, the people of Western Bielo-Russia and Western Ukraine (*i.e.* the eastern districts of Poland) voted emphatically for incorporation in the Soviet Union.' [1]

Nor was confidence increased when, on November 6th 1941, Stalin made his fighting speech on the occasion of the twenty-fourth anniversary of the Communist Revolution. 'We have not, and we cannot have, such war aims as the seizure of foreign territory, the subjugation of foreign peoples, whether it concerns the peoples and territories of Europe or of Asia' he declared. Unfortunately, the excellent impression of the statement was countered by the fact that when he enumerated the Russian provinces occupied by Germany—he included Estonia, Latvia and Lithuania among them! 'We have not, and cannot have,' Stalin continued, 'such war aims as the forcing of our will and our régime on the Slavonic or any other enslaved European peoples, who are expecting our assistance

[1] For an account of the method of voting, see the chapter on the Baltic states.

Our aim consists in helping these people in their struggle against Hitlerite Germany, and later permitting them freely to settle their own destiny in their own lands.' This would have been excellent, but for the 'plebiscites' in territory occupied by Russia, which could scarcely be described as 'free' settlements. The people who suspect Russian intentions may be wrong, but at least all grounds for their suspicion have not yet been removed.

In December 1941, however, General Sikorski made direct contact with Stalin, and the resultant declaration nullified some of the earlier apprehensions. The suspicion between Poland and Russia is not primarily one of ideologies, but of history. It cannot be dissolved in a day, but there now exists the will to real collaboration. Russian and Polish friendship would alter the whole character of the atmosphere of Eastern Europe, very much for the better. From every consideration it is to Russia's advantage to have a strong and friendly Poland on her flank. A weak Germany implies almost automatically a strong Poland.

Much will probably depend on what happens between now and the end of the war. The opinion of the British and American governments may prove to be the decisive factor. Russia has received many cruel blows; fate has allotted to her the most destructive and exhausting phase of the war: she will need the help of the civilised world in her recovery: I do not think she is likely to involve her case by a dispute over frontier provinces of limited economic interest and of great ethnic complexity. Her adhesion to the principles of the Atlantic Charter should ease the situation.

In any case, we have now covered enough ground to make possible a recoverable summing up of the problems.

VI

(*a*) The question of an independent Ukraine is largely an internal affair for Russia. Before any outside nation could offer suggestions, there would need to be far more forcible

evidence of the demand for independence than exists today
It is probable that, in the security which will follow victory
autonomous powers of local government will be delegated
more freely to the states of the Soviet Union. In such case, we
are likely to hear little more of Ukrainian nationalism—except, perhaps, from Ukrainians abroad.

(b) The German claim to Ukraine will disappear on the
day when Germany is defeated. It has no legal, historical
ethnical, ethical, economic or any other backing.

(c) The ethnic difficulties of the Russian-Polish frontier
are as involved as any in Europe. Any agreed boundary i
bound to be a compromise, for there is no suggestion of a
'natural' line of demarcation.

Since most nations look upon the Russian march into Poland
as a form of aggression, and as Russia declared that she made
the move for her own protection, it is reasonable to assume
that after victory she will retire to the original frontiers settled
by the Treaty of Riga. Russia will scarcely expect the world'
outlook to be guided by any 'plebiscites' held under war conditions and in circumstances which could scarcely be con-
strued as a reasonable expression of will.

This does not mean that the Riga frontiers are perfect, o
that any frontier drawn between Russia and Poland will eve
be perfect. We have seen that in Poland there are minoritie
of the Russian races amounting to 5 million Ukrainians and a
million White or Bielo-Russians. An exchange of population
so far as it is practicable, is obviously indicated.

This would still leave considerable Russian minorities on th
Polish side. It does not follow that all of these would prefe
to be under Soviet rule. Although of Russian or Ukrainiai
ethnic origin, their outlook is very local. When given the
treatment promised by the new democratic Polish régime
there is no reason why they should not be happy and pros
perous.

Moderate or minor rectifications of the frontier are o
course quite possible. Nevertheless, they should be negotiated

with care. Russia is so vast that the addition of a few hundred square miles to her territories is meaningless: on the other hand, even a modest advance to the west cuts the only railway in a land of already sparse communications. Where territorial considerations are of smaller importance, economic considerations become correspondingly larger.

I would like to see an early approach to this problem, even if the solution were only provisional. (No reasonable plebiscite could be held in the disputed areas until months after the war, for it will take a long time to collect all the Poles exiled in Siberia and to return them to their homes.) It may be that Russia still harbours lingering elements of her old suspicions, remnants of the days when she saw opponents everywhere. It is certain that there are still people who have not yet recovered full confidence in Russia—they do not doubt her courage and they glory in her magnificent resistance, but suspect her attitude after victory. No single act would so create confidence as a Russian declaration about her post-war frontier policy.

The sooner the boundary problems of Europe are settled after victory, the better for us all. It is going to take some time to arrange the frontiers of areas where our enemies are concerned: the least one can do is to fix in advance the lines of division between our friends.

CHAPTER FOUR

THE BALTIC STATES

I

ON ONE occasion, after a journey round the Baltic, was arguing with three members of Parliament. Some comment prompted me to challenge them to fill in the Baltic states on a sketch map. All three failed hopelessly over Estonia, Latvia and Lithuania.

The Estonians are close relatives of the Finns. A virile race they settled down to pastoral life, loosely organised in tribes. They were conquered by the Danes and reduced to a state of serfdom: yet their spirit survived—their conquerors found them such troublesome subjects that they sold the country outright to the Teutonic Knights of the Sword. They needed their swords!

In 1521 the people of Estonia voluntarily offered their land to Sweden: there followed two prosperous and happy centuries before its seizure by Russia. Not until 1917 did a new Estonia emerge, for the first time in history as an independent state.

Geographically the country is uninteresting, its low ridges relieved only by occasional lakes and many forests. Its area is only 18,500 square miles (half the size of Scotland), and its population little over a million. The birth of the new state was attended by complicated labour pains. One of the German aims in 1914 was to extend her empire over the Russian Baltic provinces. The treaty inflicted on the defeated Russians left these provinces as German petty kingdoms, with relatives of the Kaiser as titular rulers. Offices were actually opened in

Germany to enrol German soldiers as settlers in the new promised land.

Nor did the Armistice end this dream. Taking advantage of Allied distrust of the Bolshevik régime, German armies continued to operate in the Baltic states. The situation was amazingly confused. Both Estonia and Latvia had peasant armies in the field, striving to consolidate their promised independence:

COMMUNICATIONS—RUSSIA AND THE BALTIC STATES

the German Balts formed their own force, in collaboration with German regular armies: Russian 'Whites' were also present in some strength: finally, there was an Allied Mission, with naval backing. Thus the Baltic states saw the paradox of Allied forces co-operating with their enemies against Russia!

After the signature of the Treaty of Versailles the situation cleared. The Russians had withdrawn: then, after a struggle, the Estonians with Allied backing ejected the Germans. By 1920 there was a real Estonia on the map of Europe.

Russia made a generous treaty. The loss of the Baltic provinces was a serious economic blow, for much of the trade of her northwestern provinces flowed to the Baltic via the ports in the Gulf of Finland, now in foreign hands. Russia even allocated a proportion of her much-needed gold reserve to the newly founded states (15, 7 and 3 million gold roubles to Estonia, Latvia and Lithuania respectively): this was indeed a gesture of goodwill. There was now a chance for the Baltic states to settle down, to organise prosperity from the confusion which surrounded them.

Considering the geographical position, the Estonian population is remarkably compact. Minorities numbered only 11 per cent: 1.7 per cent were German Balts—descendants of the Teutonic Knights, or the merchants who followed them. These gentry had retained their lands and powers with amazing ease under Tsarist rule. They were full of complaints, of course, when their estates were expropriated for division into peasant farms: some found other middle-class occupations—but Hitler solved one problem at least when he recalled the German Balts to their 'homeland'—in Western Poland!

There is only one frontier problem in Estonia, and that of trivial importance. Just to the south of Lake Peipus live the Setus, the Estonian equivalent of the Finnish Carelians. These people are of Estonian stock, but have been Russified for centuries. They are Orthodox, while the Estonians are Lutherans. They are dirty, backward and superstitious: the government has done some good work by planting Estonian farmers in the district, to show the Setus new ways of agriculture.

There are only about 50,000 Setus in Estonia, but many thousands on the Russian side of the frontier. However, this is a boundary question never likely to be raised. Russia is not hungry for a few square miles of land, and the Estonians are scarcely likely to move to the rescue of their 'brothers' on the other side. The Setus are quite uninterested. They have no national and few tribal loyalties. All they want is to be left alone.

If the Setus are backward, some Estonian ideas are forward. A condemned man may, if he should so choose, avoid the indignity of hanging. He is presented with a cup of poison and—within reasonable limits of time!—may execute himself.

Another notion is perhaps worthy of study. Members of Parliament in Estonia are paid $50 a month. If they are absent, their salary is stopped: and even if they are half an hour late they lose $2.50!

The first Estonian constitution was the essence of democracy—but was quite unpractical: it depended so completely on voluntary agreement that the national executive had no real powers. When emergencies threatened, the weakness of the system was shown; it was ideal for a fully developed state, free from potential aggressors, but did not fit the times. In 1924 there was a Communist rising which impelled a temporary period of martial law. The real trial came after 1930, when Estonia was hard hit by the world economic crisis. It is at times like these that extremes flourish. The small Fascist party was gaining ground by finding scapegoats when the peasant leader Constantin Pëts assumed power under a new Constitution: his régime was a mild form of dictatorship; there was no terror or persecution. Indeed, it is reasonable to argue that Pëts saved Estonia from Fascism—which would inevitably have meant German dominance.

One feature of the new Estonia is worthy of note. Its treatment of minorities was excellent: the Cultural Autonomy Law of 1926 was a model of its kind: what is more, it was fully implemented. If its spirit had been translated to other disturbed areas of Europe, then our problems of today and tomorrow would have been much simplified.

Before considering the present-day tribulations of Estonia, it would be as well to glance at the neighbouring Baltic states.

II

In Riga, the capital of Latvia, there are separate cemeteries, side by side, for Protestants, Roman Catholics, Orthodox, Jews and Mohammedans. The scene is significant of the confusion of Latvia's ethnic history, which has never been so consolidated as that of Finland or Estonia.

The Letts are neither Slavs nor Finno-Ugrians, but are of Indo-European stock—with, of course, the usual admixtures of neighbouring bloods developed by history. The Latvia which emerged from the World War was its first appearance as an independent state: until it disappeared as a Russian province, the country consisted of the duchies of Livonia and Courland.

Lettish tribes peopled the land fifteen hundred years ago. In the year 1200 the town of Riga was founded by a company of German 'Crusaders.' As the Letts lived in isolated tribes, the Crusaders were able to subdue them one by one. Then in turn they were ousted by those Teutonic Knights of the Cross who were the scourge of the Baltic shores.

With the decay of the knights, the duchies became Polish territory—scene of the long combats between Germans, Poles, Swedes and Russians: combats in which the Letts had no interest, but in the course of which they had to die.

At the time of the Polish partitions, in 1795, Russia seized the provinces. It is a necessary corrective to emphasise that Latvia was a Russian province for no more than 123 years. Throughout that time the local aristocracy consisted of German Balts, descendants of the marauding knights and of German merchant adventurers. The Balts transferred their allegiance with every new master in order to retain their power and estates: in Latvia they were local governors—German, not Russian, was the official language!

(Many of these German Balts attained high rank in the Tsarist armies—which were then surprised when they were beaten by the Germans!)

When the new Latvia emerged, these Balts naturally lost their privileges. In 1914, four-fifths of the land of Latvia was owned by about five hundred people, mostly Germans. They were allowed to retain 250 acres each—and as the average Latvian farm is 25 acres, this seemed fairly reasonable. But the Balts, like all dispossessed men, were dissatisfied and dangerous.

The establishment of Latvia followed the same confused fighting as in Estonia. The Germans occupied the land at the time of the Russian collapse: when they retired in 1918, a Bolshevik army advanced. The Latvians fought back, assisted by 'White' Russians and a German force. This last was a dangerous ally; when the Bolsheviks had been defeated, it wished to stay in Latvia. But by the autumn of 1919 the land was free.

Its first government was intensely democratic. The minority population was large (25 per cent of the whole), but all were represented proportionately in the new Parliament. Latvia had to learn by experience that democracy is easier to preach than to practise. Its outward forms can be imitated, but its spirit is more difficult to capture. In fifteen years the country had more than twenty governments.

Then, in May 1934, Karlis Ulmanis established himself as Vadonis, or leader: the mildest revolution and the most paternal dictatorship ever staged. There was nothing Fascist about the régime: I saw Ulmanis among his people, a peasant leader among peasants. He had no bodyguard; he never wore a uniform.

The only suggestion of Fascism in Latvia lay in the *Aizsargi*, a corps half-way between Blackshirts and Home Guards. Its important feature was that it owed allegiance to the State, not to an individual or party.

Considering its limitations, Latvia did well in its twenty years of freedom: education was of a high standard; there were few wealthy people—but fewer paupers. External economy was the principal difficulty. The land supplied food for all, but imported manufactured goods were restricted and expensive because of the lack of foreign exchange. The spirit of progress was always apparent: the greatest need of Latvia was the one thing denied—another twenty years of peace.

III

The history of Lithuania has run along very different lines from that of its Baltic neighbours. They have been bound to the sea: Lithuanians looked towards the Continent.

Now but a small state, Lithuania was once a great empire stretching from the Baltic to the Black Sea, and Vilna was its capital. The Lithuanians of the Middle Ages were pagans, and had a great reputation as warriors, subduing the Slav tribes in what are now White Russia and Ukraine. In 1386 the thrones of Lithuania and Poland were united by marriage—at that time Lithuania was three times the size of Poland. For a time thereafter Poland and Lithuania followed a common destiny.

This consolidation of interests led directly to the problem of Vilna (or Vilno, or Wilno, or Vilnius—all the same place), which has so directly affected the fate of Lithuania. The state which re-emerged in 1919 had a population of 2½ millions: it was happy in that it escaped a great deal of the confused fighting which devastated Estonia and Latvia. Nevertheless, each time I visited Lithuania I commented upon the 'temporary' atmosphere: a feeling of uncertainty, as if no one were sure that the country had come to stay. This was the inevitable result of the inheritance of two unsolved and dangerous frontier disputes. First in importance was that of Vilna, the ancient capital.

After the alliance with Poland in 1386, the Lithuanians supplied the warriors, the Poles the culture. In particular, Polish monks were dispatched at once to Lithuania to evangelise the people. They could not speak Lithuanian, but local chroniclers report that the Lithuanian king himself interpreted their sermons! They must have been forceful, for the local people early abandoned their paganism—sacred fires were extinguished and idols destroyed, and in Vilna alone some 30,000 Lithuanians were baptised.

After the union of Lithuania and Poland, however, the political importance of Vilna declined—the Poles knew more of the game of statecraft, and the seat of government was transferred to Cracow, and later to Warsaw. Polish priests, rather naturally, proceeded to Vilna in greater numbers: here was a vast field for missionary and educational work. Polish officials and their families gradually followed. As Polish was the language of the Polish-Lithuanian court, it became the language of the ruling classes in Lithuania. If you wanted to get on, you had to learn Polish; if you wanted education, you had to know Polish to get it. Through succeeding centuries the character of Vilna changed; once predominantly Lithuanian, it became more and more Polish—and many of the remaining Lithuanians spoke Polish as their first or only language, and were already forgetting that they were ever Lithuanian.

In the partition of Poland, Vilna and Lithuania fell to the share of Russia. Vilna now experienced an influx of Russians, including Jews who were not permitted to settle in Russia proper. The city therefore became a glorious ethnic medley, of which its churches today bear full witness. They even include a Mohammedan mosque! I found several families of Tartars in the city.

Now although the Lithuanian population of Vilna dwindled, the rural districts round about were predominantly Lithuanian. When the state of Lithuania was reborn—under German 'protection'—after the Russian Revolution, she naturally claimed Vilna as her historic capital; her first post-war frontiers—the 'Curzon Line'—were well to the south of Vilna. In the confused fighting of the period, the city changed hands several times.

First the Lithuanians lost Vilna in war to the Russians. Three months later it was recaptured—by the Poles! Then the Russians invaded Poland, but were defeated on the Vistula:

unable to hold Vilna, they handed back the city and district to the Lithuanians, thus restoring the 'Curzon Line.' All this happened in 1920.

The League of Nations hoped that this was the end of the matter—the Lithuanians occupied substantially the territory first allocated to them. Such hopes appeared justified when on October 7th, 1920, at Suvalki a military agreement between the Poles and the Lithuanians was signed in the presence of the League's military control commission. The League had apparently scored one of its first successes.

LITHUANIA AND VILNA

Frontier before Zeligowski's Raid ▬▪▬▪▬

Frontier until 1938 ▬▬

Disillusion followed rapidly. Within two days the Poles had invaded the Vilna region. At first it was explained that the invasion was a private expedition organised by a 'rebel' general, Zeligowski, and an army of irregulars. But Zeligowski seized Vilna and Poland held on to it, and it is not now denied even in Poland that the 'rebel' was acting on behalf of Poland; the League, indeed, had been suitably bluffed.

The excuse put forward is that most of Zeligowski's men were Poles from the Vilna region—which was true—and that they could not bear to see their kindred in foreign hands. This explains the raid on Vilna, but it does not explain the signing of an agreement two days earlier.

The Poles claimed that it was purely a military agreement, without any international obligations, but the normal outlook of public opinion is that one form of signed agreement is as binding as another. Poland, which on the whole has played a worthy part in world affairs, lost a great deal of the world's sympathy by this trick.

However, the man in the street and his statesmen did nothing; they were weary of war and the endless strife in Eastern Europe. They were sorry for Lithuania, but that was all. A little firmness, however, and Poland might have compromised —after all, she owed her existence to the Allied victory. The League of Nations, although Lord Cecil described the episode as 'an international scandal,' after some half-hearted attempts at negotiation, eventually accepted the *fait accompli*, and Vilna remained within the Polish borders.

The Lithuanians, outnumbered by ten to one, could do little but brood in their fury. The Poles held an election in the Vilna region, which naturally favoured Poland—the election was of the 'arranged' type with which we are now familiar. The election seemed a monstrosity to Lithuanians at the time, but its conduct was mild compared with that of elections held by more 'advanced' nations ten years later.

It will not take us long to decide, I think, that the Polish method of seizing Vilna cannot be justified by any moral standards. But can the seizure itself be justified? Is Vilna Polish?

One thing is certain—Vilna is *not* Lithuanian. Today the city houses 200,000 inhabitants, and only 5000 of them are Lithuanian. Vilna is noted as a city of churches—but only one of them is Lithuanian. Even on the basis of the pre-war figures, which perhaps afford a fairer comparison, the Lithuanians (according to their own figures) claim only 2 per cent of the inhabitants of the city.

For that matter, only 30 per cent of the inhabitants were Polish, 40 per cent were Jews and 25 per cent Russians. Vilna is, in fact, an ethnic medley—it is the natural meeting-place of the Great Russian, Polish and Lithuanian tribes. Today the proportion of Poles is naturally higher, but they are still outnumbered by the Jews. Thus, unless you count Polish Jews as Poles, Vilna can scarcely be described as a Polish city. But that does not make it Lithuanian.

In the surrounding rural district, however, the position is different. When Polish priests and administrators came to Vilna, they settled the city but left the country districts comparatively undisturbed. There were colonies of Russians in the territory, and more came after the partitions. The last pre-war figures show that in some of the eastern districts of the Vilna territory some 80 per cent of the inhabitants are Russians.

At that time the Russians put forward no claim to the territory. As between Lithuanians and Poles, the situation was clear—yet difficult. In urban areas the Poles outnumbered the Lithuanians; in some of the country districts the Lithuanians formed the majority. It does not follow that national groups are strongest nearest their own frontiers, and in some districts there are strong Lithuanian settlements to the south of Vilna. South-west and north-east of Vilna are rural districts which are almost entirely Lithuanian, and further south and east are many districts where the Lithuanians outnumber the Poles. It is only fair to point out that there are many thousands of Poles in the villages on the Lithuanian side of the frontier.

The first obvious question is: To settle all these disputes about population, why was a plebiscite not held at once? The difficulty was, of course, to decide whether the plebiscite should cover town and country together, or separately. Actually two attempts were made by the League to hold a plebiscite. The first failed because both Poland and Lithuania refused to agree to it—both were apparently afraid of losing it! The other reason for the failure was more dramatic: an international force would of course have been necessary to control the plebiscite, and Russia threatened to make war if any international force assembled near her frontiers! Such are the minor difficulties of diplomacy!

The second attempt was based on a potential close alliance between Poland and Lithuania. This Lithuania refused to agree to—she was afraid of being absorbed in a greater Poland.

It was a pretty problem for armchair statesmen, but it was desperately serious to Lithuania. The blow to the national pride was intense—a country deprived of her historic capital! At first the world's sympathies were with Lithuania—until she herself legalised the Zeligowski method by the similar seizure of Memel. The same League Conference which confirmed Lithuania in Memel legalised Poland's seizure of Vilna!

Until 1927 Lithuania and Poland were in a state of intermittent warfare, with daily frontier 'incidents' (Lithuania, incidentally, still prints all official maps as including Vilna, and in Kaunas I was officially requested not to refer to the present frontier as the frontier, but as the 'temporary administrative line'). Then one day Pilsudski went to Geneva; he had none of the artificial graces of diplomacy, and meeting the Lithuanian Foreign Minister, Valdemaras, flung at him the stern question: 'Well, what do you want—peace or war?' And Valdemaras, representative of a tiny state, could only reply: 'Peace.'

But it was no more than a truce. Diplomatic relations were not resumed, and the frontier remained closed. When I crossed from Vilna to Kaunas in 1934, I passed along a main road which once carried a heavy traffic; I found it grass-grown —*and I found that I was only the fourteenth person to pass that way in twelve years!* To make the crossing, my application had to be approved personally by the Lithuanian Prime Minister, Foreign Minister and Home Secretary, to say nothing of a host of ministers and officials at Warsaw.

The 'Forbidden Frontier' caused much misery to the unfortunate peasants. One-third of the natural hinterland of Vilna was in Lithuania: but the Lithuanian farmer could not send his produce there, and must transport it expensively to Kaunas. Until 1928, when a local arrangement was made, it was even impossible for peasants to work such of their land as lay on the other side of the frontier: even then it was still difficult, for deep trenches had been cut across the unfrequented roads, railways had been torn up. There was no normal communication between. A letter posted in a Polish village to a village in Lithuania had to travel five hundred miles through Latvia or Prussia—although the two villages might be in sight of each other! In spite of my unquestioned credentials, it took me two hours to pass from one side of a trench to the other.

The Poles claimed—and I believed them—that they were keenly anxious to resume their old friendly relations with Lithuania. Pilsudski went further—he always looked upon Lithuania as the Scotland to Poland's England. He himself was a Lithuanian from the Vilna territory: Poland's national poet, Mickiewicz, was a Lithuanian. Why not resume the old alliance? said the Poles, again and again. The Lithuanians always declined; they would merely be absorbed in a greater Poland as a very junior partner. In any case, before they would talk about alliances, they wanted Vilna.

It was in connection with Vilna that I made an attempt to figure as an amateur diplomat, and since then I have never envied foreign secretaries. From bitter experience I warn armchair statesmen that it is too easy to decide that Poland should do so-and-so, and Lithuania should accept this and give up that. Logical cold-blooded reasoning is not enough in international affairs. A Spaniard can find a hundred logical and convincing arguments why England should surrender Gibraltar: but England will not surrender Gibraltar, at least, not until all possibilities of international conflict have been eliminated, and this is likely to take a long time. The Allied campaign in North Africa would have been quite impossible but for the British base at Gibraltar.

Circumstances so arranged themselves that I was in touch with people who could speak for Poland and Lithuania. With the Pole I had discussed the dangers of Vilna—in Vilna; I pointed out the importance of a friendly Lithuania in the case of combat; of a friendly Lithuania when East Poland catches up West, and becomes a trading country—at the moment it is scarcely exploited, but one day it will need the services of a port like Memel. If at war with Germany, Poland would inevitably lose Danzig and Gdynia, and Lithuanian friendship would then be invaluable.

He agreed with all these arguments, and, apart from them all, was very anxious to conciliate Lithuania. He even agreed that the seizure of Vilna was a 'trick,' but attempted to justify it by the unsatisfactory methods of the League of Nations Commission. Then, for the first time in my life, I found that I had met a *European statesman who was willing to give up portions of his country's territory*. He did not go as far as I would have done, but his outlook was so bold and novel that I took off my hat to him.

I arrived at Kaunas, therefore, with high hopes. Here was an unique opportunity of acting the peacemaker—of stopping up one of Europe's running sores, which might at any moment become a dangerous wound. I had every possible advantage, since I was without official connections of any kind.

It seemed that the question of the frontier might be reopened with a view to revision. Near Olkienki and Orany, in particular, I had found dozens of Lithuanian villages—these could be returned to Lithuania. It might mean the cutting of the Grodno-Vilna railway, but this problem could be faced; it would be well worth while spending $500,000 in settling the Vilna feud. Further to the north-east, too, the Lithuanian frontier could be pushed out as much as ten miles. If desired, Lithuanians outside the new frontier could be repatriated, or exchanged for Poles in Lithuania. Vilna, of course, would remain Polish.

This was at least an excellent compromise, *and I knew that*

Poland would accept it. But my high hopes were soon dashed in Kaunas. I was thanked for my interest, but my suggestion was turned down gently but decisively. There could be no permanent settlement without Vilna. 'How would you like it,' asked a Lithuanian statesman, 'if Frenchmen had settled in Winchester, your historical capital: and, although the country round about was English, France seized the county of Hampshire?'

No, Vilna *must* come back to Lithuania, it was explained. No government which agreed otherwise would survive for five minutes—and this, I believe, is true. Vilna may now be Polish, but it is the very heart of Lithuanian history and nationalism.

After the return of Vilna anything was open to discussion—*anything,* my Lithuanian statesman declared. He fully realised the peculiar position of Poland—the meat in the German-Russian sandwich, and that apart from other considerations the cession of Vilna would mean an important military loss. He was prepared to counter that with a military alliance—so that, in event of war, not only Vilna but the whole of Lithuania would be with Poland. Trade treaties—equal rights for Poles in Lithuania—*anything* could be discussed and arranged, once Vilna were returned.

I argued at length: agreed that the seizure of Vilna was scurvily planned, but nevertheless that Vilna was a Polish city—certainly not Lithuanian. I insisted that the quite informal and unofficial offer I made was unique—no other country had shown the slightest sign of giving up a square yard of ground. Poland's gesture ought not to be abruptly dismissed; but always we stuck at Vilna.

Then I turned to the attack: What was the alternative? I demanded. I was convinced that in no circumstances short of overwhelming defeat in war would Poland surrender Vilna. Did the Lithuanians propose to make war? The answer was no, emphatically. Quite apart from the inadvisability of making war on a country ten times her size, Lithuania hated the very idea of war—she had suffered enough in the last, when Russians and Germans in turn ravaged the country. (And I ought to add at once that this was a general feeling—I met no one in Lithuania who wanted a war: but then, there were only a few thousands among Europe's millions who did.)

Then, I continued, what did Lithuania propose to do? Wait. What for? A miracle. Was not that hopeless? No. The rebirth of Lithuania was a miracle—that of Poland a greater miracle. Who would have dared to prophesy in 1914 that first Russia and then the Central Powers would be defeated? The defeat of one or the other was certain, but the defeat of both was essential if Poland were to be recreated. Yet the hundred-to-one chance came off—and Pilsudski had foreseen it and had gambled on it. There might be another miracle today or tomorrow.

But the Lithuanian idea of a miracle was not very comforting. It involved another European conflagration, with Poland either defeated or buying off Lithuania with Vilna.

I learned one lesson from Vilna—that compromise is not enough; if a compromise is to be effective and lasting, only friends can make it. And at that time no one could claim that Poland and Lithuania were friends—they were scarcely acquaintances. The Forbidden Frontier divided them, the most nervous barrier in Europe.

This was in 1934. I was quite certain that one day a spark would be struck which might set ablaze the dangerous tinder which was piled along the Polish-Lithuanian frontiers. I was surprised when it was delayed four years. In March 1938, at the time of the German march into Austria, a Polish soldier was killed by a Lithuanian patrol.

The Poles determined on stern measures. They were convinced that the European war had already begun—that Hitler's march into Austria was a strategic jockeying for position. In *any* war Poland's access to the sea would be perilous, and an unfriendly Lithuania on her flank was dangerous. She determined to force the Lithuanians to complete negotiations which had begun in January 1938, but which were suddenly broken off by Lithuania. Poland suspected the backing of a foreign power. At this time Lithuania leaned towards Russia for support—necessarily, since her problems were with Germany and Poland.

A startled Europe learned that Poland had dispatched an ultimatum to Lithuania, couched in terms seldom used in diplomatic correspondence, and demanding an answer within forty-eight hours. The ultimatum, after dealing with the death which had provoked it, went on to demand the immediate resumption of diplomatic and trade relations. No argument was permitted. The Lithuanian Government was to accept it in full and without discussion, otherwise—

Polish troops began to mass at Vilna, and Marshal Smigly-Rydz himself went there. The city was excited by patriotic demonstrations. 'Mobilise!' 'March on Kovno!' 'Liquidate Lithuania!' cried the marchers. Tanks and cavalry moved into position along the frontier. The Polish fleet put to sea.

This was serious enough: had it not been for the more dramatic days in Austria it would have been sensational. But it was seen that this was only the beginning. It was reported that Russia was urging Lithuania to resist—and that Hitler was also massing troops on the Lithuanian frontier. If the Poles seized Kovno (Kaunas), the Germans would seize Memel.

There were excited scenes in Kaunas. There was a considerable section which would have resisted—for Lithuania is one on the Vilna question. But there could only be one end to such a one-sided war, and as German aeroplanes cruised overhead and rumours spread around, the inevitable run on the banks began. The atmosphere was familiar to old hands—it was exactly the tension which precedes a war.

The diplomatic corps got busy—they at least knew the dangers of the situation. The British and French Ministers in Lithuania took urgent action, maybe countering that of Russia. By one report, Russia withdrew at the last minute her offer of aid. At any rate Lithuania capitulated, and on March 19th the Polish terms were accepted. The following day soldiers began to fill in the trenches in the road over which I had passed.

I think the Lithuanians were wise. A grievance they certainly had, but it was childish to break off all communications with Poland for so long. For—and this is important—the resumption of diplomatic relations with Poland did not to any degree imply acceptance of the position of Vilna. Colonel

VILNA, 1939–41

Beck promised on behalf of Poland to respect Lithuanian rights and independence—but he left no doubt that if the ultimatum had been rejected the Polish army would have marched into Lithuania.

Again the judgment of the world was that Poland had done the right thing by the wrong method. However, the German menace assisted the gradual development of a new atmosphere between the estranged countries. In May 1939 occurred an event which would have been classed as fantastic two years before—General Rashtikis, the Lithuanian Chief of Staff, visited Warsaw for diplomatic and military talks. He was decorated with a Polish order, the highest mark of distinction, and on his return stated that his visit 'had resulted in a very close friendship between the two countries, revealing a complete identity of view.'

For by this time Lithuania had felt the first grip of German pressure—and Memel had been seized. There were ominous signs that this was only the beginning—the parallel of Czechoslovakia was only too obvious. It is perfectly true that 'complete identity of view' did exist between Poland and Lithuania so far as Germany was concerned. With Lithuania as well as Czechoslovakia under German control, the circle around Poland would be more than half complete. For Lithuania the question was of her very existence.

When the Russians marched into Poland, at the height of the German invasion in September 1939, Lithuanian hopes were raised high. In spite of many difficulties, she had effected some kind of reconciliation with her former rulers. The Russians recognised this by admitting the Lithuanian claim to Vilna. The area allocated only included a portion of the territory lost in 1920, but it covered the city and a strip of land along the frontier—in all about 2500 square miles of territory with a population of nearly half a million. Of this, only about one-quarter was Lithuanian.

The Suvalki region, claimed by Lithuania, was handed over to Germany and incorporated in East Prussia. Nevertheless there was intense joy in Lithuania at the recovery of the ancient capital: a joy destined soon to be dimmed.

IV

At this stage it is essential to examine the parallel problem of Memel (or Klaipeda, to quote its Lithuanian name).

Memel is a Baltic port which up to 1918 represented the eastern extremity of the German Empire. Behind it, on the right bank of the Niemen, is a strip of territory associated with Memel historically and economically. This area, at the time occupied by Lithuanian and Lettish tribes, was conquered by the Teutonic Knights during the thirteenth century. Pursuing their 'missionary' enterprise—for the local inhabitants were pagans—the knights murdered or expelled such as would not accept Christianity, and portions of the land were temporarily depopulated.

Memel itself became a flourishing port, a member of the Hanseatic League. Despite attacks and even occupations by Lithuanians, Poles, Swedes and Russians, the port remained German in population and character. Its importance, however, declined after the partition of Poland, for the greater part of its natural hinterland was included in Russia, and trade was artificially diverted through Russian ports.

The sea-coast at first envisaged for the recreated Lithuania after the war consisted of a few miles of sandy shore, devoid of a port and almost of the possibility of constructing one. Fatigued with their labours on major problems, the powers at Paris postponed this. By the Treaty of Versailles (Article 99) Germany was required to cede the Memel territory—the land east of the river Niemen—and undertook to accept its ultimate disposal, as eventually decided by the Allies. An Allied Commission, with French troops, occupied the territory, and there was a prevalent idea that Memel would eventually assume the same status as Danzig—a free city, but it is interesting to note that maritime rights were thought to be intended for Poland: at that time, indeed, Lithuania had not been recognised by the victorious powers.

The Lithuanians, however, had different views. They had heard much of the awkwardness of the Danzig situation; they had learned much from the Polish seizure of Vilna. The powers help those who help themselves, they argued, and were peculiarly susceptible to the *fait accompli*, as Vilna had proved. We must not blame the Allied Powers too heavily for their weakness: their nations were weary of war, and desired peace even at the expense of justice. What would have happened to a British government which sent an army to fight for Memel in 1922? Nor was the Polish coup at Vilna the only exemplar for the Lithuanians—the raid on Memel was directly prompted by the French march into the Ruhr.

On January 10th, 1923, Memel witnessed a strange scene. The French garrison, which had come to hold the town against Germany on behalf of Lithuania, found itself surrounded by a menacing Lithuanian army! Outnumbered and not much interested, the French troops surrendered and evacuated the port. The whole Memel-land area was immediately occupied by the Lithuanians, who promptly presented their *fait accompli* to the powers. It was represented at first as a spontaneous rising of the rural population against the occupation of the powers, but I never met any Lithuanian who believed this fiction, or any Memel-lander who 'spontaneously rose.' An Allied Commission decided very definitely that the raid was planned and executed by the Lithuanian government.

The gamble came off—the challenge was not accepted. Memel and its hinterland—about 1000 square miles—were formally handed over to Lithuania, subject to a measure of local autonomy—Memel was to be a self-governing unit under Lithuanian sovereignty, and with a governor appointed by the Lithuanian president. This solution was finally accepted by all parties, and the problem of Memel was born. Few even among the sponsors of the scheme imagined that they had heard the last of Memel. Signor Nitti, more detached in this instance than other politicians of the day, described Memel as 'one of the greatest blunders of the peace treaty.'

It is only fair to the legislators of the time to point out another of their difficulties. Lithuania was still smarting over the legitimate grievance in the Polish seizure of Vilna. The ratification of the Polish occupation of Vilna was under contemplation, and it may easily be that the desire to give some sort of compensation to Lithuania may have created a slight bias in the minds of the Conference which arranged the settlement. No plebiscite was held, but a traveling commission formed the view that union with Lithuania was *not* desired. This was a reasonable conclusion. The Germans were in a slight majority in the district, and it cannot be assumed that every Lithuanian would have voted for incorporation within Lithuania. (Indeed, subsequent elections show that quite a number of them would not—many thousands of Lithuanians voted for an *autonomous* Memel-land.)

Such, very briefly, is the history of the problem; now for the problem itself. The German case is perfectly clear: here was a stretch of territory which had been under German rule for centuries, suddenly separated from the fatherland by a dictated treaty, merely to give Lithuania a port. True, there were Lithuanians in the country districts, but Memel was and is overwhelmingly German. It was utterly wrong to put Germans under the rule of a lower civilisation—for the autonomy clauses were ignored by the Lithuanians as soon as their sovereignty was assured. If it were essential to give Lithuania an outlet to the sea, then she could have been granted special rights in Memel, as Czechoslovakia has in other German ports. At the most, Memel should have become a free city on the Danzig basis.

According to the last German pre-war figures, the population of the territory was 141,000. Of these 51 per cent spoke German as their first language, 48 per cent Lithuanian, and 1 per cent were Poles, Jews or other races. (We have seen that language is no sure guide to race, but as the German argument is founded upon it, we will accept it here for the present.) But, say the Germans, these Lithuanians are not real Lithuanians—they are no more than a tribe distantly removed; their culture and religion are German, as might be expected when their forefathers have been under German rule for six hundred years. It is further claimed that the percentages quoted above are misleading, since many German families speak Lithuanian as their first language! In mixed marriages between German men and Lithuanian women, it is asserted, the resultant families usually speak Lithuanian!

This is a remarkable claim, and would appear to admit that Lithuanian tradition and culture in the district are stronger than German. The idea of German fathers bringing up their children *in Germany* to speak Lithuanian seemed so amazing as to demand investigation. The district is not large, and I made independent inquiries, but I was unable to discover a solitary case.

Nor can I agree that the Memel Lithuanians are not Lithuanians. Naturally, long generations under German rule have introduced German words into the language and German thoughts into the mind. But no country consists of one pure stock—Germany not excepted. If the German arguments were accepted, Bretons and Normans would not be real Frenchmen, Devonians and Northumbrians would not be real Englishmen—and Bavarians would not be real Germans. The Lithuanians of Memel speak Lithuanian, say that they are Lithuanian, and were generally perfectly happy to be incorporated in Lithuania.

I have no quarrel with the German figures. By 1939 the Lithuanian proportion had naturally increased, but if at the moment of handing-over you considered the population of Memel on a fifty-fifty basis, you would not be very far wrong. But, unfortunately for those who have tidy minds, the two races were not neatly divided. Of the 71,000 Germans in the territory, over half were to be found in the town of Memel itself. Thus Lithuanians easily predominated in the country districts, though they generally formed the poorer classes of the population.

This makes clear the Lithuanian argument. Here is a rural territory contiguous to Lithuania with a big preponderance of Lithuanians—of course, it should be joined to the mother country. But if the territory comes to Lithuania, then the port of Memel must come too—admittedly it is largely German, but it has no place in the world if it is separated from its territory. In any case, to a developing country like Lithuania a port is essential, and Memel is the only possibility.

The problem of Lithuania runs parallel to that of Poland. In this region, as in other parts of Europe, invading tribes tended to occupy complete river basins, natural areas of settlement. Thus Poles grouped about the Vistula, Lithuanians about the Niemen. By the vagaries of history, Germans settled at the mouths of the rivers. It was a reasonable argument that a nation's economic outlet should not be strangled by a foreign power.

For a time the prosperity of Memel dwindled, since the links with its previous hinterland in East Prussia and Poland were broken. The Lithuanians attacked the problem boldly: new railways were built; soon it was necessary to extend the port facilities, as the tonnage handled was more than doubled.

Yet the Germans of Memel were not happy—I was soon convinced of that. They complained bitterly of Lithuanian 'oppression,' although they brought it on themselves. For the Memel scheme to work smoothly, cordial co-operation between Germans and Lithuanians was essential, and from the very first moment the Germans refused to co-operate. Do not blame them too hardly. Suppose the Germans had won the World War and had annexed Dover. Would the people of Dover have co-operated very willingly with the Germans?

The freely elected council allotted to the territory under the autonomy clauses was a farce from its inception. It had a German majority, and after a few violent rows the Lithuanian members declined to attend. Thereupon the Lithuanian government declared the local council non-effective, and for most practical purposes Memel has been treated as an ordinary portion of Lithuania.

The language difficulty was intense—there is a big gap between the German and Lithuanian tongues. With conciliation on both sides, the difficulty could have been overcome. But the Germans declined to have anything to do with the Lithuanian language: this action, if unwise, was at least understandable, for the Germans of Memel had been incorporated in Lithuania against their will. The Lithuanian government, however, decided with some justice that its own employees ought to speak Lithuanian, and ordered officials, policemen, postmen and the like to learn it. Most of them refused; the time limit was extended again and again, but in 1934 and 1935 large numbers of government employees who still proved obdurate were at last dismissed. Naturally they became martyrs on the spot—and they and their friends became doubly sensitive to 'patriotic' propaganda from Germany.

The resistance of the Germans may perhaps be justified on patriotic grounds, but it was bound to provoke retaliatory measures. A government is at least entitled to claim that its own employees shall understand the language in which its orders are issued. The dismissed Germans were very largely replaced by Lithuanians, and Memel was full of anomalies. I found Lithuanian teachers in charge of German children— the scholars understanding scarcely a word the teachers spoke. I saw people in post-offices wandering from *guichet* to *guichet* in search of a penny stamp, unable to read the indicative notices above. Memel itself lost its ancient name and became Klaipeda.

Both sides must share the blame for the unhappy atmosphere in Memel. It very nearly resulted in open combat in 1934. The news of the attempted Nazi *putsch* in Memel passed almost unnoticed in Europe, for it came at the same moment as the murder of Dolfuss. There was a widespread German plot to seize the town and hold it for Germany. Unhappily for the plotters, one of their number 'squeaked' to the Lithuanian government, and the rising was suppressed before it began. There were wholesale arrests, but only one casualty—the 'squeaker.'

His end was peculiar. He was seized by the infuriated plotters, hustled into a motor-car and hurried towards the German frontier. He was given such lurid hints as to what awaited him that on the way he died of heart failure! Technically, I suppose, this is murder, and his death was included in the charges brought against some of the prisoners.

There were 126 of them, and after long delays they were tried *en masse* by court-martial. Most of them were found guilty. Four were sentenced to death, the remainder to various terms of imprisonment. The death sentences aroused Germany to fury. German leaders made threatening speeches: irregular patriotic forces massed on the frontier, intent on a wild attempt at rescue. The moment was as acute as any since the war. England and France saved the situation by diplomatic action. They did not dispute the legality of the death sentences, but called attention to the Lithuanian neglect of the autonomy clauses of the settlement. With much good sense, the Lithuanian president exercised his prerogative of reprieve, and the problem was shelved—but not solved.

Memel was again in the news in 1938. While the Poles massed at Vilna, prepared to march into Lithuania, German troops were ready to seize Memel. Only the Lithuanian submission to Poland averted what might easily have been the first stage of the new European war.

According to German propaganda, the territory was burning to return to the fatherland—even the Lithuanians of the rural districts wanted to go back. This, by my impressions, was not true. It was not even true that all the Germans wanted to return, for some of them appreciated the new prosperity and the potentialities of the future. Yet it would be absurd to claim that they were happy under Lithuanian rule. It is a pity that the Lithuanian treatment of the Memel-landers was not more liberal: yet the difficulties were immense—propaganda ensured that the population was recalcitrant and non-co-operative. There could be no peace in Memel under such conditions: it was never the Nazi intention that there should be peace.

After Munich, Hitler declared once again that he had no more territorial ambitions in Europe. Yet the event aroused a wild wave of Nazi enthusiasm in Memel, and all the old arguments began afresh. One of the German spokesmen proclaimed that, although the Führer had disclaimed further conquests, he had not forbidden exiled Germans to clamour for return to the Reich. This claim had a familiar ring, and was not very comforting.

The end of Memel came suddenly but not unexpectedly. On March 21st, 1939, Germany presented an ultimatum to Lithuania which followed a now familiar pattern. Memel was to be surrendered within five days, and was to be a free city. (This status was conveniently forgotten a few minutes later.) There was nothing to be said, for Lithuania had no effective allies—and it was made quite clear that any refusal would involve the immediate invasion and subjection of Lithuania. Within the five days, therefore, Klaipeda had become Memel again.

There were other points in the ultimatum, which suggested that Lithuania might become a vassal state to Germany on the Slovak model. These were resisted; and, as we have seen, Lithuania turned to Poland for support. But Memel provides an excellent example of how European problems should not be solved. And nowhere outside Germany is the solution regarded as permanent.

v

The case of the Baltic states provides a strong argument in favour of federation. Here were three countries which in spite of all difficulties provided a considerable degree of prosperity and happiness to their people, which threatened no one and only desired to live at peace, but nevertheless found themselves hopelessly entangled in the turmoil of war. Their fault was that they were too small.

The status of these countries had been one of the main causes of the breakdown of negotiations between Britain, France and Russia in the spring of 1939. We had given a guarantee to Poland; it could only be of a serious practical value if backed by Russia. Naturally, the question will always be debated why Russia was not consulted *before* the guarantee was given.

Russia demanded, as an essential condition of the guarantee, its extension to cover the Baltic states. This was logical enough. If the Germans occupied these countries, then the defence of Leningrad and Northern Russia—to say nothing of Poland—was wellnigh impossible. The difficulty was that the Baltic states did not wish to be guaranteed. They argued, with some justification, that this was an open invitation to German attack.

(It is interesting to note that Russia made similar demands during the negotiations on the Franco-Soviet Pact in 1935. They were rejected by Laval.)

In the spring of 1939 few people in Britain appreciated the ruthless atmosphere of Europe. It scarcely seemed democratic to guarantee small countries against their will—especially as it became apparent that Russia meant a very practical guarantee, involving garrisons in the Baltic states. In view of our reluctance, the Russians opened simultaneous negotiations with Germany: here no scruples were encountered, and the Soviet-German Non-Aggression Pact resulted.

The incident is typical of the difficulties of diplomacy. Had we forced a guarantee on the three tiny Baltic states it would have been against all democratic precedent: yet it might have prevented the war; it would certainly have shortened it.

The outlook of the countries themselves was always the same: to avoid the war. If it spread, there was always a risk of German invasion. The guarantee involved the certainty of Russian occupation. The Baltic states wanted neither German nor Russian armies on their soil. In this unpleasant dilemma they preferred the risk to the certainty.

The Soviet apologia reads: 'Hitler was preparing to seize the Baltic States'—which is probably true. It continues: 'and the Governments of these States were preparing to put their territory at Hitler's disposal immediately he demanded it. Just as the President of Czechoslovakia, Hacha, summoned by Hitler to Berlin, in March 1939, without any resistance, put their Fatherland "under the protection of Hitler," so the spokesmen of Estonia, Latvia and Lithuania (not to speak of Finland) were only waiting a similar summons to Berlin.'

Not even Hacha's worst enemy would suggest that he went to Berlin willingly! And imagination must be strained to picture Lithuania, burning under the seizure of Memel, anxiously awaiting the further protection of Hitler!

Immediately after the conquest of Poland, Russia proceeded with the action we had refused to condone. The Foreign Ministers of the three Baltic states were summoned to Moscow and presented with demands for the conclusion of pacts of mutual assistance, involving Russian naval and air bases on their territory. Estonia, Latvia and Lithuania did not act as the Soviet apologia had suggested. ('During the last years of their existence the Governments of Latvia, Lithuania and Estonia showed by all their behaviour that they were prepared to aid Hitler in every way, and to make it easy for him to seize the Baltic States.') They could not hope to stand up to Russian might, and submitted. Russian garrisons marched in.

The Soviet policy was much criticised at the time, but it was frankly realist—which means that you must consider your own interests before those of other people, or of ethical principles. Since then the British attitude has been tempered by stern necessity. Their occupation of Iran is in principle not unlike the Russian occupation of the Baltic states.

Had this been the end, there would have been little to be said. The Russians, however, claimed that the Baltic states continued to look towards Germany. Even a military consultation between the general staffs of the three countries was looked upon as a menace—though the total population involved was only five millions, and the Russians held all strategic points! In June 1940, at the height of the Battle of France, the Soviet demanded facilities for further garrisons: then more.

'In view of the anti-Soviet policy of the Governments of the Baltic States,' the official explanation reads, 'the U.S.S.R. was compelled to demand from all three States the formation of such

Governments as would be capable and willing to ensure that the Pacts of Mutual Assistance would be loyally carried out.'

Actually, Russian commissars went to the three capitals to set up new governments of 'Left Intellectuals.' The usual mass meetings and propaganda campaigns followed: then elections were announced.

'The elections, which took place on July 14th and 15th, 1940, were held on strictly democratic lines,' runs the Soviet account. 'In Estonia, the "Alliance of Working People of Estonia," which stood for the establishment of the closest possible union and friendship of Estonia with the U.S.S.R., received nearly 93 per cent of all the votes cast. In Latvia, the candidates of the bloc of the "Labouring People of Latvia" received 97.6 per cent of the votes cast. Finally, in Lithuania, the candidates of the "Labour Alliance of Lithuania" received 99.19 per cent of all the votes cast.'

The very conclusiveness of the argument is its weakness. No democrat will ever believe that any party could poll 99.19 per cent of the votes cast by legal methods on 'strictly democratic lines.' Actually the election was of the type familiar in continental Europe. It is small wonder that the candidates named received such a high percentage of the votes cast, for they were the only ones allowed to be nominated! Voting was compulsory; it was announced that passports would be stamped, and anyone not voting would be classed as an enemy of the people. The results were claimed as a dramatic vindication of Russian policy. It was an unfortunate slip by which a London newspaper published the official results from a Russian news agency twenty-four hours before the polls were closed!

The representatives thus elected met in their respective capitals a week later. The Russian proclamations had featured the freedom of the Baltic states and their right to self-determination. Now the first item on the agenda of each Parliament was found to be along different lines. 'The representative assemblies, elected by universal suffrage, established Soviet Govern-

ARCTIC OCEAN

North Cape

NORWAY

Rybachi Pen.

PETSAMO

MURMANSK
KOLA

NARVIK

SWEDEN

HAPARANDA

LULEÅ

Soviet
KARELIA

KEM

UMEÅ

FINLAND

VASA

LADOGA

Aaland Is.

ÅBO

HELSINKI

HANGO

KOTKA

VIIPURI

STOCKHOLM

PALDISKI

TALLINN

ESTONIA

LENINGRAD

Dagoe

Oesel

WINDAU

RIGA

U.S.S.R.

LIBAU

LATVIA

(MOSCOW)

LITHUANIA

KAUNAS

WILNO

DANZIG

EAST PRUSSIA

WILEJKA

MINSK

WARSAW

POLAND

German-
Russian
Frontier
of Sept. 28
1939

CRACOW

LWÓW

**Soviet
Baltic
Bases:**

Air Bases ◉

Naval Bases ▲   Army Bases ▦

Army, Naval and Air Bases ✪

ments in the three Baltic States, met and decided on the entry of these States into the Union of Soviet Socialist Republics.'

Thus the Baltic states disappeared as they had emerged. Old leaders and opponents of the new régime met the customary fate of such people. Peasants were apprehensive lest their holdings should be collectivised: on this important question Russia wisely temporised.

Thus, when Hitler attacked Russia, the Baltic states were occupied by Russian garrisons: Latvia and Estonia were again the scene of fierce fighting, and parts of the countries were ravaged. The conquering Germans attempted to raise local armies to fight by their side, but failed. The fact is, and always was, that the Baltic states wanted 'protection' neither from Germany nor Russia, but to be left alone by both.

Among one section in Lithuania there was a different reaction. Colonel Skirpa, the last Lithuanian Minister in Berlin, secretly organised a force to help the Germans when they marched against Russia. This force sustained 12,000 casualties in its actions against the Russian garrisons. These heavy losses were not rewarded by the independence which Skirpa had proclaimed. It was made clear that Lithuania had merely exchanged one form of occupation for another.

A Lithuanian puppet governor was found in General Kubiliunas, who had led the abortive pro-German *putsch* in 1934. He has a Lithuanian Council and a military police force, but of course the Germans are masters in the land. All three Baltic states are officially part of the German *Ostland*, under a governor-general.

It is somewhat strange that Lithuania, which leaned the closest of the Baltic states to Russia during the inter-war years, should now turn to Germany. But of course the puppet council of Kubiliunas is no more representative of Lithuania than was the Soviet created by Russia. There are opportunists in all the Baltic states anxious for careers: there are others who sincerely favour one side or another, and decide for Germany or Russia according to what they think are the best interests of their countries—confronted with the awkward alternatives of accepting one master or the other. But most citizens of the Baltic states long to be free.

VI

The Baltic states ought to re-emerge in some form or other after the war. They deserve it by their record: they are entitled to it by the principles of the Atlantic Charter. Yet the situation bristles with difficulties, and may prove a stumbling-block in the preparation of peace as it did in the negotiations of 1939. Considering the outstanding problems:

(*a*) Most of the German Balts have been removed: they are not likely to be welcomed back: when they are turned out of their temporary Polish homes, room will have to be made for them in Germany. For centuries Germany has looked to the Baltic shores as an outlet for expansion, in territory and power. This dream must fade for ever.

(*b*) Lithuania has a strong claim to the return of Memel, key to her economic system. In view of their intransigeance, it might be better to move the German part of the population to the west—this is certainly a case where the few must suffer inconvenience for the advantage of the many. With reason and common sense, Memel need never have become a problem at all: the Memel-landers will have to lose because of their own folly.

(*c*) The three states will probably want to unite as something closer than a Federation: they are too small to exist alone —will always be a temptation to any predatory power. Not merely defence and foreign policy should be common, but currency and economy generally.

(*d*) It would be to the advantage of all if the new combination made economic pacts with Russia. The Soviet could pass trade through Baltic harbours to the advantage of the countries concerned. Indeed, the Baltic ports will become increasingly important to Russia as her trade develops. Russia has a legitimate interest in the defence of the Baltic states: with the disarmament of Germany, already assumed as the basis of argument, the menace would have disappeared, and it may not be necessary to establish garrisons. In any case, it has been proved that these facilities are of no avail against an armed Germany.

(e) It might be to the advantage even of Russia if a strong chain of buffer states existed between her and Germany. The new Baltic bloc, therefore, might array itself in close contact with the Central European Federation of which Poland and Czechoslovakia appear likely to be the basis.

Alternatively, Lithuania may prefer to join outright the Polish-Czech Federation, while Estonia and Latvia would continue their independent existence, though naturally they would lie in a Russian sphere of influence. This does not necessarily imply occupation. Russia is interested in the Baltic states in exactly the same manner as Britain is interested in Holland and Belgium.

Whatever her future course, it is certain that Lithuania would gain by resuming her old and intimate co-operation with Poland.

(f) In this event, the problem of Vilna would lose most of its sting. I should certainly suggest a rectification of the frontier in favour of Lithuania which would bring many tens of thousands of Lithuanians under their own rule. I think the Polish claim to Vilna today is strong. With an easier atmosphere, a damping-down of patriotic propaganda and the bond of common suffering, a new era of close co-operation between Poland and Lithuania might be at hand.

In the long run, history is likely to judge the new peace treaties by the treatment meted out to small states who have suffered through no or small fault of their own. We have argued that our admiration for Russian valour must not blind us to the fact that Russian foreign policy, realistic though it may have appeared, has not always been in accordance with the spirit of the Atlantic Charter. While appreciating Russia's anxiety that Estonia, Latvia and Lithuania should not be used as a basis of German attack, few people would attempt to justify the method of incorporation into the Soviet Union. The Russian apologia is often misleading and in parts a travesty of the actions of people who merely wanted freedom. Today they lie under the German heel. After victory, they will be entitled to ask for justice. This can and should be reconciled with vital Russian requirements.

CHAPTER FIVE

FINLAND

I

IF you can imagine a considerable slice of Northern Canada projected into Europe, you have a fair idea of the character of the Finnish countryside. There are 60,000 lakes in the country, and 80,000 islands—many in the lakes, but thousands dotted off the irregular coastline. Coastal strips of varying widths permit a scientific agriculture, and support the greater part of Finland's 3½ million population. In the interior there are stretches of grazing-grounds, of waste land and of vast forests—the prime wealth of Finland.

The comparatively small population occupies the sixth largest country in Europe. Nevertheless, the natural resources are limited, and the northern half of the land Arctic in character, and it is doubtful if the country could support a population very considerably increased. The Finns make up in quality what they lack in quantity. They are one of the finest races in the world in physical build and mental capacity. Their educational system is one of the most advanced in Europe. One Finnish child in 76 attends a secondary school: one in 420 proceeds to a university—British figures are one in 100 and one in 1150 respectively. There is a healthy passion in Finland for education for its own sake, not for what one 'can get out of it': more than once I encountered farm labourers with university degrees.

Because, until 1918, Finland was part of Russia, there is a tendency to regard it as a primitive country of eastern civilisation. This is quite wrong: Finland lay under the Russian yoke for little more than a hundred years: its cultural affinities were always with Sweden. The Gulf of Bothnia was no more effective as a 'natural' barrier than a maze of lakes and forests.

THE BALTIC STATES, 1919–39

The Finns are of Finno-Ugrian stock, akin to the Magyars and Estonians; there is a suggestion of the Mongolian in their ethnic ancestry. The original tribes probably emigrated from Russia—there are still isolated and backward tribes of Finno-Ugrians in Central Russia. The Finns have occupied their present homeland for about eighteen hundred years.

In 1155 the Swedes invaded Finland—as usual, the invasion was euphemistically called a 'crusade.' It took even the valiant Swedes two hundred years to overrun their neighbour's territory, though the Finns were bound by the loosest of tribal associations; now a common frontier with Russia was established.

The Swedish hand was light. Swedes—at this time the most advanced race in Europe—settled in the coastal districts of the south, where their descendants still survive. From the fourteenth century to the present day men have referred to their fellows as 'Swedish Finns' or 'Finn Finns.' Finland was a semi-independent grand-duchy, with its own Parliament; the king of Sweden was the grandduke, and the influence of the 'Swedish Finns' was out of all proportion to their numbers—about 15 per cent of the population.

In the continual Swedish-Russian wars Finland was a favourite battleground. Peter the Great actually conquered the entire country, but contented himself with the annexation of Carelia. In 1809, however, Napoleon wanted the help of Russia in his Continental System of counter-blockade against Britain. Always generous with other people's property, he gave Finland to Russia.

There was no question of the submergence of Finland, which still retained its local government: its allegiance was merely transferred from the King of Sweden to the Tsar of Russia. At first the Russian interference was negligible, but towards the end of the nineteenth century a vigorous attempt at Russification was made: it may have had a religious background as important as the political: the Finns were strongly Protestant.

The inevitable effect of the campaign of Russification was to provoke the nationalism it strove to suppress. Perhaps for the first time Finns began to dream of a free Finland.

The semi-independent status of Finland is illustrated by the fact that the Finns were not conscripted for the Russian army. The 1917 revolution naturally brought confusion in its train. While Finnish peasants sympathised with the struggles of their fellows across the border for freedom, the insistent demand was for the independence of Finland. There was a period of civil war: Russian garrisons became 'Red Guards,' and sought to win Finland for Communism. There were scenes of terrible slaughter before the new Finnish government made a mistake: it asked for German assistance. This was at once granted, and the Russians were driven out. The Finns have been paying the price ever since. A relative of the Kaiser was nominated as king of Finland, and only the Allied victory saved the country from the fate of a German dependency.

It is quite wrong to dub the Finns as 'pro-German.' Many of the 'Swedish Finns' preferred Germans to Russians, but most people merely wanted to be Finns. Successive Finnish governments, however, were afraid to take action which might offend Germany: there was still a reasoned fear that one day Russia would march to the west, and that Germany would be the only power which would offer protection.

The post-war development of Finland was rapid. Today one family in three owns its own area of land. In a generation primitive agriculture has been replaced by modern methods, with State banking services and co-operative enterprises and marketing facilities. The standard of living is high, and the standard of health one of the highest in Europe. In its treatment of minorities Finland set an example to the world. There might have been some resentment against the 'Swedish Finns' because of the power they had wielded. Instead, Swedish ranked with Finnish as the official language: indeed, the proportional expenditure on Swedish-speaking educational facilities was higher than the Finnish. All educated Finns speak

Swedish as a second language: apart from local use, it has literary, cultural and commercial advantages.

The economic crisis of 1930 hit Finland hard. Somebody had to be blamed: the Communists suffered. They were not numerous, but were unpopular because they made no secret of their subservience to Russia—a country naturally suspect in a land it had held by force only a generation earlier. Eventually the Communist party was outlawed, but Fascism was not a real force in Finland, never holding more than 14 seats in a Parliament which was overwhelmingly controlled by the Social Democratic party.

The basis of Finnish foreign policy was the League of Nations. Finland and Sweden provided the League with one of its first successes. There was a dispute about the ownership of the Åland Islands: these had been classed as part of Finland for a long period, but were inhabited by Swedes. The League decided that they should be allocated to Finland, with certain reservations for local rights: both parties accepted the decision loyally: here, indeed, was a precedent that ought to have been followed more frequently. The economic value of the Åland Islands is not great, but their strategic importance is very high, as a glance at the map will show.

Apart from these islands, Finland's only territorial problem lay on the eastern frontier with Russia, north and east of Lake Ladoga. Here a Finnish tribe, the Carelians, straddles the frontier.

Carelia is the most primitive corner of Finland. Here western ideas mingle with those of the east: the province was conquered by Russia over two hundreds years ago, so passed a long spell under direct Russian rule. The country is not rich, which may account for the inferior physique of the Carelians: the long years of Tsarist rule may account for their lower mentality. Yet they are still Finns, although their dialect has absorbed many Russian words. They differ from their brothers over the border in religion—they adopted the Orthodox faith while under Russian rule.

On the Russian side of the frontier are about 140,000 Carelians. Between the present frontier and the White Sea they are in scattered settlements—this is poor and sparsely populated country at the best—but there is a compact bloc

Frontier of Russo-Finland · 1917
Frontier of Finland 1921–1940
Frontier of Carelian Republic in the U.S.S.R.
Carelian Finns
Leningrad-Murmansk Railway
White Sea Canal

CARELIA

between Lakes Ladoga and Onega. Although of limited economic value, the territory was of great sentimental interest to the Finns as the region associated with their national legend, the Kalevala—equivalent, shall we say, to the saga of Arthur and his knights in England. In 1918 the Carelians wished to join with Finland. The Russians refused to admit any Finnish claim, however, and the question became dormant. The frontier was never easy, and there were many 'incidents.' It is very doubtful, nevertheless, whether it would ever have disturbed the peace of Europe. Certainly it should not have.

II

Yet Carelia came into the headlines in October 1940. Estonia, Latvia and Lithuania had been forced to admit Russian garrisons. Now it was Finland's turn.

The Russian proposals stated that they were designed to secure the safety of Leningrad, and to ensure that Finland should never be used by a third power (unnamed, but which could only be Germany) as a base for an attack on Russia. For this purpose, Russia demanded (a) a number of Finnish islands in the Gulf of Finland, (b) the movement of the frontier between the Gulf and Lake Ladoga twenty miles further north, (c) cession of the Petsamo Peninsula in the far north, (d) destruction of Finland's frontier defences, (e) a lease of the port of Hango and a small territory about it. In return for the concessions, the Russians proposed to cede to Finland about 2100 square miles of Russian Carelia, which had a large Finnish population.

(In this offer, incidentally, Russia contradicted all her previous contentions that the Finns had no claim to Carelia. But this is not unknown in diplomatic usage.)

The Finnish reply was dignified. The cession of the islands was agreed. Even the frontier might be moved, but not to the extent the Russians demanded, since it passed through a purely Finnish district. (Further, the Russian demand would have meant the complete abandonment of the Mannerheim Line of defences.) But on Hango the Finns were firm. Here was their only port which was normally ice-free throughout the winter; its loss would be a severe economic blow. Further, a foreign garrison on Finnish soil implied the end of Finland's policy of neutrality.

As further negotiations failed, the Russian attitude changed:

a new propaganda campaign opened. It was claimed that the Finnish ruling class did not desire an agreement with Russia: soon, in the fashion of propaganda, the Finnish ruling class was plotting an attack on Russia! All the while, it seemed, the Finnish working classes were most anxious to secure friendly relations with the Soviet. Actually, no government was ever more firmly backed by its people than that of Finland at the moment of crisis.

The Soviet apologia scarcely varied from the usual pattern: foreign policy is not so strongly influenced by forms of internal government as might be imagined.

There was in the immediate post-war years a strong and legitimate Russian fear of German influence in Finland. The obvious policy was to ensure that Finland never became a *place d'armes* from which an attack on Russia might be made. The Russians did not quite appreciate, however, that neighbouring states did not change their outlook instantaneously merely because there had been a revolution. To the Finns, Russians were still Russians, even if they were Communists instead of Tsarists.

Nor did the Russians realise the delicate limitations of democracy: in Finland there was possible a freedom of expression which has not yet been known in Russia. Thus several patriotic Finnish organisations were formed whose objects were viewed with natural suspicion from Moscow. One of them, for example, fervently demanded the recovery of Eastern Carelia, with its Finnish population. The Russians accused this body of fomenting incidents along the disputed frontier.

The Russians certainly exaggerated the Fascist 'menace' in Finland. The largest representation the Fascists ever achieved was 14 members—out of 200. At the outbreak of war this had actually declined to 7. This can hardly be termed a 'menace,' even if the party were as vehemently wordy as its type. While it is true that comparatively small parties of Fascists (or Communists) with economic backing from home or abroad, can have an influence out of all proportion to their numbers, no observer could ever have classed Finland even as a potential Fascist state. The Fascist newspapers—and those of other Right-wing parties—were critical of some aspects of Soviet affairs, as were newspapers in other countries. States with a controlled press often have difficulty in understanding that an outburst in an obscure and privately owned newspaper does not necessarily reflect the views of the government or the people of the country in question.

The atmosphere of suspicion was dense: on the Finnish side, because of memories of Russian domination and fears that dreams of empire might recur; on the Russian side, because the Finns never attempted to hide their gratitude for the German help which had brought them freedom. It is possible to argue with nearly anything but suspicion.

The uneasy feeling between the two countries was emphasised after the rise of Hitler. It will be remembered that at this time he proclaimed the Russians as the enemies of mankind. In Finland Nazi agents opened their campaign, using the local Fascists for their purposes. As we have seen, they were not very successful. Finnish opinion varied. Many of the 'Swedish Finns' might be accused of being pro-German: many of the peasant farmers sympathised with their fellows over the frontier who had suffered under the Tsars. Yet it is quite wrong to label Finland as either pro-German or pro-Russian. The overwhelming feeling in Finland was in favour of neutrality.

It is claimed by the Russians that Hitler was about to seize Finland and the Baltic states when their ultimata were presented. It is doubtful if that was his plan—at that time. Such a move would have provoked hostilities with Russia at the very moment when he wished at all costs to avoid it. Nevertheless, the Soviet apprehensions were only too reasonable. The world's complaint lay not so much in the character of the Russian claims or the justification behind them, as in the manner of their presentation and execution.

In Finland, once the negotiations had broken down, the

Russians announced that the Finnish government did not really represent the people: if that were true, it was amazing how the Finns fought to back a government in which they had no confidence! A puppet government was formed on Russian soil, under an expelled Finnish Communist named Kuissinen: for a brief spell he held his little stage—in Russia; in Finland he was merely an object of ridicule: then, like Henlein in Sudetenland, was promptly dropped.

The first Russian campaign was disastrous. Apparently it was calculated that Finnish resistance would only be desultory—it may be true that the Russian leaders did believe their own assertions that the Finns were not behind their government.

Local troops of the Leningrad garrison crossed the frontier at nine points. When they had penetrated a sufficient distance into the areas with sparse communications, the Finns attacked their flanks. Victory after victory went to the highly mobile Finnish forces: the first-class mental and physical condition of the Finns showed its superiority.

The Russians at least learned their lesson. After two months of humiliating defeats at the hands of a much smaller opponent, an organised attack was mounted opposite the Mannerheim Line, between the Gulf of Finland and Lake Ladoga. This was no Maginot Line of expensive fortifications, but an adaptation of natural defences—lakes and forests. Then the weather, which had hitherto favoured the hardy Finns, now changed: the Gulf of Finland froze—a sea of smooth ice, over which the Russians could move to outflank their opponents.

The sentiment of the world had been stirred by the gallant resistance of the Finns. In Britain there were loud cries for intervention; even louder cries from France, where men of all parties were anxious that the battle should be fought on any other ground but that of France. An expedition was organised. Had it not been for the refusal of Norway and Sweden to permit the passage of armed forces, the Allies would have been at war with Russia!

The Finnish army was exhausted from its struggle against heavy odds. In face of the new, overwhelming and well-organised attack, disaster was inevitable. The Finnish government accepted the situation and peace was signed on March 13, 1940.

Up to this point Russian conduct of affairs had not appeared in a pleasing light: the whole episode seemed to resemble a Hitlerian interlude. There were suspicions that Stalin was reviving Tsarist imperial ambitions. The Russian-built railways from Leningrad pointed to Narvik, an ice-free port in Norway, on the open Atlantic: Russian ambitions had always been directed towards places on warm seas. In an espionage case in Sweden, it was shown that Russia was taking especially close interest in the railways of Northern Sweden.

Now Russia had Finland at her mercy: Germany was the only power which could have aided her late friends—and she stood ostentatiously on one side. If Russia had seized the whole of Finland, no one could have stopped her. Instead, she reverted to her original demands, with some additions. The lease of Hango was forced, certain rights of way and substantial additions were made to the demanded area north of Leningrad: this now covered all the Carelian Isthmus, including Viipuri, the second city of Finland, with a purely Finnish-Swedish population.

The Finns had no choice: they had to accept and then to sit back and bide their time. In Britain, the comparative moderation of Russia was missed in the disappointment of the Finnish collapse. Yet few people would claim that the Russians had been inspired in their plans. They had gained the defensive positions originally demanded, but at the cost of nearly 100,000 dead and a larger number of wounded. These quarter of a million trained men, with their equipment, might have turned the balanced scale of force a year later.

III

The Finnish losses were severe. That the Mannerheim Line had passed into Russian hands was not so serious, since it had shown that it could not survive a prolonged assault by a resolute, well-equipped, numerically superior enemy. The

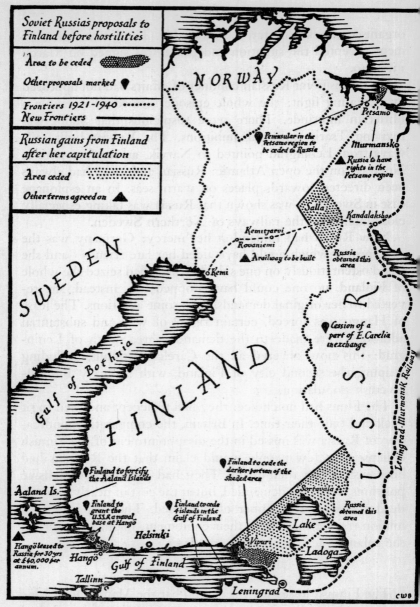

Soviet Russia's proposals to Finland before hostilities

Area to be ceded

Other proposals marked ♦

Frontiers 1921-1940 ·········
New Frontiers ——————

Russian gains from Finland after her capitulation

Area ceded ················

Other terms agreed on ▲

NORWAY

♦ Peninsular in the Petsamo region to be ceded to Russia

Petsamo

Murmansk

▲ Russia to have rights in the Petsamo region

SWEDEN

Salla

Kandalaksha

Kemijärvi
Rovaniemi

▲ A railway to be built

Russia obtained this area

o Kemi

♦ Cession of a part of E. Carelia in exchange

Gulf of Bothnia

FINLAND

U.S.S.R.

Leningrad-Murmansk Railway

Aaland Is.

♦ Finland to fortify the Aaland Islands

♦ Finland to grant the U.S.S.R. a naval base at Hango

♦ Finland to cede 4 islands in the Gulf of Finland

♦ Finland to cede the darker portion of the shaded area

Sortavala

Russia obtained this area

Lake Ladoga

▲ Hangö leased to Russia for 30 yrs at £40,000 per annum.

Hangö

Helsinki

Vipuri

Gulf of Finland

Tallinn

Leningrad

CWB

FINLAND: THE ORIGINAL DEMANDS AND THE AREAS ACTUALLY OCCUPIED BY
RUSSIA AFTER VICTORY

loss of Viipuri was a heavy economic blow; it had handled a quarter of the foreign trade of Finland: in the vicinity were important saw-mills and power stations.

The problem of evacuation was tremendous. In spite of the declarations of the puppet Kuissinen, few Finns wished to remain under Soviet rule, and over half a million fled to the main area of Finland. It is no small task to re-settle half a million people in a country where the total population is only 3½ millions. The lease of Hango was another severe economic blow—Finland's only ice-free port.

Finnish trade was crippled. Already the considerable commerce with Britain and the United States was almost stopped by the war. Possibilities of trade with Russia were limited, and Germany had little to offer in exchange for Finland's agricultural products. The consequent distress intensified the sullen resentment of the Finns. Nor were they likely to appreciate the Russian moderation in the hour of victory: to the Finns, the Russian seizure of strategic points seemed to be merely the beginning, as it had in the Baltic states.

When Hitler inevitably reverted to his original policy and decided to attack Russia, therefore, his agents found plenty of listeners in Finland. Long before the attack there were German divisions in the country—posted there by Hitler to prevent an attack on Finland by Britain! Alternative explanations were that the troops were merely in transit to Norway—or that they were not there at all! The country was now in an impossible situation. German and Russian armies were posted on its territory.

At the moment of the clash Finland hesitated. Even then, had Russia declared her intentions as straightforwardly as she did a few weeks later, Finland might have taken no part in the battle. The temptation was too great: here was an obvious opportunity to recover the lost national land.

In the early moments of a war the jingoes flourish. The patriotic societies which had aroused the suspicion of the Russians now came into their own. Not content with demanding the return of the lost provinces—in which demand they were supported by the bulk of the Finnish people—they went much further. Ancient claims, long dormant or discarded, were revived. Eastern Carelia must be returned to Finland: some enthusiasts cried for the extension of their country's frontiers as far as the White Sea—for the acquisition of the whole of the Carelian Soviet Republic. This, although including a large Carelian Finnish population, and although its character was admitted by its name, actually housed larger numbers of Russians—150,000 and 250,000 respectively.

For the second time Finland was at war: now she had a powerful ally. German-Finnish armies soon recovered the lost territory—except Hango, which held out for months against a siege not powerfully pressed. They reached the gates of Leningrad in the south: in the centre and north they were far into Russian territory. The jingoes were exuberant.

At this stage the friends of Finland abroad became anxious. There were few people in Britain who had no sympathy with the Finns: the fact that they were ranged beside Britain's enemies and against her allies was recognised as one of the strange turns of this strangest of wars. As they had not foreseen its amazing twists, they could scarcely blame the Finns for lack of foresight. Indeed, their outlook seemed logical enough.

The Russian government then made the right move—unfortunately, late in the day, as diplomacy often is. It declared that its policy had always been that implemented in the moderate peace treaty with Finland—to protect itself against German attack through Finnish territory. Now that attack had materialised and the defensive acquisitions had served their purpose, Russia had no quarrel with Finland, and was prepared to make peace based on recognition of the original pre-war frontiers of 1939.

This was a reasonable offer. It was backed (September 1941) by the British government in a note which emphasised that if the Finnish armies did not halt at the old frontiers and retire from the battle, their conduct in persisting with the fight must necessarily affect the terms of the eventual peace. This was followed later by a strong request from the United States that Finland should withdraw. Relations between Finland and the United States had always been close: the Finns in America are a virile and powerful community—and Finland was the only European country which had kept up its instalments of war debts.[1]

The Finnish position was difficult. Even if she made peace with Russia, German armies were on her soil, virtual masters of her fate. Further, distrust of Russia was still the paramount sentiment. If Russia won, who could guarantee that new demands would not be presented to a Finland unable to resist? The Finnish Labour party issued in October 1941 a manifesto which countered the jingo excesses by proclaiming that Finland sought no territorial acquisitions, but that from a military point of view it was necessary to fight on until the enemy was defeated, lest he should return. This point of view appears reasonable to all Finns; it could only be countered by a joint Anglo-*American*-Soviet guarantee of the old frontiers. At the same time there is a strong jingo element in Finland, exuberated by success and convinced that Germany will win, which still demands the extension of Finnish territory eastwards to the White Sea.

The predominant fact is, however, that the Finns are not now masters in their own house. Their policy is directed from Berlin, not Helsinki. There have been suggestions that the Finnish claims on Russia cover not only the lost territory, but include the whole of Carelia, Murmansk and the entire Kola Peninsula, bordering the White Sea, and territory as far south as Lake Ilmen—including Leningrad! If these terms are ever formally put forward, it will be important to remember that they are German terms, not Finnish.

Nor are the Russians likely to accept such terms on any conditions. Two of their 'life-lines' run through Carelia—the

---

[1] Technically they were not war debts, but American credits to Finland after the war for reconstruction.

railway from Leningrad to the ice-free port of Murmansk, and the Stalin Canal, which links Lakes Onega and Ladoga with the White Sea at Soroka, on the railway to Murmansk.

IV

The British declaration that Finland's fate at the conclusion of victory depended upon her conduct during the war was logical enough, yet it clashes to some extent with the second point of the Atlantic Charter.

Not even the Russians pretended that the Carelian Isthmus was anything but Finnish territory, historically and ethnically. Their argument was purely strategic—and was strong. There are limits to individual and national rights. If my neighbour shows a light during an air raid, then I am justified in taking strong action, since I am likely to suffer as well as he. The Russian defence of Leningrad was obviously prejudiced by the narrow hinterland to the north. It was unfortunate that circumstances of history and suspicion made it difficult for Russia to trust Finland's will to neutrality; and that, like other Great Powers, she was unduly sensitive of the influence and strength of those ultra-patriotic groups which have done so much in all lands to destroy prospects of peaceful understanding.

(*a*) In the post-war settlement it can be argued that, as the German menace has now been dissolved, the original frontiers on the Carelian Isthmus should be resumed, perhaps with minor modifications.

(*b*) The Carelian frontier, further north, ought to present no real difficulty. Ethnically Finland might be entitled to demand modifications particularly in the area between Lakes Ladoga and Onega. On the other hand, many Russian settlers have been planted in sparsely populated Carelia in recent years. It has been suggested that the Finns would not welcome these as co-citizens, since their political creed might be infectious—or that their presence would give the Russian government grounds for interference! This last phrase indicates the intensity of suspicion in this corner of Europe: even the most elementary move is examined with a view to the discovery of underlying and nefarious objects.

Apart from the question of defeat, it is doubtful if the Finns would present serious claims in a moment of sanity. Their losses have been large; they will need all their energies in rebuilding their stricken country: and, of course, they will be on the losing side. Eastern Carelia would be no great economic asset, except for its communications to Murmansk—its main interest to the Finns is one of sentiment. An exchange of populations would involve bringing many more Finns into Finland than Russians into Russia, but they would serve to make good the reduced man-power of Finland and to populate some of the semi-deserted areas.

The United States has throughout the war maintained diplomatic relations with Finland, and the policy has paid handsome dividends. Because of American influence, the Finns successfully modified German plans to use Finland as a base of attack against Russia, and the Finnish armies halted virtually on their own frontiers. America said, in effect: 'Stay there, and we will do our best for you. Move further, or allow the Germans to move further, and you take what you get.' This astute diplomatic policy not merely secured Leningrad against attacks from the north, but probably saved the important port of Murmansk. Naturally, the Germans may seek to break down the plan when conditions get desperate.

A sincere settlement is essential and by no means impossible. In Britain and America at any rate there is no animosity towards the Finns: nor is there likely to be. They have been the sports of fate, involved in cataclysms not of their own making. The average Britisher or American can put himself in the Finns' place without difficulty. If Russia, too, will agree to a generous peace, then there is a real prospect of that friendly understanding between Russia and Finland which is essential to the peace and prosperity of both. This is one of the questions which may be settled before the end of the general war or by Finland asking for terms.

CHAPTER SIX

ROUMANIA

I

ROUMANIA ought to be one of the happiest countries in Europe. It has been favoured by Nature far beyond all others of the Balkan states. Here are large areas of fertile soil, providing adequate supplies of food for the population and an ample surplus for export: fine forests, and important oil wells which by their products replenish the foreign currency which other Balkan countries lack so badly. Add to these advantages a fine sturdy peasantry. Roumania *ought* to be one of the happiest countries in Europe—but it isn't.

Perhaps the turbulent history of the land is partly to blame. The Roumanians claim that their race is of Roman origin. Certainly their language has a Latin base, even if it has now been contaminated by borrowings from neighbouring tongues. For Roumania was the ancient Roman province of Dacia: there Trajan's legions settled, to stay until the barbarian onslaught on Rome called many home. By this time the local peasant population had been partially assimilated: now it was subject to the flow of the warring tribes from the east, and each successive invasion left its mark on the culture, language and characteristics of the local people. Considering the many vicissitudes of its history, the Romanic language of Roumania is a remarkable survival.

For hundreds of years the Roumanian nation disappears from historical records: not until the thirteenth century does its authentic history begin. At that time there were two independent principalities, Moldavia and Wallachia, with very mixed populations. After centuries of intensive combat and assaults from without, and after periods of subjection to

Polish and Hungarian overlords, the provinces fell to the
Turkish invaders; for nearly four hundred years the Turks
were masters of what we now call Roumania. Their rule was
inefficient and corrupt. Governorships and official posts were
openly sold, a system which proved lucrative to their holders
but miserable for the unfortunate peasants. Not until 1774 did
Moldavia and Wallachia receive even a modicum of self-
government: for nearly a century they served as pawns in the
long contest between Russia and Turkey.

By this time, however, national consciousness had been

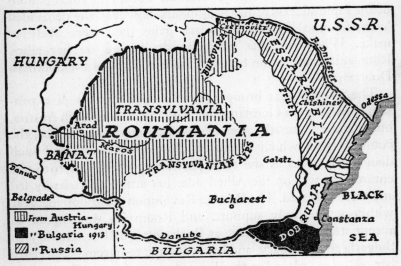

ROUMANIA, 1919–39

aroused, as the revivifying echoes of the French Revolution
reverberated even over the distant plains of the Danube. In
1857 the two principalities voted for union and freedom, and
two years later these were forced by the Great Powers from
the unwilling Turks.

At that time the country was impoverished, suffering from
centuries of misrule. Nor were the early years of the new state
happy: its politicians had been trained in Turkish courts, and

the unfortunate peasant seemed to gain little from his change of governors. Nevertheless a patriotic spirit slowly prospered, and by 1879 the full independence of Roumania was recognised.

Although Moldavia and Wallachia were predominantly Roumanian in population, they housed large minorities. Even larger numbers of Roumanians were, however, still exiled beyond the national frontiers. Vacillations of foreign policy failed to raise Roumania's prestige: nor was this heightened by her conduct during our own lifetime. She stood aside when Greece, Serbia and Bulgaria attacked Turkey in 1912: jealous of the rapid success of her neighbours, however, she demanded 'compensation' for the territorial gains they were likely to make. When Bulgaria treacherously turned on her allies, Roumania marched on her neighbour and seized the Southern Dobrudja.

The World War brought further opportunities of expansion. The king—a German—had made an alliance with Austria, but popular sympathy was overwhelmingly with France, the country from which Roumania drew her culture and such democratic ideas as she then possessed. In August 1916 she entered the war on the Allied side: her armies were badly led and were defeated. The Russian Revolution the following year withdrew her only support, and Roumania was forced to accept stern terms of peace at Bucharest. She lost territory to Bulgaria and Hungary, and her economic resources—especially her oil—were placed at the disposal of the Central Powers.

The Allied victory in 1918 relieved Roumania from her bondage—she hastily declared war again, so as to share in the benefits accruing to a combatant, and marched into Hungary. In the subsequent peace treaties she made huge territorial gains. The Southern Dobrudja was recovered from Bulgaria; Transylvania, part of the Banat, and Bukovina were taken from Austria-Hungary: Bessarabia had already been seized from Russia in the throes of the Revolution. Territory and population alike were more than doubled. But, out of her 17 million people, 30 per cent were non-Roumanians. It is the presence of these large minorities which has led to trouble in Roumania.

Nor was the post-war policy of successive governments always helpful. Democratic ideas clashed sadly with traditional interests. Elections were generally 'managed'; bribery and corruption were rife. Indeed, in the low moral sense of the governing classes lies perhaps the principal clue to Roumanian discontent: not that it is a monopoly of this unhappy land.

Bribery has always been a feature of Balkan politics. It is a Turkish legacy, and could scarcely be eradicated in a couple of generations. The men who took over the control of the reborn Roumania had been trained in Turkish methods and knew no others. Drastic reform was not considered possible, and bribery and corruption continued as a feature of official life.

We often see and hear eulogies of the British civil service. Most of them are deserved, for it is indeed the best in the world. Yet its outstanding feature usually passes unnoted, taken for granted—it is incorruptible. No one who does not know the East or the Balkans can appreciate all that this means. If you go to interview a British official it is useless to flourish pound notes—unless you wish to appear in the dock on a charge of attempted bribery. If you go to interview a Roumanian official, you don't stand much chance of getting very far unless you *do* flourish currency notes.

The people who make cheap jokes about 'soft jobs' in the British civil service ought to go to Roumania. There officials are everywhere, and some form of permit is necessary for the most trifling occasions. The law concerned is not necessarily repressive in intent, but it is useful to provide a horde of jobs for friends of politicians. There is a lot to be said for a service recruited by competitive examination: it may produce some misfits, but it excludes jobbery, which is a hundred times more serious. In Roumania one of the first acts of a new government is to dismiss its civil servants and to replace them with its own friends. The Goga-Cuza administration was only in office for six weeks, but when it fell the new government dismissed 25,000 civil servants who had been appointed during those six weeks!

Of course, Roumania is not alone in its use of the 'spoils' system—in the Balkans it is quite common. The official knows that he may lose his job at the next election, so he makes as much as he can while he is in office. With certain outstanding exceptions, many of the Roumanian politicians have set the pattern for their employees. If you think I exaggerate or that my experiences were exceptional, ask any business man of your acquaintance who has ever tried to trade with Roumania.

Corruption is encouraged by low salaries. A general gets £25 a month: while the cost of living—actual living, food, housing and service—is much lower than in England or America, on his official pay alone he could scarcely maintain the status of a provincial bank manager. Even a Cabinet Minister gets only £40 a month—officially. Civil service clerks are paid about 30s. a week, and a skilled labourer is lucky if he makes £1. That is to say, nearly everybody feels bound to add to his salary or wage by any means, illicit or otherwise. The tragedy is therefore that graft is accepted as normal in Roumania because nearly everybody practises it. When government loans are floated, it is an understood thing that a due proportion of the proceeds will go into the pockets of the ministers concerned. They can scarcely complain when their subordinate staffs imitate their methods. To the credit of King Carol, he made determined efforts in his period of dictatorship to eradicate this menace, but even he would admit that his efforts were only partially successful.

My first visit to Roumania was made in 1933. I was arrested two or three times a day as I wandered about the unfrequented countryside. There was no venom in the arrests. The Roumanian policeman was paid 12s. or 13s. a week, and his pay was often months in arrear. Whenever he needed ready cash, therefore, he arrested somebody. A shilling or so passed, and the arrest was easily revoked. Being British and pig-headed, I refused to pay the shilling, which caused me to waste a lot of time in police stations. What appalled me was the manner in which this petty tyranny was accepted by everybody as a normal thing. When I got to Bucharest and mentioned to a friend, an educated man—a university professor, in fact—that I had crossed Roumania on a bicycle without expending a penny on bribes, he refused to believe the feat possible.

I had, of course, heard many stories of Roumanian corruption, but was prepared to believe that they were grossly exaggerated for propaganda purposes. But when I complained of my own experiences, Roumanians protested that I was comparatively well treated. Many of the casual incidents of the wayside were disquieting.

I remember making a short journey by train. Armed police or soldiers were everywhere: after buying tickets, the passengers were herded into a waiting-room, under guard, only to be released when the train arrived. Once in the train both ticket collectors and detectives came along—apparently railway travel was forbidden in Roumania without a passport. In many cases you must get special permission before travelling at all. In my train were two peasants, brothers, who were journeying to visit a sick relative. The detectives discovered that one of the men had forgotten his passport and he was promptly bundled off the train at the next station, to be sent back to his home station.

I saw peasants treated in such fashion as would have raised a riot in England. I saw a peasant pleading with the police; he had brought a calf to market, and they would not let him sell it until he had paid the marketing tax. He could not pay the tax until he had sold the calf—and he had to take it back to his farm.

The petty corruption is almost beyond belief. The maze of officials is incredible. I never yet succeeded in posting and registering a parcel in Roumania under half an hour—as a Commissioner of Police warned me, unless I registered it, there was little hope of its reaching its destination. The complaints I heard on every hand were astounding—of petty bribery necessary for the simplest transaction. These complaints came from Roumanians as well as minorities. I repeat that I would not have been so concerned except that the system was accepted as inevitable by rich and poor alike. It is not unknown in other Balkan countries.

I want to be quite fair to Roumania—indeed, I am very fond of this lovely land. To her great credit must be placed the very correct conduct at the time of the Czechoslovak crisis, when she was one of the few states which did not attempt to avoid her obligations. I crossed from west to east in 1937, and I found a state of affairs much happier. My daily average of arrests dropped from three to one: if the police were warned of my coming, I had nothing but civility at their hands. The local peasants, however, complained just as frequently as before. Roumania is the worst police-ridden state in Europe, Russia not excepted. It is annoying when a village policeman holds you up for an hour staring suspiciously at your passport. As he cannot read English, you wonder why he finds it so interesting. At last you find that he can only read his own language with difficulty, a word at a time.

King Zog of Albania was up against the same problem, and solved it with the assistance of a dozen British officers. No one in Roumania has yet been brave enough to tackle it. If Britain ever felt especially friendly to Roumania, she might loan them a spare departmental permanent secretary, to reform the executive administration; an officer of the Exchequer and Audit—although the poor man would probably die of fits; a chief constable from Scotland Yard, who would be appalled as he filled his jails with his own policemen; and half a dozen second-division clerks, those handymen of the civil service. Or maybe what Roumania really needs is a Harley Street specialist. I am no friend of dictators, but a man of principle, incorruptible, just and firm, could work miracles in Roumania in five years of power.

The Roumanian government must be held responsible for the low standard of life and commerce. There are some countries in Europe where men must fight a continuous battle with Nature for a mere livelihood, but Roumania is comparatively rich. The difficulties besetting her trade are largely man-made. I can never get used to the sight of peasants who grow enough food for their families and a large surplus for sale, but have neither shoes on their feet nor a penny in their pockets.

Communications—or the lack of them—are largely responsible for peasant poverty. Over great areas of Roumania there are no real roads, but only dust-tracks. Agricultural marketing depends on rapid communications, Roumanian trade remains local. A striking exception is to be found in the German settlements. Here the peasants have not waited for the government, but have made roads for themselves.

A correlated problem is that of the Jews, who form about 7 per cent of the population. When the big estates of the landlords were carved up, little farms were handed out to the peasants. But this was not enough—a farmer needs capital as well as land. In almost every village I found one shopkeeper, a Jew. In bad times the peasants come to him for money, and he takes up mortgages on their farms. There can be few peasants in Roumania who do not owe money to the local Jew. Thus, when some fanatic extremist comes along preaching anti-Semitism, the peasants listen to him. Their outlook is very limited. They know little of tariffs or world affairs; but if the Jew is blotted out, then their debt is void.

As in Poland, the problem of the Jews is a real one in Roumania. The Jews have never been incorporated in the local population—until 1830, indeed, they were classed as vagabonds, without rights of any kind. Today they are not merely the village shopkeepers and financiers, but have something near to a monopoly of the professional posts. Some 70 per cent of the doctors and lawyers of Roumania are Jews. The universities are full of Jews. It might be argued that they deserve their success—that the Jew must be more virile and intelligent than the Roumanians. But naturally the Roumanians don't quite hold that point of view.

Roumania has been ill-served by its political parties. The Peasants' party and the Liberals (who are not Liberals, but Conservatives) followed traditional lines, and had many honest, capable and well-meaning men in their ranks. Unfortunately these were swamped by grafters and place-seekers. The extremist creeds promised little peace for Roumania. The Communists, if only because of geography, were in close touch with Russia, and had little chance of capturing the popular vote—for Russia was *not* popular in Roumania. The Fascist organisations, like the Iron Guard, ran true to type: one of their happiest expressions of political argument was the murder of a rival as he lay sick in hospital.

The weakness of democratic ideas of course played into the hands of the Iron Guard, which began as a Roumanian idealist youth organisation, gravitated towards Fascism with gangster methods, and finished as a Nazi auxiliary. For a time it was successfully countered by King Carol, who after his return from exile in 1930 was virtually dictator of the country. Today General Antonescu, who after the king's second flight in September 1940 succeeded him as dictator, openly affects the Iron Guard uniform.

From the moment the Peace Treaties were signed in 1919, it was obvious that the defeated powers harboured wide ideas about revision. Hungary was especially active. With the beneficent backing of France, the Little Entente was formed —an agreement between Czechoslovakia, Yugoslavia and Roumania for the maintenance of the *status quo* and to check Hungarian revisionism. Later, Roumania was included in the Balkan Pact, which was aimed in similar fashion against Bulgaria.

The economic crisis of 1930 seriously weakened the power of the Balkan states, and made them especially susceptible to German economic pressure after the rise of Hitler. The policy of anti-revisionism was held firmly in all the satiated states. Nevertheless there were anxious eyes turned towards France, when one after another of the clauses of the Peace Treaties were openly defied without opposition. The seizure of Austria

was viewed with justifiable alarm, for within a year the Little
Entente had been destroyed by the elimination of Czechoslovakia, its strongest member. Roumania gained a minor degree

THE BALKANS, 1919–39

of confidence from the Franco-British guarantee, but there
was always expressed justifiable doubt as to how the guarantee
could be substantiated.

At the outbreak of war Roumania had a mutually-defensive pact with Poland against Russia. She made no attempt to implement it when the Russians marched into Poland: nor can she be blamed for that, for such a move would have been suicidal. Esteeming the implications but suspicious of the practical value of the Franco-British guarantee, Roumania turned to the other Balkan powers for joint security. In February 1940 it seemed that Balkan unity had never been so strong. Both Hungary and Bulgaria had intimated that they did not propose to press their revisionist claims until after the war, and a genuine desire was obvious among the south-eastern states to keep clear of the war.

At the same time, serious attention was given to Roumanian defences. The long frontiers provided few natural obstacles, but hundreds of thousands of conscripts laboured on the making of the defensive system popularly known as 'Carol's Moat.' The country could not afford fortifications on the Maginot scale, but a vast system of works began after Munich. The main feature was an enormous ditch, fed by water from adjacent rivers, and alleged to be a permanent obstacle to tanks. The defensive plan was almost melodramatic; oil was to float on the surface of the water, to be set alight at the critical moment.

Behind the moat was a series of trenches, pill-boxes and strong points. Like nearly all the fortifications erected in Europe at such vast expense, Carol's Moat was never used. The strongest fortifications in the world are useless unless held by men of stout heart, well-equipped and well-led. In any case, Hitler avoided frontal assaults: like ourselves, the Roumanians did not read *Mein Kampf* seriously enough. They devoted much to the strengthening of their frontiers but ignored the threat to their inner defences; their national unity was disintegrated by a mixture of personal ambition and foreign intrigue. Carol's Moat was really forced, not on the frontiers, but in Bucharest.

The summer of 1940 saw the situation completely changed.

The collapse of France did more than wreck the slender security of the Allied guarantee; it was a moral shock to Roumania, so long dependent on France for cultural and practical ideas. If France, idealised beyond her real strength in Roumania, could not stand up to Germany, who could? The entry of Italy into the war altered the whole strategic situation. The German seizure of Denmark, Norway, Holland and Belgium had already shown that small countries no longer had any 'rights.' There were signs that Russia held expansionist ideas, and German economic pressure was becoming intense.

In the following sections we shall discuss subsequent events by which the territory of Roumania was roughly reduced by half. In vain she appealed to Germany, hastily dropping all semblance of sympathy with defeated France or fighting Britain. The Allied guarantee was denounced (July 1st, 1940), and a 'reorientation' of Roumanian policy foreshadowed 'as determined by the new European order in course of establishment.' That is to say, Roumania was now under German influence and control.

Nevertheless national pride was severely wounded by the loss of Roumanian provinces—which only a few weeks earlier had been emphatically proclaimed as 'Roumanian for ever, to be defended with the last drop of our blood.' Humble people often believe the grandiloquent assertions of politicians. King Carol, who had been the dominant figure in the land, became the scapegoat of the hour. On September 8th he abdicated in favour of his son Michael. The Iron Guard had taken the lead in the anti-royal indignation, and, true to its type, attempted to murder him as he left the country. General Antonescu now became 'Leader of the Roumanian People,' virtually dictator: Roumania found itself a Fascist state, with the Iron Guard as the only political party. It was soon obvious that the new 'Leader' was little more than a puppet, the controlling strings being manipulated in Berlin.

First, German 'technical experts' arrived to train the Roumanian army. Doubtless it needed the training, but the 'experts' soon assumed the proportions of an army of occupation. Before 1940 was out, there could be no further dissimulation. Roumania was completely in the German grip: from her plains German armies passed into Bulgaria, eventually to attack Yugoslavia and Greece. The Balkan Pact, so strong a year earlier, was now implicitly dissolved: 'one by one' the Balkan states fell to the aggressor.

When Germany attacked Russia, the Roumanian government found itself forced into the war it had tried so warily to avoid. Roumanian troops moved willingly enough to the recovery of Bessarabia. Then it became obvious that they were pawns in the German game. They were flung against the defences of Odessa, ill-armed and ill-trained. They were heavily involved in the disasters at Stalingrad and in the Caucasus. Their tremendous losses caused a wave of disillusion and anger to sweep over Roumania. Were it not for the forbidding presence of German garrisons, it would be reasonable to prophesy early revolution in Roumania. It can only be delayed: and it is badly needed.

Before considering the prospects of the new Roumania, it is necessary to examine in general detail some of the territorial problems which have first to be solved.

II

On June 26th, 1940, the Russian Foreign Minister handed an ultimatum to the Roumanian Minister in Moscow; it was short but severe. Within twenty-four hours the province of Bessarabia and the northern half of Bukovina were to be handed over. If this demand (described as 'applying peaceful methods to diplomatic issues') were not met, then there was no room to doubt the character of the next move.

Bessarabia, the land between the rivers Pruth and Dniester, was an outlying province of the Roman Empire, the easternmost part of Dacia. It was strongly fortified to resist barbarian invaders, and traces of its ancient walls still survive. After the usual Balkan vicissitudes, it was settled by Roumanians in the fourteenth century, and Roumanian princes ruled the land until the coming of the Turks.

Under Turkish rule Bessarabia was part of the principality of Moldavia, which was allowed a modicum of self-government under its own princes or governors—sometimes Roumanians (or Moldavians—at this period the terms were synonymous), sometimes Turks or Greeks. In 1812 the province became Russian—the transfer was represented as the delivery of the Christian Roumanians from the tyranny of the Moslem despots. The peasants were not so sure; they had at least some personal freedom, whereas the Russian peasants were serfs. Fearing the same fate, the 'delivered' peasants began to move west, back to the 'tyranny of the Moslem despots.' The Turks, indeed, were overwhelmed with immigrants. They settled the difficulty in the fashion of the day. Declaring that there was an attack of plague in Bessarabia, they massacred the unfortunate peasants who tried to cross the river Pruth.

The Russian population in Bessarabia was never very large; it consisted mainly of landowners, together with the soldiers and officials required for the administration of the province. The towns were rapidly occupied by Jews—who, as we have seen, were banished from Russia proper to the provinces. The peasants, however, were largely Roumanians, with important minorities of Bulgars, Germans, Ukrainians and others. Once they found that serfdom was not to be introduced, a change of sovereignty meant little to them—peasants only want to be left alone. They made no attempt to resist the prevailing Russification, and by 1914 less than 15 per cent could read or write the Roumanian language. Tens of thousands could not even speak it. Under the Russian régime, no one was allowed to learn to read and write in Roumanian unless he had first learned to read and write in Russian. Priests were compelled to conduct their services in Russian. Another half-dozen generations, and the people of Bessarabia would have been classed as Russian. This in spite of the fact that only 30 per cent of the population was Russian or Ukrainian, including troops and officials: for that matter most of the other Russians and Ukrainians in Bessarabia had entered the province since its conquest.

For once there is no serious dispute between figures as to the racial characteristics of the province. Russian figures at the taking over in 1812 showed it as 86 per cent Roumanian: by 1862 this had been reduced to 75 per cent—by the introduction of Russian and German colonists. Even in 1897, when the Russian census counted as Russians all those who understood any Russian, the figures showed 47 per cent of Roumanians, as against 19.5 per cent Ukrainians, 11.8 per cent Jews, and only 8 per cent Russians. In 1915 the Russian figures showed over 70 per cent of the population of Bessarabia as Roumanian. Thus, despite the process of Russification, Bessarabia has always been predominantly Roumanian in its racial character.

In the early stages of the Russian Revolution, Kerensky recognised the principle of autonomy for Bessarabia. A National Assembly was convoked at Chishinev, the capital. Naturally, it was not elected—revolutionary assemblies never are. Subsequently, the Bolsheviks complained that the Council was composed exclusively of big landlords. At the same time Russian Imperialists claimed that it was a Bolshevik organisation! Actually, it was formed of bourgeois elements—teachers, lawyers, farmers and the like—the men who normally lead a peasant community at a time of crisis.

Ukraine was at this time a separate republic, under German influence, so that Bessarabia was cut off from Russia. Disbanded Russian soldiers were looting in Bessarabia, and the National Council appealed *both to Russia and Roumania*. Russian troops were sent but promptly joined the pillagers. A Roumanian force helped to restore order, but the original declaration of an independent republic could scarcely be implemented. It was threatened by the new Ukraine, and the Roumanian army was in occupation by invitation. On April 8th, 1918, the National Council passed a resolution demanding union with Roumania by 86 votes to 3; there were 36 abstentions, but most of them were men who were anxious to proceed more leisurely and by democratic methods. There is little doubt that the vote represented the prevailing wish in Bessarabia.

This summary of events is rather important. It shows that there was no question of a 'seizure' of Bessarabia by Roumania, but a voluntary act on the part of its people.

Ethnically, the Roumanian claim could scarcely be questioned, considering Bessarabia as a whole. The withdrawal of troops and officials lowered the proportion of the Russian and Ukrainian population to little more than 20 per cent, while Roumanians form nearly 60 per cent. The remainder are divided between Jews and the other minorities.[1]

For fifteen years the Soviet government utterly refused to recognise the transfer of Bessarabia. The railway bridge over the Dniester at Tighina remained in its war-time condition of ruin, and there was no communication between the two countries. There was suspicion in Roumanian circles that Russian agents fomented discontent among Bessarabian peasants, but this was probably due to the appalling economic conditions— and to suspicion that other provinces were more favourably treated by the central government.

More than once Russia demanded a plebiscite, but Roumania refused. She could be confident as to the result, but refused to admit the Russian claim at all. She could point to successive election results, which showed no trace of separatist sentiment. Russian official maps, however, still continued to show Bess-

[1] The census of 1930 showed the following amazing medley of races in Bessarabia and illustrates the difficulty of frontier-drawing in Eastern Europe.

Roumanians	1,610,757	Greeks	2,044
Russians	351,912	Albanians	1,809
Ukrainians	314,211	Armenians	1,509
Jews	204,858	Hungarians	829
Bulgars	163,726	Turks	541
Germans	81,089	Czechoslovaks	540
Gagauz (*Christian Turks*)	98,172	Yugoslavs	345
Gypsies	13,518	Others	10,438
Poles	8,104		

arabia as Russian territory temporarily alienated. Nor did the Roumanians seem convinced that the return of their inheritance was permanent.

When I wandered about this depressing province, I wondered why either country should be so eager to possess it. Its bare ridges and valleys are almost treeless, and the biting winds of the steppes can add treachery even on a sunny day. Not even in Albania have I seen worse roads. As I struggled on a bicycle from Jassy to Chishinev it was incredible to think that this dust-track was the main road between two important cities. Villages were infrequent, and often I would ride—or push—for two or three hours without meeting a human being. There was an air of neglect about the countryside: vineyards ill cared for and unproductive: fertile land lying fallow: drainage and irrigation schemes abandoned. What was the use of anything? peasants asked me. I could not answer. What *is* the use of working hard to produce more food if it is simply to rot in your barns? There is no starvation in Bessarabia, but an appalling lack of all other essentials. I passed through one village and saw only one pair of boots. These belonged to a young mother who was carrying her baby to church to be blessed. She was carrying her boots too—they were too precious to be worn except for the actual ceremony in the church.

I have argued—without opposition, I think—that many of the troubles of Europe are fundamentally economic. The pity is that many of them are so completely unnecessary. There must be thousands of families in Britain where an extra loaf of bread every week would be a godsend: in Bessarabia there are barns full of rotting grain. In Northamptonshire it often happens that there are thousands of boot- and shoe-makers out of work: in Bessarabia there are hundreds of thousands of people who walk barefoot, or with a piece of old automobile tire fastened to their soles. This is called an economic problem: world conferences are called to solve it, and fail. If you were a Northamptonshire shoemaker and I were a Bessarabian peasant we should solve it in about ten minutes—if we could once get into touch with each other. But the moment nationalism enters the scene, the most simple problem becomes immensely complicated.

I was not surprised at the peasant's grumbles. He lives in a shack of mud and timber, often built in a day: usually one room has to serve his large family. Meals are monotonous—although he has an ample supply of food, it is all of a kind: I ate *mamaliga*—boiled grain, very podgy—till I never wanted to see it again. Only in the fruit season is there real variety of diet. Of modern conveniences the peasant has none: his home is furnished in primitive fashion—when I arrived in Bessarabia I had ridden across Europe from Holland, and many a Dutch cow is better housed than honest Bessarabian peasants. The policemen patrolling the streets are fully armed, and inspire fear rather than confidence. The peasant is inevitably in debt to local Jews: but the Jews themselves are hard-pressed since trade is so negligible. The government has instituted a system of State loans, but as is usual in the Balkans excellent paper schemes seldom materialise.

I found grave discontent throughout the land. Bessarabian peasants complained that they had not been treated as long-lost brothers, but as a subject tribe. Their local councils were abolished and the province was administered by the central government at Bucharest. Taxation was high, and economic distress was rampant. While it is true that thousands of peasants shared in the division of the land, their natural market was gone. Prior to the last war, Bessarabia had been part of the granary of Russia. Now a closed frontier prohibited natural exports, while hopeless communications hindered trade in the opposite direction. In any case, Roumania already had a large surplus of the agricultural products which Bessarabia offered.

Communications are the economic key to Balkan problems. In Bessarabia there are only 530 miles of railway track to serve its area of 17,000 square miles. Most of this is of modern construction. The Roumanians were certainly unfortunate. For years they put off complaints by saying that all would be well when the railway to Chishinev was completed. As soon as this was done, the world slump intervened, and the Bessarabian peasant was worse off than before. There is only one bridge connecting Roumania with Bessarabia over the marsh-lined valley of the river Pruth. Without exception the roads are appalling. Only 60 miles are scheduled as 'passable' in all weathers, which means that they are approximately equivalent to an English country lane. The rest are just dust-tracks, negotiated only by wooden carts drawn by unshod ponies. When I crossed Bessarabia on a bicycle, I found it quite impossible to ride along the roads. My only hope was to make a precarious passage on the verge, where thousands of bare feet had beaten out a narrow path of moderate firmness.

It was claimed that the neglect of Bessarabian communications was deliberate; that Russian invasion was inevitable, and the advancing army would be hampered by the poor roads. The argument was unjustifiable, for Roumanian fortifications were concentrated along the Dniester, which offered a strong natural defensive position. Thus, had it come to a fight, the Roumanians and not the Russians would have had the disadvantage of poor communications behind them. My own impression was that the Roumanian neglect of Bessarabia was dictated largely by fear—by uncertainty about the designs of their powerful neighbour.

I found that the trade of Bessarabia was largely in the hands of the Jews—the Balkan peasant is seldom a good man of commerce. Some of the towns house a Jewish majority, and every village has its shop, owned by a Jew who is more than a retailer—he is the local financier, and a keen financier at that. Any village Jew would change a pound note for me, usually giving more than the official rate of exchange. His commercial ability and his inherited tradition as a money-lender implied that he held mortgages on many peasant properties. This meant inevitably that he was unpopular. The anti-Semite party of Professor Cuza won striking victories in Bessarabia in the last 'free' elections.

Cuza was also violently anti-Communist. I must record that

I found little leaning towards Communism in Bessarabia—except among the younger generation of Jews. Even the Russians and Ukrainians were seldom Communist in their outlook—although culturally they still looked to the eastern bank of the Dniester. I heard Russian music played in the towns and villages: the few books available in the Russian districts were pre-Revolution classics. The Slav is inherently sentimental, and the exiled tribes in Bessarabia still looked to Russia as their homeland even though they might not appreciate its political system.

This tends to confirm the theories of Marx and Engels, that Communism would arise in the industrialised lands and that the backward peasant states would be the last reactionaries. That in fact it actually arose in Russia was due to two unpredictable factors—first the war with its reaction on Russian *morale*, and secondly, the genius of Lenin. Moreover, even Russian Communism was essentially a product of the town proletariat—the peasant communities took to it only with reluctance.

At the same time there were complaints among the Russians in Bessarabia of harsh treatment by the Roumanian police. So far as I could trace, these were justified—but not in the sense that the Russian peasants were selected for special persecution. To me the behaviour of the Roumanian police to their own peasants was unpardonable.

By 1938 there were signs that the tension over Bessarabia was easing; it seemed that Russia and Roumania might find themselves fighting on the same side. The outbreak of war, following the Russian-German pact, almost immediately brought the issue again into the foreground. On December 6th, 1939, the organ of the Comintern declared: 'A policy of minority oppression and exploitation of the masses exists in Transylvania, Bessarabia, the Dobrudja and Bukovina. The Communist international urges all workers to take up the decisive fight against those who inflame the Roumanian people against the oppressed minorities.'

This was a plain warning of events to come—and an open

invitation to Hungary and Bulgaria to join in the sharing of the spoils. It was followed by an ambiguous speech by M. Molotov on March 29th, 1940: 'Of the southern neighbouring states I have mentioned Roumania as one with which we have no Pact of Non-Aggression. This is due to the existence of an unsettled dispute, the question of Bessarabia, whose seizure by Roumania the Soviet Union has never recognised, although we have never raised the question of the recovery of Bessarabia by military means.'

Roumania was by this time thoroughly alarmed. The district on the eastern bank of the Dniester had been formed into a Moldavian Soviet Republic—an adoption of the ancient Roumanian name with the obvious idea of an expansion of its territory.[1] The Roumanian king and ministers made the usual proclamations about protecting Bessarabia with their lives. The atmosphere was intensely disturbed.

Not until the collapse of France did the drama develop. For some time there had been no Russian diplomat in Roumania—a Minister had 'disappeared' from Bucharest under mysterious circumstances in 1938. Now, on June 20th, 1940, a new Soviet Minister was accredited to Roumania. The tension was eased; apparently normal relations were to be restored. Then, six days later, came the brusque ultimatum: a demand for the return of Bessarabia to Russia.

In the absence of French and British aid, Roumania turned to the Axis Powers, with whom her rulers had long flirted on a 're-insurance' policy. But Hitler at this time was only too anxious to pacify Russia—this was the year during which the Soviet was represented by Nazi propaganda as a pillar of peace and sense, and before it became once more the home of war-mongers and scoundrels.

There must have been some consternation in Berlin. The Russian move into Bessarabia has often been represented as the

[1] This policy was bound to be dangerous, in that it aroused irredentist ideas in Roumania—ideas which the Russians made legitimate, in effect, by their use of the word Moldavia, implying the Roumanian ethnic character of the country.

fruits of Russian-German agreement, but this seems doubtful. The Germans had in recent years invested huge sums in Bessarabia in the cultivation of the soybean, which is so useful for fodder and the manufacture of margarine. They could not have relinquished their holdings with any pleasure. At the same time Russia had to be pacified—for the moment.

Roumania was helpless. The patriotic declarations had to be abandoned and forgotten. The Russians marched into Bessarabia at twenty-four hours' notice, even before the Roumanian troops could retire from the scene. There was some resistance to the Russians from units which had not received the order to withdraw.

At the same time the Soviet demanded the cession of Northern Bukovina. Here the ethnographic claim was stronger, the historical claim weaker. The whole province was acquired by Austria from Turkey, in the convulsions of the Russian-Turkish war, in 1774, and Bukovina formed part of the Austrian Empire until 1918. (It had never formed part of Russian domains.) Then it was transferred to the enlarged Roumanian kingdom. At that time its population consisted of—

Roumanians	273,000	Poles	36,000
Ukrainians	305,000	Hungarians	10,000
Germans	168,000	Others	12,000
Jews	130,000		

It will be seen that the Ukrainians outnumbered the Roumanians—though for propaganda purposes the Jews were often counted as Roumanians.[1] Since 1918 the Roumanian proportion has increased, and today the Roumanian and Ukrainian populations are approximately equal.

A thousand years ago Bukovina was largely inhabited by Ukrainians. Then Roumanians, pressed by successive Turkish

[1] This is a common trick, and explains some of the wide variations of figures between disputants. In this case, for example, the Roumanians counted the Jews as Roumanians, while Soviet figures counted them as Ukrainians.

invasions, moved northwards—the ancient capital of the Moldavian principality, Suseava, is in Bukovina. The Germans in the province are of comparatively recent settlement, since it came into the possession of Austria.

On the collapse of Austria-Hungary, the last Austrian governor handed the province over to local Ukrainian leaders (October 25th, 1918). But then, four days later, local Roumanians met at Cernowitz and voted for union with Roumania. They had the potential backing of the Roumanian army: the Ukrainians had none—not even the prestige of a national state. So Bukovina became Roumanian.

Today the Ukrainian section is largely concentrated in the northern portion of the province, and here it heavily outnumbers all other races. It has resisted all attempts at Roumanisation. Under the comparatively mild Austrian administration there were over 200 Ukrainian schools in Bukovina. The Roumanians closed these, and Ukrainian children had to learn their lessons in Roumanian. Nevertheless their culture was kept alive. For many centuries this district had existed without schools at all—they were a comparatively modern innovation. The Uniat Church was the principal cultural and racial organisation.

In this I found the basis of the potential Russian difficulty in Bukovina. The Ukrainian peasants strongly favoured union with their brothers over the Polish and Russian borders, but were very suspicious of the anti-religious activities of the Soviet.

Taken by and large, the frontier established by the Russians in Bukovina in June 1940 corresponds approximately with the line of ethnographic division. This is, however, not the case in Bessarabia.

An important feature of the Russian advance lay in the fact that the Soviet frontiers now reached the Danube. One of the first Russian demands was for a share in the control of the vital river traffic. It may be that this acted as a provocation to the Nazis, who have always pretended to regard the

Danube as a German river; or it may be that they were suspicious of further Russian encroachments. A move a hundred miles south, and the whole of the Danube delta would be in Soviet hands: further, Russia would have a common frontier with Bulgaria, and in view of the affinity between the two races such a move might have effects which would counter Hitler's Balkan plans.

For long Nazi activity in Roumania had been intense, and in October 1940 German forces entered the country. From that time General Antonescu, the Roumanian 'dictator,' has been little more than a puppet.

When the Germans attacked Russia, it was not difficult to raise some enthusiasm in Roumania, where national pride had been deeply hurt by the successive mutilations of the country. Obedient to his masters, Antonescu declared war. Nevertheless, the first moves were hesitant, and it was not until the Russians were retreating that the Roumanians seriously took the field. Their first heavy actions were fought outside Odessa. Roumanian troops appear to have been callously used by the German command to take the first shock of battle, and their casualties were very heavy. Their army was ill-equipped and badly officered. The Roumanian peasant is sturdy and is potentially a good soldier, but he needs good leadership. He has seldom enjoyed this advantage.

Under the cold douche of heavy losses, enthusiasm for the war rapidly waned. The greater part of the Roumanian people looked upon the campaign for the recovery of Bessarabia as a righteous crusade, but there were no ambitions beyond. The Fascist press, German-inspired, went to amazing lengths to whip up enthusiasm for adventures in Russia. It was reported that not only was the Russian republic of Moldavia to be added—this in spite of the fact that its population was 90 per cent Ukrainian—but the Germans had promised the 'pure Roumanian city' of Odessa! This claim was the most fantastic of all. The only Roumanians to see Odessa were those who fled there as refugees during the last war.

One Fascist newspaper, *Porunka Vrema,* was unusually frank: 'Frontiers which no longer satisfy Fascists cease to exist. Who affirms the great stupidity that the Roumanian people wish to live calmly and peacefully within the present frontiers?'

I do. When the time of reckoning comes, I hope it will be remembered that the Roumanian people had no wish to venture beyond their old frontiers; they were driven by their masters, and had small opportunity of resistance. Difficult as is revolt against a dictatorship, I shall be surprised if it does not happen in Roumania before this war is through. I hope that the feelings of the Roumanian peasants, and the cruel losses they have suffered under the reign of force, will be taken into account on the day of judgment.

The attitude of the Roumanian leaders, though inexcusable in its opportunism, can at least be understood. Some are pure adventurers and plunderers. Others are not; they were determined to recover Bessarabia, which they believed was part of their national territory. Why did they not halt, then, when Bessarabia was reconquered? If they had, who could guarantee that the Russians would not recover the province at the first opportunity? it was argued. Only by Russia's total defeat could Bessarabia be regarded as permanently Roumanian. Therefore Roumania must march beside Germany towards a common victory. The argument has a superficial logic.

Nevertheless, there is every sign that Antonescu has fallen into a Hitler trap. Since the 'capture' of Odessa he has boasted of the 'reconquest' by his troops of the old Roumanian province of Transdnistria—the Soviet republic foolishly called Moldavia. Hitler backs the Roumanian claim and possession. Antonescu ought to know that when Hitler gives something, he takes more. We shall see that neither Hungary nor Roumania is satisfied with the partition of Transylvania. The most fervent nationalist in the Roumanian ranks would consider himself cheated if he were fobbed off with Transdnistria and robbed of Transylvania!

It may be that the future of Bukovina will be settled by plebiscite, in the spirit of the Atlantic Charter. In such case, my own opinion is that Northern Bukovina would vote for incorporation with Russia, and that the frontiers established by the Russians in June 1940 would be approximately correct.

Bessarabia is more difficult. Were the province considered as a whole, I am confident that the Roumanians would secure a majority. It might be more equitable, however, to take the plebiscite in districts, for the Ukrainian minority is reasonably compact in the north-east and the south. In these areas the vote would be likely to go solidly against Roumania.

It will be objected that a boundary following ethnographic lines would spoil the 'natural' frontier of the river Dniester. We have already considered 'natural' frontiers. Further, modern war has shown that a river is no longer even of serious strategic importance. The Dniester frontier was useless to Roumania when she was pressed by Russia in 1940. It would be equally useless in another time of tension. A wise man would make an accommodation to ensure that no cause of quarrel was likely to arise again.

With the Russian frontier extending to the west of the Dniester in the north-east and the south of Bessarabia, about 85 per cent of the Slav minorities would be gathered with their kin. It would not be a serious matter to exchange the rest for Roumanian peasants at present in the areas to be incorporated in Russia. The other mixed minorities would cause no trouble: apart from the Jews, they are peasants attached to their plots of land, without any strong national consciousness. The one potential cause of trouble, the German minority, has already been removed. In the days when Hitler was accommodating Stalin, he withdrew the greater part of the 80,000 Germans from Bessarabia (much against their will: many of them were moved by force) and re-settled them in Poland.

Economically, the division of the province would leave it at least no worse off than it was before. The Roumanians would retain the centre of Bessarabia, and would need to develop communications about Chishinev, the capital.

The problem of Bessarabia is capable of equitable solution. The method of approach may depend very largely on Roumanian conduct during the remainder of the war. An eventual overthrow of the dictatorship might lead to a new atmosphere of understanding.

III

This war has brought amazing surprises in its train. Not even the most far-sighted prophet would have suggested in 1939 that Roumania and Hungary would soon be fighting side by side. For here are two countries where mutual enmity has been steadily encouraged, and between which there is a real and bitter problem to be settled. Were I to turn prophet myself, I would say that the moment the Axis Powers are beaten, then Roumania and Hungary will begin to fight between themselves.

It is from 1848 that the real quarrel between Hungarians and Roumanians can be traced. Until that time the Roumanians were peasant farm labourers—almost serfs. (The historic social divisions followed nationalities: the Magyars were the warriors, Germans the traders, Roumanians the peasants.) In 1848 the eddies of revolutionary thought swept conservative Hungary: new liberal and democratic ideas were freely proclaimed. A new constitution was adopted for Transylvania —but it was held that the Roumanians were too backward for a share in democracy. The franchise was based on qualifications, and the Roumanians found themselves still without representation. They had absorbed some of the spirit of democratic ideas, and were bitterly disappointed and disillusioned.

It might be true that the Roumanians were unfit for a share in government, but they have a legitimate complaint in that the Hungarians took no steps to fit them. The Magyars tend to live in history: the Roumanians had always been peasants— no Magyar could envisage anything different. Count Stephen

Tisza, for so long ruler of Hungary, was only expressing a common autocratic sentiment when he declared: 'I know of no such thing as a Roumanian nation.' Even so late as in 1918 Roumanian parliamentary representation in Hungary was still virtually denied.

The emergence of a Roumanian state from the Turkish tyranny roused its inevitable repercussions among the Roumanians in Transylvania.

In another section [1] I have outlined the problem of the Magyar minorities just inside the Roumanian frontier. This is sufficiently difficult, yet it is simple compared with the Magyar 'island' in Transylvania, the great western province of Roumania, seized from Hungary in 1918.

Transylvania is a lovely land. It forms a plateau, roughly circular: the mountains at its western fringe are modest enough, but the eastern boundary is the great sweep of the Carpathians. Here are valleys of breathless beauty: more than once I have sat in their green depths or on the passes above, almost overcome with sheer emotion at the loveliness about me. Even its name is intriguing, for Transylvania means 'beyond the woods.'

It is a land of colour. Its medley of races have retained their picturesque costumes, and the drab process of westernisation is happily slow. On any day a Transylvanian village is colorful, and on a Sunday evening the scene rivals the plains of Hungary.

There are unimportant industries and coal mines, but Transylvania lives up to its name, and is a pastoral land. The wide valleys are fertile, and the mountain slopes offer grazing for millions of sheep. The great landlord has now almost disappeared, exterminated by the expropriation laws; 'intellectuals' are comparatively few in a land where a generation ago 60 per cent of the people were illiterate. Transylvania is a peasant land, even if its sons are of many races.

Maybe the limited educational facilities explain the extraor-

[1] Page 455.

dinary survival of superstition in Transylvania. Ideas which were abandoned centuries ago in Western Europe are still firmly believed. I remember sitting up one night in a Transylvanian village with a wooden beam across the door to bar the entry of blood-sucking vampires—the priest and I were the only people in the village who did not believe in this ancient superstition. I have heard stories of vampires, werewolves and mandrakes, told by ignorant but sincere peasants with such conviction that I thought my hair would stand on end, and where I had to fight to disbelieve such impossible yet credited stories. Apart from its political interest, Transylvania is a fascinating ethnic study, and the student of ancient folklore and survivals will find it unsurpassed in Europe. Scenically its charm is beyond all words but those of a poet. If Roumania were a happier country, and if Transylvania were more accessible, it might easily become one of the show places of Europe.

It was part of the Roman province of Dacia. When the Romans withdrew, they may have left behind a Romanised population; but the next mention of Transylvanian history is of a population of Vlach shepherds. The Magyars overran the district in 1003; little attempt was made to interfere with the indigenous inhabitants, but strong bodies of settlers were sent to guard the Carpathian frontiers. To the south-east were planted the Szeklers, a Magyar tribe: [1] further north were German colonists—they are popularly called Saxons, but most of them appear to have come from the Rhine valley. For five hundred years Transylvania was a Hungarian province, though with wide powers of self-government. Then, when the Turks overran Hungary, it became an independent state —and thousands of Hungarians fled thither for refuge. The defeat of the Turks before Vienna in 1685 eventually brought Transylvania under Austria; there were many clashes between

[1] Although the Szeklers are now claimed as Magyars, Hungarian historians of bygone generations derided this claim and declared that they were the descendants of Huns. If so, they are thoroughly Magyarised and are generally in the forefront of the clamour for reunion with Hungary. For practical political purposes, therefore, they should be classed as Magyars.

the many shades of the population—first, peasants against overlords, irrespective of nationality, then Saxons and Roumanians against Magyars. In 1868 Transylvania was placed by the Empire under Hungarian rule. In Roumania proper the people looked across the mountains with sympathetic interest. Transylvania had been described as the cradle of the Roumanian race: here, during the centuries of Turkish oppression, the Latin tradition was never extinguished; here Roumanians took shelter from the blast of war, to return to the plains in times of peace. An official account, published as late as September 1940, read: 'It is there that the first light was kindled, that the warm love of our country, the consciousness of our national unity, the sentiment of freedom and honour were born. It is the men of Transylvania who made these revolutions for social justice, national freedom, and the union of all Roumanians. The graves of our marytrs are there in Transylvania, our first libraries, the cradles of our first political organisation.'

Nevertheless, in the decades prior to 1914 all patriotic and nationalistic aspirations were sternly discouraged by the Roumanian government—which was allied to Austria-Hungary! Not until the end of the war was it possible for the people of Transylvania to express their own wishes. As the Austro-Hungarian Empire crumbled, the Roumanians of Transylvania naturally declared for union with their brothers beyond the Carpathians. The Saxons, in January 1919, agreed to join the new 'Great Roumania.' This decision was sensible enough. It was quite impossible for them to form a kingdom of their own, scattered as they were, and they were hopelessly isolated from any other considerable branch of their own kin. The German settlers in the Balkans had always been loyal to the régime of the day; they were workers and traders, not politicians, and as soon as it became obvious that Transylvania was to be allocated to Roumania, they accepted the situation with excellent grace. The Magyars, naturally, did not.

For the historic and sentimental importance of Transylvania

was as strongly impressed in Hungary as in Roumania. During the Turkish occupation of Hungary proper, Transylvania was the province where Magyar as well as Roumanian culture was kept alive. From Transylvania came most of the Magyar heroes of the liberation: the province has played a stirring and leading part in Hungarian history.

The ethnographic medley is amazing. The population includes—

Roumanians	1,876,000	Gypsies	30,000
Magyars	998,000	Others (Russians,	
Germans	248,000	Ukrainians, Bulgars,	
Jews	52,000	Czechs, Slovaks)	14,000

These are official Roumanian figures assessed in 1936. The Hungarians claim that the proportion of Roumanians is exaggerated. This may be true, but it is also a fact that thousands of Magyarised Roumanians have reverted to their original racial group since 1918.

The Hungarian official statistics for 1910 perhaps offer a fairer guide—

Roumanians	1,472,000	Gypsies	25,000
Magyars	918,000	Others	15,000
Germans	234,000		

Thus for once there is no statistical argument. If Transylvania is to be considered as a whole, the Roumanians are in a considerable majority and always have been.

The figures above are for Transylvania proper—there are in addition hundreds of thousands of Magyars in districts just inside the Roumanian frontier.[1]

Tens of thousands more are scattered in isolated groups all over Transylvania, especially in the towns. But in the east there remains a considerable homogeneous block, occupying substantially the same territory as the original Szekler settlers. The exact limits of this Magyar 'island' need not concern us

[1] Page 455.

here: according to their drawing, wide or near, they would enclose anything from half a million to three-quarters of a million Magyars. The indisputable fact is that there is a considerable area of Transylvania which is Magyar—it does not house a mere majority of Magyars, but is almost entirely Magyar: in places the Magyars form over 90 per cent of the population—a remarkable proportion in so medley a land. And this Magyar 'island' is separated from Hungary by a wide stretch of territory which is predominantly Roumanian.

It would be absurd to pretend that the Magyars in Roumania were happy and contented. They had always looked down on the Roumanians as an inferior race, and had treated them accordingly—and now they were ruled by the race they despised. From 1919 onwards they declined to co-operate with the régime, and openly clamoured for reunion with Hungary—this latter naturally enough. Yet their non-acceptance of the situation necessarily complicated their condition. They were denied their proportion of government posts. 'How can we appoint a man to an official job when he is an open enemy of the régime?' asked the Roumanians pertinently.

Culturally at least they were better off than the Roumanians were under Hungary. The majority of the schools were, however, run by the Church, and paid for by the Magyars direct. It is unfair that a man should pay a State education tax, and then pay a private education tax in addition. But it was also unfair in 1913.

The Magyar press was as free as any other in Roumania, which at any given moment may not mean very much. Their cultural societies were very active, and their economic situation was at least higher than that of the neighbouring Roumanians. Nevertheless, I felt exceedingly sorry for the Magyars of Transylvania. Irredentism seldom makes for happiness.

The quarrel between Hungary and Roumania was a bitter one. That between Hungary and Czechoslovakia was like strife between two intellectuals, with sarcastic wit predomi-

nating. Hungary and Roumania were more primitive in the
fashion of their quarrel, and the reason is to be found in history. There has always been a tendency in the Balkans to confuse patriotism with hatred of the other country.

If you wander over any part of Roumanian Transylvania,
and talk with the older generation, you cannot but be impressed at the sincerity of their complaints of the old Hungarian régime. They were a repetition of those of Slovakia,
but with greater force. The Roumanians were treated as an
inferior subject race, and only those who did not resist the
process of Magyarisation could hope for success. The State
schools were entirely Magyar: challenged at the Peace Conference of 1919, the Hungarian delegation was unable to mention
a solitary State school where instruction was given in Roumanian (or, for that matter, in Slovak or any other non-
Magyar tongue, except German).

The Hungarian case was that their culture was higher than
that of their subject nationalities, so that it was her duty to
draw them up to her level—which could only be done by
Magyarising them. There were, of course, local Roumanian
schools run either by the Church or paid for by the peasants
direct. As they lived on the edge of poverty, they could
scarcely afford to pay out considerable sums for the education
of their children. Thus they had to choose between education
in Magyar or none at all. Most of them chose none, and in
1914 no less than 78 per cent of the Roumanian population of
Transylvania was illiterate. (Even then, it is important to
note, the level of culture and education among the Roumanians of Transylvania was higher than that of their brothers in
the Old Kingdom of Roumania, so recently under Turkish
rule.)

The political system of Hungary resembled that of England before the Reform Bill. Only 6 per cent of the entire
population voted, and of the Roumanians only 3.2 per cent
had the franchise. Nor could they vote with freedom, for the
open ballot had always been favoured in Hungary. It was a

brave man in those days who would vote against his feudal landlord!

Roumanian parliamentary representation was a farce. The maximum number of delegates was 5—whereas by proportion of population the number should have been 120. The Roumanian press was maltreated and frequently suppressed.

(I should emphasise that I am here summarising the more moderate of the Roumanian complaints. Actually, Magyar Socialist papers were freely suppressed as well by the old régime.)

Roumanian meetings were banned or dispersed, often with violence. Roumanian peasants were exploited, treated almost as feudal serfs. And so the list goes on.

After 1919 the picture was reversed. Passing to the districts of Transylvania preponderantly occupied by Magyars, I found another set of complaints. The Magyars claimed that they were facing a complete policy of Roumanisation—the minority clauses of the Peace Treaty were largely ignored. Street signs had all been changed from Magyar to Roumanian —and if a letter was addressed in the Magyar style, it might not arrive: the street is 'not known.' Roumanian was exclusively used on the railways and post-offices, and the policy was being introduced into the State schools. The national cultural activities of the Magyars were repressed—Hungarian songs and dances were strictly forbidden. It was not permitted to import modern Magyar books from Hungary. Magyars were ill-treated by the police merely because they were Magyars. Practically the whole of the civil service was Roumanian, and thousands of Magyars were dismissed. When the great Magyar estates were expropriated, they were almost entirely divided between Roumanian peasants, the claims of the Magyars being ignored.

There is a pathetic similarity between these two sets of complaints. Both have foundation, but are pathetic because they prove the utter lack of tolerance. In one of my first hypothetical problems I warned readers that they must not make the easy answer—that if the two nations would settle down, a little tolerance would minimise their grievances to vanishing point. I have looked in vain for signs of tolerance in Transylvania.

It was obvious to me, as I wandered Transylvania, that while there was a firm basis for many Magyar complaints, the Roumanians also had a point of view. If a minority is to be happy, it must co-operate with the ruling power. The Magyars have never pretended to do this: on the contrary. The political argument was that co-operation would imply satisfaction with their lot, which they would never admit. So they preferred obstructive methods, putting up with dozens of personal grievances so that Hungary should be able to claim with truth that her exiled sons were unhappy and yearned to return to the fatherland.

(It would be as well to answer one obvious sub-question. Admitting that the Hungarians did not treat their minorities too well before the World War, what is the position today? There are about 550,000 Germans, 150,000 Slovaks, 80,000 Yugoslavs and 50,000 other minority nationals inside pre-1939 Hungary. The Germans, by my observation, were quite contented: they ranked equal with Magyars. The Slovaks and Yugoslavs complained still of the policy of Magyarisation and the repression of their own national cultures. There were still no non-Magyar schools, and a Slovak press was forbidden. Slovak peasants also point enviously to their cousins over the border who had achieved their life's ambition in the possession of a piece of land. Nevertheless the complaints were petty compared with those of older days. I have seen worse conditions in many European countries, including those which claim high civilisation.)

The complaints of the Magyars in Czechoslovakia were much exaggerated; but in Roumania the standard of government and of political life have been much lower—I have referred to this in the appropriate section. Corruption and inefficiency on a vast scale have made life in Roumania very difficult. The Roumanian peasant is one of the finest fellows in

Europe, but he has been mighty unlucky in his politicians. I have said that I would willingly have lived in Czechoslovakia, but I would firmly decline to live in Roumania, particularly as a member of an unpopular minority. Many of the stories of persecution of Magyar minorities by petty officials are unfortunately true—I have seen enough for myself for conviction. No one in clean-governed Britain can imagine what a hell can be made of life by an oppressive village policeman. And if that policeman who orders you about, demands bribes for the slightest service, forbids everything you want to do—if twenty years ago he was one of your own servants, classed as unintelligent at that, your discomfiture today can be imagined. I should hate to be a Magyar in Roumania: I feel that I should become a rebel, and would shout my loudest for reunion with Hungary.

Nor have the Transylvanian Roumanians always appreciated their new conditions. The enlarged state was centrally administered from Bucharest, and many Transylvanian privileges disappeared. Local patriotism always ran high, and there were signs of a growing and vigorous movement demanding federal home rule—not separation from Roumania, but self-government in local affairs. This was reasonable enough, and such a move might have added to the strength of the Roumanian state.

(On the other hand, many influential Transylvanians held different ideas. They held that they were more advanced and 'western' than the Roumanians east of the Carpathians, and tried to 'capture' the Bucharest government. They did not succeed—but Transylvania has always been very well represented among Roumanian leaders.)

At the outbreak of the present conflict, the principal objective of the small countries of South-Eastern Europe was to avoid being involved. Hungary, while never abandoning her claims to Transylvania, made it clear that she would postpone the issue until the end of the war. There is cause to doubt that this undertaking was given honourably.

The Russian seizure of Bessarabia and Northern Bukovina

in June 1940, however, shattered the atmosphere of reason. If Roumania were to be dismembered, then Hungary must have her share—must move quickly before a rival appeared. Who could tell whether Hitler would claim Transylvania as German territory? The population included 7.7 per cent of Germans: 'where there are Germans, there is German land,' runs the Nazi creed.

For once even Hitler must have considered himself in an awkward dilemma. For years he had wooed and flattered Hungary, fanning her revisionist aspirations. More recently he had been pushing Roumania away from her democratic obligations on to the Axis side. Now both his protégés, Hungary and Roumania, appealed to him for protection against the other!

The Hungarian threat certainly united Roumanians of all parties. Nevertheless, weak and isolated, it was obvious that concessions were necessary. Conversations with Hungary were opened at Turnu Severin in August 1940. The Roumanians offered considerable cessions of territory in the border districts, which would have returned approximately half a million Magyars to Hungarian rule. At the same time an exchange of population was proposed: Roumanians should be withdrawn from the ceded districts and replaced by Szeklers from the Transylvanian 'island.'

The flaw in the proposal lay in the fact that the number of Magyars to be settled far exceeded the number of Roumanians to be withdrawn. Nevertheless, the offer was a reasonable basis for discussion. Indeed, had it been made five years earlier, in an atmosphere of peace and reason, it would probably have been accepted.

The negotiations broke down almost at once, for the Hungarians demanded the greater part of Transylvania, over 26,000 square miles: 2,200,000 Roumanians would thus have become Hungarian subjects. No Roumanian of any party could consider such an exorbitant claim for one moment. Hungarian troops began to mass on the frontier.

By this time the weakness of Roumania was apparent. Extreme elements in Hungary were dominant, and reason fled. The dispute had to be referred to German 'arbitration,' and Ribbentrop [1] made his Award on August 30th, 1940.

There was no argument; he dictated his orders at Vienna. I have a photographic copy of the map on which he hastily sketched the new frontier in heavy blue pencil. It paid little attention to ethnic or economic requirements, but was largely

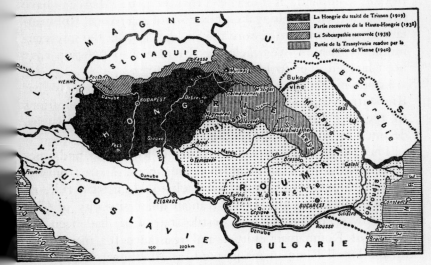

PARTITION OF TRANSYLVANIA

An official and accurate Hungarian map which shows the extension of Hungarian frontiers since 1938, and in particular the section of Transylvania seized from Roumania. The Szekler 'island' is formed by the tip of the Hungarian tongue now extending south-east into Roumania; the population between this area and 1938 Hungary is largely Roumanian.

strategic in its division. He allotted the northern half of Transylvania to Hungary—a tongue of land deliberately stretched to the east so as to enfold the Magyar 'island.'

Hungary gained 17,500 square miles, with a population of 2,370,000. Of these, 48 per cent were Magyars, 43 per cent Roumanians, 2.5 per cent Germans and 6.5 per cent of other

[1] Count Ciano was also permitted to sign the 'Award.'

nationalities, according to Hungarian estimates. Roumanian figures, based on the census of 1930, are different and important:

Roumanians	1,370,000	Jews	131,000
Magyars	893,000	Germans	66,000

The difference in the statistics is probably explained by the process of de-Magyarisation followed since 1919. The Roumanian complaint is therefore that 893,000 Magyars have been returned to Hungary at a cost of 1,370,000 Roumanians; that, in order to restore the Szekler 'island,' the intervening areas with an overwhelming Roumanian population have been handed over to Hungary.

Economic difficulties were ignored—it was obvious that Ribbentrop was thinking in terms of German communications to the east, and of a new flanking frontier with Russia, destined to be useful at the moment of attack.

The Award was received with fury in Roumania, and especially among the Transylvanian Roumanians. Apart from the million Roumanians transferred back to Hungarian rule, of unhappy memory, the Transylvanian university city of Cluj was now incorporated in a hostile state. Cluj had been the centre of Roumanian culture and resistance for many centuries. To all Roumanians it stands as affectionately as Winchester or York to the English.

So far from being a 'settlement,' the Vienna award only created new problems and whetted extremist appetites. The resentment in Roumania was countered in Hungary by whole-hearted agitation for the return of the rest of Transylvania and the other lost provinces: there still remained 400,000 Magyars in Roumania. Immediately came bitter complaints of terrorism from both parties. The Roumanians taken over by Hungary complained that they were immediately restored to serf-level, and that preparations for the Magyarisation of the native population were in hand. The Magyar landlords, dispossessed of their lands after 1919, flocked back to Transylvania; the Roumanian peasants faced that crowning tragedy, the loss of their land. The Hungarians complained that the Roumanians were venting their spleen on the Magyars still remaining under Roumanian rule. There was certainly a basis of truth in both allegations. Ever since there has been a continuous sequence of 'incidents,' and neither side pretends to accept the 'settlement' as final. Each hopes that the other will be so weakened during the war that it will form an easy prey. At the moment of writing, the Roumanians seem to be fulfilling this condition, for they have been driven to the conflict in Russia, with very large casualties. The Germans are, however, demanding much larger contingents from Hungary as a contribution to the 'crusade against Bolshevism.'

It is a reasonable anticipation that, unless firm action is taken, Hungary and Roumania will be at each other's throats when the main conflict is over. Roumania is certain to denounce the Award at the first convenient moment, and few could blame her: Hungarians show no signs of abatement of their larger claims. At present their aspirations are submerged under their common domination by Germany. When this is removed, then they will revert to primitive methods. Yet such a course would only emphasise the tragedy and aggravate the problem. Even at the best, with conciliation on both sides, the question of Transylvania is intensely difficult.

If the new Hungary joined a Balkan Federation, the atmosphere would be eased. Generations of nationalistic excess cannot be eradicated by a stroke of the pen, however, and I would prefer a firmer basis of settlement. It might be well to revert to the Roumanian plan, suitably extended: the movement of the Hungarian frontiers to the east, with a subsequent exchange of population. There would be bitter opposition from the people concerned, especially the Szeklers, but they cannot have it both ways. If they are content to live under Roumanian rule, they can stay where they are, among the mountains they love. But if they insist on political union with Hungary, they must move nearer to the Hungarian border.

Transylvania above all the disputed areas of Europe needs an ethnic sorting-out. Racial enmities are too deep: Roumanian peasants hate the Magyars who have oppressed them in the past, Hungarians despise the Roumanians as an inferior race. If peace could be enforced in the region for fifty years, the Roumanian and Magyar might settle down side by side. But I would prefer to ensure that peace by removing so far as is humanly possible the basis of quarrel. No perfect settlement is possible; in any case, the problem must be considered in conjunction with that of the other Magyar minorities in Roumania, described in the Hungarian chapter.

IV

In such a welter of difficulties it is a relief to turn to one Balkan frontier problem which has been solved, and whose solution has all appearances of being permanent. For thirty years the Dobrudja has played an important part in the disturbance of Europe—its influence has been vaster than many thinking people realise. Millions of others, of course, have never heard of it.

The Dobrudja was a province of South-East Roumania, between the Danube and the Black Sea. It is not distinguished physically—there are some ranges of low hills, great swamps bordering the Danube and waterless plains in the interior. It is very fertile, however; it can support a considerable peasant population and can even supply considerable quantities of grain for export. Its history is typical of the Balkan medley. The Greeks colonised it; Roman and Byzantine emperors ruled it in turn; but in the seventh century the invading Bulgars settled there, intermarrying with the local population. For four hundred years it was part of the Bulgar Empire; then, after a short period under independent Wallachian princes, it was incorporated in the Turkish domains, and remained so for five hundred years.

During this period it was considered as part of submerged Bulgaria. Nevertheless, it should be explained that at no time was it ethnically Bulgar—there was always present a considerable minority of Petchenegs and Cumans—both tribes of Turkish origin—and Wallachians (now known as Roumanians). Under the Turkish Empire, naturally, still larger numbers of Turks settled in the Dobrudja.

For five hundred years the Dobrudja, like Bulgaria, was no more than a name—a half-forgotten name at that. But the Russian-Turkish War of 1875 restored the Dobrudja to a place

BULGARIA AND THE DOBRUDJA

on the map, to the subsequent dismay of a whole succession of diplomats.

They arranged things remarkably in those days. The Roumanians had been happy in the gain of Southern Bessarabia, which included a large Roumanian element. But the powers gathered in Berlin in 1878 suddenly said to Roumania: 'There are Russians in Southern Bessarabia: the Russians won the war—you must give up the province to Russia.' When the Roumanians not unnaturally grumbled, the powers said: 'Very well, we'll give you compensation—you shall have the northern half of the Dobrudja.' The Roumanians did not particularly want the Northern Dobrudja—in which Roumanians formed only a minority of the population—but they were told to be good boys and do as the older folk said. Quite legitimately, therefore, they began to colonise their new province. This, at the time, was easy to accomplish without injury to the Bulgar majority, since thousands of Turks left the country at the break-up of the old empire.

Thus, when the Balkan allies flung themselves on the Turks in 1912, the northern half of the Dobrudja was part of Roumania, the southern half belonging to Bulgaria.[1] Roumania did not join in the coalition against the Turks, but when Bulgaria turned on her allies at the moment of victory Roumania hurriedly declared war on Bulgaria.

Unhappy Bulgaria was soon beaten to her knees, as might have been foreseen. Not only did she lose Macedonia, but the Roumanians demanded—and received—the Southern Dobrudja as their pound of flesh. The ethnic and historic claims to the territory were flimsy, but this was a land-grabbing age —legal claims to the land were not of great importance; and Roumania was on the winning side.

We see now how this miserable Dobrudja has already affected world history—its story for the moment becomes identical with that of Macedonia. In 1914 Bulgaria was sullenly licking her wounds, looking longingly on the Dobrudja, now completely incorporated into Roumania, and Macedonia, largely occupied by Serbia. Bulgaria's natural inclination was to come into the war on the side of her allies—to fight *against* her ancient enemy, the Turk, not with him. Her aid would have been invaluable. The Bulgar is a fine fighter, and the army had been well 'blooded' in continuous Balkan wars. For the first year of the war the Serbs held the Austrians, and with Bulgar help could have done more. Most important, Bulgaria was between Turkey and the Central Empires. With Bulgaria on the side of the Allies, the early collapse of Turkey was certain.

[1] See map on page 231.

But the diplomatic situation was weakly handled. It was easy to bribe Roumania into the war. Gt. Britain could promise her territory belonging to enemy states. To get Bulgaria into the war on her side, as we have seen, she would have to promise territory occupied by her allies. Nor would they listen to reason—states seldom do when their 'national pride' is involved. Gt. Britain could have argued with Roumania as she did with Serbia: 'We *must* win this war. When that is done, you shall have Transylvania, which you want so badly. But to win the war the help of Bulgaria is essential. You give up the Dobrudja—just the Southern Dobrudja, say—to Bulgaria, and she will come in. The Dobrudja is not a tenth as important as Transylvania, so you will gain heavily.' Actually, she *did* put that argument, but not sufficiently forcibly. Roumania would not give up a square yard, and thereby nearly committed suicide, for she was utterly beaten within a few weeks of entering the war.

She was now in the hands of the Central Powers, and had to give up several square yards. Germany and Austria, however, recognised that there was now a considerable ethnic difference between Northern and Southern Dobrudja. The northern half had been Roumanian for nearly fifty years, and had been so colonised that there was now a Roumanian majority. The Central Powers, therefore, reserved Northern Dobrudja temporarily under their own rule until the map of Europe should be finally redrawn, when its fate should be settled. Southern Dobrudja, however, was immediately handed over to Bulgaria, whose ethnic and historic claims were indisputable—the half-province had been Roumanian only since 1913.

Bulgarian aspirations were satisfied. Even at this stage Britain could have withdrawn Bulgaria from the war by promising that she could hold what she held. She had done a lot of damage, out of all proportion to the size of her army. She had played a big part in the defeats of Serbia and Roumania, bitter blows to the Allied cause. *This almost insignificant Dobrudja, with the equally insignificant Macedonia, had certainly pro-*

longed the war by a year—by more, in the eyes of some competent judges. Who will say that we should take no interest in obscure corners of Europe?

Roumania, vanquished, hurriedly re-entered the war in its last hours, so as to be in at the kill. She demanded as her reward for failure not only the promised Transylvania, but the return of the Southern Dobrudja as well. And, by the Treaty of Neuilly, she got it.

Since that time Bulgaria did not cease in her efforts for the peaceful revision of the treaty. She refused to join the Balkan Pact—which offered her many advantages—because it assumed the permanence of the present frontiers. That Bulgaria would never admit. Its people, from Fascists to Communists, were united on that point.

Bulgaria, presumably on the common principle of asking for more than you expect to get, claimed the whole of the Dobrudja. I do not think that her claim to Northern Dobrudja can today be admitted. The territory may have housed a majority of Bulgars in 1878, but such is not the case today. The Bulgarian claim, in fact, is based on a figure of 100,000 Bulgars out of a total population of 300,000. The Roumanians, needless to say, do not agree with the Bulgar figure, and say that the number of Bulgars is less than 50,000. In any case, the Bulgars are today in a minority—for once we can agree on that.

A further complication is introduced by the fact that the only railway communication between Roumania and the Black Sea lies through the Northern Dobrudja. With this railway in enemy hands, a considerable portion of Roumanian trade might be paralysed—particularly in winter, when the Danube is frozen.

I do not think we need consider seriously, however, the problem of Northern Dobrudja. Only extremists among the Bulgar irredentists pursued this claim. The real problem of the Dobrudja lay in the south.

In 1913 the Bulgars formed more than half the population

of the Southern Dobrudja. The next largest ethnic group was formed, not by the Roumanians but by the Turks. The Roumanians, in fact, were an insignificant minority. They claim that this is no longer the case. Certainly they strove hard in the last ten years to make the district Roumanian. Their methods were not pretty, as I saw for myself.

Some of the steps taken were unhappily normal to the situation. Bulgar schools were closed,[1] newspapers and societies suppressed—even choral societies came under the ban; it was never an actual crime to speak Bulgar, but it was certainly dangerous. Elections in Dobrudja villages were a bigger farce than Balkan elections usually are—armed gendarmes guarded the ballot boxes and refused to allow Bulgars to approach!

This, unfortunately, is a familiar picture, and I had seen it in other parts of Europe. But I was not quite prepared for the methods of the colonising campaign. I did not blame Roumania for colonising the Dobrudja, assuming that she meant to hold on to it. In the event of war, Roumania would have found on her own doorstep a band of fierce, callous warriors who hate her even more than they once hated the Turks. This happened in 1916, when the Bulgars of the Dobrudja were openly treated by the Roumanians as enemies, and it might happen again. So the Roumanian government began to settle the Southern Dobrudja.

The settlers were of two classes. When Greece received from Turkey her million Greeks, room had to be found for them. Among others, Greek Macedonia housed over 100,000 Roumanian Vlachs, who were promptly returned to their own country. The Roumanian government decided, quite legitimately, to plant these men in the Dobrudja. The other settlers were not so well chosen—some of them were ex-convicts, chosen to hold the dangerous corners of this outpost of Roumania.

I have seen something of twenty-six countries of Europe, but never have I found such an unhappy land as this Southern

[1] The number of Bulgar schools was reduced from 276 to 4.

Dobrudja. Bulgars glared at Roumanian settlers literally across the hearth. The tiny farms of the Bulgars were seized, and a half presented to an incoming Roumanian. The Bulgar must even house his enemy until he could build a dwelling for himself. The Roumanians were armed, the Bulgars were not; the Roumanians had the backing of the armed police, the Bulgars had not. And the Bulgar of the Dobrudja is far fiercer and less restrained than his brother over the border.

There were armed police everywhere. An English hamlet is content with a weekly visit from a passing policeman; the same hamlet in the Dobrudja needs four or five armed men—with soldiers within call. True, if it were not for the overwhelming force opposing them, the Bulgars would probably have made short work of their enemies. The loss of their land was the bitterest cut of all; when you take a peasant's land, you take his heart.

Had I not seen for myself, I would have suspected the reports of terrorist activity as exaggerated propaganda. But I could not fail to sense the atmosphere of gloom and furious despair. People who had never heard the word propaganda told me frightful stories of torture and death. More than once I saw for myself.

There was one unhappy period of six months when over two hundred Bulgars of the Dobrudja lost their lives. At this time I would have classed the Dobrudja as the site of the fuse for the European powder-house. For these murders were terribly dangerous. Each was fully reported in the Bulgarian press—and you may be sure that atrocities were always embellished in the telling. A dozen times patriotic societies of Bulgars were on the point of raiding the Dobrudja—were forcibly restrained by their own government. I would never have been surprised at a Bulgar outbreak in the Dobrudja with support from Bulgaria. Then war would have been inevitable. The death of one man has started off a war before now.

It is not my intention, of course, to cast Roumania as the villain of the piece. Had the positions of Roumania and Bulgaria been reversed, the story would probably have been the same—or worse. Despite their great advance during the last generation, Balkan codes of conduct do not yet approximate to western standards: this particularly applies to political methods.

The Roumanians claim that the Bulgar population of the Dobrudja is now only 38 per cent of the whole. The Bulgars fiercely dispute this, and in any case point to the thousands of families of recent Roumanian settlers. On the other hand, there are at least 75,000 Roumanians in Bulgaria, where their treatment has not been especially happy. There is an obvious case here for the consideration of exchanges of population.

Economically, the loss of Southern Dobrudja hit Bulgaria hard. Roumania was large and potentially rich; Bulgaria was small and poor. The surplus grain of Dobrudja merely added to Roumania's already large surplus for export; Bulgaria had no surplus at all.

While Southern Dobrudja formed only 2.5 per cent of the area of Roumania, it was 10 per cent of the area of Bulgaria. Its agricultural economy was richer. In Southern Dobrudja alone the agricultural machinery exceeded a quarter of the entire total for Bulgaria. This means a lot in a land where many peasants still use the wooden plough, the hand sickle and the winnowing floor, and whose ambition is the possession of modern machinery. In the Balkans questions of land and corn take the place of our tariffs and means tests as subjects for political discussion: and tempers are as primitive as arguments.

There were, of course, extreme elements in Roumania who still adhered to the 'not a yard, not a stone' policy. Others were more moderate; they might have been persuaded to meet the Bulgarian claim, but believed with justice that such a step would have provoked immediate demands from Hungary and Russia. So the miserable deadlock continued.

Happily, from 1935 the situation improved. Even Bulgars admitted that the atmosphere was easier. Provocation and reprisal alike were milder in their forms. Yet the Czechosloval crisis showed that Bulgaria was simply biding her time. The break-up of the Little Entente, and the virtual isolation o Roumania, prompted patriotic demonstrations in all parts o Bulgaria; the problem was only shelved. Frontier incident became a commonplace.

Nevertheless, the official Bulgarian attitude in the early days of the war was correct enough. Due largely to the steadying influence of Turkey, Bulgaria agreed to postpon the issue of the Dobrudja until the end of the war—there wa no anxiety to spread hostilities to the Balkans. It was mad plain that a claim *would* be preferred when the war ended but it is probable that the Bulgarian pledge was honourabl intended.

The situation was changed by the Russian seizure of Bess arabia and the subsequent Hungarian demand for Transyl vania. It was scarcely human to expect Bulgaria to stand by patiently while all other claimants satisfied themselves a Roumania's expense. The Russian move was approved, and Bulgaria's own claims promptly revived and presented.

Roumania was helpless. She turned in despair to her newl appointed Axis 'protectors,' but they could only advise her t agree to a settlement with Bulgaria. Then the British govern ment stated that it would regard favourably an amicabl settlement of the Dobrudja question—which was a diplomati way of stating that it backed the Bulgarian case. *If this state ment had been made ten years earlier, Bulgaria might hav been satisfied, the Balkan Pact might have become complete and the war would certainly have taken a very differen course.* It is idle to allot all the blame to pre-war govern ments for their indifference to Balkan affairs; they only re flected the general attitude of the country—an attitud destined to prove very painful and expensive in the long run

On August 21st, 1940, agreement was reached betwee Roumania and Bulgaria. The Southern Dobrudja was cede immediately to Bulgaria, and arrangements were made fo exchanges of population—Bulgars from Northern Dobrudja exchanging farms with Roumanians in the south. The occupation was carried out without serious incident.

Indeed, the whole episode was a credit to both parties. The Bulgars in their hour of triumph showed a wise restraint. Had they demanded the whole of the Dobrudja, the Roumanians could scarcely have resisted, for it is probable that the Bulgar claim would have been supported by Russia—which would then have had a common frontier with Bulgaria near the mouth of the Danube. The moderation of the Bulgars must always be recalled to their credit.

The only fault with the whole transaction, indeed, was its date. Had the agreement been concluded in 1930 instead of 1940, the whole course of history might have been changed—for the better.

It has since been revealed that the British government, acting through the intermediary of Turkey, attempted to settle the problem in 1939, prior to giving their guarantee to Roumania. The attempt failed, largely because Roumanians believed that concessions would be considered as a sign of weakness by her other neighbours, Russia and Hungary, who also had territorial claims at her expense. Nevertheless, early in 1940 King Carol informed King Boris that he was prepared to return Southern Dobrudja after the war; he only asked that the question should not be pressed publicly at the moment, so as to avoid other claims.

The fact that Britain has approved a settlement initiated by her enemies is in itself an admission of the justice of the Bulgarian cause. Yet I still regret that the step was not taken earlier. It is a pity that justice to Bulgaria was secured by German backing, not British. Because in 1933 I wrote an article, not favouring the Bulgarian case, but stating it, I found myself *persona grata* all over Bulgaria. A little more interest and enterprise in British government circles, and her influence in Bulgaria might have been vastly increased.

Both sides appear to have accepted the settlement loyally.

While Roumania makes no secret of the fact that her aims include the recovery of Bessarabia and Transylvania, there is every indication that the problem of the Dobrudja is considered as settled.

M. Tilea, President of the Free Roumanians, met in London in 1941 M. Kosta Teodoroff, leader of Free Bulgaria. They agreed on the principle of the cession of Southern Dobrudja, and no one is likely to quarrel with it.[1]

This is a decision we can heartily endorse: indeed, it may prove a useful precedent for parallel cases.

v

As if the ethnic medley of the Balkans were not sufficiently involved, it received additional complications from the action of local monarchs, who scattered German settlers through their domains. For many generations these Germans were an asset to their adopted countries: today they are a menace, and tomorrow they will still be a problem.

Settlement began in Hungary. The Magyars were land-owners and serfs, with little interest in urban occupations. German artisans found a ready livelihood in Hungarian towns; German—and German-Jewish—traders almost monopolised Hungarian commerce from the thirteenth century onwards. These townsmen gradually became Magyarised—a remarkable development which will call for further comment.

In Roumania, however, the situation was very different. Here the Germans settled not only as artisans and traders, but as peasants. At the invitation of successive Hungarian kings thousands of German families emigrated to Transylvania. They were colloquially termed 'Saxons,' but actually most of them came from the Moselle valley and from Luxembourg. They were given special privileges of self-government in their own communities—their first charter was in 1224. This was in

---

[1] They also agreed on one minor special clause. Balici is to be a free port and Roumanians are to be entitled to use it without passport or customs restrictions.

accordance with mediaeval practice. St. Stephen, king of Hungary, demanded: 'What Greek would rule Latins by Greek laws, or what Latin would rule Greeks by Latin laws?'

Although the passing generations have seen the persistent whittling-down of German privileges, the descendants of the original settlers are still Germans, living in their own communities. They have maintained themselves as a race apart from their neighbours, looking upon themselves as a superior people. Differences in religion—the Transylvanian 'Saxons' were Protestants—helped in the continuance of racial separation. Their standard of life and of education was and is considerably higher than that of their neighbours. On the other hand, in spite of their adherence to a primitive *herrenvolk* idea, the 'Saxons' have always loyally supported the régime of the day, appreciating that they could demand no more than local self-government.

In pursuance of this practice, they accepted the Roumanian state on the break-up of the Austrian-Hungarian Empire in 1918. During the frequent Roumanian-Hungarian clashes their attitude was one of diplomatic aloofness. They resisted Hungarian bribes. A representative German assembly in Transylvania declared that the Germans were neither the enemies nor the friends of the Hungarians. History had decided their fate, and it seemed that they could only return to Hungary by violence, which they declined to consider. This was an eminently sensible point of view, typical of the history of these settlers. The 'Saxons' gained by their moderation. They retained their own schools and local government: they enjoyed a comparative prosperity; they were as happy as any people in the Balkans—until the rise of Hitler.

The emphasis of the Nazi doctrine on race, and its encouragement of irredentism, had wide repercussions in Roumania. In one of his Reichstag speeches Hitler referred to South-Eastern Europe as being 'full of splinters of German nationality'—not of German race, be it noted, but nationality. Actually the splinters numbered two million Germans or German-speaking people, and of these three-quarters of a million were living in Roumania.

At first there was little enthusiasm among the 'Saxons' for the Nazi creed. Then the inevitable 'organisation' began. Hitherto the German settlements in Roumania had been local, with little but cultural affinity as a bond. Now they were welded into a political whole.

The original Nazi party in Roumania was banned, but in the fashion of the day it merely changed its name to the Deutsche Volkspartei. It is significant that the greatest opposition came from local German leaders, who saw how the new movement must upset their traditional mode of life. The younger generation, however, was swept off its feet, and since 1936 the Nazification of the 'Saxons' has made violent strides.

Nevertheless, the 'Saxons' were much disturbed by Hitler's policy of mass-transference of populations. They were deeply attached to their lovely homeland, and had no wish to be moved to a strange Germany, or to be settled in a hostile Poland. The only Germans who accepted the new policy were some of those in Bessarabia and Northern Bukovina, who did not wish to remain under Russian rule. The majority of these were removed in the autumn of 1940. They have not been happy. Naturally, in such a backwater of Europe, their development has been retarded, and they complain that their 'brother' Germans in the fatherland ostentatiously look down on them as inferior beings.

The lines of the Vienna award may have been dictated to some extent by the 'Saxon' reluctance to move. Although the 'Saxons' form 7.7 per cent of the total population of Transylvania, the proportion in the area ceded to Hungary is only 2.5 per cent. This has the appearance of deliberate policy. Maybe Hitler plans to leave a large German population in the rump Roumania to justify a subsequent claim as German territory. Or it may be that he does not wish to transfer a large German population to Hungarian rule, for history has shown that the Hungarians are the only Danubian nation which has successfully assimilated Germans. This is all against the Nazi creed.

There was one significant feature about Hitler's 'holy' war against Russia. Although sacrificing Roumanians freely, he has left the German settlers on their farms. True, an appeal was made for volunteers, but it was not pressed. Indeed, out of three-quarters of a million Germans in Roumania only 67 volunteered for the 'crusade.' It may be the German plan to kill off as many Roumanians as possible, while retaining the German population intact. More Machiavellian schemes than this have been seen during recent years.

After a German defeat, and with a new Roumania, the problem of the 'Saxon' settlers will become acute. The Roumanians are not likely to look kindly on the Germans who abused the hospitality and privileges which Roumania gave for so many years, and who proved willing to act as a Fifth Column for a foreign power. If there is any place for Germans to go to, there will certainly be a demand in Roumania that they should be expelled from the land.

VI

It is now possible to summarise the problems of Roumania and to make suggestions for post-war solutions. The difficulties outlined in this chapter do not exhaust the perils of this unhappy country. The problems of the Magyars living just inside the Roumanian frontier are dealt with in the Hungarian chapter. Perhaps the outstanding problem of all is likely to be the internal state of Roumania itself.

Confining ourselves to our declared limitations of frontier rectification, we can reasonably decide—

(a) The present frontiers between Roumania and Bulgaria can be considered as permanent: Roumania should retain Northern Dobrudja, Bulgaria Southern Dobrudja. The present process of exchange of minorities should be continued until this problem no longer exists.

(*b*) Russia has an ethnic claim to Northern Bukovina—not a historic claim, be it noted, for this province has never previously been part of Russia. If the people of this province vote in plebiscite in favour of union with their fellow Ukrainians—as is possible that they will—then the frontier fixed after the Russian coup of July 1940 is reasonable.

(*c*) Bessarabia is more difficult. Neither the Pruth nor the Dniester forms a natural boundary between different races, and the strategic basis of a river frontier has been reduced or removed.

If a plebiscite is held after the war in Bessarabia, it would be fairer to take it by districts. If the voting followed ethnic distribution, the Russians would be allocated a considerable area in the north, adjoining Bukovina, and a second large area in the south. Such a carve-up would not affect existing economic arrangements too seriously, as they are already very primitive. Subsequent exchange of Russian and Ukrainian settlers for Roumanian peasants would help to stabilise the new frontier.

Once the ethnic principle is invoked, however, the Roumanians are bound to point out that there are considerable numbers of Roumanians in Soviet Russia, in the so-called Moldavian Republic. Aggressionist ideas installed by Germany have been faithfully followed by Antonescu, who has renamed the occupied Republic 'Transdnistria.' Moderate Roumanian opinion, naturally, does not back his claim. It does suggest, however, that Roumania should recover Bessarabia, and that the Russian elements in that province should be withdrawn into the Moldavian Republic, while people of Roumanian stock from the republic should replace them in Bessarabia.

If the decision were to hold local plebiscites in Bessarabia, and a division of the province resulted, such an arrangement would leave about 80 per cent of the Jews of Bessarabia on Roumanian soil. This might not be their own choice. It must be admitted that there is a strong anti-Semitic sentiment in

Roumania, and that this is not solely due to the activities of modern Fascist parties. There is some anti-Jewish feeling in most countries, including Britain. In Roumania it has been especially strong, owing to the peasant dependence on local Jewish financiers.

It is highly probable that in any case Jewish financial dealings of the type which have embittered the peasantry will be restricted or made unnecessary by the extension of State banking and loan facilities. Already a beginning has been made even in Roumania, and the process is bound to spread. We can legitimately foresee a large-scale application of the co-operative agricultural systems which have been so effective in Scandinavia. In such case the Jewish village shopkeeper, merchant and financier would find his occupation gone.

I should emphasise that while anti-Semitism in Roumania is active—it has been deliberately aggravated by the Iron Guard and General Antonescu, who affects a slavish imitation of his master in most things—moderate Roumanian opinion is on another basis. It was disgusted by the massacre of Jews in January 1941. It distinguishes between the Roumanian Jew proper and the large numbers of Russian Jews who have entered the country during the past few generations. It proclaims that there is no animus against the Roumanians of the Mosaic Confession, as it terms the Roumanian Jews; these men have always played a leading part in Roumanian affairs, often intermarrying with Roumanians. The Russian Jews are, however, considered as foreigners who must be expelled. Where are they to go? They form part of the vast problem of the unwanted Jew—which has to be solved just as surely as any frontier dispute in the Balkans.

If Russia and Roumania felt like taking a long-term view, they could solve the problem of Bessarabia and the difficulty of the Jewish population by forming Bessarabia into a Jewish state. Russian and Ukrainian peasants could be withdrawn into Soviet territory, Roumanians into Roumania. The number of Jews in Roumania would not suffice to populate the whole of

Bessarabia: in any case, thousands of Roumanian Jewish families of long standing would remain in their own country: but there are likely to be hundreds of thousands of Jews in Central Europe who will require alternative accommodation.

Such a scheme would probably meet with opposition from the Jews who would have to leave their shops, who have lived exclusively by trade. Nevertheless, most of them would agree that their lot has been unhappy for many years; and, in spite of their capacity for withstanding oppression and suffering, most would admit that the future is not bright.

A strong Jewish objection would be that Bessarabia could only absorb a fraction of the Roumanian Jews in the professional or commercial callings they have previously followed. This is true: the bulk of the Bessarabian settlers must be farmers, but it is an elementary error to assume that the Jew cannot be a first-class agriculturalist. On the contrary. He was noted for his skill on the land three thousand years ago: in Palestine today he has shown that this ancient application has only lain dormant, and has not died. There are districts in Sub-Carpathian Russia, or Ruthenia, where all the inhabitants are Jews—not merely the traders, but foresters and peasant farmers. A strong Jewish settlement in Bessarabia is not a fanciful suggestion: the land can support a considerable population, and urban development would afford full opportunities for the organising genius of the race.

A Jewish Bessarabia would not be an independent state, but would have local self-government. It would affiliate either with Roumania or Russia. The decision would be strongly influenced by the trend of anti-Semitic feeling in Roumania, which will not subside in a day. If Roumania's present rulers continue for much longer in power, the answer to a Jewish plebiscite would probably be Russia.

(d) Transylvania is probably the most difficult of all Roumanian problems. The Vienna award has few claims to justice, and in any case satisfies neither party: the Transylvanian question is bound to be raised at the Peace Conference.[1] As both Hungary and Roumania are on the other side, we are entitled to insist that they shall settle their differences permanently. There will be no lasting peace in Central Europe until this danger spot is removed. A Spartan plan has been suggested— to lock up Hungarian and Roumanian delegates in the same room until they reach agreement, but the real difficulty is to find a solution likely to be accepted by the two peoples. No perfect solution is possible, and give-and-take is necessary on both sides. Hitherto all the giving has been done by the side which happened to be the under-dog at any particular moment. After the war Hungary and Roumania are likely to be companions in misfortune, part of the wreck left in the trail of a Nazi defeat.

As a basis of discussion, an expansion of the Roumanian plan for the cession of territory along the Hungarian frontier might be considered. It would involve considerable exchanges of population. The Magyar minority in Transylvania would certainly object strongly to removal from its historic home. It would have to make a final decision: either it would pass permanently under Roumanian rule, or else move itself bodily to Hungary or the ceded territory.

A plebiscite in this area might yield interesting results. So far neither Hungary nor Roumania has wished to apply this method—perhaps for different reasons: on the one hand, because it does not follow that a man in recording his vote will follow the prompting of his racial origin; on the other, because a plebiscite might have set a dangerous precedent. This latter difficulty at least can now be resolved.

[1] The British government made its position quite clear. Lord Halifax, then Foreign Secretary, after approving the cession of Southern Dobrudja to Bulgaria as a result of negotiation, stated that the partition of Transylvania was in another category because it had been enforced. 'The British government were unable to accept the solution now announced, since it was the result of dictation by the Axis Powers and has been imposed on Roumania under duress. We do not propose during the war to recognise territorial changes unless they have been freely agreed between the parties concerned.' This is an important and essential statement of principle.

I have suggested that the problem of Transylvania is intimately connected with that of the mixed populations about the old frontiers. Final judgment might therefore be suspended on this point until Chapter Eleven has been perused. My own opinion is that Transylvania is one of the areas where firm handling of minority problems is essential. There are districts in Europe where, in a period of peace, a man might be a willing member of a commonwealth in which his race is a minority. The racial clash between Magyars and Roumanians seems to exclude this happy solution here. Even if the two countries were members of a federation, the problem would still remain. I am convinced that Hungary and Roumania are unlikely to be members of the same federation *until* the problem is solved.

(*e*) The Germans in Roumania are not likely to be popular after the war. Are they to remain there, brooding over their racial creeds, waiting for the next Hitler to arise? It is the younger generation which has embraced most fervently the Nazi creed; it will take a long time to grow out of it.

The removal of the ancient German settlements would be a severe loss to the prosperity of Transylvania. Yet it is bound to be demanded when Roumania recalls the harm these men have done. Their accommodation depends largely upon the shape of the new German frontiers.

Naturally, any settlement is likely to depend upon the character of the new Roumania. I believe it is destined to differ a great deal from the past and the present. The old Roumania carried too many unfortunate legacies of Turkish rule at its worst: the present country is in the hands of a careerist Fascist clique. I believe that Antonescu represents Roumanian feeling even less than Mussolini represents Italian ideas. I am confident that a large majority of Roumanians are with us in spirit. It was not over-difficult to drive them into war against Russia, who appeared to them as an aggressor. We must not judge them hardly for that—England nearly went to war with Russia in 1940 over the aggression in Finland.

I have said that the collapse of France stupefied Roumania, since for some generations France had been the cultural source from which Roumania freely drew. In recent years, however, an increasing number of Roumanians were sent to English and American schools and universities, and these men are now likely to have a big influence in the conduct of affairs. The British Council's work made an excellent beginning: there were real signs of Anglo-Saxon interest in Roumania.

British policy has not been very happy recently. We have automatically included Roumania among Hitler's 'jackals'—while actually she was driven directly to her present position by the failure of her policy of appeasement. It would be far more sensible to say to the Roumanians, often and loudly, that we are sympathetic with their troubles, that we want to help them to clear Fascist dictators and foreign aggressors from their country, that we will help them to start again.

The former British Minister in Bucharest estimated that 86 per cent of Roumanians were pro-British. Britain cannot afford to neglect these people; she needs their help and friendship, now and after the war, just as they need hers. Already they are distressed by the heavy losses in unwanted battles in Russia: a strong propaganda offensive might detach them from the trail of the German war machine, and make of Roumania another land to be held down by force until the war is over. Whatever happens, the sufferings of this unhappy country are bound to be intense, but from them may be born a new spirit which will propel this potentially-great land into a worthy place in the New European order.

CHAPTER SEVEN

YUGOSLAVIA

I

YUGOSLAVIA is the land of the South Slavs. When it emerged from the war it was called the Kingdom of the Serbs, Croats and Slovenes, but this title was cumbersome. Yugoslavia was a sensible choice, though to British eyes and ears it was regrettably confused with Czechoslovakia.

It is a fascinating country. If any land in Europe can claim to be the meeting-place of East and West, that land is Yugoslavia. The term 'land of contrasts' has been used so often that it is now a cliché, but it is readily applicable to Yugoslavia. Scenically the country is an amazing medley, and more than once I have wandered from frontier to frontier, delighted continuously with the changing scene. In the north are the Slovene Alps—a continuation of the Alpine group. This is a lovely land, reminiscent of the Tyrol at its best, and inhabited by a friendly and virile peasant people. Immediately to the south is a region of green hills, bordering the valleys of Danubian tributaries. This is the land of the Croats, pleasant rather than magnificent. Next follows a wilder country, known in olden days as Serbia and Bosnia. Sometimes the mountains are green and friendly, enclosing fertile valleys; sometimes they are gaunt, forbidding ridges, with intervals of desolate *karst*—a rocky desert. The *karst* is seen at its best— or at its worst!—in the old kingdom of Montenegro, to the south of Dalmatia. Here at least is one stretch of Yugoslavia which appears in the British map, for thousands of tourists frequent Dalmatia every summer. Its innumerable islands, ancient towns and bathing beaches make it an admirable holi-

day centre, but for interest it cannot compare with its hinterland. Who would loiter too long on a Dalmatian beach when
but a hundred miles away is Sarajevo, capital of Moslem
Europe? In Turkey, the ancient protector of Islam, the picturesque side of Moslem religious life has vanished, but in
Sarajevo the muezzin still calls the faithful to prayer from the
minaret, and the women are heavily veiled.

Nor are the contrasts confined to scenery. In no land of its
size is there such wide variety of peoples. Serbs and Croats are
own cousins, but a casual stranger can distinguish them.
Serbs and Bosnians are own brothers, yet the manner of their
lives differs strangely. Here in Yugoslavia is a range of national
costumes and customs which are a delight to the student and
the lover of the picturesque. A south Serbian village on a Sunday morning is like a scene from a romantic highly-coloured
play.

You would never guess from their jolly, inconsequential de-
meanor that the Serbs rank high among the fighting races of
Europe. Their history has been written in blood; nor has the
last page of the book been completed.

The South Slavs came from Southern Russia in the sixth
century and settled across the Central Balkans. Two hundred
years later came the more virile Bulgars. The South Slavs were
disunited, lived in isolated tribes. For succeeding centuries the
Serbs were under Bulgar or Greek rule, while Croats and
Slovenes sought the protection of Venice or Hungary. In the
twelfth century, however, a Serb kingdom was founded, and
endured until the coming of the Turks. These Asiatic warriors overwhelmed the Balkans: in a fatal battle at Kossovo in
1389 the Serbs were overthrown, and passed under the Turkish
yoke for nearly five hundred years.

A dozen times the Serbs struck for their freedom, but not
until the last century was it achieved. In successive wars more
provinces were freed from the Turks, always at a price in
blood. By 1913 practically the whole of the purely Serbian
territory had been recovered, with the exception of Bosnia

and Herzegovina, which had been annexed by Austria-Hungary. The kindred provinces of Croatia, Slovenia and Dalmatia had been incorporated in Austria-Hungary since mediaeval days.

The Serbs of 1913 burned for a reunion with their cousins, but conflict with a powerful Austria-Hungary was a vastly different proposition from one with a decadent Turkey. Maybe the term 'reunion' is too decisive, too, since previous unity between the branches of the Yugoslav race had been of the slightest, and had been broken for six hundred years. Yet, as we have said, while Croats and Slovenes were cousins of the Serbs, Bosnians were the Serbs' brothers—and the people of Bosnia were Serbs, under a foreign ruler. It was not President Wilson who invented the political theory that peoples should live under the rule of their own kin—it has been a natural urge throughout history. The World War was the direct outcome of the determination of the Bosnian Serbs to join their brothers.

Yet the development of the new country was beset with difficulties. Hungary in the north and Bulgaria in the south claimed areas of Yugoslavia: there were Albanian and German minorities in the land—and Yugoslav minorities in Italy. There were internal dissensions between the important tribes which made up the kingdom of the South Slavs. Indeed, before we can appreciate the modern history of Yugoslavia, it is necessary to halt to examine the internecine feud between Serbs and Croats.

II

It might once have been considered that the problem of Croatia was purely a domestic affair, affecting only Yugoslavia —just as it might have been argued that the military rising of General Franco against the Republican government was purely a domestic problem of Spain. We have seen more than once that domestic difficulties and weaknesses are open invitations to dictators who are adepts at fishing in troubled waters, and who understand the technique of dividing a nation against itself. Croatia may not have aroused much interest in Britain, but in Berlin and Rome its possibilities were always rated as of first importance. If at any time the province appeared to be sinking into a state of satisfaction, prompt and incendiary methods were at once applied. In the event, the dictators were disappointed at the response to their efforts; but already they

HISTORIC PROVINCES OF YUGOSLAVIA

had added seriously to the trail of problems demanding solution in the South Slav state.

The country which emerged in the last days of 1918 was more than an enlarged Serbia. The addition of Bosnia and Herzegovina absorbed another million Serbs, but Dalmatia, Croatia and Slovenia, all incorporated in Yugoslavia, were inhabited by people of common origin but of different outlook from the Serbs. The Croats of Dalmatia and Croatia speak the same tongue, Serbo-Croat, but Slovene is another dialect of the basic Slav language.

Years before the war, Serbs, Croats and Slovenes had dreamed of reunion—for they had never forgotten that they were all South Slavs, closer in kinship than men of Northumbria and Wessex. Patriotic societies revived the glories of South Slav history and culture; they were periodically suppressed by the Austrians, but always appeared again in a new form.

Now one of the few personal opinions I have advanced in this book is that a policy is preferable to a nebulous idea. History produces ample proofs, but enthusiasts tend to ignore the cold lessons of history in favour of its romances. Before the war most Serbs, Croats and Slovenes dreamed of a united South Slav kingdom, but no one had the foresight to plan out the form of the new unity: there would be ample time to settle details like this when victory had been achieved. This was a vital error. It may be wrong to count your chickens before they are hatched, but it is only prudent to decide what you are going to do with your chickens *if* they are hatched.

The last days of 1918 were so full of emotional excitement that few people worried about forms of government. The Croats and Slovenes, to say nothing of the Serbs of Bosnia and Herzegovina, had achieved their freedom—the South Slav tribe was united again after eight hundred years. Now everybody was going to live happily ever after.

But a honeymoon cannot be indefinitely prolonged; sooner or later the happy couple have to decide how they are going to live—most couples wisely prefer to do this before their marriage. Very soon the sentimental phrases of rejoicing merged into economic argument. If anything is calculated to upset the blissful atmosphere of a honeymoon, it is economic argument.

The new country needed money, desperately. For three years Serbia had been ravaged by enemies: its portable wealth had disappeared; its fields lay barren, and only a few miserable cattle roamed its parched hills. Croatia and Slovenia, however, were unscathed and comparatively prosperous—their soil had escaped the deadly touch of war. In the new taxes, therefore, the comparatively well-off Croats naturally found themselves paying more than the bankrupt Serbs. Such a realisation has killed many a promising friendship.

Nor was ethnic kinship enough. It was quite true that the Croats spoke the same language as the Serbs, but for eight hundred years the two branches of the tribe had lived under vastly different conditions—under different civilisations. Nationality *can* be submerged by long existence in an alien land: the descendants of the Huguenots and the Flemish weavers are as English as I am. The marvel is, indeed, not that there were differences between Serb and Croat outlook, but that after so many centuries they retained much in common.

Croats and Slovenes lived under Austrian and Hungarian rule, generally beneficent and comparatively just; Serbs lived under Turkish despots, inefficient, corrupt and sometimes brutal. Croats and Slovenes were christianised from Rome, Serbs from Constantinople. Thus today Croats and Slovenes are Roman Catholics, Serbs Orthodox. And although a Croat can understand every word a Serb says, he cannot understand a word he writes, for Croats use the Latin alphabet and Serbs the Cyrillic.

Croats and Slovenes enjoyed the moderate educational facilities of Austria-Hungary; the Serbs had to make their own. Croats and Slovenes were peasants of peace—although the Austrians esteemed them as soldiers when the occasion arose. The Serbs were bred on war—their life under the Turks was one long desultory guerrilla campaign, and the last hundred years a ceaseless battle for liberty. Croats and Slovenes made accommodations with their civilised masters, and some of them attained the highest military, political and cultural rank; the Serbs were almost serfs, hating their Turkish masters. The culture of Western Europe permeated Croatia and Slovenia, but could not cross the Turkish frontier. The Croat is polite and refined, a companion for conversation; the Serb is vigorous and tough, a companion for battle.

Is it marvellous, then, that after eight hundred years the outlook of the South Slav brothers differed vastly? If a Huguenot descendant should return to France, would he not have difficulty in adjusting himself to French conditions? And the differences between the civilisations of England and France are minor compared with the vast gulf between those of Austria-Hungary and Turkey.

The Croats made the surprising discovery that they were outnumbered—there were six million Serbs and only three million Croats and Slovenes. Thus the Serbs could always outvote the Croats and Slovenes. One would have imagined that this might have been foreseen! Further, by a weird electoral law typical of the Balkans, a party which polled one-half of the total votes received 75 per cent of the seats. But was it essential to form parties along racial lines—why not the Conservative-Liberal-Labour alignment?

With amazing rapidity the quarrel came to a head. As so often happens, it was complicated by its personalities. The Prime Minister, Pashitch, was a grand old warrior with a vast experience of Balkan combat, a man accustomed to bitter enemies and treacherous allies. He had fought throughout his life for the freedom of Serbia—he was too old to think of Yugoslavia. His opponents claimed that he regarded Croatia and Slovenia merely as conquered Austrian provinces, and some of his actions supported this view.

The Croatian leader was just as implacably dynamic. Stephen Raditch was an educated man of peasant stock, and became one of the outstanding orators of our generation. True, he had a ready-made case for presentation, for the new country was seething with complaints. Actually the whole of Europe was seething with complaints—you cannot turn the world upside-down for four years and then expect it to be normal immediately afterwards. But Raditch did not emphasise this legitimate argument—he preferred to blame Belgrade. True, there was plenty to say: world conditions in 1920 were hopelessly chaotic, but nothing happend in Yugoslavia to ease their effect. The Serbs have always been noted as soldiers, but never as administrators. Raditch blamed Belgrade for everything—and the peasants believed him.

Raditch travelled abroad, preaching the justice of the Croat-Slovene cause, and exaggerating its potentialities for danger. Considerable foreign opinion was attracted to his side—he was a good linguist, and could be persuasive in several languages. And, even his enemies believed, he was sincere.

Then someone in Belgrade made a great tactical mistake—Raditch was flung into prison. He emerged with the redoubled glory of the hero who had suffered for his cause.

Was he sincere? After denouncing Pashitch as a tyrant and the king as a murderer, Raditch joined the government at Belgrade. True, he did not stay in it very long. Even this flirtation with authority did not destroy his popularity. By this time he had worked out a more practical programme—he demanded a federal union of the historic provinces of Yugoslavia. The scheme appeared at first sight to be reasonable enough, and his following increased.

Then, on June 20th, 1928, came the tragedy which was to make a domestic argument become a serious quarrel. Balkan politics have always been virile, and more than one parliamentary chamber has seen a pitched battle across the floor of the house. A Montenegrin deputy on the government side emptied his revolver into the Croatian benches. Two members were killed outright, and Raditch was mortally wounded. His death was as dramatic as his life, with every peasant in Croatia and Slovenia sharing the pains of his dying hours. Death brought him a martyr's crown—and gave a religious significance to his cause: a martyr *must* be right.

Parliamentary government was suspended, and King Alexander became virtual dictator of Yugoslavia. True, Yugoslavia had not reacted strongly to democratic methods—the king had had twenty-five ministries in seven years. But his action had one untoward result: when a people has grievances, a scapegoat must be found. Hitherto the Belgrade government had shared this onerous position: now Alexander filled it alone.

The Croats and the Slovenes were not the only ones to grumble—indeed, in those days there was plenty of cause to grumble in Yugoslavia. Nor were some of the accusations flung against Alexander without foundation—yet the principal Croat-Slovene complaint was in the main unfair.

The Croats and Slovenes were now firmly demanding a federal union—that is to say, the continuance of the state of Yugoslavia with full financial, defence and diplomatic powers, but with a large measure of autonomy allotted to its constituent provinces—Serbia, Croatia, Slovenia, Dalmatia, Montenegro, Voyvodina,[1] Bosnia and Herzegovina. The Croats pointed out that even under Austria-Hungary they had enjoyed a considerable measure of home rule. At the Croat capital, Zagreb, were local ministries of Justice, Education, Agriculture and Police; and a local Parliament—all subject, of course, to that at Vienna. It was urged that a similar scheme was easily workable in Yugoslavia: the Croats claimed that this was their underlying idea when they agreed to reunion in the last days of 1918. They were bitterly disappointed with conditions in Yugoslavia. The accidents of history had treated Croats and Slovenes in friendlier fashion than Serbs. Croats and Slovenes were far more advanced in culture, education, commerce and agricultural methods, they declared, but they were rapidly being reduced to the level of the backward Serbs. 'Who could deny that the cultural standards of Croatia and Slovenia were the highest in Yugoslavia? Who could be happy when even our ancient folk-songs are banned by the police? And this because the police are all Serbs! Here is the Croat race, self-governed for generations, now ruled entirely by Belgrade, with scarcely any of its people among the civil service or the police. We are ruled by force; we have no say in

[1] Comprising the Backa and the Yugoslav share of the Banat.

affairs. The only men who count in a Croat village are the
Serbian police. Croatia is absolutely united in its opposition to
Belgrade rule—in the last election ever held, sixty-three of the
sixty-seven seats went to the Croat peasant party. Is it right
that millions of people should be ruled against their will—and
that by an inferior race?' So ran the Croat complaint.

Alexander's opposition to the federal scheme was inexorable.
He believed that Yugoslavia could only exist as a united country: that any loosening of the central authority would be an
open invitation to intervention by interested neighbouring
states—and in this he may have been right. The idea of unity
dominated his thoughts and actions. But it was quite a mistake
to interpret his dreams as directed against Croatia and Slovenia;
rather, their aim was for unity of Yugoslavia. The Croats
complained bitterly when he destroyed the historic entity of
Croatia by dividing it up into a series of provinces—but he did
precisely the same to Serbia. It was made a crime to fly the
ancient Croat national flag—or the Serbian flag. Alexander's
approaches to the problem may not have been tactful, but at
least his aim was sincere—he was not trying to make Croats
into Serbs, but to make both into Yugoslavs.

The first relief to the tension came, by the irony of history,
with the murder of King Alexander. The horror of the crime
aroused widespread revulsion. Although Croats had talked
freely about the probability of such an assassination, the Croat
terrorists who were largely responsible for its execution were
violently denounced; many of the more extreme 'patriotic'
societies suddenly found their influence gone. Unlike the
Serbs, trained in the hard school of merciless struggle with
the Turks, the Croats were unfamiliar with the weapon of
political murder. In death, many of the faults of Alexander
were forgotten; it was agreed that his real mistake had been to
hurry history, instead of allowing the Yugoslav medley to
settle gently. His magnificent war record was recalled, and
lost nothing in the re-telling.

Croats and Slovenes are less restrained and far more emotional than the Serbs. Their hearts bled for the widowed queen and the new boy king—at least these had done no wrong. There was a remarkable scene as Alexander's body was halted at Zagreb, the capital of Croatia. There was to be a scheduled halt of half an hour, to allow officials to pay their last respects. But this had to be extended to twenty-four hours, as hundreds of thousands of peasants swarmed into the city to do homage to their dead king.

For a moment it seemed that grief would reunite the South Slav races. Dr. Matchek, the Croat leader, saw Queen Marie, and promised a truce. The moment was ripe for conciliation, but no one seized it. Emotion plays a deceptive part in politics, and pacts founded on sentiment seldom endure. Soon the old situation was restored—the demand for federation, with even wider powers for the constituent provinces. It should be explained, however, that at no time was there any demand whatsoever for return to Hungarian rule.

A second relief was more effective—the Abyssinian war. It was revealed to Yugoslavia as to the world that Mussolini's threats were no empty phrases. His references to Dalmatia were recalled with apprehension: nor was the plight of the Croats and Slovenes in Italy forgotten.

Nevertheless, in 1935 Italian policy towards Yugoslavia suddenly changed. The threatening speeches of yesterday were forgotten, and fair words substituted. Important trade treaties were signed. The Yugoslav government quite naturally was glad to accept assurances of amity from its peaceful neighbour: the common people were not so sure. They had been brought up on distrust of Italy and affection for France, and public opinion cannot change as quickly as the policies of dictators. The government did its best, by Balkan standards. France was the ally of Yugoslavia, had trained and financed her army. But when the French Foreign Minister visited Belgrade, peasants who dared to shout 'Vive la France!' were beaten up by the police.

Italy's reasons for her change of front were soon apparent

—to secure the widest influence in Yugoslavia before Germany got there first. The rivalry between the Axis forces came to a head after the seizure of Austria—when, for the first time, Germany and Yugoslavia had a common frontier. German economic activity in Yugoslavia, already considerable, was heightened. The government at Belgrade appeared to favour German pretensions—while proclaiming friendship with Italy. The many machinations, some open, but most behind the scenes, brought the problem of Croatia and Slovenia out of the parochial into the European class. After the fall of Czechoslovakia it became desperately urgent.

The parallel was only too obvious. The Slovaks, to gain autonomy, had 'invited' the intervention of Germany. Might not the Croats be used in similar fashion? Their complaints against the Serbs were deeper and more forceful than any Slovak complaints against the Czechs. Here was a unique opportunity for Machiavellian politics. The Italian seizure of Albania, in April 1939, brought the danger nearer home.

Neither the Serb nor Croat leaders missed the signal of danger. M. Tsvetkovitch, the Prime Minister of Yugoslavia, entered into negotiations with Dr. Matchek, the Croat leader: this was in April 1939—immediately after the seizure of Czechoslovakia. At an early date it was announced that the principle of a federal state had been agreed; unhappily, the negotiations broke down on details. There was a surge of feeling in Croatia, and for a moment it appeared that ugly events were pending. Again restraint was imposed by external influences. Germany appeared to be playing a double policy—wooing Croatia, on the Slovak model, but alternatively preparing a new Sudetenland. For there are already 400,000 Germans in Northern Yugoslavia, and their instructions from their organisations were far-reaching. They were to buy land wherever they could in the Danube, Save and Drave valleys. The Croats were described as semi-barbarians; mixed marriages were discouraged—and the sale of strong drink to the

Croats recommended. There is a strange repetition in propaganda methods.

The approach of desperate crisis in Europe again prompted renewed efforts, and on August 24th, 1939—just one week before the outbreak of open war—a final agreement was signed. The Croats were to have a Parliament at Zagreb with full autonomy for local affairs—finance, defence and foreign affairs remained under the control of the central government. The Yugoslav Cabinet was reconstructed to include six Serbs, six Croats and six representatives of other racial organisations or political parties. Dr. Matchek became Vice-Premier to M. Tsvetkovitch.

The new Croatia exceeded the boundaries of the ancient kingdom—its extent had been the principal cause of failure of the earlier conversations. Besides Croatia-Slovenia, it included most of Dalmatia and the northern part of Bosnia; altogether, it comprised 26.6 per cent of the Yugoslav territory. Naturally, it was impossible to fix boundaries which accorded exactly with ethnic frontiers, for the branches of the Yugoslav tribe are freely mixed. It was estimated that the population of the new autonomous state was about 4,425,000: of these 3,220,000 were Croats and 890,000 Serbs—these latter including 165,000 Bosnian Serbs, who were Moslems.

The agreement—generally termed the Sporazum—was a great triumph for common sense. Nevertheless, all difficulties were not resolved. Die-hards on both sides bitterly expressed their resentment—some Croats demanding complete independence, some Serbs declaring that the federal scheme was a weakness. Other Croats, though more moderate, claimed a still greater share of control, especially over expenditure—to which Croatia, as being naturally richer than Serbia, contributes more than its share. Proud Serbs, living in history, recalled bitterly that it was they, not the Croats, who won freedom for Yugoslavia, and were especially incensed that the agreement placed Serbs under Croat rule. Details of the agreement brought long and bitter arguments, and German and Italian agents were always at hand to create discord. The dictators recognised from the first that a strong federal state might be as useless to them as a strong unified Yugoslavia, and took steps to hamper its development.

However, the external dangers seemed likely to ease the internal difficulties. At least a start was made in the organisation of the new state. Given a few years of peace, in which the barriers of suspicion could have been broken down, the new Yugoslavia might have strode firmly ahead. This suspicion had hitherto been one of the weaknesses of the state. Because it held that the loyalty of the Croats was not beyond doubt, successive governments had refused to appoint Croats to high places in the army or administration: this weakened the services—and presented more grievances to the Croats.

Naturally enough, the Serbo-Croat agreement raised other problems: most urgent was that of Slovenia. The Slovenes are a South Slav tribe, of ethnic kinship to the Serbs and Croats, but their language differs considerably. They had lived for many centuries under Austrian rule, reasonably content, and Austrian influences continued to be strong even after the formation of the Yugoslav state. There are about a million Slovenes in Yugoslavia, in a remarkably compact homogeneous block, habiting a lovely mountain land; nearly half a million Slovenes live over the Italian frontier—where, as we shall see, their lot has not been happy; there are a further 80,000 just over the old Austrian frontier. These have been Germanised to some extent, since their ethnic basis has been ignored.

It can be reasonably assumed that local autonomy for Slovenia is not far distant. Indeed, rule from Belgrade was an anachronism after the Serbo-Croat agreement. There should be no serious dispute on this point when the war is over. In a following section we shall argue that the new Slovenia is likely to extend beyond its present borders.

More difficult is the problem of Bosnia. Here again, fired by the Serbo-Croat agreement, a long-latent demand for autonomy has been put forward. The Bosnians and Herzegovinians are mostly Serbs except in the extreme north, where the large Croat admixture led to the incorporation of some areas in the new Croatia. The Bosnian Serbs lay longer under the Turkish yoke than their brothers: many of them made accommodations with their masters, and adopted the Moslem religion. Thus, while the Turks were repressing and ill-treating the Serbs, they classed the Bosnians almost as their equals. For three centuries Bosnia was one of the most settled corners of the Turkish Empire.

Then in 1878 Austria-Hungary marched into Bosnia and Herzegovina, neighbouring provinces. The Russians, natural protectors of the Slav peoples of the Balkans, had to accept the occupation as the price for Austrian neutrality during the Russian-Turkish War. Nevertheless, the Bosnians fought hard against the new invaders. The Serbs would have come to their aid, but were exhausted by a disastrous war; and, of course, they could have been no match for the overwhelming might of Austria—the only possible result would have been the loss of their newly gained independence. The Austrian occupation of Bosnia and Herzegovina lasted for forty years—forty years of continuous strife, for there never was any question of acceptance of the régime by the local Serbs. Indeed, in 1907, despairing of union with Serbia, a representative assembly of Bosnian Serbs demanded the end of Austrian occupation and a position as an autonomous province of the Turkish Empire!

In many ways the Bosnians were better off under Austrian rule. The country, one of the most backward in Europe, was developed, and roads and railways were built. Education was introduced almost for the first time, and an efficient and incorruptible administration took charge. Nevertheless, the Bosnians were unhappy and dissatisfied—the star of freedom was now high in the Balkan heavens, and liberal ideas travelling from other redeemed countries found a ready hearing in these obscure provinces.

It had been assumed by the rest of Europe that the Austrian occupation was merely temporary, to guard her Adriatic interests while the Balkan ravel was untangled. Soon, however, it became apparent that Austria's idea was not the liberation of Bosnia, but the subjection of Serbia. There were prominent Austrians, including the Archduke Franz Ferdinand, who looked upon this as a Liberal mission—the creation of a tripartite Empire in which the South Slavs should rank equally with Austrians and Hungarians. At any rate, in 1909 Bosnia and Herzegovina were formally annexed, despite the verbal and armed protests of the inhabitants.

Obvious ideas took their inevitable course. The union of Serbs and Bosnians was one of the most natural movements in the world. The rapid success and emergence of the greater Serbia from the Balkan Wars of 1912–13 raised Bosnian hopes to the highest state of expectancy. Reunion became frankly a prime object of Serbian policy: in Bosnia men worked towards that end in true Balkan fashion. There can have been few Bosnians who were not implicated in some rebellion, or were not members of some secret society directed against Austrian rule—which had now become almost military in its necessary severity.

It was, of course, one of these secret societies which organised the assassination of the Archduke Franz Ferdinand at Sarajevo on June 28th, 1914, and precipitated the first World War. After the Allied victory, Bosnia and Herzegovina joyfully joined their brother Slavs in the new Yugoslavia.

Since then difficulties have arisen, though not nearly so pronounced as those between Serbia and Croatia. Religious questions provided acid arguments. Some Serbs look down on Bosnian Moslems as weaklings who would not stand up against oppression for their faith—though it is unreasonable to blame a man because his great-great-grandfather became a Moslem. The rift between Christian and Moslem creeds was never wider than in Bosnia, which is the last stronghold of fervent Mohammedanism in Europe. The Bosnian Moslems at least deserve respect in that they are faithful disciples of their creed. Today they look down on the Turks, their erstwhile tutors, as backsliders! While it is true that there is a demand for local autonomy today, it is equally true that Moslems dislike being governed by Christians, and Christians have an even greater objection to government by Moslems. The two religions are hopelessly mixed, and any separation is quite impossible. In any case, there are limits to the subdivisions of local autonomy.

The Bosnian problem is not urgent, however, and should be capable of solution in the relief of the post-war atmosphere, when new ideas of security may banish demands for local privileges. The Croat question, however, was destined to lead to dramatic events, amply proving that its dangers had not been over-estimated. Before examining the causes and effects of the German onslaught on Yugoslavia—involving the setting-up of a puppet 'kingdom' of Croatia under Italian domination—we should first enumerate other Yugoslav problems which have been and will be well in the news.

III

In 1914 Italy was the ally of Germany and Austria-Hungary. Nevertheless she declined—quite legitimately—to enter the war on their side. Aggressive action was in no case contemplated or condoned by the alliance, and in any event Austria had plunged into the war without any attempt to co-operate with Italy. Further, the Treaty of Alliance, made in 1882, stated that it was not in any case directed against England. This saving clause was not inserted because Italy's extensive coastline put her at the mercy of the British fleet, but because of the traditional friendship between the two countries. Italy had never forgotten British moral and material support in her long struggle for freedom, and the idea of war with Britain was unthinkable. Consideration of these pre-war sentiments makes recent history unhappy reading!

At first it was assumed that Italy would remain neutral, but powerful factions saw an opportunity for the completion of Italian unity. Considerable numbers of Italians still lived under

Austrian-Hungarian rule, and if they were to be freed the time was now or never. As in other instances, it was easier to negotiate with the other side. Demands to Austria brought unsatisfactory responses, but Britain and France were quite prepared to give away Austrian territory. By the Treaty of London, in April 1915, it was agreed that Italy should enter into the war on the Allied side, and that on its successful con- clusion she should be allocated the Trentino, Istria and the Julian March, Northern Dalmatia, Valona (in Albania) and a share of Asia Minor. It is unnecessary to point out that these areas far exceeded those inhabited by Italians.

At the Peace Conference, therefore, Italy duly demanded the fulfilment of her bond. President Wilson, however, op- posed her claims with unusual firmness—he went even so far as to issue a personal appeal to the Italian people over the heads of their government. He argued that he knew nothing of these secret treaties—which scarcely abrogated them, nevertheless! Much more forcible was the contention that Italy had accepted his Fourteen Points, and that these principles overrode any previous arrangement. If this were so, then certainly the Italian claims needed substantial modification, for the Brenner frontier and the Julian March could not be reconciled to any degree with 'the rectification of the Italian frontiers on clearly recognisable national lines,' or autonomy for the peoples of Austria-Hungary. President Wilson's appeal had unexpected results: previously the Italians had been divided, moderate opinion favouring agreement with the new Yugoslavia; but now practically all parties, angered by the accusative tone of Wilson's appeal, were so indignant that the hand of the gov- ernment was vastly strengthened—against Wilson!

A glance at the sketch map of the Julian March is worth while. The Julian March is the term applied to the Istrian Peninsula, and the provinces of Gorizia, Trieste and Fiume— that is to say, all the north-eastern territory gained by Italy. It has a considerable Italian population—but actually the greater part of the district is preponderantly Yugoslav! Most

of the towns, particularly in Istria, are largely Italian, togethe
with the western coastal strip. The remainder, if Presiden
Wilson's principles were to be followed, would certainly hav
been allocated to Yugoslavia.

The Yugoslav government was not slow to assert its claims
No sooner was the war over than Italian and Serb patrol
were involved in 'incidents,' some of them alarming. Th
Yugoslavs demanded practically all the territory up to the old
Italian frontier. They agreed that Trieste and several Istriar
towns were largely Italian, but insisted that the surrounding
countryside was entirely Yugoslav. Further north the Yugo
slav claim was clearer, for west of Gorizia and Trieste there
was no substantial Italian element.

The Italians were aghast—it appeared that they had fough
the war for nothing! The Yugoslavs drove the wound deepe
when they pointed out that 50,000 Croats and Slovenes wer
actually enclosed within the pre-war Italian frontier. This i
quite true—until quite recently the district north-east o
Udine was called Italian Slavia, and had an overwhelmingly
Slav population. This was worse and worse! So far from gain
ing territory, President Wilson's principles would actually de
prive Italy of a corner of one of her frontier provinces!

In the Julian March complete there were slightly more Croat
and Slovenes than Italians. If you took the figure of Croat
and Slovenes as half a million, you would not be far wrong
Recent Italian figures are quite untrustworthy, for anybody
who could speak any Italian was classed as Italian. In one
Croat commune the Italian census figures claimed that out o
its considerable population there were only thirteen adul
Croats and three Slovenes. Yet these were credited with 306c
children! Croats and Slovenes are reasonably fertile and have
large families, but at least Nature has her limits!

Even a census by these methods gave a total of 377,00c
Croats and Slovenes. The Yugoslav figure is 600,000, sc
500,000 is a reasonable compromise. A few thousands more or
less do not affect the principle of the argument.

THE JULIAN MARCH. 1939

Despite President Wilson, Italy obtained a considerable proportion of her demands. Britain and France were uneasy; they had made specific promises to obtain Italy's support in the war, and now they wished to honour these promises so far as they could. Already Italy was disappointed in that only a microscopic share of the conquered African territory was allocated to her, and any aspirations to Asia Minor soon disappeared. The Peace Conference salved its conscience, too, by awarding Dalmatia to Yugoslavia.

There was little to be argued against this course. The Dalmatians are definitely Yugoslavs, a branch of the Croat family. On the sea-coast, however, there are small Italian settlements, remnants of the days when Venice dominated the Adriatic. One of these, Zara, was handed to Italy, but the remainder of the coastal area joined its natural hinterland. In all the ports there are Italian colonies, and many of the local Croats, by long cultural and commercial association, speak Italian as well as their own tongue.

The Yugoslavs made no secret of their dissatisfaction over the allocation of the Julian March to Italy. Complicated by the question of Fiume—to which we shall return later—the two countries were for many years engaged in bitter controversy, not unmixed with violence on both sides. Let us follow for the moment the fortunes of the 500,000 Croats and Slovenes included within the Italian frontier—three-quarters of them, naturally, are Slovenes, since the greater length of the frontier adjoins Slovenia.

As I wandered about Europe, I heard many complaints from minorities in all countries. In the aftermath of war you must expect them: I have pointed out that it is too easy to say that if peoples would only work together with amity and toleration, then their troubles would never occur. Toleration is the rarest phenomenon in continental Europe. Even applying the necessary considerable discount for exaggeration, I had to agree that the lot of the Yugoslavs in Italy has not been too happy.

Now when small states were created or expanded at the Peace Conference, minority clauses were inserted by the Great Powers in the treaties of peace. By these, the small nations had to guarantee to their minorities the rights and opportunities available to their own nationals. I agree that in some cases the clauses have not proved worth the paper they were written on, but that is a matter of regret rather than of surprise.

But Italy, being a Great Power, was called upon to sign no minority agreements. A historic state of such wide culture and ancient civilisation needed no legal safeguards to enforce liberal treatment of its subject peoples. The Italian government at once confirmed this impression: 'The people of alien nationality who are united with us must realise that every idea of oppression or of denationalisation is foreign to us; that their language and their cultural institutions will be respected, and that they will enjoy all the privileges of our liberal and democratic constitution.

It would scarcely be denied, even in Italy, that this pledge has not been fulfilled. On the contrary, the imposition of Italian cultural and political thought on the Slav minorities has been firmly pursued. I would have taken small count of excesses in the months immediately succeeding the war, when moral values were low and neglected. But the Italianisation of the north-eastern province has been systematic and continuous, and has occasioned anxious moments to the peace of Europe. Much of the bad feeling between Italy and Yugoslavia can be traced to this disputed area.

A mere catalogue of the complaints would be startling. At first represented in the Italian Parliament—the province of Gorizia returned four Slovene delegates out of five—gradually the minority was barred from public life, and for many years the half-million Croats and Slovenes have not had a single representative in any official assembly. The scenes at the early elections were unworthy of any civilised power—first d'Annunzio's *Avanti* and then Mussolini's Blackshirts made the free ballot impossible.

In 1913 there were 321 Slovene and 167 Croat schools in the territory: these were not sufficient, for 10,000 children were unable to go to school. But today there are no Slovene or Croat schools—they are all Italian. A child which dares to speak its own language in school is punished; Croat and Slovene teachers have been dismissed and replaced by Italians. The printing of Yugoslav primers, or even fairy stories in the Yugoslav languages, is a crime. Since the establishment of the Fascist régime, Croat and Slovene children are forced into the Balilla and Avanguardisti, and propaganda is poured into their receptive minds; they are even taught to scorn their own parents and race.

Of the excesses in the first flush of Fascism I say nothing, since they were common all over Italy, and merely intensified in the Julian March. It is important to explain that the process of Italianisation was well under way before the rise of Mussolini, although under his régime the pace has been quickened. The petty persecutions have more than local importance, however: if an Italian Fascist seizes an Italian Socialist and beats him up, or forces him to swallow castor oil, or preaches his creed in any similar fashion, that is primarily a domestic affair. But if an Italian Fascist maltreats a Yugoslav, that is a different matter. Ten million Yugoslavs are living next door, and you may be certain that no tale of persecution loses in its journey over the frontier. I traced one or two back, and found that they had been exaggerated 100 per cent. The point was, however, that they had a firm basis of fact.

Social and cultural life in the Julian March was active in Austrian days: now all Croat and Slovene clubs which have not been set on fire have been closed down. The Slav press was completely suppressed by 1920. Names have been Italianised—more than one civil servant has been dismissed because he christened his child with a Slav name. It is sad to record that in Italy, home of the Catholic Church, Slav priests and monks have been maltreated and practically all of them have been driven from the country. Slav prayers and hymns are heard no more in Slav churches. Thousands of Croat and Slovene peasants have been driven from their homes, to be replaced by Italian settlers. The last twenty years, in fact, has seen a vast and organised programme intended to change half a million Croats and Slovenes into Italians, their own wishes being of no account whatsoever.

Such, very briefly, are the complaints of the Yugoslavs of the Julian March. I have stated them at their mildest—any spokesman among them would accuse me of hopelessly understating the case. In Yugoslavia itself my catalogue would be considered as absurdly inadequate.

'Put yourself in our position,' said a Croat of Zagreb. 'You are an Englishman living in Italy, let us say. You are surrounded by other Englishmen, living in English territory seized by Italy. Yet you are not allowed to teach English children in English; you will never see an English newspaper. You must not give your child a fairy-book in English: even if you did, it could not read it, since it is taught in Italian. If there is an election, you may not stand as a candidate; you are permitted to vote, but only as you are told. Otherwise you will be beaten up, maybe murdered. Your cultural life disappears—the English library in your town is deliberately burned, your social club wrecked. You are a religious man, but church service is a farce, since you cannot understand the sermon and the priest cannot understand your confession. If you dare to speak English in the streets, you may be arrested. If you are a party to a law case, then your suit is lost before it begins: in any case, you will not understand what is happening. If you meet your friends and sing some of your lovely old English folk-songs, the police will break into your house. Dare to say one public word in defence of your English traditions, and you are promptly exiled to the Lipari Islands. Your children are forced to wear the uniform you detest, the uniform of tyranny. Your only privilege is to wear a uniform yourself—to be conscripted as a soldier and to die in the highlands of Abyssinia, helping to establish a Fascist Empire. Would you like to live like that?'

My answer was naturally emphatic. It is quite certain that the question of the Slav minority in Italy will be raised when the Axis powers are beaten. Already the Slovenes have made their dissatisfaction perfectly clear. Long before the war turned to the Balkans, Slovenes were deserting from the Italian army —not because they were cowards, but because they saw no reason why they should be slaughtered to make a Mussolini holiday.

At the moment the Slovenes in Italy can do nothing. After the war they will certainly demand justice. In 1919 we did not give it to them because of the clauses of the Treaty of London by which Italy was bribed into the war. This time we can approach the problem with an open mind.

It is not insoluble. A plebiscite will reveal the Slovene wishes, for the Slav element is fairly compact. There will naturally be a reasonable demand that Italians who have been 'planted' in the district shall not be allowed to vote. In our anxiety to give justice to the Slovenes, we must not deny it to the Italians. If the frontier were drawn along purely ethnic lines, the hinterland of Trieste would be ridiculously reduced—the port might be ruined. It might be advisable to allocate to Italy a wider section of the Istrian Peninsula than her native population justifies, remove the local Slovene population from the additional strip, and replace them by the unfortunate Italians who have so recently been 'planted' on Slav lands. This solution assumes that the plebiscite would favour the incorporation of the district with Yugoslavia. I do not know the situation today, but when last there in 1936 my estimate was that a very considerable majority of Slovenes would favour that course. Little that has happened since can have tempted them to change their minds.

And, as we shall see, if there are thousands of Italians who will have no legitimate right to vote in the plebiscite, there are tens of thousands of Slovenes who have now been expelled from their country, and who will have to be brought back to vote—if they are still alive.

IV

Coupled with the problem of the Julian March is that of Fiume. Now in the Treaty of London which induced Italy's entry into the war, Fiume was definitely excluded from the promised rewards. It was the natural port of Croatia and Slovenia, and was to be held either for the Croatian state which some people then envisaged, or for the new Yugoslav state. Immediately after the armistice both Italian and Yugoslav troops entered the town, with many resultant clashes. Eventually Fiume was occupied by an international force pending its disposal.

Now although Fiume was a Hungarian port until 1918, its population was 60 per cent Italian—although many of the Italians were recent settlers. Here was the basis of the Italian claim. The Treaty of London had promised Northern Dalmatia to Italy: President Wilson had refused, since Dalmatia was Yugoslav. Very well; by his own principle of self-determination Fiume was Italian. Nevertheless, the hinterland of the port was almost 100 per cent Yugoslav, and its prosperity depended entirely upon Yugoslavia.

But economics means little to fervent nationalists. In September 1919 the Italian poet Gabriele d'Annunzio raided Fiume with an irregular band of legionaries and defied everybody, the newly-born League of Nations included. Without official Italian backing, he 'ruled' Fiume, and his fanatic creed exasperated friends and opponents alike. Although eventually flung out of Fiume, he achieved his end. Italy and Yugoslavia eventually entered into direct negotiations. Fiume became part of Italy, connected with the Julian March by a narrow corridor. On the other hand, its eastern suburb, Susak, went to Yugoslavia.

D'Annunzio's raid was a black day for Fiume. When eventually the city was legally allotted to Italy, there were processions of triumph through the streets. The Italian merchants, however, sat brooding in their homes; many of them had advocated the status of a free city for Fiume, working harmoniously with Yugoslavia. They were right, for d'Annunzio's nationalism spelled the ruin of Fiume.

It was an absurd position. Fiume was a joke or a tragedy, according to your outlook. Twice I wandered round its harbour—excellently equipped, with many natural advantages and with its rail communications deliberately planned to serve the Croatian plain. It was like a stroll round a dead city. Some wharves bore such a look of desertion that obviously they had not been used for years: I fell over a railway line because it was covered in grass. One afternoon I made a census—it did not take long. In Fiume five vessels were loading or discharging. In Susak there were twenty-six.

In Fiume-Susak you had the most ironic situation in Europe: Fiume half dead, bankrupt, a pauper living on Italian charity; Susak vigorously alive, expanding rapidly. New docks were built in Susak every year—and half a mile away in Fiume were miles of unused quays and rotting machinery! Susak trebled its population, and is now considerably bigger than Fiume! Furthermore—and this is surely the crowning farce— since Fiume is bankrupt and Susak thriving, thousands of inhabitants of Fiume were glad to find work in Susak!

I stood on the notorious barbed-wire bridge which connects Fiume and Susak. It took me longer to cross this bridge than any other open frontier of Europe. I was surrounded by barbed wire. On either side of the bridge long queues of people waited while leisurely and surly officers conducted amazing processes of formality. The simplest transaction was deliberately made difficult: real business was almost impossible. The suicide of Fiume did not merely help the rise of Susak: other Dalmatian ports, like Split and Dubrovnik, have overcome some of the physical difficulties of trade with the interior and have considerably extended their commerce.

Yet, if that were all, Fiume would be of purely local account. As I have said, however, it must be classed with Vilna as one of the black spots of Europe. D'Annunzio's gospel of force inspired Mussolini, yet that was its least effect. The tragedy was that the first exponents of the doctrine of force won, and were allowed to retain the spoils.

It is idle to blame the statesmen of the day, leading their war-weary nations along the troubled road towards peace. They must have cursed these fanatic firebrands who added new problems to a fantastic world, but hesitated to meet force with force. Actually it was unnecessary; the force opposed to them was puny, and could have been met with firmness. The trouble was the old one—drift, lack of policy, compromise with principle, indecision. It ought to have been obvious that one successful defiance of a decision by conference would lead to others. The examples of Fiume and Vilna have served as models for events beside which they themselves were puny. If d'Annunzio had been flung headlong out of Fiume, and tried and maybe executed as a rebel and murderer, then the history of Europe since 1919 would have been vastly different. D'Annunzio was the forerunner of the Hitler type. If he had received his due reward, other swashbucklers would not have been encouraged to emulate his example.

Now when Italy declared herself in favour of treaty revision, she was not thinking of the woes of Germany or Hungary; she was still rankling over the way in which she had been cheated of Dalmatia. 'Dalmatia, Italian in its origin, ardent as a saint in its faith, had been recognised to be ours by the Pact of London. Dalmatia had been waiting for the victorious war with years of passion, and, holding in its bosom still the remains of Venice and of Rome, was now lopped off from our unity.' So wrote Benito Mussolini. More than once he echoed the same sentiments: 'We had won the war: we were utterly defeated in the diplomatic battle. We were losing —except Zara—the whole of Dalmatia, our land by tradition and history, by manners and customs, by the language talked and by the ardent and constant aspirations of the Dalmatians towards the mother country.' It is not necessary to examine the claims in detail—for, except for scattered populations in the coastal towns, the Dalmatians do not speak Italian, but Serbo-Croat, as their first language, and certainly have no aspiration to 'return' to the mother country. And if the 'tradition and history' argument were admitted here, it would assume Italy's right to the return of the entire Roman Empire —even England could scarcely escape!

The point is that Mussolini and millions of Italians believe that the claim of Italy to Dalmatia is more than justified. A strong patriotic Dalmatian League has maintained enthusiasm —and also the necessary fury when Yugoslav patriots, in a foolish excess of zeal, disfigured ancient Venetian monuments in Dalmatian towns. Mussolini himself has appeared at demonstrations of the Dalmatian League, waving a Dalmatian flag. A dozen times he has made speeches in far more flamboyant vein than the extracts quoted above.

The dictators are fond of proclaiming that they mean what they say—and one must recognise that Mussolini usually did. Consequently, he could scarcely blame the Yugoslavs because they took him at his word. His speeches about Dalmatia and the revival of the glories of the Roman Empire could scarcely be misinterpreted on the other side of the Adriatic. And, in spite of his sentimental references to Venice or Rome, Dalmatia is overwhelmingly Croat in its population. The Croats and Slovenes are acutely politically-minded, and the signs of the times needed little consideration. And men who had discussed the rival merits of rule from Vienna, Budapest or Belgrade had only one opinion on the idea of rule from Rome!

It was perhaps significant that the first Italian demand on the collapse of Yugoslavia was Susak. Probably Fiume was jealous of the success of its rival. Today Susak has reverted to its ancient position as a suburb of Fiume. The Italians are reported to be moving some of the dock installations to the older port, to help to restore its ancient glories.

Such moves need arouse but little heed. Whatever solution of the Julian March problem is adopted, it can surely be assumed that Fiume will now recover its rightful place as the natural port of Croatia and Slovenia, the Italian portion of its population being transferred to Italian towns if it does not prefer to remain under Yugoslav rule.

v

In this chapter are summarised Yugoslavia's internal problems and her relations with Italy. In other chapters are some details of the quarrel over Macedonia with Bulgaria, and of the problem of the Albanian minority in South Serbia.[1]

It will be convenient at this stage, however, to outline the course of events in Yugoslavia since the outbreak of war. At that time its commitments were identical with those of Roumania: the Little Entente had been killed by the seizure of Czechoslovakia, but the Balkan Pact still held. The natural anxiety was to escape the war, and there passed many months of precarious neutrality. The commercial dependence of Yugoslavia on Germany—half the total exports and imports of the country—made it inevitable that the economic life of Yugoslavia was gravely strained. Germany was only too happy to take Yugoslavia's agricultural and mineral produce, but had little to supply in exchange.

Gradually the strategic situation became impossible. With German troops in Hungary, Roumania and Bulgaria, Italians in Albania, the country was virtually surrounded by Axis armies. As German pressure became stronger, Yugoslav realists looked at the map. Their frontier extended for over 2000 miles: the greater part was hopelessly exposed, and it was quite impossible for the gallant but ill-equipped Yugoslav army to guard it all.

Economically, the position was serious. Yugoslavia now had large 'frozen' credits in Germany, and was almost completely dependent on the Axis Powers for trade: since the collapse of France and the entry of Italy into the war, commerce by Mediterranean ships had virtually ceased. Not only military

[1] See pages 336 and 361.

realists, but hard-headed business men, began to favour an understanding with Germany.

Internally, the situation was bad. The Serb-Croat agreement had not yet had time to prove its worth: old antagonisms still remained. There was a considerable Communist element (and a much larger section of the population which looked to Russia with sentimental affection), and in the spring of 1941, it should be recalled, the Soviet foreign policy was still directed to the appeasement of Germany. The Communists, therefore, tended to weaken Yugoslav resistance, as they had done in France a year earlier. When realist Yugoslav statesmen surveyed their country, they might well be dismayed. If strong powers could not stand up to Germany, what would be the chances of a small power torn within itself?

Considerations like these led Yugoslavia along the fateful 'crocodile' path which enabled Hitler to take his victims one by one. A firm military alliance was suggested between Britain, Turkey, Greece and Yugoslavia. It was turned down in Belgrade: in justification, it should be observed that such a pact would certainly have been interpreted as a threat by Germany, and that geographic reasons ensured that Yugoslavia would get the first and full force of the retaliatory blows.

Of the sympathies of the people there never was doubt. Nor were all the Yugoslav leaders prepared to submit tamely to the approach of danger. In November 1940 the Yugoslav town of Bitolj was bombed by Italian 'planes. General Neditch, the Yugoslav commander-in-chief, wished to drive the Italians out of Albania before the Germans arrived—a sound strategic stroke. It was obvious to Neditch, as to all keen observers, that the German march into the Balkans had begun, and Yugoslavia must eventually be involved.

His advice was not accepted. He resigned. The incident showed quite clearly to Hitler that the Yugoslav government was determined on peace at any price; he likes dealing with such governments—he has had long practice. It is too easy to blame the Yugoslav leaders, except that they should have learned from the mistakes of others. Nevertheless, they showed no signs of subserviency; indeed, they had dealt firmly with provocative elements financed by German and Italian sources.

They were apparently relieved by the comparative mildness of the German demands which eventually were presented —had perhaps never read the step-by-step policy argued in *Mein Kampf*. Hitler's next stroke was planned against Greece. Already his armies were in position in Southern Bulgaria. There was some difficulty over maintaining their supplies, however—all had to be carried across Hungary into Roumania, then south in Bulgaria by second-class railway lines—and not even a bridge over the Danube: there is no bridge between Belgrade and Czernavoda, near the Black Sea. The main line from Germany to the Balkans runs across North-Eastern Yugoslavia. The use of this line was essential to major operations.

On March 25th, 1941, the Yugoslav Prime Minister (M. Tsvetkovitch) and his Foreign Minister were 'invited' to Vienna. They agreed to sign the Axis Pact, and to allow the use of the railway line for the passage of German 'supplies and hospital trains.' The Germans were quite satisfied: this would do very well for a beginning. Troops were already detailed to occupy Yugoslav stations and junctions, to organise the passing of the 'hospital trains.'

Then followed the drama in which Yugoslavia found its soul. The Yugoslav people are realists in politics; they knew that such a surrender was the beginning of the end. They appreciated the appalling difficulties of the strategic situation, with their country virtually surrounded; they knew that in this war courage alone is not enough—that an army must have arms. They were dependent upon supplies from Britain and the United States to supplement their meagre resources. There was only one route by which such supplies could come—by the single-track railway up the Vardar valley from Salonika: and the Germans in Bulgaria were only thirty miles from that railway. That is to say, supplies could not come at all.

In spite of the hopeless situation, the Yugoslav people made a decision of courage and honour. The government which had agreed to the surrender was overthrown by a wave of popular feeling. Prince Paul, the Regent, left the country: the youthful King Peter took over his troubled inheritance. General Simovitch became Prime Minister, with a cabinet representing all parties and races of Yugoslavia. At first there was some doubt about Dr. Matchek, the Croat leader, who had not resigned when the government had decided to sign the Axis Pact: but he resumed his post as Deputy Prime Minister. Party and tribal squabbles were forgotten in the common cause.

The new government was conciliatory enough. It offered to sign a non-aggression pact with Germany, without adherence to the Axis: but it was not willing to surrender its sovereignty by allowing the passage of German troops. This settled the issue. In any case, Hitler's pride was outraged; he had already decided on a stern revenge.

On April 6th—ten days after the overthrow of the government—the attack began: long before the new cabinet had time to get a firm grip of the reins. Britain and the United States at once promised assistance—that this could only apply to the future, not the menacing present, can only be blamed on the previous Yugoslav régime. One very interesting event took place a few hours *before* the German attack: Yugoslavia and Soviet Russia signed a pact of non-aggression and friendship: a shadow of events to come.

The military campaign could only be a matter of days, the odds were so enormous. The Yugoslavs fought with their traditional courage—and are still fighting. When organised resistance was broken, tens of thousands of men took to the mountains, whence they operate as guerrilla raiders. A spate of terror and revenge, of frightfulness unknown even in Balkan annals, was Hitler's reply. Yet a thousand tortures and executions have not been able to end the Yugoslav war.

Immediately the mutilation of Yugoslavia began—its rapidity betrayed long and careful preparation. Slovenia was divided in two portions, the northern half absorbed into Greater Germany, the southern seized by Italy. The Slovenes bitterly resented their fate, and from this lovely mountain region have come continuous stories of sabotage and rebellion, with consequent reign of terror, massacre and deportation.

In the first six months of the new régime over 150,000 Slovenes had been herded out of their province into the rump Yugoslavia, already devastated and half-starving. Deliberate attempts were made to set one branch of the Yugoslav family against another. Slovene students were compelled, under threats of rifles and machine-guns, to work on the demolition of the Serbian Orthodox Church in Ljubljana. The subsequent film—with rifles and machine guns deleted—was then exhibited in the Serbian provinces to stir up Serb hatred against the Slovenes—who were being planted among them as refugees.

An intense policy of denationalisation has been followed in both parts of the unhappy province. The use of the Slovene language has been proclaimed a crime. The German admission has been brutally frank: Northern Slovenia is German land, and always will be. Hence the necessity to expel its inhabitants and re-settle the country with Germans.

(In passing, it is interesting to note that there is a small overflow of Slovenes—about 80,000—in the adjacent Austrian province of Carinthia. These have always been treated as Germans!)

Croatia, with enlarged boundaries, was formed into a 'kingdom' under Italian protection. The chosen king was the Duke of Spoleto—who was so confident of his throne that two years later he had not even visited his kingdom! In this at least he was prudent. The whole scheme, of course, was but a camouflaged annexation of the province by Italy.

The quisling premier of the puppet kingdom was a specimen of his class even more disgusting than most. Ante Pavelitch was a Croat who had set up a terrorist organisation called the Ustashi: it might be called a Balkan I.R.A.: it stopped at nothing. Its proclaimed objective was an independent Croatia, but as it was financed from German, Italian and Hungarian resources it was naturally suspect in Yugoslavia. In any case,

THE DISMEMBERMENT OF YUGOSLAVIA, 1941

1. Northern Slovenia, annexed by Germany. 2. Southern Slovenia, annexed by Italy. 3. Backa and Baranja, with 3a, annexed by Hungary. 4. Banat, 'reserved' by Germany. 5. Croatia-Slavonia, a 'kingdom' under Italian protection. 6. Dalmatia, annexed by Italy. 7. Montenegro, another 'kingdom' under Italian protection. 8. Serbia, the rump kingdom under German domination. 9. South Serbia, allotted to Bulgaria, except for two small districts, added to Albania.

it did not believe in discussion: its arguments were bombs and bullets, or daggers in the back.

It was Pavelitch and his gang who organised the assassination of King Alexander of Yugoslavia. Pavelitch was sentenced to death by the French courts, but he was in Italy, and Mussolini refused to surrender him to justice: wisely, perhaps, for had he talked there would have been sensations in Europe. For years he wandered between Rome and Berlin, a hireling assassin, constantly stirring up strife in Croatia. Now, after an experience almost wholly confined to the organisation of assassination, he found himself Prime Minister of Croatia.

(Dr. Matchek went to Zagreb at the outbreak of war to be among his own people as the blow fell. He was unable to rejoin the government in time to leave the country. So far as is known, he is held a prisoner by Pavelitch.)

The present status of Croatia is of course purely temporary, and is of small importance except for the miseries of the inhabitants. Pavelitch is now in his element; he can organise murder on a scale he never before envisaged. Guerrilla warfare continues, with consequent repression and massacre.

(The terrors in Croatia will have their repercussions after the war. The idea of Pavelitch is to clear Croatia of its large Serb minority, and his methods equal those of the Middle Ages or the worse days of the Turks in their ferocity. Appalling scenes of torture and murder are daily occurrences. Serbs have long memories. When they look back, they will remember that their friends and relatives were murdered by Croats—they may not stop to consider their political colour. The greatest efforts at alleviation will be necessary, both on the part of the Serbs and especially of the mass of Croat peasants, disgusted at the terror executed in the name of their country.)

Another Italian experiment was the revival of the kingdom of Montenegro. When the Serbs were defeated on the fatal Field of Blackbirds, some of the surviving Serbian families withdrew to the inaccessible Black Mountains, just to the north of Albania. Here their descendants, Serbs of Serbs, maintained their independence for five hundred years: not even the Turks could subdue this tiny state in its mountain fortress.

During the World War, Nicholas, the last king of Montenegro, flirted with the Central Powers, and lost his throne. In any case a Yugoslavia, land of the South Slavs, without Montenegro would have been absurd. The ancient kingdom was incorporated in the new. There were many teething troubles —as when the Montenegrins were called upon to pay taxes for the first time in their lives!—but there never was any question about solidarity of interests. Now the Italians proposed to revive the primitive glories of Montenegro again. It was unfortunate that they should find the Black Mountain Serbs as unconquerable as ever. If the Turks could not subdue the Montenegrins, it is quite certain that the Italians cannot. Six months after the creation of the new kingdom, they had been unable to find anyone courageous enough to become king of such a sturdy state.

The Italians are treated as an unfortunate joke. In September 1941 they issued a stern order that all arms must be handed in at once. The 50,000 warriors of Montenegro produced a total of two rifles—neither of which would fire!

The remainder of Yugoslavia exists under a mixed German and Italian military control. In some areas of the mountain lands of South Serbia, Bosnia and Herzegovina this control exists only in name. Guerrilla forces occupy towns, vacate them when enemy troops arrive, then capture them again. Communications are precarious, disorder universal. The Yugoslavs are not merely waiting for the day of freedom; they are fighting for it.

VI

It is not difficult to foresee the shape of the new Yugoslavia.

(a) Internally, the state will probably develop on federal lines, with local autonomy for Croatia and Slovenia and—if it is genuinely demanded—by Bosnia and Montenegro. The greatest care must be taken that the power of the unified state is not weakened: autonomy should apply only to purely local affairs.

(b) The Slovenes and Croats left under Italian domination

after the last war clearly deserve warm consideration after all their trials. In 1919 plebiscites were avoided, since Italy had been promised the territory outright as part of her bribe for coming into the war. Now there is no such difficulty.

The plebiscite should be held district by district. If its results follow ethnic lines, the countryside would be overwhelmingly Slav, the towns largely Italian. In this instance the countryside outweighs the towns in numbers and importance. An exchange of population appears inevitable, and the resultant frontier will probably cut the Istrian Peninsula in two from north to south.

(c) Any adjustment of the frontier involves automatically the return of Fiume to Croatia.

Zara is an obvious anachronism, living only on Italian pride and ambition to make the Adriatic an 'Italian lake.' The port would develop rapidly under the impetus of Yugoslav trade— it has been almost killed by its nationalism. Its inhabitants will have to choose between national pride and prosperity.

(d) Yugoslavia's frontier disputes with Hungary, Bulgaria and Albania are discussed in the appropriate chapters.

CHAPTER EIGHT

BULGARIA

I

BULGARIA may be classed among the more backward countries of Europe, but a more interesting land I never hope to visit. Scenically its attractions are only moderate. The mountains that emerge from the Danube plain are stolid rather than majestic, and the rivers are insignificant. Some of the southern valleys are, however, unforgettable—the famous Valley of Roses, whence comes most of the world's supply of attar of roses, is unique. Bulgaria is almost entirely pastoral or agricultural. Its peasants cultivate their strips of land by methods which have scarcely changed since Biblical days. They are a fine, sturdy race: of great reputation in battle, but friendly and hospitable. The great lack of Bulgaria to date has been leaders: or, alternatively, luck, for she has backed the wrong horse with unenviable consistency.

The history of Bulgaria runs parallel with that of Serbia. In the sixth century the country we now know as Bulgaria was settled by the Serbs or South Slavs. The Bulgars arrived a hundred years later. They were a tribe of horsemen of Turanian stock, akin to the Huns. They were pagans, fierce and barbarous; they lived by war and loot. From their Asiatic home they had passed into Russia, and thence they descended upon the Danube plain.

The agricultural Slav tribes were in no condition to meet such warriors; nor could the Byzantine Empire withstand their violent onslaughts. Rapidly the middle Balkans were overrun and a Bulgarian Empire was established. It crumbled and fell, in the fashion of its day, weakened by internal dissension, but in the twelfth century a second empire emerged, with its capital at Trnovo.

There may be a more fascinating city in Europe than Trnovo, but I have yet to find it. The little river Yantra forms almost a figure 8 in forcing its way through the northern range of Balkan mountains, and the city is built on the slopes, so that the roof of one house touches the foundations of the next. One day archaeologists will excavate the rest of Trnovo and reveal its ancient splendours: on its now deserted hills, did I but rip up a sod with my boot, ancient stones were revealed beneath. And opposite the ruins of the emperor's castle is a Forest of Nightingales.

For two hundred years the Bulgarian Empire was supreme in the central Balkans: Albania, Macedonia, Serbia and Northern Greece lay within its domain. At that time, on the authority of our own Crusaders, Bulgarian civilisation was as high as any in Europe. This is extraordinary, when it is recalled that the Bulgars entered the Balkans as pagan plunderers.

Even more extraordinary is the manner in which the conquered imposed their culture upon the conquerors. The civilisation of the settled Serbs was naturally higher than that of the nomadic raiders who conquered them. The Bulgars did not exterminate the Serbs in the fashion of their day, but, after using them as serfs, intermarried with them, and in the course of generations adopted their culture and language. Thus the Bulgarian race as we know it today are actually descendants of Serbs and Bulgars, the Serb element probably overwhelming its rival. The Bulgarian language today is akin to Serb: both might be regarded as branches of an original Slav tongue.

From the advance of the Turks into Europe the stories of Bulgaria and Serbia have a melancholy similarity. For five hundred years the Bulgars lived miserably under Turkish rule, and not until the inevitable series of campaigns had been fought did the third Bulgarian Empire emerge—a tiny fragment of its ancient glory. We have already seen the worthy part she played in the final wars of freedom in 1912–13—and how she ruined everything in her treacherous turn on her allies to gain the coveted Macedonia. These Balkan wars left more than one evil legacy of potential danger.

Western opinion on Balkan states is frequently scathing. It is quite true that standards of living are low and education backward. More disconcerting is the standard of government, for most Balkan countries have an appalling record of conspiracies, assassinations and corruption. Yet judgment must be tempered with fairness. The long Turkish rule must never be forgotten. The Balkan peoples themselves had no rights— except the right to pay extravagant taxes. Most of them were completely illiterate, and the few educated men were those who had adopted Turkish culture.

When, after bitter struggles, these peoples regained their freedom, almost automatically they adopted democratic systems. But democracy is not so simply installed. It is the most difficult political system to work: it demands an intelligent and reasonably educated electorate; and it stands on tradition. In the Balkans it never had a chance. In most of the new countries power was immediately seized by the few professional politicians available—trained in the Ottoman school. These men were a bitter legacy.

Bulgaria was no better served by her statesmen than any other Balkan country. Here and there arose a fervent patriot, but most of them were of the type only too common in their district and day. Even in the last generation, when the other Balkan states have been assimilating western political morals, Bulgaria has not always been happy. The influence of Macedonia can be traced—the Macedonian is sharper-witted but much less scrupulous than the Bulgar, and has achieved remarkable representation among official and influential positions. It is difficult for a Westerner to credit Balkan corruption. Between 1878 and 1926 Bulgaria had ninety-six cabinet ministers. Of these exactly one-half were tried and condemned for embezzlement of public funds. But most of them were amnestied by the Tsar.

Despite her many changes of government, which continued during the inter-war period of 1919–39, Bulgarian ideas were united on the question of treaty revision. To raise an argument in Bulgaria, I found that I had only to mention the Dobrudja, Macedonia or Dedeagatch. In no state was the natural outlook so fierce and uncompromising as in Bulgaria: the Bulgarian intransigeance on the subject of recovery of her lost provinces wrecked all prospects of that united Balkan Entente which might have kept the tide of war away from South-Eastern Europe.

Her foreign policy was quite simple: the Bulgars had strong sentimental and racial affinities with Yugoslavia and Russia; apart from these, the outlook of the country depended almost entirely on her aspirations. Since Britain and France led the anti-revisionist group, Bulgaria turned instinctively to Germany—which country naturally favoured treaty revision! It is also true that Bulgaria's economic dependence on the Reich was very marked—nearly 70 per cent of her trade flowed to and from Germany—but I do not believe that this would have been such a vital consideration had not Germany backed her revisionist claims.

The country, unlike Roumania, is not naturally rich. Bulgaria is about the size of England (without Wales), but 30 per cent of the land is barren. The population is only 6½ millions, and the standard of life is low. There are only 93 towns in the whole country, and of these only 10 have populations larger than 25,000. Bulgaria is a land of village communities. Each village has its council of elders: often there is a suggestion of the collective spirit which is the basis of Russian rural life. Most peasants have their own plot of ground (usually very small: three-quarters of the holdings are less than 18 acres), but the elders allocate the communal grazing, direct the consumption of timber from the local forest—and even give permission for young people to marry.

They *are* young when they marry. It is not uncommon for a Bulgar woman to be a grandmother at forty. Babies are often born in fields—and in a few days the mothers are back with the harvest gangs, a wooden cradle slung under a tree. There are no rich in Bulgaria, by our standards, though there are by their own. The Prime Minister gets $250 a month. A civil servant considers himself well off on five dollars a week. A labourer can be hired for 50 cents a day. Of course these figures are meaningless except in relation to what they can buy. I remember in one Bulgarian town getting an excellent seven-course dinner for 18 cents! On the other hand, an ordinary five-cent bar of chocolate costs twenty cents. The explanation was that the food for the dinner was home-produced and therefore cheap; the chocolate imported and heavily taxed and therefore dear.

Bulgaria, indeed, offers a sample of the problem of under-consumption which upsets the economic life of the world. There is usually food to be had in Bulgaria, even if the peasant diet is very plain, but many manufactured goods are almost unpurchasable. (We hear a lot about the possible effects of radio propaganda in occupied countries. The 6½ million people in Bulgaria have only 50,000 radio sets between them!)

Bulgaria's loss of her fringe territory means that she has the most composite block of population in the Balkans. It includes only 160,000 people of other races—an amazing figure among the Balkan jumble: the principal minorities are Serbs, Jews, Roumanians, Armenians, Turks and Russians. Most of the Roumanians are likely to be repatriated shortly.

The sturdy Bulgarian peasants have a great reputation as fighters, and the Bulgar has often been described as 'the gentleman of the Balkans'—if he stabs you, it will be in the front, not the back.

It is a pity that this national characteristic has not been transmitted to successive governments. The pre-war government was predominantly pro-Axis—Italian as well as German influence was profound in Sofia. It was replaced on the outbreak of war by a non-party government, for it was quite obvious that the Bulgarian people did not want war. The new government made friendly arrangements with Russia, Turkey and Yugoslavia, and by agreeing to hold back her Dobrudja claims until the end of hostilities gave proof of her peaceful intentions.

The collapse of France altered the whole atmosphere: the Russian seizure of Bessarabia prompted an immediate claim for Southern Dobrudja. Now latent ambitions were fanned by Germany. In the summer of 1940 even some of her best friends thought that Britain would not win, so it was scarcely remarkable that Bulgaria should lean to Germany—already bound by strong economic ties, by promises of treaty revision, and by fear and respect for the mighty German war machine.

The autumn of 1940 saw Bulgarian subservience increasing. A series of Fascist measures—including anti-Semitic laws—were introduced. Nevertheless, British successes in North Africa and Greek victories over the Italians prompted caution, but early in 1941 the Germans forced a decision. It could only go one way. A huge German army was already in Roumania: Britain could give no help, and Russia was unwilling to move from her position of precarious neutrality. Even before Bulgaria's adhesion to the Tripartite Pact on March 2nd, 1941, German forces were already in control of Bulgarian airfields. While the German army continued to march in, the Bulgarian Prime Minister pathetically protested that the presence of German troops 'changed nothing of Bulgaria's policy of peace.'

It was from Bulgarian soil that the German attacks on Greece and Yugoslavia were launched on April 6th. At first Bulgaria played the part of a passive spectator, but, when the German drive was successful, old ambitions could not be restrained. Bulgaria joined hurriedly in the scramble for territory, and a few weeks later her troops and administrators were in occupation of Yugoslav Macedonia and Greek Eastern Thrace.

At this stage, therefore, it is advisable to consider these two problems: the parallel case of the Dobrudja is included in the Roumanian chapter.

CONFLICTING INTERESTS IN THE BALKANS AT THE OUTBREAK OF WAR

II

If my father and my grandfather could have picked up this book and read a section headed, 'The Macedonian Problem,' they would have felt quite at home. Nor would its contents have added much to their enlightenment, for the story of Macedonia since their day is little more than repetition of an over-familiar theme.

It is not a particularly attractive country, and I have often wondered why its possession should have occasioned such continuous bloodshed. In the west are mountains, bleak and barren, with wide valleys—green in spring, but parched in autumn. To the east the mountains fall away till they merge in rolling uplands and monotonous plains. In short, it is typical Balkan country, and in Western Europe would be permanently classed as a distressed area. To add to its distractions, it lies on both the earthquake and the malaria belts of Southern Europe.

In ancient days Macedonia was, of course, the centre of a mighty empire, but its power depended more on the personality of its emperors than upon the character of the country. At the time of Christ it was an unimportant Roman province. Then followed the successive swarms of invaders common to most Balkan countries. The Bulgars were the only ones to hold the district for sufficient length of time to impress their character upon it, and in 1371 it fell to the Turks.

A hundred years ago, when the Christian races of the Balkans began to throw off the Turkish yoke, the problem of Macedonia was already appreciated in Western Europe. It housed one of the most complicated ethnic medleys in Europe—the word *macedoine*, a culinary mixture, was coined from Macedonia. Greeks, the traders of South-Eastern Europe, were to be found in large numbers in all towns—in Salonika they had to contend with a lively colony of Jews who were descended from refugees from the Spanish Inquisition. The great landlords and richer peasants were mostly Turks, as were the officials—except the tax-collectors: these dangerous positions were sub-let to Greeks or Armenians. In the west were considerable districts occupied by Albanians, and in the north by Serbs. There were thousands of families of *vlachs*—landless men, shepherds, who moved with their flocks from lower to higher pasturages according to the seasons: they were mostly of Roumanian origin. But in addition to these assorted nationalities—and a dozen less significant minorities—there was a much larger indigenous population which called itself Macedonian. The people classed themselves as a Bulgarian tribe, and looked to the Bulgars for aid in the struggle for liberty. Indeed, it is significant that at this time Serbia took little interest in Macedonia.

By the beginning of the present century, Serbia, Greece, Bulgaria and Roumania had achieved their freedom in part, and the attenuated Turkish Empire consisted in the main of the district about Constantinople, Albania and Macedonia. Conditions of life in Madecdonia were pitiful under Turkish

MACEDONIA

misrule, with murder and starvation as its salient feature. By this time the freed Bulgars were working hard for their brothers—or cousins—in Macedonia. Hundreds of schools were established: and eventually terrorism replied to terror. In 1893 two Bulgar schoolmasters founded the Internal Macedonian Revolutionary Organisation—the famous I.M.R.O. These men, Damian Gruev and Pere Toclev, were ardent patriots, and were esteemed as such by the liberal states of the west. Their war-cry was 'Liberty or Death for Macedonia'— and in view of the subsequent argument, it is necessary to emphasise the words 'for Macedonia'—there was no mention of Bulgaria, Serbia or Greece. They fought an underground war against the Turkish tyranny, returning blow for blow. Yet their movement had a moral basis, the cause of liberty. It flourished exceedingly: patriotism was its religion—recruits had to swear eternal loyalty on a revolver and a dagger in the form of a cross. The Turks were well served by their spies; they tortured, raped and massacred. The patriots formed komitadji or irregular bands and took to the mountains, and a guerrilla warfare of intense ferocity began.

Now when, in 1912, Serbia, Bulgaria and Greece formed a coalition to drive the Turks out of Europe—or at least to liberate the surviving populations of their own races—very wisely they divided the prospective spoils before they began. But over Macedonia they could not agree—all three had serious claims. The Greeks were emphatic that Salonika was Greek—which was largely true—and claimed that the Macedonian hinterland should go with its port. The Serbs pointed out that Macedonia had been an integral part of the great Serbian Empire; that the people were a Slav tribe akin to the Serbs; and the access to the Aegean Sea was vital to the new nation—Greece already had a hundred harbours, while Serbia had none. Bulgaria claimed that Macedonia had formed an integral part of *two* Bulgar empires; that the Macedonians were a Bulgar tribe, much nearer ethnically to the Bulgars than the Serbs; that they spoke a Bulgarian dialect, and that culturally they leaned to Bulgaria. Further, Bulgaria had done the greater part of the work of making the Macedonians freedom-conscious.

So, although other potential conquests were apportioned, the major part of Macedonia was left unallocated until victory was achieved—the line of 'autonomy' was to be followed, and this in Macedonia meant nothing. The success of the campaign was unexpectedly rapid. By virtue of their geographical position, the hardest fighting fell to the Bulgars, who were never wanting in courage. While they were pressing towards Constantinople, Greece and Serbia occupied Macedonia—and when Turkey was beaten, it was obvious that they did not intend to budge.

Then Bulgaria made an appalling error of judgment, turning suddenly on her former allies. After initial victories, she was speedily beaten—Roumania joining in with a flank attack. The victorious allies parcelled out Macedonia between themselves. Salonika and the south went to Greece, the north-west to Serbia, and Bulgaria was allotted only a minute area of Macedonia. Licking her wounds, the scowling Bulgaria sat back with dark thoughts of revenge.

Now there is a serious school of thought in Great Britain which argues that European squabbles have nothing to do with Britain or anybody else. Its exponents would laugh at me if I suggested that the Macedonian problem was a matter of vital importance to Britain. Yet, if I wished for a thesis for this book, I would undertake to prove that every one of these European danger spots is a matter of real concern to us. Apart from the fact that Balkan quarrels have a nasty habit of spreading, Macedonia has already cost the lives of half a million British soldiers, and the maiming of a million more.

This is not conjecture, but solid fact. Consider the situation at Christmas 1914. England was at war with Germany, Austria-Hungary and Turkey. Of these, easily the weakest was Turkey. Further, the defeat of Turkey would have had most important strategic consequences, since the Dardanelles would be opened to admit supplies to hard-pressed and ill-equipped Russia.

In such circumstances she looked about for allies in the Balkans. The natural enemy of the Balkan states was Turkey: the natural protector of the little Slav nations of Serbia and Bulgaria was Russia. The Bulgars had already shown what they could do against the Turks: a Bulgarian onslaught towards Constantinople, and a British demonstration at the Dardanelles, and Turkey was doomed. The subsequent potentialities are obvious—not merely the reinforcement of Russia,

but a favourable opportunity of attacking Austria-Hungary in
the rear. No military knowledge is necessary to appreciate
this—a glance at the map is enough.

England approached Bulgaria: her task should have been
easy, for popular opinion was overwhelmingly with Russia
and against Turkey. Bulgaria's demands were simple—she
wanted Macedonia. Great Britain put the point to Serbia:
'Give up your share of Macedonia, so as to bring in Bulgaria:
It is a tract of no outstanding importance, since there is now
no question of your having Salonika. But if we win this war,
you are to have Croatia and Slovenia—territory incomparably
richer—to say nothing of Bosnia and Herzegovina. And in
place of Salonika you shall have ample ports in the Adriatic.
All this can come about *only* if we win the war. So give up
Macedonia to Bulgaria, and make victory certain.'

But Serbia said no. Until this time she had repelled Austrian
invasions with comparative ease—considered that victory *was*
certain without Bulgaria's aid. She refused to yield a yard of
the disputed territory.

Naturally, German and Austrian diplomats were not idle—
and their bargaining hand was far stronger than Britain's. They
were at war with Serbia—could give away her territory with
equanimity. They argued with Bulgaria: 'Come in on our
side: we are bound to win, and then you shall have your Macedonia.' And, since England offered nothing and the Central
Powers offered exactly what the Bulgars wanted, small wonder
at the eventual decision.

Bulgaria came in on the side of Germany and Austria. The
tottering Turkey was propped up by the supplies which could
now pass to her; Serbia, smitten by the Bulgars in flank, was
rapidly overrun by invaders. An immobile army had to be
assembled at Salonika—sarcastically termed by the Germans
their 'greatest internment camp'—watched by Bulgarian jail-
ers. Is it too much to claim that the Bulgarian decision
lengthened the war by a year? Most competent military critics
would say *two* years, with their toll of frightful slaughter.

That is to say, but for miserable Macedonia, American entry into the last war might have been unnecessary. Who shall say that the whole world is not affected by the troubles of Europe?

Yet once again Bulgaria had backed the wrong side, and at the end of the war her case was worse than before, with further fragments of Macedonia nibbled from her territory. In vain she put her ethnic and historic arguments to the statesmen of the peace conferences. In these days it does not pay to make war and win—it is disastrous to make war and lose. Bulgaria had gambled recklessly, and had lost. But the problem of Macedonia still remained.

There was nothing to do but accept the situation, and the government did it. Not so I.M.R.O., which was not bound by the judgments of Paris. In the rump of Bulgarian Macedonia bands of desperate men gathered; they called themselves patriots, but others called them brigands. They kept up a state of intermittent warfare, and claimed to 'rule' their own corner of Bulgaria in the name of the Macedonian people.

At first they were treated as an irritating nuisance, an extremist cult whose atrocities would soon lose their novelty. But in 1922 the komitadji bands received reinforcements.

Now hitherto the Greek section of Macedonia had seen surprisingly little trouble. But, it will be recalled, the Greeks had been allocated a huge expanse of territory in Asia Minor by the powers at Paris: the agreement was that Smyrna was essentially a Greek port, and must have an adequate hinterland. The new dictator of Turkey held vastly different views; his armies swept the Greeks from Asia Minor: then, so that it might never again be claimed that Smyrna was a Greek port, he cleared all Greeks out of Turkish territory. The Greeks, of course, retaliated by clearing all Turks out of Greece. The exchange, however, was very unequal—200,000 Turks against 1,500,000 Greeks. That meant that homes had to be found for a surplus of 1,300,000 Greeks—a colossal task.

After a period of chaos, the Greeks tackled it boldly. Greek Macedonia was an obvious area of settlement: the towns were largely Greek, but the villages included large foreign elements. There were tens of thousands of semi-nomad *vlachs*, of Roumanian origin—they were promptly transported to Roumania. There were even larger numbers of Macedonians who claimed to be Bulgars; they were taken at their word, and bundled into Bulgaria.[1] Naturally, they were disgruntled at this sudden uprooting from their ancestral homes—and the young men gravitated automatically to the komitadji.

It might be said, therefore, that the problem of Greek Macedonia was solved—amicably, from the official point of view, for treaties for exchange of population had been arranged between Greece and Bulgaria, under the aegis of the League of Nations. As a result of the exchange and resettlement, 90 per cent of the population of Greek Macedonia became Greek, which is a remarkable percentage for this part of the world. Except for the resentment on the part of the emigrants, therefore, the Macedonian quarrel was now almost exclusively between Bulgaria and Yugoslavia.

I.M.R.O. dominated the scene. It even levied its own taxes—in addition to the government dues—in its district. Its headquarters at Petritch were a mixture of civil government and field force. The cabinet at Sofia professed itself helpless—was actually overawed by the terrorists. One minister, Tsankoff, replaced the weathercock on his house by a machine-gun! Any minister who opposed I.M.R.O. was speedily assassinated.

The policy of Yugoslavia did not help. It was the intention

---

[1] There are about 60,000 Macedonians left in Greece today. They have been intensely loyal, and fought with traditional courage against the Italians in Albania. Their area is at present under German occupation, and it is significant that they have made no request for Bulgarian protection—although the Bulgars occupy nearby areas. This contrasts vividly with the attitude of Macedonians in Bulgaria. The explanation is to be found in religion. These 60,000 stayed behind in Greece because they were faithful to the Greek patriarch, and did not wish to transfer their allegiance to the Bulgarian branch of the Orthodox Church. This is not the only case of the claims of religion overriding those of nationality.

to Serbise the population of Yugoslav Macedonia. Bulgar schools were forbidden, and every form of Bulgar or Macedonian patriotism was ruthlessly suppressed. When first I travelled in this district, it was a crime to be found in the possession of a Bulgarian newspaper!

The murder of the Macedonian peasant leader, Stambouliski, in 1923 brought the conflict into the open. He had attempted to settle the quarrel with Yugoslavia—and I.M.R.O. condemned him. First he was made to dig his own grave; then his ears and nose were cut off, before he was mercifully killed. This was the beginning of a series of atrocities which were to cause the deaths of thousands of people, many of them without active part in the quarrel.

I felt desperately sorry for the wretched inhabitants of Yugoslav Macedonia, or South Serbia, as it had been rechristened. Komitadji bands would swoop over the frontier in some desperate raid of pillage and murder: if the peasants aided the raiders—and their natural sympathies were often with them— then they could look for trouble when the avenging Yugoslav soldiery arrived. If they refused their aid, then the komitadji were past masters in the arts of torture and murder.

From what I could see, there was little to choose between the two sides. In one village I saw a man who had 'talked'; the opposite side had made sure that he would not talk again, for his tongue was slit down the middle. In the same street was a woman who had refused to talk; she bared her shoulder to show me her armpit, where a red-hot brand had been thrust. Another man showed me his fingers, where wedges of wood had been driven between the flesh and the nails.

Every atrocity provoked a dozen others, for reprisal is the commonest of instinctive passions. Except that it was far more ferocious, the guerrilla warfare in Macedonia was akin to that in Ireland at the time of the Black and Tans. When I talked to komitadji, they protested strongly that they were not murderers—they were patriots; their object, they claimed, was to attract the attention of the chancelleries of Europe to Mace-

donia. If so, they certainly succeeded! You must not blame
them too hardly for their choice of method. Far too often have
civilised governments ignored problems peacefully presented,
only to capitulate to armed disorder.

The two governments were inevitably involved. The Yugoslavs complained that the Bulgarian government connived at
the komitadji raids—that it made no effort to suppress the
bands. The Bulgars retorted that if the Yugoslav government
had allowed to its minorities the rights to which they were
entitled, then the trouble would never have arisen. There was
an acute state of tension akin to the moments preceding war.
The Yugoslav frontier was a mass of barbed wire, with
machine-gun posts every kilometre.

For ten years the appalling record of slaughter continued.
I.M.R.O. was well supplied with money and arms—apart
from the 'taxes' it levied, it boasted that it received subsidies
from Italy, the 'historic' enemy of Yugoslavia. But in 1933
there arose a Bulgarian government which was appalled at this
warfare between cousins: the influence of King Boris was
flung into the scale, in the cause of peace.

The komitadjis eased the situation by quarrelling among
themselves—and they were no more gentle in their internecine feuds than in their guerrilla warfare. Taking advantage
of the situation, the government exiled the leaders. A new
atmosphere developed. King Alexander of Yugoslavia paid a
state visit to Sofia which had far-reaching effects in the cause
of friendship. Yet a few weeks later King Alexander was dead.

I would revert here to my previous contention—that the
Balkan quarrels do concern us very intimately. Mr. Eden in
his first term at the Foreign Office did a good deal of first-class
work—and no one doubts that he will do a good deal more.
If I were able to put to him a poser: Which was the most
delicate moment for European peace during that term? he
might prefer to make more than one answer. I am confident,
nevertheless, that one of the moments he would choose would
be that which followed the murder of Alexander—when

Yugoslavia and Hungary were straining at each other's throats, and when war was nearer than we knew. The lowering of the tension must be counted among Mr. Eden's major feats of diplomacy. And the man who caused the trouble was named Chernozemski. He was 'borrowed' by a Croat terrorist organisation to murder Alexander, but actually he was a Macedonian komitadji.

After 1935, however, the situation eased. The power of the komitadjis may not have been broken, but at least it was subdued. In spite of a new spirit of co-operation between the two Balkan Slav countries, Bulgaria never pretended to abandon her claims.

Her demand for Macedonia and the Dobrudja kept her outside the Balkan Pact. Nevertheless, the fact that she was surrounded by potential opponents held her extremists within reasonable bounds. Gradually relations between Yugoslavia and Bulgaria became easier. A Pact of Friendship was signed in 1937, and as late as February 1940 there were discussed not merely closer economic relations, but a full customs union. The position was, of course, that German pressure was driving the Balkans towards unity; it is a tragedy that an emergency was necessary to produce this result—which was still incomplete when the emergency arose. Had France remained in the fight but a few months longer, a very different story might have been told in the Balkans.

As we have seen, immediately after the collapse of France came the Russian demand for Bessarabia. This promptly stimulated the dormant and legitimate Bulgarian claims to Southern Dobrudja. The attainment of this aspiration prompted the revival of ideas which were gradually dying among the more reasonable sections of Bulgaria. Was there not now a real chance for the recovery of her other lost territories?

The Germans fanned these ideas assiduously: as usual, they were very ready to give away what did not belong to them. Bulgarian economic dependence on Germany helped in the process: from the German point of view, Balkan unity of any description was dangerous, and must be halted.

With the German armies in Roumania, and with German influence in Bulgaria already profound, the Bulgarian government could have done little even had it wished. It was completely overawed by German force: the powerful army clique had always been attracted by German military might, and King Boris was of German descent. Soon began the familiar infiltration of 'tourists' and technicians. By the spring of 1941 it was apparent that Bulgaria was virtually in German occupation. New aerodromes were being prepared under German direction; poor communications were being improved. Bulgarian ministers did not pretend to be comfortable in their minds. Twice in a generation they had backed the wrong horse. Now they had again to try to pick a winner—when they would have preferred to abstain from betting at all.

The attack on Greece opened a new chapter. Hitherto Bulgaria could represent herself as a small state unwillingly and temporarily surrendered to a mighty power: now she had ranged herself openly among Britain's enemies. It was purely a question of opportunism. The Nazi creed never struck the same horror in Balkan countries as it did in Britain, for some of its methods are painfully familiar there. Anyway, here was a chance of recovering coveted territory: the phrase 'possession is nine points of the law' has many Balkan equivalents. The Bulgarian government probably had a majority of its people behind it when its armies marched in the wake of the aggressors into Greece and Yugoslavia.

Yet there are Bulgarians who see history being repeated. In 1917 all the lost territory had been regained: by the end of 1918 it was lost again. Only a German victory can assure Bulgaria that the territory she holds today will be more than a temporary occupation.

As soon as Yugoslavia was prostrate, therefore, Bulgaria marched into Macedonia. Some of her leaders would have marched even further. Already they had seized strategic positions on the common frontier—now they wished to press on to the line of the river Morava;[1] that is to say, they were prepared to assist in the total destruction of Yugoslavia. In Macedonia ready and primitive passions were aroused, and again the unhappy valleys witnessed murder and pillage. The Serbs will not forget this lightly—the third attack by their neighbours within thirty years. Nor are they disposed to throw all the blame on the Bulgarian government. Even a dictatorship must have a substantial proportion of its people behind it.

Yet in spite of all difficulties I do not believe that the problem of Macedonia is insoluble. It will need great patience: people in the Balkans are noted for their long memories—and they have a lot to remember.

I recall one scene: two peasants, sleeping on a hillside. Yet, as I approached them, I saw that they were not sleeping, but dead: murdered. Close by their families were mourning. Those peasants were nothing to me, but I have never forgotten the overwhelming grief of their children. I do not think a little elementary schooling in Serbian is likely to make the children forget. As they grow older, they are bound to ask why their fathers died.

These two men had been killed by Serbs—this was in 1935. Now the situation is reversed—and is just as grim. Nevertheless, I do not despair: I foresee a Yugoslav-Bulgar entente in our time—perhaps within a Balkan Federation. It will need endless goodwill in the making, but it is not impossible. Then the exact status of the Macedonian people would recede in importance, and should cease to be a menace to peace.

We must not expect every desirable thing to happen immediately the war ends. The terror and massacre will not be forgotten so easily. The Yugoslav and Greek governments in London are working on a scheme of federation which may be as close as that of Poland and Czechoslovakia. They plan it deliberately as the beginning of bigger things. This is sound

---

[1] The Germans refused this plea, as it would have involved handing over mines which they wished to keep themselves.

statesmanship. Both countries have much to forgive of their neighbours, but they have made it clear that friendship and not eternal enmity is their aim.

III

We have seen that after the Balkan wars of 1912–13, Bulgaria lost most of her gains because of her treacherous attack on her allies. One only was she allowed to keep—a corridor of territory through Thrace to the port of Dedeagatch. After the World War, the territory was claimed by and awarded to Greece. Like most Balkan borderlands, it had a mixed population—Greeks, Turks and Bulgars. The latter numbered only 69,000 out of 213,000 and on ethnic grounds the Greek claim could not be denied.

(The Bulgars claimed a figure of 81,000, but this included officials and troops not indigenous to the region. In fairness it should be pointed out that the population included 70,000 Turks who were later replaced by Greeks under the arrangements for exchange of population. Today the Greeks of Eastern Thrace outnumber the Bulgars by three to one.)

Economically the Bulgars were hit nationally and locally: nationally, by the loss of their only port on the Aegean; locally, because the shepherds of the Rhodope mountains had for many centuries driven their flocks down to the Thracian plains for winter pasturage. Now this was prevented by a closed frontier.

The Treaty of Neuilly undertook 'to ensure the economic outlet of Bulgaria to the Aegean Sea.' Irredentists argued that this implied territorial access to the sea: the men who drew up the treaty said that it did not. Instead, they proceeded to carry out their intentions. By the Thracian Treaty of August 10th, 1920, Bulgaria was allotted a free zone in the port of Dedeagatch, and the full use of the connecting railway. The treaty was not ratified by Bulgaria.

The Greeks were anxious to be conciliatory, but the Balkan atmosphere was one of suspicion and opportunism. First Bul-

garia asked for a more convenient port four miles west of
Dedeagatch, which had but a poor natural harbour. The
Greeks agreed. The Bulgars then claimed that such a port
would be useless unless it were under Bulgarian control: the
Greeks agreed. The Bulgars next demanded control of the
railway: the Greeks agreed. Having gained all the essentials,
the Bulgars now demanded a territorial corridor.

The Greeks, with Allied approval, made Bulgaria an alternative offer—a free zone in Salonika, a port far superior to
Dedeagatch in every way. When the Bulgars refused, it became apparent that their objective was not the economic
outlet promised by the Treaty of Neuilly, but the recovery
of territory.

This ought not to have been a serious problem: with no
strong ethnic claim, all Bulgaria's reasonable demands could
and would have been met by special facilities in Greek ports.
Nor, it should be emphasised, did the loss of Eastern Thrace
rankle sentimentally as did the cession of Southern Dobrudja
and Macedonia. Here was no historic Bulgarian territory—
the Thracian corridor was under Bulgarian control for no
more than five years, from 1913 to 1918! But for the German
attack on Greece, it was unlikely to disturb the peace of
Europe.

As in the case of Macedonia, however, the rapid German
victories aroused dormant passions. Bulgarian armies occupied
Eastern Thrace from the Maritza to the Struma—far beyond
the original claims. The fundamental control was of course
German, but Bulgarian troops could be usefully employed on
communications and other preparations for an eventual attack
on Turkey, while the Bulgarian government exercised a shad-
owy and uneasy authority over the reoccupied region. The
situation fitted admirably into the German plan—to get the
largest possible number of countries and people dependent
on a German victory.

IV

A separate chapter has not been allocated to Greece since she has not claims to make on other countries, and is singularly free from troubles likely to affect the peace of Europe. One or two notes are, however, advisable.

The present position of Greece is desperate. The country is almost useless to the Germans, with small industrial and agricultural resources. They have therefore looted everything they could—even to the seed for sowing—and left the country to its fate; most of the occupying garrison is Italian. Now Greece faces starvation. Already the death-carts make a daily round of Athens, where the mortality from starvation reached 500 a day by the end of 1941. The situation is aggravated by the fact that the areas under Bulgarian occupation are the most fertile in Greece. The Italians make no move to alleviate the distress. Their aim is to depopulate the country so that they can occupy it themselves.

I have referred to the proposed federation between Greece and Yugoslavia. It is likely to mature. Yet the Greeks have always tended to look upon their country as Mediterranean rather than Balkan. Certainly the Hellenic culture differs from that of the Slavs and the Turks. If a plebiscite could be taken in Greece, the overwhelming demand would be for the closest collaboration with all their neighbours—but for inclusion within the British Empire, or in association with it, like Egypt. Probably we shall have to face such requests from many quarters after victory. The possibility was envisaged at the Ottawa Conference years ago.

I have said that Greece has no territorial demands in Europe. (After the defeat of Italy, she will presumably receive the Dodecanese Islands, twice promised to her. Turkey is likely to favour this move.) In my conversations with Greeks of many classes, however, I have found a strong desire for one territorial adjustment; the demand will probably never be preferred, because it affects a friendly power.

There is an historic route of invasion of Greece—by the Monastir Gap. The Germans followed it faithfully in 1941. The Greeks, who after their long wars of defence think in strategic terms, would like to garrison this immensely strong point themselves; to the Yugoslavs it is an unimportant pass in the southern extremity of their country; to the Greeks it spells security. However, with a closer union between the two countries, these apprehensions may be lowered or removed.

v

To no Balkan country will the defeat of Germany bring such disillusion as to Bulgaria. The economies of these nations are so closely linked: the Bulgarian leaders have banked everything upon German success.

The German attack on Russia occasioned real misgivings in Bulgaria. There is a strong Communist element in the land: miserably, it had played into the hands of the ruling political and military cliques in the days of German-Russian collaboration. Now, of course, it reversed its policy and advocated violent resistance to Hitlerism. By this time, however, the Germans were undisputed masters of Bulgaria and dealt with Communist opposition savagely; thousands of Bulgars were arrested, hundreds executed.

Yet all the opposition to the new aggression did not come from Communists. The Bulgarian peasant has a deep-rooted sentimental affection for Russia, his 'big brother.' Was it not with Russian assistance that he gained his freedom from the Turks? Even if 'ideological' differences existed, Russia was still of sacred memory in Bulgaria.

Then, as their losses mounted, the Germans pressed for Bulgarian divisions to serve in Russia. In this they had not the wisdom of their predecessors in 1915. At that time, when pressing the Bulgars into the war, the Germans were careful to send them into action against Serbs, Greeks, British and French—*not* Russians. As I write, even the puppet Bulgarian government resists the demand. It would supply troops for labour services, but if matched against the Russians in battle the government is afraid that half their men would desert to the other side. I think such apprehension is well founded.[1]

Disappointed in his attempt to drive the Bulgars into action against the Russians, Hitler has tried to mobilise them against the Turks. This is quite a different proposition. Although relations between Bulgaria and Turkey have been friendly for some years, most Bulgars were reared on the idea that the Turk was their hereditary enemy. Further, the possession of Istanbul is a long-cherished Bulgarian dream. What is Dedeagatch, or even Salonika, compared with Istanbul? (They must be innocents indeed if they imagine that Germany would leave such a prize in their hands. But it is an excellent inducement.)

As I write, there is news of German and Bulgarian concentrations along the Turkish frontier. It will be remarkable if Turkey escapes the attention of the aggressionist powers for much longer, and Bulgaria may well be used as a tool.

Again Bulgaria has gambled and lost. Her punishment will not be severe, for she has very little to lose.

(*a*) She is likely to retain Southern Dobrudja, regained from Roumania.

(*b*) She will have to restore to Greece the portion of Thrace she now occupies. On the other hand, the promised economic outlet to the sea can still be arranged.

(*c*) She will retire from that section of Macedonia she has occupied by force. Subsequent developments will depend very largely on her future relations with Yugoslavia. If the two joined to form an enlarged South Slav state, then the problem of Macedonia might solve itself. The new state would probably be federalised, and might include provinces like Serbia,

---

[1] In August 1941, General Sukeach, the newly appointed Bulgarian Chief of Staff, was inspecting an engineer regiment. He asked that the men who sympathised with Russia in her struggle against Germany should take three paces forward, and promised that no harm should come to anyone who thus demonstrated his opinions. Only one man remained in his place!

Bulgaria, Croatia, Slovenia, Bosnia-Herzegovina, Montenegro —and Macedonia.

One of the obstacles to such union hitherto has been the existence of two royal houses. King Boris—of German descent —may have to pay the price of defeat, as his father did in 1918, and may lose his throne. King Peter has the advantage of being a South Slav. There are strong tendencies towards closer unity: nowhere in Europe is neighbouring kinship so closely marked. I recall one vivid commentary on the rival Serbian and Bulgarian claims to Macedonia. In one village near Skoplje I met two men who were brothers: *one called himself a Bulgar, the other a Serb*. Yet this family provided my brightest outlook on the Macedonian problem.

'Are you a Serb or a Bulgar?' I asked the son of one of these brothers.

'Neither,' he answered. 'I am a Yugoslav!'

A magnificent answer! He was neither Serb nor Bulgar, but a Southern Slav.

'And you?' I asked of his sister.

'I am a Yugoslav too,' she said, *'if you include Bulgaria as well.'*

CHAPTER NINE

ALBANIA

I

FOR a country so small, Albania has already occasioned a surprising amount of argument in the chancelleries of Europe.

It is a remarkable land. Except for a narrow coastal strip, it is entirely mountainous—high ranges enclosing some of the loveliest valleys in Europe. For centuries the Albanians have lived a primitive life in their isolated highlands. Foreign invaders came and went, occupied the coastal strip, and claimed to hold the land, but their authority ended where the mountains began. Even the Turks, who 'ruled' Albania for four hundred years, did no more than utilise the tribal organisation of the Albanians for their own purposes.

During that time the only law in Albania was found in the code of Lek, an Albanian Moses. It was based on blood for blood, and although full of protestations of honour it included the worst features of the vendetta. Thousands of Albanians were killed every year in family feuds, and sometimes whole tribes were exterminated. Western civilisation and culture were unknown, and the life of the Albanian scarcely differed from that of his ancestor in mediaeval days.

Although Albania suffered less from the Turks than other Balkan states—for 70 per cent of the people accepted the Moslem religion—there were periodic rebellions. In 1913 independence was at last regained, and a German prince, William of Wied, became first king of Albania. He had scarcely begun to rule when the World War broke out: Austria eventually occupied the north of the little kingdom, Italy the south. After the war Albania became an independent republic.

At once it was in the news. Its boundaries were not demarcated, and there were bitter quarrels with the neighbouring
Yugoslavia and Greece. In 1920 the Yugoslavs actually invaded Albania. Their army was eventually held by a scratch
force of tribesmen raised by a young man who was Home
Secretary of Albania: his name was Ahmed Zogu.

The port of Valona and its hinterland, in the south of
Albania, had been promised to Italy by the Treaty of London.
It is a mediocre port, but its possession gave Italy complete
control over the Adriatic—the Yugoslav seaboard was completely hemmed. The Albanians held different ideas. Exploit-
ing the arts of guerrilla warfare which had served them so well
against the Turks, they drove the Italians from Valona. Italy
still held the adjacent island of Suseno, however.

In 1923 an Allied commission was fixing the southern boundaries of Albania. Its leader, an Italian general, was murdered
by a Greek fanatic. By this time Mussolini had achieved
power. The incident, he decided, needed more than the normal diplomatic usage—it demanded an exhibition of the new
energy of Fascist Italy. Within forty-eight hours a division
of infantry and half the Italian fleet had assembled off the
Greek island of Corfu and bombarded it. For hectic moments
Europe trembled on the verge of war; then Greece was induced to pay an indemnity which was sufficient solace to
Italy's honour.

By this time, too, more had been heard of the young Home
Secretary who had resisted the Yugoslav invasion. He had
become first prime minister, then president; and in 1928 he
declared himself King Zog I of Albania. Since that time he had
to face almost annual insurrections, most of them led by
tribal chiefs jealous of his rise to power. On the whole, however, his rule became stabilised, and his control of Albania was
more real than that of any other ruler had been for a thousand
years. He worked energetically for the modernisation of his
little land. With the aid of a remarkable corps of British officers he organised an efficient gendarmerie. His army was

trained by Italians, and schools and public buildings were built—with Italian money—and new roads, primarily of military importance, connecting the principal towns, and radiating to the Yugoslav frontier.

Mussolini never disguised his real interests in Albania. Its oil is important, and its metals may be useful, but the real value of Albania is strategic. Italian control of her coast compensates for the 'loss' of Dalmatia, and makes the Adriatic Sea into an Italian lake. In the event of war with Yugoslavia—a very real possibility until a year ago—Albania offered a serious threat to the Yugoslav flank; and the Albanian army, small though it might be, was a valuable reinforcement—the Turks used to esteem the Albanians highly as warriors, and we shall see that they have no friendship for the Yugoslavs. Although it is only the size of Wales and has a population of less than a million, Italian strategic conception was quite sound—Albania has an importance far beyond its size.

But Mussolini had to learn a lesson which has been taught to us by bitter experience—that a benefactor is seldom loved. Even if his intentions pass the highest moral standards, he is apt to outstay his welcome—and the humblest Albanian highlander was under no delusions about Italian interest in his country. There was a clash of temperament, too. In spite of all the Italians have done—and their material achievements have been considerable—the Albanians do not like the Italians. That is all there is to it, but it is important. I heard bitter complaints of the arrogance of Italian officers, who acted as if they ruled the country. When one of them arrested me, the Albanian police released me at once, simply because I had been arrested by an Italian.

Zog had turned to Italy almost without choice. His country was undeveloped and needed heavy financial backing. His immediate neighbours, Yugoslavia and Greece, could not give it—and, in any case, were hereditary enemies, until recently engaged in open conflict. Italy was the only alternative, for Britain—Zog's first choice—was not interested.

In 1926 the bonds between Albania and Italy were drawn closer. Faced with a rebellion more serious than usual, Zog turned to Mussolini for help. It was given—at a price. Italy acquired the right to intervene in Albania's internal or external affairs whenever the latter so requested.

The following years were spent by Zog in attempts to lessen Italian influence. A customs union was rejected in 1932, and two years later Zog attempted to control Italian commercial penetration and to remove Italian officers and instructors from the Albanian army. Mussolini's reply was a naval demonstration off the Albanian coast.

Then a strange scene was played. Without official appeal, Albanian tribesmen streamed from their mountain valleys, ready to defy the whole might of Italy!

Nevertheless, in succeeding years Italian influence was strengthened again. Albania's oil and metal resources were entirely under Italian control; Italian officers trained the Albanian army, and a firm alliance was made. Apparently Italy had everything she could possibly want.

On April 5th, 1939, there was wild rejoicing in Albania. Singing and cheering crowds mobbed King Zog's modest palace in Tirana, and in the wild valleys highlanders discharged their rifles in a *feu de joie*. Always his subjects had looked to him to marry and found a dynasty. There were difficulties, for Zog was a Moslem, and not every noble family would consider such an alliance. But a year earlier the king had delighted his country by taking as his wife a lady of distinguished family, half Hungarian and half American. And now she had duly presented him with a son and heir. Here was the one thing needful to consolidate Albania—the certainty of succession after centuries of unrest.

The new prince was two days old when his inheritance was rudely stolen from him. On Good Friday Italian troops landed without warning. Resistance was desultory—the Albanian army totalled only 12,000 men, and within a week Albania was overrun. King Zog and his invalid queen made a precarious journey over the unfriendly mountains to seek refuge in Greece.

The real reason for Italy's act of aggression is not yet known. The Italian apologia declared that Albania was occupied because King Zog had proposed that Italy should send troops to Albania for the purpose of attacking Yugoslavia. No one outside Italy, and not many people inside, attached any credence to this fantastic plea.

It is more probable that Italy was attempting to force King Zog into a closer collaboration than he or his people wished, and that he adopted his attitude of 1931. The moment of 1939, however, was sterner and morals lower, and he was promptly bundled off his throne. It was given out that Italy had been invited to take Albania under her protection, and a new government of Albanian 'patriots' was set up—most of them were Zog's opponents, including the aforesaid jealous tribal chiefs. A few days later, in the fashion of these things, all pretence of Albanian autonomy was dropped and the initial promises forgotten. An Italian lieutenant-general ruled the land with the assistance of an army of 70,000 men. As a measure of assurance, part of the Albanian army was removed to Italy. Sections of the Fascist party were formed throughout Albania, and the Italian legal and penal codes were introduced immediately. Albania became, in fact, no more than an Italian province.

Is this the end of Albania? I doubt it. I lived for a while among the Ghegs of High Albania and I never saw anything to equal their fierce unyielding courage. I would not care for the task of holding Albania down, even with 70,000 soldiers. Death is only an ordinary risk to an Albanian tribesman. I recall a story told to me by a Serbian officer. During the terrible retreat of 1916, the Serbs were harassed by Albanian irregulars. My friend captured a band of seven of them, who were duly court-martialled and sentenced to death. Ammunition was scarce, so it was decided to cut their throats. After the first two men had died, the remaining Albanians obligingly lifted their heads to expose their throats, so as to make the task of the executioner easier, and went to their death with a grim jest. I would not care to visit High Albania today—the tribesmen are the best guerrilla fighters in Europe, and I might be mistaken for an Italian.

Albanian resistance continued, in spite of stern repression. In August 1940 there was a serious anti-Fascist rising. Then came the Italian attack on Greece.

Mussolini's idea was obvious. Hitler had already indicated that he proposed to turn to the Balkans, which he considered as Germany's sphere of influence. Mussolini had other ideas. He held that Dalmatia, Croatia *and Greece* should fall to Italy's share of the spoils. Hence he must get in first.

Already suspicion had been aroused. Not only was the Italian garrison in Albania unduly large and constantly increasing, but tens of thousands of Italian workmen were also brought over, to work on new communications under semi-military conditions.

The excuse given for the wanton attack on Greece was even more feeble than is usual in these cases. It was alleged that Albanian minorities in Greece were being ill-treated. Then a certain Albanian brigand, Daut Hoggia, a man with many murders to his 'credit' and a price on his head, was himself killed by two Albanians on Greek territory. The two men were promptly arrested and held for trial. Mussolini did not want justice; he wanted war.

At least, he wanted victory—preferably without fighting. His intelligence service was strongly represented in Greece, but woefully misled him. He was confident that the Italian armies, strongly reinforced and far superior to the Greeks in equipment as well as numbers, would rapidly overrun Greece. Instead, they were held, defeated and soon pushed back into Albania: as gallant a campaign by a resolute people fighting for their homeland as the war has shown.

Mussolini hoped for Albanian backing in his adventure. It is true that feeling between Albanians and Greeks was not friendly—largely a relic of earlier feuds, particularly of the confused days of 1912–14, when armed bands of brigands ranged both sides of the Greek-Albanian frontier and when each side accused the other of atrocities. Yet Albanian support was lukewarm. Most of the tribes had never taken kindly to Italian rule; they had been irritated beyond measure by continuous forced requisitioning of their cattle and crops. The incentive of fighting a traditional enemy was not enough: in spite of Mussolini's declarations, the Albanians liked the Italians as little as they did the Greeks.

At an early stage of the campaign most of the Albanian troops had to be withdrawn from the battle zone as 'unreliable,' and were employed subsequently on labour services. In Albania there were continuous acts of sabotage. The Greek government made a proclamation to the Albanian people, promising them liberation after victory. True, this was discounted by the talk in some Greek quarters, in the exuberance of success, of annexing the 'liberated' Albanian territories. Nevertheless, there was a real chance that if the campaign had continued and the Greeks had penetrated further into Albania, they would have been joined by thousands of hardy tribesmen. Probably not until the end of the war shall we know how near was Mussolini to disaster in the spring of 1941. Then his partner's attack on Greece developed. A German armoured force burst through the Yugoslav lines, streamed down the Monastir Gap, got behind the Greek army in Albania, cut off its supplies and compelled it to surrender. The victory was celebrated with fervour all over Italy: but the reports of the scenes of enthusiasm scarcely mentioned Albania.

II

As Albania was last of the Balkan states to emerge from the ruins of the Turkish Empire, it is not surprising to find that its frontiers are compressed, since other people had first choice. Consequently, about 600,000 Albanians live outside

Albania—and as the population of the parent state is only a million, the proportion of exiles is large.

Nearly 100,000 Albanians are to be found in North-Western Greece. They are hopelessly intermixed with Greeks, and no redrafting of the frontier would be any improvement. Indeed, Greek claims for a frontier readjustment is at least as strong as the Albanian, for there are about 45,000 Greeks to the north of the boundary. Further, this is one of the areas of Europe where nationality is most fluid. Over 100,000 Albanians are of the Orthodox faith—and to many of them this means more than the fact that they are blood brothers to their Moslem neighbours. Indeed, in 1914 the inhabitants of Northern Epirus revolted when the area was allocated to Albania. Greeks and northern Albanians have mixed freely for centuries: indeed, it is remarkable how many of the outstanding Greeks of history have boasted Albanian blood.

But for the intervention of the Italians, this would never have become a problem at all. Race consciousness is not strongly developed among the Albanians, whose state only so recently found a precarious independence. Most of the scattered Albanian families in Northern Greece only asked to be left alone: the Greeks in Albania were mostly engaged in commerce—they were strongly represented in the region of Koritza, the most important manufacturing town of Albania.

If the problem is pursued, however, it is capable of reasonable solution by minor modifications of the frontier and exchange of populations.

More serious is the case of the Albanians in Yugoslavia, for here is a direct clash between ethnic and historic interests. Down to the south of Yugoslavia, verging on Macedonia, is a district which is almost sacred to the Serbian race. Here is an upland plain, surrounded by a ring of gaunt mountains: this was the site of the Serbian battle of Hastings—a battle which had effects a hundred times more decisive than our own, for the Serbs went into serfdom to the Turks for five hundred years. This is the plain of Kossovo, the Field of the Blackbirds.

In the thirteenth century Serbia was a great empire, occupying a considerable part of the Balkans, with the city of Prizren as its proud capital. The Serb armies fought desultory battles with the advancing Turks over a period of a generation, but on St. Vitus Day, 1389, the Tsar Lazar faced the full army of the Sultan Murad. Weakened by internecine strife—part of

ALBANIANS AND MACEDONIANS IN YUGOSLAVIA

the Serbian army marched off the field at the critical moment of the battle—the Serbs were hopelessly beaten. For nearly five hundred years the Turks ruled the Serbian lands, with the Serbs as their slaves.

The dread field of Kossovo was introduced into every Serbian legend and folk-song: naturally, it was a plain of blood and terror, of gloom and despair. Peasants fled from its unhappy memories, and others were exterminated by roving, uncontrolled bands of Turkish irregulars. For three hundred years the district was almost deserted, peopled only by families of wandering herdsmen. Then the Turks settled Kossovo with Albanians; they, being Moslems, were not subject to the 'evangelising' drives which had helped to depopulate the plain. Thus a new problem was born.

Now in some European countries, as we have seen, there is occasional argument as to a man's nationality. The Kashubians and Mazurians, for example, are claimed as both Germans and Poles. But at least there is never any quarrel as to whether a man is a Serb or an Albanian. As I wandered about Kossovo, the white skull-cap of the Albanian was in evidence everywhere, and all about I heard the Albanian tongue. The few Serbian families were mostly recent settlers, living miserably under housing conditions unfit for cattle, reclaiming land which had lain fallow for five hundred years. In the infrequent towns, however, the Serb element is much more apparent. Prizren, the ancient capital, has a population of 25,000, almost equally divided between Serbs and Albanians.

Prizren retains a few traces of its ancient glories, for it was actually Turkish until 1912 and was one of the most eastern cities in Europe. Drainage is augmented by streams diverted down the middle of the streets, carrying off a quantity of refuse but depositing more by its flanks. Moslem mosques and minarets dominate the skyline—some of them built with the stones of demolished Christian churches. Conditions of life are frankly primitive, and make Prizren one of the most interesting cities of the Balkans.

Here, then, is a problem analogous to that of the Julian March. Adjoining the Albanian frontier is a considerable area predominantly inhabited by Albanians—by the pre-1914 figures this statement goes without argument. Yet it is part of Yugoslavia, and Albania has never ceased to voice its complaint.

Kossovo is an excellent subject for a debating society. The arguments would run:

ALBANIAN: The land is ours, because it is inhabited by Albanians.

SERB: Yes, but they are an artificial population—they were planted there by the Turks after the indigenous inhabitants had been expelled or exterminated.

ALBANIAN: Indigenous inhabitants! Why, Albanians occupied the whole of the Balkan Peninsula long before the Serbs ever heard of it! When they replanted us in Kossovo, the Turks were merely giving us back our own.

SERB: Maybe you were there thousands of years ago, but we held Kossovo for five centuries. Then we were defeated by the Turks, not the Albanians—why, at Kossovo, Albanians fought beside us! Besides, how can you expect us to give up ground which is steeped in our history?

There we have the crucial argument. Economically, Kossovo is of no great account, but historically it is the outstanding district of Yugoslavia. Including both its greatest battlefield and its ancient capital, how can Yugoslavia—the new Serbia—be expected to relinquish it? so it is argued. Suppose France, on however well-reasoned grounds, claimed a district including Hastings and Winchester—what would an Englishman say? The argument is more forceful than it appears at first sight: there is more sentiment in most of us than we know.

Naturally, however, the Albanian view-point was not the same. Further, the traditional Albanian argument is not conducted with words. For four years after the Armistice the Yugoslav-Albanian frontier was not settled, and there was a period of desultory warfare. After the frontier had been demarcated, and Kossovo allocated to Yugoslavia, local strife continued. The Macedonian terrors were repeated here. The Albanian tribesmen are masters of the art of guerrilla warfare. Yugoslav patrols were ambushed with consistent regularity. It was almost impossible to catch the murderers, for the wild mountain country was almost entirely populated by Albanians. The administration of the region was intensely difficult. A Yugoslav official who volunteered for service at Prizren was adjudged to have committed suicide. A military post was established at every kilometre of the roads, but the lawlessness continued.

Then the Yugoslav government adopted a measure England has found efficacious on the North-West Frontier of India. The Albanian organisation is tribal, and the Yugoslav government made each tribe responsible for its own area. If it kept the peace, then it was paid a subsidy; if violence occurred within its area, then the whole tribe was punished. This was the kind of justice the wild tribesmen could understand, and the disorders rapidly diminished. Nevertheless, even in 1930, it was quite unsafe to travel here, for there were numerous bands of komitadji—or brigands, if you will—at large in the mountains. One of these eventually went too far. They caught a well-known Yugoslav general, stripped off his uniform, and sent him back to Prizren in his birthday suit. Shooting soldiers is one thing and stripping generals is another. Punitive expeditions were organised and the brigands rounded up. I saw one very salutary method of warning—the bodies of the dead brigands were paraded through the street for others to observe and ponder.

When I revisited Kossovo in 1935, the district was 'pacified' —or shall I say cowed? There were still periodic outbursts, but most of the trouble was caused by exiles from Albania, rebels against King Zog. The Yugoslav government watched these gentlemen very carefully, and it became possible for any man to travel to Kossovo and Prizren without the slightest fear of danger. Yet even then the local police were fully armed: nor when I looked at the tall, tough Albanian highlanders did I blame them.

Kossovo has already affected the course of history. When Albania decided to westernise, it looked around for a friendly neighbour to finance the operation—for there was scarcely so much as a road in Albania. Obviously, the country which advanced the money would have a hold and influence over Albania. There were only two countries interested—Albania's neighbours, Yugoslavia and Italy. The Italians were not popu-

lar in Albania, but the Yugoslavs were anathema—were they
not holding tens of thousands of Albanians in thrall in the
plain of Kossovo? Had they not utterly refused Albania's
claim to her rightful frontier? Perforce, therefore, Albania
chose Italy as her protector. Soon Albania owed Italy millions
of pounds which it could never hope to repay. Consequently,
when Mussolini chose to defy the League of Nations, he could
always depend upon one vote—Albania would always cast
its vote on his side. After he had left the League, Albania held
a very useful watching brief—until its forcible seizure in 1939,
by which time votes by the League of Nations were of small
account.

The potential dangers were not overlooked in Yugoslavia.
As protector of Albania, Mussolini might hear the call of the
oppressed Albanians of Kossovo. It was perhaps an accident of
history by which the call of the much smaller Albanian
minority in Greece caught his ear first!

The conquest of Yugoslavia brought no solution to the
problem. Yugoslav Macedonia was allocated to Bulgaria,
whose new and temporary frontiers now include tens of thousands of Albanians, so generous were the boundaries drawn.
The Albanian frontiers, however, were enlarged by two small
strips only—a small area in the north-east, about Djakovica,
and a strip from Debar to Struga, on the north shore of Lake
Okrid. Both these districts have predominantly Albanian
populations, but the main Albanian population of Kossovo still
lives in the rump Serbia, under German rule. Evidently Hitler
does not wish Mussolini to extend his sphere of rule. Indeed,
it is reasonably certain that if Hitler won he would promptly
turn his partner out of the Balkans altogether.

III

It is most difficult to estimate the character of the post-war
Albania—and consideration of the frontier problems involved
depends largely on this.

There is one school of thought which argues: Albanian

national consciousness is not yet developed—the people are still in the tribal state. Therefore there is no reason why they should not be happy under beneficent foreign rule. There are two main tribal divisions: the Ghegs to the north of the little river Skumba, and the Tosks to the south. There is a great difference between the character of the two divisions. The kilted Tosks are feudal, the trousered Ghegs are still tribal. Let the Ghegs place themselves under the protection of the Yugoslavs, the Tosks under that of the Greeks. The Albanians are the descendants of one of the oldest of the Balkan races; they are like the Basques in Western Europe—and the Basques have been divided for centuries in France and Spain.

The objections to this argument are: (*a*) the Albanians have at least begun to acquire national consciousness, and the process has probably gone too far to be halted; (*b*) the proposal suggests that the Albanians should place themselves under the protection of people they class as their hereditary enemies—a term which means much more in the Balkans than in Western Europe; (*c*) for that matter, there is a strong racial campaign for autonomy among the Basques.

By the terms of the Atlantic Charter, the first objective is to discover the wishes of the Albanian people. My own impression is that they would poll heavily in favour of a free Albania. Yet a small, undeveloped state could scarcely exist unsupported. There is an obvious protector in the Balkan Federation which is proposed and ought to mature. Albania would be the most junior member, but the others might take a legitimate pride in assisting their weaker cousin.

In such case, frontier questions would present few difficulties. We have seen that the minority problem in the south could be solved by minor rectifications of frontier, with small exchanges of population. In the north-east it would be possible to extend the Albanian boundaries a reasonable distance before touching any vital Yugoslav interest. The extended territory would provide a settling-ground for other Albanian exiles in Yugoslavia.

If Italy were still allowed to hold Albania after the war, then both Greece and Yugoslavia would be justified in maintaining a purely strategic outlook, which would mean that the old frontiers would stand in their essentials.

One feature of the Atlantic Charter must be understood by us and all our friends. It is intended for all-round application. We have seen that the Yugoslavs have a strong claim against Italy in the Julian March: the Albanian claim against Yugoslavia is on substantially the same basis.

CHAPTER TEN

CZECHOSLOVAKIA

I

OF ALL the countries created or confirmed by the peace treaties of 1919, none justified its existence so completely as Czechoslovakia; perhaps for this reason it was the first to disappear. The land was an oasis of tolerance and freedom in Central Europe: such ideas as tolerance and freedom have a nasty habit of crossing frontiers into neighbouring states. Here alone was ample reason for the elimination of Czechoslovakia by the Nazis. Dr. Goebbels might be able to persuade his docile Germans that democrats in Britain and the United States were starving, but here was a prosperous democracy next door, to be seen by all; a living proof that democracy gave better results than totalitarianism. Such a vicious example must obviously be uprooted.

Perhaps the greatest handicap to Czechoslovakia was its name: even today it is indiscriminately confused with Yugoslavia by people who do not look at a map often enough. One can understand that the principal partners in the new state should desire to share its name: the name itself was some sort of argument against the Austro-Hungarian Empire, from which the provinces forming the new state were carved. But to the rest of the world Czechoslovakia appeared as a state artificially created rather than as a reunion of a long-separated family. It would have paid the Slovaks to have sunk their pride, as the Moravians did, so that the new state should have revived the ancient and honourable title of Bohemia. Sentiment, especially historic sentiment, counts a lot. If I buy up the old-established grocery business founded a century ago by

Mr. John Brown, I am more likely to keep the goodwill if I carry on with the name; it would be folly to describe myself as Messrs. Smith, Jones & Robinson, and worse still to put up a sign like Amalgamated Grocers, Ltd.

Bohemia we know—the home of Good King Wenceslas. (There was a good King Wenceslas, by the way, but he died at the age of twenty-two, so the white whiskers on the Christmas cards are an anachronism.) The home, too, of that gallant old blind king of Bohemia, who rode into action at Crécy with his horse harnessed to that of four of his knights: since that day our princes of Wales have used his motto and device. From Bohemia, too, came great names like John Huss, fourth in religious influence only to Luther, Calvin and Wycliffe. Britain was strangely uninterested in Czechoslovakia—until recent events have compelled attention—but a reborn Bohemia must have had a warm welcome. American interest was much greater, maybe because the state was actually born on American soil.

President Wilson plainly suggested that ethnic considerations are not the only determinants of a frontier, but that history, geography and economics must have their share of influence. The historic argument must be accepted only when tempered by the severest common sense. If every European state were to claim its historic frontiers, war would break out tomorrow. The Balkans, for example, have at different times been under the sway of Greeks, Serbs, Bulgars and Turks, but fortunately none of these peoples demand a return to the days of its ancient glories. A revival of the historic claims of Bohemia would arouse even greater complications, for at one time the boundaries of the old kingdom extended to Berlin!

The Czechs, a Slav tribe, appear to have penetrated into Bohemia in the earliest centuries after Christ. Their origin is obscure, but it is probable that they came from Ruthenia—the eastern province of Czechoslovakia—by tradition the cradle of the Slav race. At the time when England was fighting the Danes the Bohemian kingdom was firmly established.

It suffered all the vicissitudes of its time, of course. Occasionally it lost or gained a province in battle or by marriage: occasionally the king was murdered by a rival noble, who then usurped the crown. By the end of the twelfth century, however, the monarchy was firmly enthroned. The glories of Bohemia varied with the character of its rulers. At one time the Bohemian kingdom stretched from Northern Italy to Southern Poland, and included a considerable slice of Germany. The kings were elected, and some of them were of German, Austrian or even Polish origin.

Although Bohemia was essentially a Slav country, there were many German settlers, especially in the towns. The religious associations between Bohemia and Germany were always close; further, successive Bohemian rulers invited German settlers, for in those days the Germans were famed for their skill as miners, artisans and traders. The descendants of these settlers provided Czechoslovakia with one of her biggest problems. In the unenlightened days of the thirteenth and fourteenth centuries, however, a man's race was considered unimportant. The University at Prague, one of the oldest in Central Europe, was indeed an international settlement. It was divided into four 'nations'—Bohemia, Poland, Bavaria and Saxony.

The Hussite wars weakened Bohemia; there is no conflict so fierce as a religious quarrel. John Huss, Rector of Prague University, was a Czech Wycliffe (it is interesting to note that the bride of King Richard II was a Czech princess who brought with her Czech scholars to England, where they came into contact with the ideals of Wycliffe and his followers). Huss protested against the abuses of the Church of his day. Nevertheless, his influence soon strayed far beyond the religious questions involved, for by this time there was rivalry between the Czechs and their German neighbours. The Hussite movement became identified with Czech nationalism as well as with moral purges, and plunged Bohemia into the interminable religious wars of the sixteenth and seventeenth centuries.

One of the direct consequences of the wars of religion
which devastated Central Europe for a century and a half was
the loss of Bohemian independence. Many of the kings of
Bohemia were also emperors of Austria, but the two offices
were entirely separate. The election of a Protestant monarch
led to the war with Austria, and at the fateful Battle of the
White Mountain, in 1620, Bohemia became merged in the
Austrian Empire. The country at this time comprised the
provinces of Bohemia, Moravia, Silesia and Lusatia.

Soon the degradation of Bohemia was complete. Religious
persecution ravaged the country, and all nobles who refused

PROVINCES OF CZECHOSLOVAKIA

to accept Catholicism lost their estates. They were replaced
by Germans—Austrian Germans, that is to say—and soon the
entire government of Bohemia was in the hands of foreigners.
German became the accepted language of social and official
life, and Czech was spoken only by the unfortunate peasants.
The old Czech culture, which in its day had been as advanced
as any in Europe, fell into decay, and at one time it appeared
as if even the language might disappear. There was every
inducement for a man who wanted to get on to change his
outward nationality from Czech to German. If he wanted
education, influence or position, he could only get it by adopt-
ing the German tongue.

Those were rural days, and the welfare of the Czechs was probably dominated by the agricultural policy of the successive rulers; the greater part of the landlords were Germans; the Czechs formed the peasant class, little better than serfs. While it is true that their treatment was no worse than that of peasants in other parts of Europe, the very fact that the landlords were foreigners made subsequent recriminations the more bitter.

In the eighteenth century the slow gathering of democratic ideas began to permeate the Austrian Empire. As has so often happened in Slav countries, the men who saved their language and culture from destruction were poets: under the influence of their fiery verses, what remained of the old Czech nobility regained its spirit, and Czech became once again a language of culture.

Now all this time Slovakia had been a province of Hungary, not Austria, although at times it was subject to the Austrian crown. Its people were of the same stock as the Czechs, and originally spoke the same language. We know, of course, that languages change in form—if you care to turn up an English document of five hundred years ago, you will only understand it with great difficulty. It can be understood, therefore, that although Czechs and Slovaks began as members of the same tribes, after a few hundred years under different foreign rulers —Germans and Magyars respectively—the language developed in different ways.

Actually the Czech renaissance began in Slovakia, not Bohemia. The Czechs of Bohemia were allowed to use their language, but the Slovaks had to face a Hungarian campaign of Magyarisation. To counter this, poets began to sing the glories of their own tongue, and a strange Czech movement swept both provinces. A further explanation of the Slovak origin of the Czech revival is to be found in the greater religious freedom of the Hungarian régime.

Now at this time Czechs and Slovaks spoke many dialects of the same common language. In Slovakia, especially, the peasants in their isolated mountain valleys used dialects which differed as considerably as those of Durham and Somerset. In the middle of the nineteenth century a young Slovak poet raised one of the dialects of Central Slovakia to the rank of a literary language—until that time there had been no standard tongue, but only dialects. It may have seemed unimportant then, but it was unfortunate that a few years earlier the Czech language had also been standardized by a group of intellectuals. It might have altered the course of history if one common language had been adopted for both branches of the tongue.[1]

These are the two languages spoken today. They differ in details, but not in essentials. A Czech and a Slovak can converse without difficulty, and can read one another's newspapers. It may be that the Czech and Slovak tongues will one day re-fuse into one common language: a standard tongue half-way between the two dialects may eventually evolve. Even today it is far easier for a Czech and a Slovak to converse than, say, a Breton and an Alsatian. It is perhaps important to point out again that Slovak is not really a dialect of Czech, but that both are dialects of a common ancestor.

It was about this same time that dreams of independence floated before Czech eyes, probably encouraged by the emergence of Serbia, the first Slav state to gain its freedom from the Turkish yoke. Early ideas were moderate enough: Bohemia asked for a Parliament in Prague and local home rule, under the Austrian crown; in effect, the emperor of Austria should be king of Bohemia—there was no question of complete independence. In fact, an opportunity to transfer allegiance to Germany was refused. Friendly feelings of the Czechs towards the Austrians were increased by the oppression of the Slovaks by the Hungarians, provoking an armed peasant rising. Had the Austrian government pursued a more liberal policy, and given Bohemia the moderate measure of

[1] This only happened among the Yugoslav peoples by accident—the Serb and Croat sages who fixed the language happened to choose the dialect of the same district of Herzegovina.

autonomy which was repeatedly promised, then an emperor might be ruling in Vienna today instead of Hitler.

The fate of Czechs and Slovaks which placed them under Austrians and Hungarians had far-reaching effects on other things than language. The rule of the Austrians was far more beneficent than that of the Magyars. The Czech language was allowed its full freedom, and in the purely Czech districts was the language of education and culture. Czechs represented Bohemia in the Parliament at Vienna, and could be as outspoken as they wished. Slovakia, on the other hand, was represented at Budapest only by Magyars or Germans. There was a definite attempt to stifle the Slovak language in favour of Magyar, and cultural and educational opportunities were few. In Austrian Bohemia Liberal tendencies gradually spread, so that peasants and workmen enjoyed elementary rights, while in Slovakia the conditions which prevailed were almost feudal. The wide differences were to have profound effects when the new state of Czechoslovakia was born.

The upheavals of 1848 brought new promise to the subjected races of the Hapsburg Empire. The subjected races—Czechs, Slovaks, Poles, Roumanians, Serbs, Croats and Slovenes—had never lost their national consciousness, and had been thoroughly aroused by the ideals of liberty preached by the French Revolutionists; nor did they fail to appreciate the difficult position of the Hapsburg rulers.

Austria, the leading member of the Federation of German States, was now faced with a formidable rival—Prussia. There was at this time a serious project for the formation of a Hapsburg Federation of South German States, with the addition of the western Slav groups. Had it materialised, then the course of European history would indeed have been changed.

In the years before 1914, the Austro-Hungarian Empire was the scene of constant political turmoil. Democratic ideas could scarcely be resisted much longer: from Italy and the Balkans spread the spirit of self-determination of nations, born long before President Wilson, and freely encouraged in Britain; Czechs and Slovaks had decided that their destinies should run hand in hand. It is significant, indeed, that the propelling spirit of the new *Czech* renaissance was a *Slovak* professor named Masaryk.

At the outbreak of war the Czechs were of course conscripts in the Austrian army. It seems incredible in these days that anyone expected them to fight for the Germans against their fellow Slavs—against the Serbs, whose fight for freedom had so inspired them, and against the Russians, big brothers of all the smaller Slav races. Some of the critical moments of the Austrian campaigns were caused by Czech regiments which passed over to the Russians *en bloc*. There were active secret organisations working for the Allied cause, while the hundreds and thousands of Czechs and Slovaks abroad were especially active.

(The 'treachery' of the Czech troops raised another bone of contention with their Sudeten neighbours; the German soldiers from the Bohemian borderlands were reckoned as being the best in the Austrian army, and were often brigaded territorially with units of Czechs. This meant inevitably that when the Czechs—although quite legitimately—went over to the Russian side, Sudeten units were left with their flanks exposed, and suffered severe casualties in consequence.)

Masaryk, with keen foresight, decided that he could best serve his cause by working abroad—there was a warrant out for his arrest anyway. In 1914 he came to the conclusion that the war would be a long one, and that it would reach its decision in the west. He began to organize forces of Czechs and Slovaks from American emigrants and from the troops who had deserted. The Russians resisted his efforts, and refused to use the Czech troops until after the Revolution—the Russians always did refuse anything which was likely to help them to win the war. Eventually large numbers of Czech troops were transported from Russia to France, where they fought honourably beside the French army.

In the meantime Masaryk and his friends had been working

furiously. It is curious that for the first year of the war, so benevolent was the outlook on Austria-Hungary in the west, the only aim the Allies would admit was autonomy! By 1916, however, the Allies had been persuaded to include the liberation of Czechs and Slovaks among their war aims, and the events of 1918 consolidated this opinion.

The adventures of the Czech legion in Siberia must rank among the major romances of history. At long last Czech divisions had been formed, but then the Bolshevik Revolution ended the war in the east. Withdrawing across Siberia with a view to transfer to France and Italy—all round the world to fight for freedom—the Czechs found themselves masters of the Siberian railway. Provoked by the Bolsheviks and supported by the Allied governments, the Czechs opened hostilities and won amazing victories over the Bolshevik armies. At one time there was an outside chance that they might have captured Moscow, but Allied direction was confused. However, the Czech legions held Siberia, a vastly important operation. Not only were the Germans unable to reach the Siberian sources of raw materials, but over half a million German and Austrian prisoners were held there by the Czechs, and prevented from rejoining their national armies. This remarkable feat on the part of 80,000 determined men, operating thousands of miles from their homes, did immense service to the Czech cause.

In August 1918 the British government recognised the Czechoslovaks as an Allied nation, and soon all the Allies were negotiating with Masaryk as the leader of a National Council. In October a formal government was constituted in Paris— a government without a country! The Czechs and Slovaks at home were playing their part, however, and long before the end of the war there was scarcely a peasant whose mind was not imbued with the new spirit of nationality.

On the collapse of Austria-Hungary events moved swiftly. On October 28th, 1918, a National Committee at Prague proclaimed the independence of the Czechoslovak state: two days later a Slovak National Council made the same decision. These councils naturally were hurriedly summoned on an 'irregular' basis—in Slovakia no other method was possible. The idea was that men representing all ranks, districts, shades of opinion, professions and religions should be called into consultation. It is futile at this stage to claim that these assemblies were illegal. Every fight for freedom is illegal—until it is won. It is quite certain that the decisions of October 1918 were unani-

THE BREAK-UP OF AUSTRIA-HUNGARY

mous among the Czechs and Slovaks. The Germans and Magyars in their provinces naturally held different opinions!

The difficulties of the new government were enormous. In Bohemia there were attempted insurrections in the German-speaking districts; in Slovakia there was more serious disorder, aggravated by the departure of the Magyar officials—and there were no Slovaks to take their places. To add to the confusion, Hungary set up a Communist régime, and its troops invaded Slovakia. Nevertheless all difficulties were firmly faced, and by the time the Peace Conference met, the new state was already stable and had already passed a remarkable volume of democratic legislation—and, what was more important, had implemented its decisions.

I have said that of all the countries born, reborn or enlarged as a result of the war, Czechoslovakia most signally justified itself. It was utterly absurd to describe it as an outpost of Communism—the Czech or Slovak peasant is of virile individuality. Its alliance with Russia has been misunderstood and perverted: when a little man is threatened by a big man he looks for allies, if he is wise. And Germany certainly used threats of a startling character, and events have proved that the only fault in Czechoslovakia's precautions was that they were not sufficiently far-reaching.

Despite its success and its stability, Czechoslovakia had many major problems still unsolved. Many of them concerned her minorities, for the accidents of history had freely scattered many nationalities in this central district of Europe. We approach a difficult problem of national pride, for there is no history of persecution to complicate it. Indeed, I would like to make an emphatic observation at once: that if every country in Europe, including Germany, had treated its minorities with the same tolerance they received in Czechoslovakia, then the condition of Europe would not be nearly so desperate today.

II

Around Bohemia, except in the south, runs a fringe of mountains. Here is a lovely land: the northern range especially is of great beauty, and the valley of the Elbe rivals that of the Rhine at its grandest. To the north of the watershed the Germans call the district the 'Saxon Switzerland,' to the south the Czechs term their share the 'Bohemian Paradise.' There is a shade of grandiloquence in these titles, attractive as the country may be. There is nothing Alpine about the Saxon mountains, and the Bohemian side is no paradise—political complexities see to that. This is the land of the Sudeten Deutsch, one of the most discussed areas in Europe.

If there had been a 'natural' frontier in Europe, then Bohemia would have been happy, for her boundaries are almost as decisive as the Pyrenees. We have seen that the kingdom of Bohemia expanded and contracted in the complex course of mediaeval wars, but the old kingdom always remained stable —the frontiers of Bohemia proper never changed.

About eight hundred years ago Saxon and Bavarian tribes began to trickle through the valleys and over the passes, to settle on Bohemian land. In those days frontiers were no great barrier, and it was not considered an insult to race to live under another flag. The first settlers were insignificant numerically, but the rate of immigration quickened with succeeding centuries. We have noted that the Bohemian crown was elective, and that German princes sometimes held it. On their invitation more Germans entered Bohemia: most of them settled in the border valleys but some penetrated into the interior, where they were successful as traders and artisans. Quite a number of these immigrants were refugees, for in those days Germany was a maze of petty kingdoms, usually at war with one another.

The Germans settled comfortably under the Bohemian crown: although they were theoretically a subject race, they held equal privileges with the Czechs. After 1620, of course, the Austrian emperors were masters in Bohemia, and the importance of the Bohemian Germans increased, since they were so closely akin to the Austrians. The deposition of the Czech nobles and the repression of the Czech culture soon made the Germans pre-eminent in Bohemia. There were further immigrations, this time from Austria, particularly of the middle classes, who supplied professional men and officials: from this time the Czechs were very definitely the subject race.

In considering this problem it is easy to be misled by our overfree use of the word 'German.' The Germans of Bohemia were of the German ethnic stock, but they were never Germans politically. Like the Austrian Germans they had sprung from a common stock, but after the fall of Bohemia they gravitated to Vienna. They had never drawn their culture from Berlin, which at that time was an insignificant village.

For centuries, then, Germans and Czechs lived side by side. In some districts Germans predominated, in others Czechs. Relations between the races changed with the course of history: there was frequently tension, but it was lowered by mutual interests—although the rulers were of German stock, most of the Germans were peasants, and suffered alike with the Czechs in the feudal days. In spite of tension, Czechs and Germans did manage to live together side by side for eight hundred years, and it is one of the tragedies of our day that not until the coming of Hitler did Czechs and Germans discover that they had really hated each other all this time. Mr. G. E. R. Gedye, who knows Central Europe as well as any man—he was expelled from Nazi Vienna because he knew too much of the truth—wrote of Czechoslovakia in 1932: 'The most hopeful racial situation in Czechoslovakia is that between Czechs and Germans.' A year later the emergence of Hitler had altered all that.

Then came the war, and with its end the break-up of the Austro-Hungarian Empire. The Germans of Bohemia rubbed their eyes in wonder and alarm—what was to happen to them? Unthinkable that they should pass under the rule of the Czechs—however amicable the relations between mistress and maid, there is bound to be uneasiness if the maid is suddenly promoted to be mistress.

They were Austrians, these Germans of Bohemia, and for many centuries had looked to Vienna as their capital. Even in the dark hour of defeat they had no thought of abandoning their brothers in Austria proper. A claim was made, backed by a considerable section, that the Germans of Bohemia should not be separated from their Austrian brothers—that a ribbon of territory, right round the Bohemian frontiers, should be added to Austria. One glance at the map shows how impossible such a state would be—the small body of Austria with an irregular tail five hundred miles long. Political geography will stand freakish shapes up to a point, but this was manifestly impracticable. One of the German leaders recognised this in a decision of common sense: 'The eight territorial districts in which Germans are settled, separated from each other by gulfs of Czech lingual districts, cannot form a single State or a single administrative area, for such State or area must after all be a united economic area. To form the German districts into a unit would be without parallel in the world and would be the greatest State-political nonsense.'

This quotation emphasises one of the most important features of the Germans in Czechoslovakia, and one frequently distorted by partisan maps. The Germans inside the Bohemian frontier did *not* form a continuous ribbon, but were found in eight preponderant groups. These largely or purely German areas were separated by districts which are partially or wholly Czech. A glance at the map on page 382 makes the position immediately clear.

Altogether there were some three and a quarter million people of German stock in Czechoslovakia. Two and a half millions of these lived in the shaded districts near the frontier, while the remaining three-quarter million were scattered in oddments all over the country. Mingled with the Germans in the frontier districts were some 400,000 Czechs.

The statesmen who gathered at Paris in 1919 had no hesitation. There were only two solutions: either the 'ribbon' area should be created and added to Austria—which was impossible by elementary geographic conditions: or Bohemia should be allotted its historic frontiers. *It is significant that no section of the Bohemian Germans demanded union with Germany.* The decision did not conflict with the Fourteen Points. An ethnic frontier being clearly impossible, the statesmen could legitimately turn to the historic, geographic and economic considerations mentioned by the President. The ideas of the

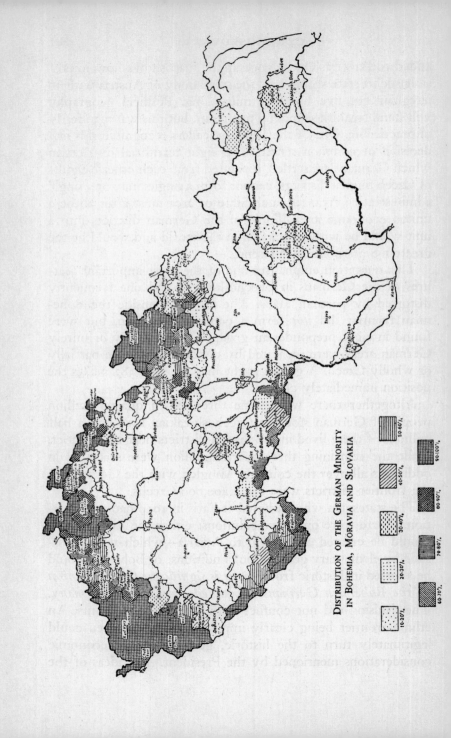

DISTRIBUTION OF THE GERMAN MINORITY
IN BOHEMIA, MORAVIA AND SLOVAKIA

50–60%	90–100%
40–50%	80–90%
30–40%	70–80%
20–30%	60–70%
10–20%	

Allied statesmen, indeed, were quite firm on this point. Dr. Masaryk, the Czechoslovak, was a scholarly realist who had no delusions as to the magnitude of the problem. Knowing that there could be no perfect solution, he proposed a moderate compromise. In the north-west corner is a triangle of territory about Karlovy Vary (Karlsbad) which is almost entirely German: in the north-east are two 'horns'—about Varnsdorf and Frydlant—similarly populated. But in Germany proper is a smaller area about Glatz where lived from 20,000 to 30,000 Czechs—relics of the conquest of Silesia two hundred years ago. Masaryk was anxious to include these Czechs in the new Czechoslovakia, so he suggested an exchange—the two north-eastern 'horns,' together with the north-western 'horn' about Eger, with well over a million Germans, should go to the German Reich, while the district about Glatz should revert to Czechoslovakia. This magnanimous offer was turned down by the Allies on the grounds that the Germans of Bohemia had never been part of Germany! This is important.

It can be imagined that the position within the new state was a difficult one. The German portion of the population, brooding over the change of fortune, was in no mood for co-operation. It is fatuous at this stage for the Germans to claim that they had no share in the planning of Czechoslovakia —at the time they preferred to stand aside. It is, of course, quite easy to understand their feelings, but the fact remains that for some years after the war they refused all co-operation with the Czechs. There were many complaints of petty persecution, for a reversal of fortune is bound to lead to incidents. The Czechs were not deficient in statesmen, but many of their officials were tactless, and the temporary feeling of insecurity bred intolerance. But the new Czechoslovakia settled down remarkably quickly, and her record of conduct is very mild compared with that of any other Continental power.

So long as the German Reich was weak and disorganised, so long were the complaints of the German minority in Czechoslovakia purely local. I investigated many of them, but my impression was that compared with minority complaints in other countries they were trivial. If a Pole domiciled in Germany had the privileges of a German in Czechoslovakia, he would count himself a happy man.

We have noticed in our hurried glance at European problems that one of the principal minority complaints is that organised efforts at denationalisation were being made: these complaints unfortunately do not lack foundation in many countries. In Czechoslovakia, however, the cultural activities of the Germans were undiminished. Of 446,000 German children in 1935, 423,000 attended German schools: the remainder lived in districts where there were only a few Germans in a Czech territory, and where separate schools would be impossible. There was never any attempt to repress the German language. By the terms of the minority clauses of the peace treaty, in any district where two-thirds of the inhabitants were German, all State documents and communications, and proceedings in courts, were made in the German language. In districts where the Germans formed from 20 to 66 per cent, both German and Czech languages were used. Where the proportion of Germans was less than 20 per cent, official communications were in Czech, but if a German did not understand Czech he was entitled to an official interpreter. This appeared to be a reasonable compromise in a difficult situation. Actually, of the three and a quarter million Germans in Czechoslovakia, two and a quarter millions lived in districts where the German language was used, and a further 600,000 in districts using both German and Czech.

The Germans were also fully represented in the Czechoslovak Parliament, and at the moment of crisis had 72 representatives in the Chamber of Deputies and 37 in the Senate.

The principal cause of discontent amongst the Germans in the pre-Hitler years was simple enough. In the early days of the republic the Czechs did not trust the Germans. This may have been a mistake, but at least the German attitude at the time was not very helpful. Consequently, local officers administering the German districts were usually Czech—they were German-speaking, of course, but not Germans. Now in an outlying district the local men—the policemen, magistrates and tax officers—are every bit as important as members of Parliament. The Germans claimed with reason that such posts should be filled by Germans—the Czechs argued that they could scarcely appoint Germans as government officials when their loyalty to the government was suspect.

I came across many cases of petty irritation. I recall a Czech postman in a village preponderantly German. His life was made a misery—and, being human, he retaliated. When the Germans refused all forms of co-operation, even ostracised him, he replied by working fiercely by rule and regulation—and there is no more effective form of strike than the strict adherence to rules intended as a general guide.

But Dr. Milan Hodza, the Czechoslovak Prime Minister, did a very brave thing—he admitted himself wrong! In February 1937—a year before Hitler's march into Austria—Dr. Hodza undertook that in future the Germans should receive their full share of government posts, and a new law was put into immediate operation. Naturally, it was impracticable to appoint Germans suddenly to 22 per cent of official jobs, but the task of replacement was immediately commenced. Here at last was a chance of real conciliation.

It was accepted by three of the four German parties. At that time Herr Henlein and his party could claim 55 per cent of the German population as followers. The remainder were divided between the German Social Democratic, Agrarian and Catholic parties, each proportionately represented in Parliament, *and each with a minister in the cabinet*. These three parties were known as the Activist Group: instead of pining over the past or planning for the unknown future, they accepted the present position and prepared to make the best of it.

I wandered about the Sudeten Deutsch country in September 1937 and was pleasantly surprised at the difference in the atmosphere. The change in a few months was all for the better, and I came away very optimistic. The Activist parties were now co-operating loyally with the central government at Prague, and the effects of the new law were already obvious. Henlein's stock was definitely falling—the growing recovery of trade assisting. Opposition parties flourish when times are bad. Hitler could never have emerged from a prosperous Germany.

Then came the march into Austria, and in a night the new hopes faded. Two of the Activist parties withdrew their support from the government and went over to Henlein. One of their arguments was obvious. Hitler had marched into Austria —next he would march into Czechoslovakia. We know what happens to his opponents—let us therefore get on the right side quickly.

We must carry some responsibility for the sudden *volte face*. These men were Germans: if they were convinced that Czechoslovakia was a stable state, likely to endure, they were willing to co-operate; but if Czechoslovakia were to disintegrate without the backing of her friends, why should Germans fight the battle of an alien race?

It was a major feature of the tragedy in Czechoslovakia that, had the administration of the previous years persisted— as it might, had firm encouragement been given at the time of the crisis—then Munich might never have been necessary.

III

Hitler's agent in Czechoslovakia was a teacher of physical culture named Konrad Henlein, who is almost forgotten in these days. It is difficult to appreciate that in 1938 and 1939 he was headline news, with Europe waiting on his next pronouncement; he was, of course, no more than the mouthpiece of Hitler—although in 1937 he assured me that he had never even seen Hitler, and that his party had no connection whatsoever with the German Nazi organisation! I hope he interpreted correctly my glance of disbelief.

At that time, too, he emphasised that territorial revision of treaties was no solution to the problem of the Germans in Czechoslovakia—that it was impossible to detach the German-speaking parts of Czechoslovakia from the republic, and that a Pan-German menace was at least as dangerous as Pan-Slavism, and would lead to catastrophe. In fact, he produced a perfect imitation of Hitler's methods—a tentative opening of moderation, so as to disarm his adversary, showing his true hand when opportunity developed.

The German march into Austria made it obvious that Czechoslovakia was Hitler's next objective, so that further discussion was impossible. The man who had never seen Hitler now flew periodically to Berlin for instructions.

His demands were comprehensive. He wanted an autonomous German state within the Czechoslovak republic—entirely self-governing, almost independent of Prague, and in full 'cultural relation' with Germany—with full freedom to adopt and implement Nazi 'ideology' (including Jew-baiting and concentration camps for opponents). The Czechs resisted this demand. First, they claimed with justice, the scheme was as impossible geographically today as it was in 1919. As we saw, the Germans lived in eight groups, with intermediate Czech territories: a 'ribbon' state today would now include well over half a million Czechs with two and a half million Germans.

The Czechs argued that a Nazi state within a democracy is impossible—that the clash of ideas and ideals would make the scheme unworkable. Further, the Czechs believed that such an autonomous state would soon be absorbed into Germany, and they were readily able to quote confirmatory chapter and verse from Hitler's speeches and book. 'The German Empire must, as a State, include all Germans. . . . The frontiers of 1914 mean nothing for the future of the German nation.' So wrote Hitler, and he can scarcely grumble if the Czechs believed what he said.

Not only would the loss of the German-speaking districts be a great economic blow to Czechoslovakia, but the strategic position would be impossible. The mountain barrier was readily defensible, and could only be forced by a considerable army. With the Germans over the mountains and in the plains, it was reasonably claimed, the threat in war-time would be overwhelming.

Defence was foremost in men's minds in those disturbed days, when the German menace had become so apparent. Now that Henlein's connection with Hitler was so open and obvious, it can scarcely be wondered that the Czech government suspected his protests of loyalty. How could they admit him to the cabinet, as he claimed? At each cabinet meeting, defence was the major subject of discussion; could they discuss defence schemes in Henlein's presence—when he might next day make a present of their secrets to Hitler?

The march into Austria altered the entire tempo of the Czech piece. Hitler's sense of timing was uncanny. The problem was natural, but the crisis was artificial, stirred to the surface at an appropriate moment. The march into Austria provided the moment, the trade depression the theme.

It is a matter of pure chance that some of the trades hardest hit by the world economic depression—textiles, glass and porcelain—happened to be located in the German-speaking districts. Actually, the man who impelled the biggest hardships to the Bohemian Germans was Hitler! Before his rise Germany was the largest importer of Czech manufactures, but new import restrictions made trade exceedingly difficult: Czech exports to Germany fell by 70 per cent.

I found many districts where unemployment was acute because of the deliberate closing of works—German-controlled—in order to keep up 'ring' prices or to avoid excessive competition. This may be legitimate business—it is common in other countries—but it was scarcely the fault of the Czechs.

The Germans deliberately choked the trade-flow of Czechoslovakia by their control of rail-borne communications. In pre-1914 days Bohemia had been one of the major industrial districts of the Austrian Empire: it had found ready markets for its products in the agricultural provinces of the empire. The high economic barriers of the post-war days had turned the flow of Czechoslovak commerce to other quarters, and a flourishing export industry had been built up. The most favourable route to overseas markets was through German ports, where, by clauses in the peace treaties, Czechoslovakia should have enjoyed special zones and transit rates. These privileges were now curtailed, and in some cases stopped altogether. Hitler's idea was only too obvious; he would strike at the economy of Czechoslovakia. In doing so, he would hit hardest at the industrial regions—including the Sudeten areas. Thus grave discontent would arise amongst the Sudeten Germans, and it would be easy to turn this discontent against the Czechs. Men suffering under economic distress are notoriously susceptible to the suggestions of propaganda.

The Czechs are, however, resourceful people; when imports and exports became difficult through Germany or countries under German influence, they explored the Polish route through Gdynia. Unfortunately, the longer journey involved made the transport of their goods to overseas markets unduly expensive.

It is important to emphasise again that, prior to the march into Austria, the demand for union with Germany was absurdly exaggerated by propagandists. If the Sudeten claim in 1937 had been a straightforward demand for union with Germany, I could have understood it. But it was not; then, at any rate, the greater part of the German protest consisted of denunciation of the Czechs. 'Germans are unable to secure fundamental human rights or freedom of political opinion and action.' This was nonsense. There was far wider political freedom in Czechoslovakia than Germany. In Prague I was received in Henlein's offices and handed literature which almost came under the category of sedition. There was no Socialist office in Berlin where I might collect information! The Germans of Czechoslovakia had over 150 daily and weekly newspapers, and some of their articles would have been classed as seditious even in England. How many journals were at the disposal of opposition parties in Hitler's Germany?

Officers of the Henlein organisation took me on the stock propaganda tour, which was written up from many points of view by journalists in every country in the world. It is a great pity that some British writers, who should have known better, believed all that Henlein told them without making further inquiries.

One of the exhibits, for example, was a derelict factory in the Sudeten area. This was represented to me as a typical piece of Czech repression of German interests. Unfortunately for the Henleinists, I was able to ascertain locally that the factory had been closed down in 1914—by the Austrians!

I was taken to see a large glass-works, owned by a German. The works were now closed, and the case was again presented to me as one of Czech victimisation. Actually the trade of the factory had been destroyed by customs duties imposed by Germany; probably deliberately destroyed, so as to arouse the necessary fury and distress.

Nor could I agree with my Henlein guides that the Sudeten Germans had no fundamental rights, ordinary liberties or freedom of political opinions. In the little towns where the propaganda banner had scarcely been raised, life went on serenely and calmly. German children went to German schools. Among my mentors were German members of the Czechoslovak Parliament—which hardly consorted with their denial of 'freedom of political opinions.' Certainly these men expressed their opinions at every conceivable opportunity.

Nor was German opinion anything like being united. As I wandered around the country in 1937, I found that the demand for union with Germany had been absurdly exaggerated. The younger and noisier elements were emphatic, but they are never as important as they think they are. Most sections of the people demanded some sort of autonomy, but even here ideas were mixed. Many of Henlein's supporters agreed with his public professions—though from a different standpoint, economics, not politics: times were good or bad, according to your trade, but union with the Reich would scarcely improve them. More moderate opinion favoured making the best of the situation, and co-operation with Prague. There was a frankly expressed apprehension of the extension of Nazi rule over Northern Bohemia, and its methods had no appeal. Not for nothing had these people drawn their culture from Vienna, and not from Berlin. A hard world of drills, concentration camps and one-way mental traffic did not appeal to these easy-going Bohemian-Austrian Germans who would rather dance than goose-step.

I must record that I found a different atmosphere a year later. Propaganda thrives on difficult situations, and these persisted in Sudetenland. The tragedy was that some respectable British journals assisted directly in the dismemberment of Czechoslovakia.

The whole unhappy business was helped by one of the features of a democratic political system, which persuades some politicians that it is their duty to oppose their opponents on all issues. Thus, after the seizure of Austria, one political group demanded a firm pledge to Czechoslovakia, already marked out as the next victim; almost automatically the other school of thought, so it appeared, was ready to jettison the country. Politicians, who a few weeks earlier had been talking about the sanctity of treaties, now made speeches which might have been interpreted as an open invitation to Hitler to march across the frontier. The dangerous thing was that they were so interpreted, and that they were represented by German propaganda as the views of responsible British statesmen.

If you ever feel in a mood for exploration, turn up the files of some of our newspapers for the summer of 1938. 'All the minorities in Czechoslovakia,' wrote a well-known correspondent of one responsible Sunday newspaper '—Germans, Slovaks, Magyars, Ruthenes—are discontented at their treatment by the Czechs, and all want to manage their own affairs in their own way, and to speak their own languages.'

I have already dealt with this point at some length. The Germans did speak their own language and generally no other. Except for their demand for autonomy or union with Germany, there was nothing barred to them: I have already quoted the Czech arguments against autonomy.

It was quite absurd to class the Slovaks as a minority— they were the partners of the Czechs. If they wanted autonomy, they had only to ask for it. Before September 1938 only one-third of the Slovak members favoured autonomy; the others firmly supported a centralised government. If all wanted self-government, it could not have been refused. In the 1935 elections autonomists in Slovakia polled only 489,641 votes out of an electorate of 1,623,000. To talk about Slovaks wanting to speak their own language is sheer nonsense. They always did: in all their schools, newspapers, books, the Slovak dialect was used. To suggest oppression of the Slovaks when the founder of Czechoslovakia, Dr. Masaryk, was a Slovak, and *when the Prime Minister of the day, Dr. Hodza, was a Slovak*—the reader will agree is somewhat ridiculous. I will return to this point, and to the question of Magyars and Ruthenes, at a later stage.

'The minorities have submitted over twenty petitions to the League of Nations, not one of which has been investigated on the spot, and not one of which has led to any amelioration of grievances.'

I recalled one of these petitions. It complained of a Czechoslovak regulation discriminating against the employment of Germans in public works. This did not require investigation, for it was proved in a few minutes that the regulation simply did not exist! I have since inquired about the other petitions. I find that they were carefully investigated by the successive Minority Committees set up by the Council of the League— which included British representatives—and were turned down without exception on sufficient evidence being given to disprove the complaints. It would have been in the better traditions of British journalism to have mentioned these facts.

'It is true that the Sudeten Deutsch have been promised 22 per cent of all government positions, under an agreement dated February 1937, but today, more than a year later, it is admitted on all sides that this attempt at conciliation has been a failure.'

If so, whose fault was that? In February 1937 the Germans occupied 14 per cent of all official positions. Subsequently the proportion was increased as the co-operation of Germans made this possible—and as suitable men offered their services. It is interesting to note that among the judicial and scholastic professions the Germans held more than 22 per cent of all posts. That is to say, there were not only enough German judges for the German-speaking districts, but there were German judges in Czech districts as well.

'Even Christmas presents for Sudeten Deutsch children from relatives in Germany are not allowed into this region.'

This is, of course, a clumsy propaganda lie which no cub reporter would swallow. It is a hardy annual among the grievances of minorities, but, like bayoneted babies in war-time, disappears before investigation. In Czechoslovakia it was grotesquely false. I bought German newspapers freely in all parts of Czechoslovakia—at a time when practically every *British* newspaper was *forbidden* in Germany.

'Big new Czech schools are in evidence, but the Government has found no money for the schools of the Sudeten Deutsch. They are four-fifths of the population, but their schools are small and old.'

This is a half-truth far more dangerous than a lie. It is perfectly true that most of the new schools in the Sudeten Deutsch country were Czech—I noticed that myself. But why? Because, prior to 1918, when the Germans were masters there, they provided no schools at all for Czech children! If Czechs wished to learn they had to go to German schools. Naturally the Czechoslovak government had to redress this injustice—and that is why most (but not all) of the new schools were for Czech children. We have already noted that practically all German children in Czechoslovakia went to German schools.

A double tragedy lies in the fact that statements like these were published. First a body of British readers was seriously misled; second, and far more serious, statements of this character, and of this character alone, were reprinted in German newspapers to prove to the German people that British public opinion was with them in their demand for the release of the Germans from their Czech 'masters.' This tragic situation was repeated in practically every country in the world. Men were so anxious for peace that they did not want to look at anything which might conceivably disturb it.

IV

The very shape of Czechoslovakia suggested an artificial state; the old Bohemia, surrounded by its mountains, was an obvious geographical entity. The new Czechoslovakia represented the outcome of a conflict between geographical and economic interests. We have seen that Czechs and Slovaks were closely related, of common stock; that their culture had survived all depression and vicissitudes, and was so strongly alive that it dominated all thoughts in the new movement of freedom. At the same time, the unfortunate accident of history which had placed Czechs under Austrian rule, and Slovaks under Hungarian rule, did more than to inculcate different mental and cultural standards. The economy of Bohemia-Moravia was based on Vienna, that of Slovakia on Budapest; even after the formation and consolidation of Czechoslovakia, communications between Slovakia and Budapest naturally were much more easy than between Slovakia and Prague. Geographical conditions had combined with political considerations to bring this about: the mountains of Slovakia formed part of the circular hedge about the Hungarian plain: it is natural for communication to flow to the centre.

We have seen too that the long sufferance of Hungarian rule had left Slovakia in a lower state of development than the

Czech provinces, and this was destined to have unfortunate results. The fall of Czechoslovakia was yet another illustration of the old truth that the strength of the chain is the strength of its weakest part.

Within its rim of mountains Bohemia is a land of low hills and broad valleys. Slovakia, on the other hand, is almost entirely mountainous. In the north the Carpathians reach their highest peaks in the Tatra group. With no bigger gap than a single valley, the Little Tatras run parallel with their big brothers, even the juniors topping 6000 feet. Further south, the mountains are less severe and imposing, but the plain is not reached until the Hungarian frontier. The Slovak people are taciturn and slow of thought, but they are virile and intelligent; their peasant costumes are a delight, rivalling the colourful displays of Hungary.

At one time in history it is probable that Czech and Slovak tribes occupied the plains of Hungary. They were driven to the north and north-west by the Magyars. The invaders, however, halted at the approaches to the mountains—the Magyars have always been a people of the plains. Nevertheless, in the course of centuries a simple but definite economic link between mountain and plain developed. The Slovak peasants in their poor mountain valleys could scarcely have maintained even a modest livelihood; it was therefore necessary for hundreds of thousands of them to descend to the Hungarian plains for agricultural work during the harvest seasons: the small payments to them in cash and kind meant the difference between starvation and existence.

The creation of Czechoslovakia, and the hostility of Hungary towards the new state, destroyed this economic link and imposed considerable hardships on the Slovaks. The Czechs did their utmost to counter the resultant distress—not only by administration of a higher degree of efficiency than had ever been known in Hungarian times, but by the establishment of local industries in Slovakia. The difficult problem of communications was firmly tackled, the east-to-west railways and roads being improved so that Slovakia could supply its products to Bohemia instead of Hungary.

German and Hungarian propaganda gave the impression that Slovakia was a subject land groaning under the Czechoslovakia yoke; this was quite absurd. We have seen that Bohemia, after its centuries of independence, passed under Austrian rule, while Slovakia was under Hungary. I shall describe in the Hungarian chapter the nature of the Hungarian rule. There was little persecution or physical oppression, but the Slovaks were definitely treated as an inferior race, and the educational system was grossly inadequate. The Czechs, on the other hand, were allowed some political rights, and in their own districts education was reasonably organised. They gained in efficiency, too, by contact and competition with Germans —for efficiency is not a national Slav trait. Consequently, when the new Czechoslovakia was formed, apart from their numerical preponderance it was only natural that the Czechs should carry a large share of the burden of administration, since their facilities for education, commerce and political experience had been so much greater. Because the Scottish educational system was, until recent years, superior to that of England, Scotsmen occupy far more than their proportionate share in the civil service or other professions dependent upon competitive examination. Ready equivalents could be quoted in the United States.

This does not mean that the Czechs ruled Slovakia—far from it. I have already pointed out that Masaryk [1] and Hodza were Slovaks. At the moment of crisis the Czechoslovak ministers in London and Paris were both Slovaks.

At the time of the crisis, only one-third of the Slovaks demanded the autonomy promised them by Masaryk at Pittsburgh, in the United States, where he laid the foundations of the new Czechoslovak state during the war. They could have had autonomy any time they persuaded the other two-thirds

[1] Actually, Masaryk was even better fitted by birth to be the creator of the new Czechoslovakia. He was the son of a Slovak father and a Czech mother, and was born in Moravia. The population of Moravia, by the way, is Czech.

to agree with them. After the seizure of the Sudetenland, however, the demand for autonomy grew—and was actually encouraged by the Czechs. In a night Slovakia became an autonomous province of Czechoslovakia. It was an astute move on the part of the Prague government. The Hungarians were fiercely demanding revision of their frontiers—and most of their claims concerned Slovak territory. The new Slovakia, it should be noted, was loyal to the federal Czechoslovak state, and suggestions that the Slovaks should be incorporated in Poland or Hungary were fiercely resisted. The new government had a strong Catholic basis.

The Church had always wielded a powerful influence in the mountain communities (and it is important to add that most of the leading prelates had received their early training in Budapest), and the despair of the hour impelled some authoritarian usages, always more tendencious in peoples of small political education. But the government never had a chance to settle down—was never allowed to settle down. Its role was already cast, probably without its knowledge.

V

Certainly there was no demand in Ruthenia (or Sub-Carpathian Russia) for return to Hungary. Here was quite a different problem from that of Slovakia. The Ruthenes are neither Czechs nor Slovaks, but are distant relatives—both descendants from the same Slav stock, as French and Italians are from Latin. They are blood brothers of the Ukrainians, of whom there are forty millions in U.S.S.R. and three millions in Poland.[1] They were assigned to Czechoslovakia because a poverty-stricken people of 600,000 could not possibly exist by itself, because union with the Ukraine was geographically impossible, and because there was no reason on earth why they should be handed over to Poland. Most important to the powers at Paris, Ruthenia formed a strategic link between Czechoslovakia and Roumania.

In his American negotiations Masaryk met Ruthene repre-

[1] See map on page 151.

sentatives and agreed that Ruthenia should be granted a modified autonomy. This self-government was delayed until October 1937, and the delay gave ample fodder to foreign propagandists. Yet the difficulties were immense, as I saw for myself.
If educational opportunities in Slovakia were poor, in Ruthenia
they simply did not exist. The Ruthenes were not oppressed,
but simply neglected. Their standard of life was appallingly
low—easily the lowest in Central Europe. They did not merely
know poverty—they lived on the edge of starvation. Even in
1937, although I was assured by the peasants that conditions
had greatly improved, I was appalled at what I saw. I lived for
days in timber cottages on a diet of maize bread and potatoes,
with milk and an occasional egg. The low mentality of the
people was pathetic. Hungarian officers told me that in the pre-
war days Ruthene recruits were so unintelligent that they did
not know their right from their left: the difficulty was surmounted by sticking a wisp of hay in one boot, straw in
another, and giving the command: 'Hay turn! Straw turn!'
Immediately after the war the Ruthenes were starving, and the
American Red Cross rushed out supplies of food. In one valley
the people were given slabs of chocolate; they did not know
what they were, or what to do with them: eventually they
dissolved them in water and painted the outside of their timber
shacks with them! These stories—and they are an indictment of
a thousand years of Hungarian rule—sound incredible, but are
true.

You do not expect a high standard of judgment and intelligence from illiterate feudal serfs, newly liberated—especially
as the Ruthene peasant had an unfortunate tendency to drown
his sorrows in a villainous home-distilled spirit. Nevertheless,
there is no cause for despair in Ruthenia. In the immediate
post-war years the Prague government devoted no less than
70 per cent of the tax receipts from Ruthenia to education,
and the policy has paid. The Ruthene children of today cannot be compared with their parents: a new generation of young
men and women has passed through Czech and Slovak univer-

sities: limited autonomy at last began to function, Czech officials being replaced by Ruthenes, and in another generation
the Ruthenes would have controlled the local government of
Ruthenia.

No one who wandered Central Europe could fail to be
impressed by the efficiency and impartiality of the Czech
administration. Socially and culturally Ruthenia made immense
strides in the two post-war decades. Economically the situation
was more difficult. Ruthenia had fitted easily in the economy
of the Hungarian plain. The lot of its people was never easy,
for the mountain valleys were narrow and not fertile, but there
was always a good demand for seasonal agricultural labour on
the plain. Now this opportunity of livelihood was cut off by an
artificial frontier, rigorously maintained by the Hungarians,
although it hit themselves as hard as the Ruthenes. The Czechs
approached the problem boldly, and by the active development of the local timber industry helped to bring better conditions to Ruthenia.

I heard many complaints as I passed along the beautiful but
pathetic valleys of Ruthenia. In hard times it is quite customary
to blame the government—we do it in our own country. There
were complaints about poor agricultural prices, and low rates
of wages paid by the Jews: although the greater part of the
development bill has been paid by Bohemia and Slovakia, the
Ruthene peasant does not understand that schools and new
roads cost a lot of money, and that self-government implies
self-support as well. These are passing complaints, without
depth. It was significant that I heard not a solitary sigh for a
return of the 'good old days.'

I found my greatest hope in the children of Ruthenia: the
young men have a vigorous and virile outlook, and a surprising
knowledge of affairs. The older generation is not interested.

'I know nothing of these things,' said an old forester to
whom I talked of Central European affairs. 'I don't understand
them. I only understand trees.'

But he *did* understand trees. The churches in the Ruthene

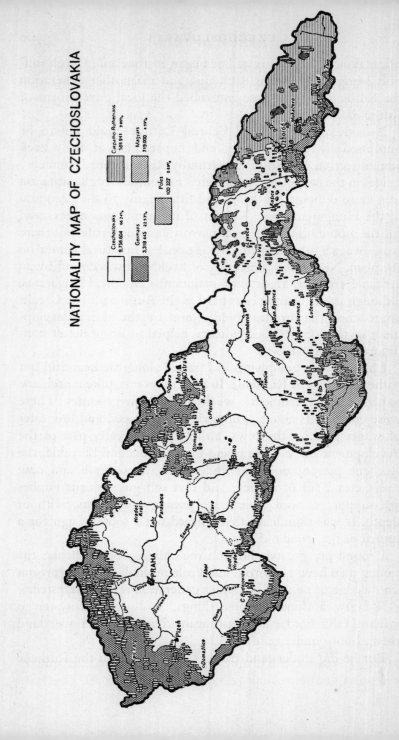

NATIONALITY MAP OF CZECHOSLOVAKIA

Czechoslovaks 9,756,604 66.24%

Germans 3,318,445 22.53%

Carpatho-Ruthenians 589,941 3.80%

Magyars 719,000 4.57%

Poles 100,327 0.59%

villages are entirely constructed of timber, without so much as an iron nail—designed and erected by men who could not read or write. If you and I, with all our education, set to work with no other tool than an axe, we could not produce things of beauty like these. There must be a submerged intelligence and culture in the Ruthene mind.

There is certainly faith. Bohemia takes its religion casually, Slovakia is devout, but Ruthenia is fervent. In 1918 most of the people belonged to the Uniat Church. Since then, however, priests of the Orthodox Church expelled from Russia have made thousands of converts. Religious freedom in all parts of Czechoslovakia was absolute. In Ruthenia religion was an accepted solace for poverty: heavenly prospects a compensation for a hard life on earth. No article of faith has been so misused as this, but in Ruthenia it was at least genuinely held by the people, not imposed by their masters. I tramped with the Ruthenes on a pilgrimage: for three days we walked over mountain paths, and mine were the only feet which were shod. I was deeply moved by what I saw, and heard, and felt. Here was a simple faith which is almost impossible in our complicated western world.

Today Ruthenia is again in Hungarian hands. (The circumstances leading to its reincorporation will be considered in the Hungarian chapter.) For a brief moment high hopes were raised as the new Russian frontiers marched with those of Ruthenia. All cultural ties were remembered and embellished. All Slavs have a deep vein of sentiment, and Ruthenia is the traditional birthplace of their race: here all their folk legends have their centre. Pan-Slav ideals found an ample response in the simple minds of the Ruthenian peasants. I gather from Ruthenes who have recently escaped that few people look upon the Hungarian occupation as more than temporary.

VI

In 1938 events moved with gathering speed. After the seizure of Austria, the chancelleries of Europe were alarmed by reports of the massing of German troops on the Czechoslovakian frontier. By May these reports approached an alarmist phase: Prague daily expected the German air fleet overhead, and part of the Czech army was mobilised, the frontier defences manned. At the last moment the Germans denied that there had been any massing of troops at all!

An increasing flood of propaganda was now loosed, in scope and ferocity unequalled in history. The dignified figure of President Benes was signalled out for vituperous abuse. 'Incidents' of a familiar pattern occurred daily in the Sudeten districts. Extremist elements, spurred by words and supplied by arms from Germany, began what was in effect guerrilla warfare with the Czech police and frontier posts. When any of the guerrillas were killed, the incident was represented as another outbreak of Czech 'terrorism.' Actually, Czech discipline and restraint were remarkable—it is significant that the Czech casualties were far higher than those of the Germans.

In such an unhealthy atmosphere the British government made a new move—it sent Lord Runciman as an 'unofficial mediator' between the two sides. The Czechs made in all four offers to the Sudetens, each more liberal than the last. The final offer, indeed, gave Henlein practically the whole of his eight points. Negotiations on this basis were opened and for a brief moment Europe hoped again.

When Hitler addressed the Nuremberg Congress on September 12th, 1938, the whole world listened. After announcing the new might of Germany, and gigantic fortifications in the west, Hitler indulged in the customary abuse of Czechoslovakia; then he announced that he was 'not willing to look on without aid while Germans in Czechoslovakia were persecuted.' Unless this ceased, he declared, 'serious results will ensue.' As the only man who could stop this 'persecution'—at a word, by stopping the provocation—was Hitler, Europe feared the worst.

Then we were given a sample of the new diplomacy on which the precarious edifice of European peace was to be built. Given practically all they wanted, the Sudetens demanded much more. And, on the pretext of another 'incident' in which lives were lost—an incident directly followed Hitler's provocative speech—they broke off negotiations and threw themselves openly into the arms of Hitler.

The situation was unprecedented in history. Thousands of Sudetens, fearful of the outbreak of armed conflict in their valleys, fled to Germany. Young Sudetens passed into Germany to form a 'free corps.' Armed and trained, they carried out 'irregular' invasions of Czechoslovakia from German soil.

The restraint of the Czechs under unparalleled provocation deserves and will receive the praise of history. By this time the question was at least in the open—it was revealed not as a question between Beneš and Henlein, but between Beneš and Hitler. From August 1938 onwards, if not earlier, Henlein was a mere pawn in the terrible game. And in the middle of August Hitler had prepared to back his demands by mobilising one and a half million troops. Foreign ambassadors were assured that the vast army exercises had no political significance, but this 'diplomatic' assurance was given the credence it deserved. The democracies may be gullible, but they are not simpletons.

The last fortnight of September was reminiscent of 1914, except that the pace was much more furious. Again Czechoslovakia manned her frontiers, while vast German armies prepared for overwhelming invasion. The Sudeten Germans were almost forgotten—the affair had now become a matter of national pride.

In the meantime, on September 7th, a significant leading article in The Times had suggested for the first time the cession of the Sudeten districts. Although it was promptly denied that this was the policy of the British government, acute observers were profoundly uneasy. It is now known that Lord Runciman had come to the conclusion that such a state of tension had been reached that settlement on terms of autonomy was impossible.

'Responsibility for the final break must, in my opinion, rest

upon the shoulders of Herr Henlein and Herr Frank and upon
those of their supporters inside and outside the country who
were urging extreme and unconstitutional action,' he reported.
'. . . Directly and indirectly, the connection between the
chief Sudeten leaders and the Government of the Reich had
become the dominant factor in the situation; the dispute was
no longer an internal one.'

It was, in fact, quite clear—as Dr. Goebbels has since admitted—that no concessions would have halted the situation.
An anxious Europe saw war stalking from the near horizon.
Sides were hastily formed, with much confusion. Poland prepared an ultimatum for the surrender of Teschen: Hungary
demanded a drastic frontier revision. France and Russia re-
declared the validity of their treaties with Czechoslovakia.
Roumania and Yugoslavia, while not anxious to go to war
with Germany, promised the utmost fulfilment of their liabilities if Hungary moved. Italy was silent, probably most anxious
of all the states of Europe.

Disaster seemed inevitable when Mr. Chamberlain made his
dramatic gesture (according to Paris, at French suggestion)
and flew to see Hitler at Berchtesgaden on September 15th.
He found the situation even more urgent than he had supposed, and was convinced that Hitler had determined that
'the Sudeten Germans must have the right of self-determination and of "returning," if they wished, to the Reich. . . . If
they could not achieve this by their own efforts, he said, he
would assist them to do so, *and he declared categorically that
rather than wait he would be prepared to risk a world war.*'

The phrase I have italicised is the key to the situation. Mr.
Chamberlain, convinced that Hitler was about to invade
Czechoslovakia, came home to consult his colleagues and the
French government. The French commitments to Czecho-
slovakia were stronger than the British and the internal condi-
tion of the country was such that they were desperately anx-
ious to avoid war. Proposals for 'self-determination' in the
Sudeten areas were placed before the Czech government.

The Czechs saw the ground fall away beneath their feet in a night. To date they had had the moral backing of England, the firm alliance of France and Russia. They naturally protested. Without being consulted they were to hand over to Germany their richest areas. They appealed to their Arbitration Treaty with Germany—which had been specifically reaffirmed by General Goering 'on his honour' only six months previously. The British and French governments persisted; no choice was left to the Czechs, who could scarcely fight Germany alone. 'Under intolerable pressure' they agreed to the dismemberment of their country.

The Russians, for all their alliance with Czechoslovakia, took no part in the negotiations and were not consulted. The fog of suspicion between Russia and the west was never deeper than at this time. Russian obligations were dependent upon those of France, and they declared themselves ready to honour them. France was not: the crisis had revealed weaknesses long apparent to outside observers. Most of the French were not interested in Czechoslovakia, but only in France, or in themselves. When a people becomes short-sighted, calamity lies ahead. The easiest way out of the crisis was the sacrifice of Czechoslovakia.

Mr. Chamberlain flew back to Germany with the good news. But at Godesberg he found himself facing another development of the new diplomacy. He expected merely to discuss with Hitler convenient ways and means of carrying out the agreed proposals. Instead, he was presented with an ultimatum far wider in its scope. The Germans demanded to occupy at once the Sudeten provinces—the mask of self-determination was already dropped: such an occupation would have left the Czechs at Hitler's mercy, for their 'Maginot Line' would be in his hands. Further negotiations would be useless.

Naturally, Mr. Chamberlain declined to accept the ultimatum. Indeed, he 'bitterly reproached' Hitler for his action. He could not press the Czechs to accept the new conditions, nor could he advise them to delay further their mobilisation.

At this stage there was no more hesitation—at least the situation was clarified. France prepared to honour her pledges and mobilised her army. It was announced that England would support France: air raid precautions were organised and improvised; the fleet mobilised. The situation was exactly equivalent to the last days of July 1914.

The German army was ready to march, but at the eleventh hour and fifty-ninth minute it was halted. President Roosevelt sent a powerful appeal to Hitler: Mussolini moved swiftly and decisively—no one doubted that he was intensely anxious to avert a war from which Italy could gain nothing, even if she chose the winning side. In one of the most dramatic moments the House of Commons ever witnessed, Mr. Chamberlain interrupted his recital of the events which were about to plunge Europe into war: there was fresh news—Hitler, Mussolini, Daladier and Chamberlain would meet at Munich on the morrow.

Each of the statesmen was mobbed by cheering crowds when he returned to his own country. For war was averted: a compromise had been reached—which, although it gave Hitler practically everything his Godesberg ultimatum demanded, did obtain a few concessions as to time and method. These at least were something—the first of their kind. The peoples of Europe did not worry over the rest; they had almost forgotten the root cause of the problem, and were only concerned with its effects. A great wave of relief swept over Europe. Only in Czechoslovakia was there no enthusiasm. 'The Czechoslovakian Government, after having considered the decisions of the conference in Munich, taken without it and against it, finds no other means but to accept, and has nothing to add.' No more poignant official communiqué was ever penned.

On October 1st, German troops marched into the Sudetenland and within a week the 'predominantly German' districts were occupied. The final frontier was to be arranged by an international commission nominated by the four Great Powers.

The Germans claimed that the Czech census of 1930 included thousands of Czech officials and troops in the Sudeten areas, and demanded the 1910 census as the basis of demarcation— although at this time there were thousands of German (*i.e.* Austrian) officials and troops in the same areas. Further, the 1910 census was conducted on a basis of speech, not nationality—if a Czech spoke German, he was classed as German. All Jews were entered as Germans. A famous British journalist, resident in Bohemia at the time, could speak German but not Czech—so appeared in the census as German! The net result of the adoption of the 1910 census as the basis of the new 'ethnic' frontier was that Germany claimed and received considerably more than even the Godesberg demands! Districts containing 99 per cent of Czechs were handed over to Germany.

(It will be noted that there was no pretence at implementing the morally sound doctrine of self-determination; no plebiscites were held. Nearly three million Germans were added to the Reich, but with them went nearly 800,000 Czechs. Further, among the three million Germans were some hundreds of thousands who had shown that they preferred democratic Czechoslovakia to Nazi Germany.)

I have summarised the drama of the autumn of 1938 very briefly, but it deserves a far deeper study. Yet it scarcely falls within the limits of this book, wide though they are. As we have seen, the fate of Czechoslovakia was an incident in the revival of the old game of power politics. The basis of the problem was lost in the fury of wild emotions. Statesmen who had proclaimed the sanctity of treaties and the common interests of democracies forgot their high sentiments in the overwhelming desire to avoid the horrors of war. It is easy to blame, but no one would envy their responsibility.

Not everybody in Britain and France joined in the wave of rejoicing which swept over Europe—passing Czechoslovakia by. There were men who knew the German mind better than Mr. Chamberlain did; they did not attach much importance to the scrap of paper which Hitler had signed, and which the British Prime Minister waved to the vociferously welcoming crowd. And, besides the men who could see more clearly ahead, there were few who could avoid some feelings of shame. Whatever the rights or wrongs of the case, no one could doubt that the Czechs had been betrayed. We had encouraged them to resist, then had suddenly withdrawn our support. There was an uneasy feeling that we had not played the game.

When Mr. Chamberlain referred to Czechoslovakia as 'that remote country, of which we know so little,' he emphasised a double tragedy in a phrase: a tragedy of short-sighted leadership, and another of ill-informed or uninterested public opinion. Worst offenders are those who now complain bitterly of the Munich 'settlement,' but who cheered the loudest when Mr. Chamberlain brought home 'peace.' Few publicists in any country would care to have their 1938 speeches quoted in evidence against them. True, some American politicians strongly condemned the Munich agreement—but always with the reservation that America was not prepared to take an active part herself.

Nor was the conduct of the democracies impressive. We sought to salve our consciences by a substantial gift and a loan to the mutilated country. Even these were strenuously opposed by some people who called themselves 'hard-headed business men'; this may mean that their outlook seldom extends beyond their business, and that their moral scruples are limited only by customs of their trade. In this country they were the leaders of the peace-at-any-price movement; their strongest supporters were the people who were completely uninterested.

VII

Berchtesgaden and Munich left the Czechs in a state of dumb amaze. There was a natural reaction against the democratic powers; we may talk about dictators whose word is worthless, but the bond between Czechoslovakia and France was the firmest in Europe. And now it had broken at the first strain! There was widespread disillusion and resentment. The Czechs argued that it was utterly unfair that the democratic Great Powers should support them up to the critical moment and then desert them. They would have been better off without that support, it appeared, since then they must have made earlier—and better—terms with Hitler.

The democratic government resigned: with it President Benes, whose dignified restraint under unprecedented provocation ensures his niche in history—one untoward word from him, and the hounds of war could not have been held back. A new government of the right was set up, its frank object being

CZECHOSLOVAKIA, BEFORE AND AFTER THE MUNICH AGREEMENT

to make the best possible arrangement with Germany. Slovakia and Ruthenia were promptly allocated a substantial measure of responsible autonomy.

At first sight the new situation appeared impossible. The complicated and efficient economic system of the country was shattered. Main-line railways were cut by protrusions of new German territory. The armament works of Pilsen were brought within range of German field guns. Prague was only 27 miles from the German outposts, and the bottle-neck about Brno was only 40 miles across. If the new frontiers had been specially devised to make Czechoslovakia militarily indefensible, they could scarcely have been better drawn.

As the weeks passed, I noticed a great change in the demeanour of my Czech friends—a change I expected. This people is too virile to throw up its hands because it has received a serious blow. Their attitude was a brave one: 'Well, the past is past. Now we must begin again.'

Both Herr Hitler and Mr. Chamberlain expressed the view after Munich that a prosperous future was possible for Czechoslovakia. They were right. In spite of the grievous blow it had sustained, Czechoslovakia's resources and energy were such that she might have survived economically and politically. All she needed was assistance in making a new start. Unfortunately —nay, disastrously—this was not forthcoming.

At Munich all the powers had agreed to guarantee the frontiers of the new Czechoslovakia as soon as they were finally settled. The guarantee was soon and conveniently forgotten. This was a disaster: not merely for the good name of Britain, but for the future of Czechoslovakia. Strategically the country was now indefensible; it depended entirely upon outside guarantees, and any chance of economic recovery and development was lost without them. The Germans spent a short time in organising the Sudeten provinces: by that time it was obvious that Britain and France had forgotten the proposed guarantees. This was excellent: the 'bit by bit' policy could continue without opposition.

After a short respite to make certain that no support for Czechoslovakia was likely to be forthcoming, Germany developed an intense internal campaign in the stricken state. Special rights were claimed for the 300,000 Germans still left in the rump of Czechoslovakia, and these were given their instructions to act as superior beings, even at the expense of provoking disorder. It was demanded that Czechoslovakia should enforce the Nuremberg laws against the Jews, should accept a military alliance and common foreign policy with Germany, and should surrender a proportion of its gold reserve. In other words, Czechoslovakia was to become a satellite state.

The Czechs resisted. Powerless and unsupported as they were, they gave way only on minor matters, always postponing further concessions. By February 1939 the Nazis were indignant at the slow 'progress' in Czechoslovakia, and hinted that if the process of alignment with Germany were not accelerated, 'certain measures' would be necessary. One word of support from outside and the situation might have been faced, but Europe was no longer interested in Czechoslovakia. Actually the ship was still sound, but it appeared to be sinking. Not only the rats, but some of the crew, prepared to leave.

We have seen that Slovakia is a mountainous country inhabited by a peasant people. As in the Balkans, their leaders were professional politicians—most of whom had been educated at Vienna or Budapest. To say that many of them were under foreign influence is to put it mildly. (When the first Prime Minister of the newly-autonomous Ruthenia was arrested on a charge of accepting bribes from Hungary, he was not brought to trial 'owing to Hungarian objections.')

It is not easy for an Englishman or an American to understand the mentality of these men. He has never known but one allegiance, and could never acknowledge any other. Picture a Slovak, born a subject of Austria-Hungary; he becomes a citizen of the new Czechoslovakia, is discontented, and wants events to move quickly; he turns from his cousins, the Czechs, to his older acquaintances.

This was especially noticeable in Slovakia, where clerical influence was so strong—and the clerics *had* powerful friends in Hungary. It was remarkable that successive political leaders in Slovakia were three priests. They were no advertisement for the often-debated alliance between politics and pulpit.

It is unnecessary to relate in detail the events of March 1939. Slovak leaders planned a complete secession from Czechoslovakia. Already they had the complete autonomy some of them had demanded—only common matters like foreign affairs and defence were left in the hands of the Czech-Slovak-Ruthene Parliament at Prague. But they were not satisfied.

German influence had been active in Slovakia for many years; it was a cardinal point of policy to weaken a prospective opponent by internecine strife. Any recalcitrant Slovak faction could get financial support from Germany, even before Munich. Fascist ideas, too, find a favourable breeding-ground wherever there is an element of distress or discontent. The Hlinka Guards, founded by Father Hlinka, the Slovak leader, bore a suspicious resemblance to foreign prototypes.

The Slovak government after Munich contained some high-minded men; some were bent on continued co-operation with the Czechs, others were not: but at least they were sincere. Unfortunately for their country, they were easily outnumbered by men who took their orders from abroad. It is now known that the cabinet contained a sufficient number of men in the pay of Berlin and Budapest to dominate its decisions. The Germans were quite content to let the Hungarians play the more showy part in the drama of intransigeance. The recovery of historic Magyar territory was a good placard to the world. Yet Slovakia had always been one of Hitler's major objectives. From it Poland could be outflanked—and her Central Industrial Area immediately threatened.

At the moment dictated by Berlin, therefore, the Slovak leaders moved to throw off the 'yoke' of the Czechs. The president of the republic acted promptly. The secession of Slovakia meant the death of the entire state—that was certain. Slovak leaders were arrested and Hlinka guards disarmed. The action of the German minority was significant—they took the lead in organising demonstrations against Prague. The next step was inevitable. A number of Slovaks appealed openly to Hitler for protection. They got it.

President Hacha was summoned to Berlin to discuss the situation. He was prepared to offer almost capitulatory terms —but while he was on his way, the Germans invaded his country. Resistance was useless: in September 1938 Czechoslovakia had powerful allies: in March 1939 she had none. Within two days German troops were parading in Prague, where the people could do no more than hiss them. 'Thus died Czechoslovakia,' wrote an eye-witness: but he was wrong.

Germany's economic gains were considerable. The very active industries included the Skoda arms factories, the Bata shoe works, and important glass, leather, cement and other establishments. Among the mines were iron ore, manganese, lead, silver and zinc. Yet the Sudeten Germans found to their dismay that their new 'freedom' brought no relief. Many of their factories were promptly closed—they were akin to German industries, and their competition could not be permitted. Within two years 8 per cent of the Sudetens had had to leave their own pleasant valleys to seek employment in Germany.

From the military point of view the advantages were greater. At Munich the formidable Czech army was neutralised: now it was eliminated, and part of the debit became a credit, as the vast stocks of first-class armaments fell to German hands. An awkward salient, pointing at the heart of Germany, was also eradicated.

From the equipment seized, the Germans were able to organise at once three complete panzer divisions which were to play a prominent part in the defeat of France. Of the first four German tanks to be captured by the French army, three were Czech!

VIII

Present conditions in Czechoslovakia are bound to have some bearing on the final settlement. The German aim was parallel with that in Poland. They will allow Slovakia, an agricultural area, to remain as a satellite state, but they must make industrial Bohemia-Moravia an integral part of the Reich, which is to be the factory of Europe.

A puppet government still functions in Prague, but the real authority, of course, is the German Governor-General. Some of the Czechs who clung desperately to their offices were probably inspired by patriotic motives: apparently abandoned by the world, they would make the best possible terms for their people. They were mistaken, however: the Germans have merely used them as pawns, always trying to direct popular discontent to the native officials.

Even to them the situation is now quite clear. Himmler on one occasion declared openly that if necessary he was prepared to have the whole Czech nation exterminated. There is a grandiose plan for the transfer of all the Czechs to Siberia—after the defeat of Russia, of course. Another scheme envisages the resettlement of Ukraine farms with German masters and Czech labourers.

In the meantime, apart from the continuous executions, over a million Czechs have been transported to Germany for forced labour. One of the first Nazi blows was struck at the Czech trade unions. In Czechoslovakia social services were as advanced as any in Europe: the method of administration of some differed from the British, naturally enough. In particular, unemployment insurance was administered by the trade unions, which received the contributions and paid out the benefits. (This method has been suggested in Britain.) Thus large liquid funds were at the disposal of the trade unions—an added incentive to Nazi attack.

Perhaps even more forceful was the onslaught on Czech culture. All secondary schools and universities were immediately closed: the Czechs, one of the best-educated races of Europe, were to become a people of labourers. For once Frank, the German Governor-General, lived up to his name: 'If you win, you will have all the universities you need. If we win the war, you will no longer need Czech schools at all!'

Yet the Austrians found the Czechs indigestible a generation ago: the Germans do so now. The battle of Czechoslovakia has scarcely begun. All observers report on the amazing spirit of resistance of the oppressed Czechs. Sabotage is rife—even the Germans have had to admit this. A Norwegian general commented on the proportion of 'duds' among the German bombs, and found that they were made in Czechoslovakia. Even with armed guards everywhere, and with German foremen looking on, a clever workman can occasionally omit some part of a bomb's delicate mechanism.

Resistance was so widespread that Heydrich, deputy chief of the Gestapo, was sent to rule Czechoslovakia. His policy of terror and murder provoked inevitable reactions, and he paid for his brutality with his life. Subsequent reprisals went beyond all previous precedents. Because it was alleged to have sheltered one of the assailants, the village of Lidice was razed to the ground, and its male population massacred. But still the Czechs wage their underground war. Some have weakened, and made half-hearted accommodations with their masters; most are implacable, waiting for the day when they can rejoin the armies of liberation.

A Czech army and air force fights in the open. A provisional government, in exile, has been formed by Dr. Beneš. It includes Slovaks and Ruthenes, who are emphatic about the necessity for reviving Czechoslovakia when victory is won. They are supported not only by those who have escaped to fight in the open field, but by millions who carry on the underground campaign in Czechoslovakia, undeterred by the terrors of the late Heydrich, the Gestapo chief designated to restore 'order' in the land.

IX

A complete summary of the problems of Czechoslovakia is not advisable here, for some of them pertain to the Hungarian section, where they are considered. We can, however, summarise our ideas on the subject treated in this chapter.

(*a*) We shall agree that Czechoslovakia must be re-established after the war: this is no more than elementary justice. The British government has already announced it as one of its war aims—without, however, necessarily guaranteeing the restoration of the former frontiers. This also represents substantially the American view. If ever a country deserved sympathetic treatment, that country is Czechoslovakia; not only for its progressive record in days of peace, its dignified moderation in times of strife and provocation, its courage under intense persecution, but above all for the essential justice of its cause.

(*b*) The first, and most serious, subject of debate concerns the Germans in Czechoslovakia. The small scattered settlements can be transplanted to Germany—in their own interests. For their little day they have strutted the stage, German citizens overlording Czech serfs. They can scarcely grumble if they find that they are not wanted when Czechoslovakia re-emerges: they should consider themselves fortunate that the moderation of the Czechs is likely to ensure that nothing worse than deportation awaits them.

The real problem, of course, is that of the two and a half million Sudeten Germans inhabiting the fringes of the Bohemian mountains. The Czechs have a strong claim to their historic frontiers: if it is conceded, what is to happen to the Germans there? They ruined the state in 1938; there will never be any guarantee that they would not do it again at the first available opportunity. A number of them have proved themselves anti-Nazis; it would be too much to expect the Czechs to trust the rest.

The first thought is that the obviously intransigeant Germans shall be ordered to emigrate into Germany. Yet there are limits to this policy. There is scarcely any direction in which German territory can be equitably extended, and already we have envisaged the return of hundreds of thousands of Germans to the Reich. If another two millions are to be added in one consignment, Germany will get somewhat overcrowded—even allowing for the making-up of her substantial casualties. We shall have to consider whether there is a case for the redrafting of the Czech frontiers in the north.

The point of view that the mountain barrier was and will be the real strategic frontier deserves consideration, but not over-emphasis. The real defence of Czechoslovakia will not depend upon mountain forts, but upon collaboration with other states—and on the permanent disarming of Germany.

Perhaps we shall be asked to consider the cession to Germany of (1) the north-eastern and north-western corners of Bohemia about Cheb and Liberec, where German population is predominant, (2) a smaller fringe in the south-west, (3) the quadrilateral north-west of Opava. Even then there would be a lot of ethnic tidying-up of the frontier to be done. Further, these districts would represent a serious economic loss to the Czechs—and, proportionately, not such a great gain to the Germans. When a new and artificial frontier is being created, economic conditions rank equal in importance to any others. In this respect Bohemia-Moravia is a remarkably complete economic whole, and only minor frontier modifications—such as those suggested by Masaryk in 1919—could be made without upsetting the balance.

At first sight our inclination would be to restore the 1938 frontiers of Czechoslovakia without question. Yet we have argued that the duration of European peace may depend on the degree with which we can persuade the Germans that they have been justly treated. The Eighth Point of the Atlantic Charter applies to Germans as well as to Czechs. A plebiscite among the Sudeten Germans after the chastening of defeat might be revealing. Certainly no area should be ceded to Germany except on the wishes of the inhabitants. The Sudetens have not experienced the long course of Nazi racial 'culture' afforded to their northern brothers; they may forget it the more readily.

(c) The people to decide on the relations between Czechs and Slovaks are obviously these races themselves. Bohemia-Moravia could exist as an independent state—could be even prosperous as such: Slovakia very definitely could not. A mountainous country, with limited natural resources, she is bound to collaborate either with Hungary, in the manner in which her limited economy developed, but with whose people the Slovaks have a very definite ethnic clash; or with the Czechs, with whom they have cultural ties and bonds of common interest steadily forged between 1918 and 1938. My own impression is that the Slovaks will decide heavily in favour of the latter. The present puppet government is no more than a German-controlled sub-committee. Influential Slovak leaders are by the side of Dr. Beneš in London. It may be that Slovaks will prefer that Czechoslovakia shall again become Czecho-Slovakia, with autonomous rights for their own province. On the other hand, the stern hand of adversity may prompt them to put first things first and omit the hyphen. In either case, the future of Czechoslovakia should be secure, for the delegation of limited regional powers need be no weakness.

(d) Ruthenia, or Sub-Carpathian Russia, is another problem. The strategic reason for its disposition—as a connecting link between Czechoslovakia and Roumania—has now disappeared. In view of the proposed Polish-Czech Federation (to be discussed in the next section), it might be administered jointly by both countries, with local autonomy for domestic affairs; or it might link up with another area, Polish Ukraine, to the north of the Carpathians. The first thing to do is to ascertain the wishes of the Ruthenes themselves: nor would this be as easy as it sounds, in view of the limited outlook of most of these peasant people.

X

To thinking men, one of the significant developments of the early months of the war was the *rapprochement* between Poland and Czechoslovakia, resulting eventually in an announcement that a federation of the two countries was envisaged after the war. Were he still alive, no man would have welcomed this sensible move so warmly as Thomas Masaryk, wise beyond his generation. 'Without a free Czechoslovakia there can be no free Poland,' he declared more than once; 'and without a free Poland there can be no free Czecho-slovakia.' If the present federal idea had taken firm root in 1919, the course of world history would have been changed indeed. Even Hitler would have hesitated before a Polish-Czech state with Masaryk as political leader and Pilsudski as Commander-in-Chief!

I have already mentioned the miserable source of resentment which forbade this happy union—Teschen, that disputed country about which so many in England had never heard. So far back as the ninth century the Duchy of Teschen (in the south-eastern corner of Silesia) was the subject of dispute between Bohemian and Polish rulers. Its population was mixed, and although only 850 square miles in extent it is very rich in minerals. In the seventeenth century it came under Austrian rule, and long before the end of the war both Czechs and Poles laid claim to the ancient duchy. They agreed to settle the dispute amicably, but in January 1919 Poland 'jumped a claim' by electing members of Parliament from Teschen. The Czechs promptly marched in, and for a year there was serious tension.

No small share of the blame for the unhappy atmosphere must go to Pilsudski, who did not like the Czechs. On the other hand, he was aiming at a Polish-Hungarian alliance—and Hungary gazed with undisguised hatred at the new Czechoslovakia.

Then Polish sentiment was outraged when the Czechs refused to allow transit of munitions across their territory during the Polish-Russian war in 1920. While Poland was actively occupied, a division of Teschen was affected, and Pilsudski always maintained that it unduly favoured Czechoslovakia. The policy of mutual annoyance continued, aggravated by the clashing personalities of the leaders—Masaryk, a democrat of democrats; Pilsudski, a dogmatic authoritarian.

The incident of Teschen rankled in both countries, and its effects proved to be far beyond its original importance. Relations between Poland and Czechoslovakia were never as cordial as they should have been, and the Poles continually reverted to the settlement. In Teschen and the small adjoining strip of Silesia allocated to Czechoslovakia were some 80,000 Poles, but these formed only 15 per cent of the population. Compared with the bigger issues like the Polish 'Corridor' and the Sudeten Deutsch, this seemed a senseless prolongation of a quarrel over a comparatively trifling cause.

Pilsudski apparently maintained the rupture long after it might have been healed. It was not difficult for him to foresee trouble in Europe, and he wanted to divert it away from Poland, to Czechoslovakia. Trouble between Germany and Czechoslovakia had been anticipated for many years. There were cynics who declared that Poland was waiting for this conflict, and would then demand a slice of Czechoslovakia as the price of her support or neutrality. Yet Poland was allied to Roumania, which country was closely bound to Czechoslovakia. It was all very confusing.

The cynics were right. At the height of the Sudeten crisis, Poland pressed an ultimatum on Prague; the Czechoslovak government, apparently abandoned by its allies, could scarcely resist, and Polish troops marched into Teschen—occupying not merely the Polish strip, but Czech districts beyond. It is quite clear that Poland's claim to Teschen was far stronger than Germany's claim to the Sudeten country. Nevertheless, the moment and manner of her action aroused deep resentment abroad—it savoured of kicking a beaten man while he was down.

This was an unpleasing episode. It was unfortunate that among the politicians of Poland were men who were ready to sacrifice principle for opportunity. General Sikorski never held such opinions, and when he became the Polish leader he immediately took steps to remedy the situation. It was good in those days to hear the frank discussion between Poles and Czechs: sins of the past were freely recalled—not for purposes of recrimination, but for a frank avoidance of similar mistakes in the future. Today Teschen appears as an insignificant trifle: Poles and Czechs are bound close in a common martyrdom. They have learned their lesson—have again recognised their traditional enemy, who conquered them by dividing them.

On November 11th, 1940, the Polish and Czech leaders in London made a joint declaration; it expressed not only their determination to fight till victory was won, but afterwards to collaborate closely to the defence of their common interests and to the establishment of a democratic 'new order' in Central Europe. The new *entente cordiale* developed rapidly. Mixed committees were appointed to work out plans for economic, political, defensive and cultural collaboration. The degree of unity in the projected federation has not yet been decided. Defence and foreign policy are essentially for common control: probably an inter-state Parliament will be necessary: presumably a president to represent the federation in public life must be elected and provided with a staff.

These steps should present few difficulties in countries which have already suffered for lack of unity. Bigger problems lie in the economic sphere. At the moment, agricultural and industrial standards differ—taken generally, those of Czechoslovakia are well in advance of its neighbour's. The annual value of production in Czechoslovakia is $340 per head of the population; in Poland it is only $120. The wealth of Czechoslovakia can be taken as two-thirds mining and industrial, one-third agricultural; in Poland the figures are reversed.

At first sight this seems a useful basis for economic federation—Czechoslovakia finding the manufactured goods, Poland the agricultural products. The situation is complicated, however, by the fact that the farm lands of Poland are much overcrowded: she needs a considerable measure of industrialisation herself in order to find work for her surplus agricultural population.

The results of immediate and complete economic federation can therefore be foreseen. Just as British farmers, with their high production costs, cannot compete with farmers in South America, so the Czech farmers would be undercut in price by agricultural products from Poland. Further, the necessary progress of Polish industrialisation would be retarded. The first aim must be to raise the standard of living in eastern Poland until it is level with that in Czechoslovakia. Otherwise there is a danger of Czech factories being flooded by cheap Polish labour; and the certainty that the poorer Poles could not pay for Czech manufactures.

These difficulties are not insuperable, however. A transitional period would probably be necessary before a full and complete customs union was possible, but in the meantime political collaboration would be changing the entire atmosphere.

In the welter of ideas, reactionary and visionary, affecting post-war Europe, in the proposed Polish-Czechoslovak federation we have something definite and solid, a basis for bigger things—for we shall argue that other countries would like to join the new combination, particularly once it had proved its worth. From time to time, even as the war progresses, it is probable that new decisions of collaboration will be made. They should be studied carefully, as a sign of the shape of things to come.

Dr. Beneš has made it clear that he regards the proposed Polish-Czechoslovak federation as a beginning, not an end; it may prove to be the first of those regional federations we have envisaged as stepping-stones to wider schemes. Certainly this one is impelled by that essential force, mutual interest. Membership of the new federation will be open to neighbouring states. We are likely to see some sort of revolution in Hungary after the war—certainly an agrarian revolution. A democratic Hungary would be warmly welcomed into the Polish-Czechoslovak federation. The case of Austria is more difficult: a democratic Austria would be welcomed just as warmly, but only a plebiscite can show whether Austria would prefer this course to membership of a German federation. Many Austrian exiles, to their own regret, believe that their country is now too firmly caught in the net of nationalism ever to escape, and that continued association with Germany is inevitable. If this is true, it is a tragedy, economically as well as culturally. With Austria and Hungary united with Czechoslovakia and Poland, the economic strength and unity of the old Austro-Hungarian Empire would not merely be restored, but extended.

Dr. Beneš has also indicated further extensions. The Yugoslavian and Greek governments in exile are conducting conversations with a view to the closest possible ties after victory. In the appropriate section the near relationship of Yugoslavia and Bulgaria has been emphasised. The course of events in Roumania is likely to be parallel with those in Hungary: the present authoritarian régime will not survive many hours after defeat. If the Balkan states joined in close federation with a Polish-Danubian bloc, then not even a future Hitler would dare to attack. The Baltic states, Estonia, Latvia and Lithuania, may also be attracted to the new association—which in turn desires to maintain the closest bonds with Britain. There are vast possibilities; when so many neighbours have the same intent and face the same dangers, minor difficulties can be smoothed away.

These projects are not dreams: their basis is already established: for the rest, time is required. In the meantime, mixed crews of Poles and Czechs pilot bombers over Berlin.

CHAPTER ELEVEN

HUNGARY

I

ONE of the tragedies in this war is that among our opponents are to be found people whom we like. We have no animosity against the Roumanians or the Bulgars: many British people have a deep affection for the Finns and the Hungarians. Much the same state of affairs prevailed in the last war. Then, though the Hungarians were ranged with our enemies, they seldom came into conflict with us; they made no secret of their pleasure at this. Generations earlier, ideas of freedom and tolerance had flourished in Hungary, and their leaders turn for inspiration to the traditional home of democratic thought, Britain. So absurd was the state of 'enmity' between Hungary and Britain that, when we won a victory, British prisoners of war in Hungary were allowed out of their prison camps to celebrate the occasion in local restaurants!

The much-reduced Hungary which emerged after defeat in the World War was a small country, about the same size as England. Except for hills in the north and west, the greater part of the country consists of one vast plain. Here roam herds of long-horned cattle and half-wild horses, tended by cowboys in picturesque attire—there were cowboys in Hungary long before America was discovered. In the sluggish streams are water-mills, of precisely the same pattern as have been used for a thousand years—most of them owned, it is interesting to note, by millers of German descent. In spite of scenic monotony, the Hungarian plain is of vast interest: in the spring it is green and pleasant, but by the autumn the plain is parched and dusty. Tiny particles of sand ascend to the air to form a back for a natural mirror, and I have seen in Hungary, as in the Moroccan desert, the *Fata Morgana,* the mirage, of indescribable beauty.

Except for the capital, the towns of Hungary are comparatively unimportant. Yet Budapest is one of the most beautiful cities in the world: two cities really—the ancient city of Buda on the right bank of the Danube, the modern city of Pest on the left. Pest is all commerce and modernity, but Buda holds the peace of history, with monuments of Hungary's thousand-year story.

Yet the greatest interest of Hungary is in its people. Budapest of course is up to date, but many of the country districts wisely cling to traditional costumes, gaily embroidered. A Hungarian village green on a Sunday evening is like a scene from a comic opera: gypsies are playing traditional dances in their own eerie style, and hundreds of men, women and children are dancing. The green is a blaze of colour, for not a drab western costume is to be seen. Here are the joyous costumes of Hungary— brilliant reds, blues, greens and yellow, beautifully embroidered, flowing over a multitude of petticoats. Nor do the men betray the scene, for their attire is the most brilliant in Europe.

The character of the people appeals to the British temperament. It has been said that you do not know what hospitality is until you have been to Hungary. Twice I have wandered about its broad acres, overwhelmed with the kindness of complete strangers. When I arrived in a village, there was no question of seeking an inn—the inhabitants almost fought for the honour of entertaining me. The fertile fields assure that there is no hunger in Hungary, even in the most modest households. After the infectious gaiety of the Sunday evening dance I would have sworn that here was a people without a care in the world. Then I would glance at the lintel of the door, where was affixed a notice, '*Nem, nem, soha!*'—'No, no, never!' We must understand what this means before we can approach the problems of Hungary.

Who are these Hungarians, crowded in their plain between

German and Slav masses? They, together with the Finns and Estonians, are a race apart from the remainder of ethnic Europe. The early history of the Magyars is in doubt, but it is reasonably certain that they emanated from Central Asia. Maybe they found their way to Central Europe with the Huns; certain it is that they were doughty warriors, then as now famous for their horsemanship. In the tenth century they settled in what is Hungary today, and although they raided sporadically and made temporary conquests of neighbouring territories, the Hungarian plain became their permanent home.

For a thousand years the Hungarian kingdom survived, but with many vicissitudes. Then, in 1526, the Hungarians were defeated at Mohacs by the advancing Turks, who occupied the great plain for two centuries. Only in Transylvania was there some semblance of an independent Hungarian kingdom: the Magyar lands to the west were seized by Austria and served as a protective belt against the Turkish menace.

The Turkish policy in those days was particularly grim. If a district resisted, then all its inhabitants were put to the sword. Thus whole areas of Hungary were depopulated. Some are still desolate today. Others were repeopled under Turkish direction—but not by Turks. Instead, Roumanians and Serbs were brought in to farm the land for Turkish overlords—and to form the basis of some of the complicated ethnic problems of today.

The process was continued when the power of the Turks declined, and the Austrians pushed to the south-east. Successive emperors deliberately settled subject peoples in Hungarian lands. The principal idea was to keep the Magyars weak: if they were a united and homogeneous people, then they might object to a mere change of masters, Austrians for Turks. Thus Germans, Serbs, Roumanians, Croats, Slovenes —even Czechs and Bulgars—were all planted in Hungary, especially on the southern and eastern fringes of the plain.

At the same time many thousands of Jews settled in Hungary. They were being persecuted in Western Europe, and gladly escaped to a newly-freed land, ripe for development. Generally they were welcomed. The Hungarian noble, like his Polish neighbour, despised trade, and allowed the Jews an almost complete monopoly. Many Hungarian towns actually had a Jewish majority, and today there are few Magyar families which have not some strain of Jewish blood. Most of the Jews were thoroughly Magyarised, and with the passing of generations it became difficult to distinguish them from their neighbours.

The Magyar peasant was as little interested in commerce as was his landlord. He was—and still is, to a remarkable degree—a man of the countryside, with a natural distaste for town life. He was employed under semi-feudal conditions on the great estates—conditions which still prevail to a limited extent in many parts of Hungary, and which will probably be changed radically or even violently when the war is over.

Thus, when the time came for the development of Hungarian industry, Jewish brains and capital provided the control, while it was often necessary to import urban labourers from neighbouring countries, in view of Magyar reluctance, combined with feudal difficulty, to leave the land. At first this system of immigration worked well enough. Later, as Hungarian nationalism became forceful, a campaign of Magyarisation was launched. The descendants of the settlers, widely separated from their own kith and kin, did not always resist. Consequently, and especially in the towns, there are today thousands of families who speak the Magyar language and proclaim themselves Magyars—often with fervour—but whose great-great-grandparents were all of foreign stock.

The ideas of liberty engendered by the French Revolution had their repercussions in Hungary, where men began to discuss and to plan an independent land. Kossuth [1] led a fierce revolt in 1848, and the Austrians could only repress it with Russian assistance. (To this may be traced directly the anti-

[1] The patriot Louis Kossuth, it is interesting to note, was of a Magyarised *Slovak* family!

Russian sentiment in Hungary today; it is based on memories rather than ideologies.) Then, in 1866, weakened by their defeat at the hands of Prussia, the Austrians decided that it would be better to come to terms with their most important minority population. By the 'Compromise' of 1867 Hungary became an equal partner with Austria—in theory, at any rate: the Parliament at Budapest had full authority over Hungarian affairs, and shared with Vienna control of defence, finance and foreign affairs.

The tragedy was that when the Magyars had secured freedom for themselves, they denied it to the subject people placed under them. A Nationalities Law was agreed and passed, but was never put into execution. Its generous provisions allowed full scope for the minority peoples: had they been implemented, there might have been an Austro-Hungarian Empire on the map of Europe today. Instead, both the language and culture of subject peoples were sternly repressed in a vigorous effort of Magyarisation. The immediate aim was not really directed against the unfortunate minorities: the idea was to build up a large and solid 'Magyar' block which could ultimately demand complete independence from Austria.

Now it is important to realise that a change of frontier today is much more complicated than it was a century or more ago. Had the principle of ethnic frontiers been adopted after the Napoleonic wars, the problem of their demarcation would have been comparatively simple. Today, with the complications of communications and economics, any considerable change of frontier means an upheaval, larger or smaller. The point is that during the century of material progress Austria-Hungary had been organised as one economic whole. Railways, roads, the flow of trade, customs barriers—everything was duly planned, so that some wit remarked that if the Austro-Hungarian Empire had not existed it would have had to be invented.

Within the empire, the Hungarian economic field was remarkably self-contained. This was due to natural and to

political causes. The mountains and plains formed comple-
mentary physical regions, and the natural line of communications centred in Budapest. Further, Magyar nationalists deliberately aimed at Hungarian self-sufficiency in economic affairs
against the day when Hungary should be free.

The Hungarian share of the empire was a territory of
325,000 square kilometres, with a population of over 20
millions. The principal frontier was the 'natural' boundary of
the Carpathians, a mountainous semicircular enclosure. In the

THE DISMEMBERMENT OF HUNGARY

south-west, Hungary dominion spread over Croatia, to reach
the Adriatic Sea at Fiume. Here then was a country ruled by
the Hungarians, but of whose population only 10 millions—
50 per cent—were Hungarian. To the north of the Hungarian
plain were 2 million Slovaks with half a million Ruthenes; to
the east were 3 million Roumanians, and to the south 3 million
Serbs and Croats. In addition, there were 2 million Germans
scattered about Hungary. Many of these regions inhabited by
minorities had been under Hungarian rule for hundreds of
years.

Nevertheless, when Hungary found herself on the losing side in 1918, it was certain that the dismemberment of the ancient kingdom was inevitable. President Wilson's Tenth Point read: 'The peoples of Austria-Hungary, whose place among the nations we wish to see safeguarded and assured, should be afforded the first opportunity of autonomous development.' There would be few people in Britain or America who would quarrel with this principle. Since one of the most persistent and reasonable pleas by the defeated powers is based on the Fourteen Points—that they laid down their arms on this basis, and then were cheated because they were not applied—our problem is to examine the Hungarian claim that the Tenth Point was hopelessly perverted in its application.

The drafters of the peace treaties were under no delusions —they knew very well that the frontiers they suggested would leave two or three million Magyars outside Hungary. The problem was intensely difficult. Hungary, as we have seen, is a vast plain almost surrounded by a circle of mountains. The Magyars are people of the plain, and their preponderance ceased abruptly at the approach of the mountains. Thus, if a true ethnic Hungary were created, it would consist of the entire plain, right up to the mouths of the mountain valleys. But this would make life impossible for the mountain people. Here are two parallel mountain valleys; they can only trade by bringing their trade down to the plain. If the plain were in foreign hands, then the mountaineers might be ruined—even starve.

There seemed to be only two possibilities. Hungary could be left as she was, a geographical and economic unit—but including millions of other nationalities to which freedom had been promised; the other—the one adopted—was to allow the new states a small fringe of plain so as to allow communications between the mountain valleys. This fringe is the area of dispute, for it is largely occupied by Magyars.

Certainly in its immediate post-war years Hungary was in no condition to protest against any terms the Allies cared to offer. A Socialist republic was proclaimed under Count Michael Karolyi, but his government was unable to keep order in the months of stress following defeat and despair. In the general confusion power was seized by the Communists. The notorious Bela Kun and his 'Lenin boys' terrorised Hungary, which experienced months of murder and chaos. The 'White' counter-revolution which followed was no more gentle in its methods. A Roumanian army marched on Budapest, nominally to suppress the Bolshevik menace, actually to secure Roumanian gains; its behaviour on Hungarian soil did not ease the inherent friction between Magyars and Roumanians. After a period of internecine strife and bloody reprisals, a conservative group under Admiral Horthy obtained command and suppressed its rivals.

(It was unfortunate that Bela Kun was a Jew. Generally, Hungarian treatment of the Jews had been reasonable. Bela Kun and his Jewish associates were made the pretext for a growing force of anti-Semitic feeling, culminating in Fascist measures. Had it not been so tragic, there would have been comedy in the reflection that many of the Hungarians who so bitterly reviled the Jews were themselves of Jewish origin! Imredy, the Hungarian Prime Minister who passed the first restrictive measures, subsequently resigned because he or his opponents discovered that he was a part-Jew.)

It was an exhausted Hungary which was compelled to sign the Treaty of Trianon without discussion. The terms certainly implemented the Tenth Point—from the point of view of the subject races. Slovakia and Ruthenia were to join hands with Bohemia and Moravia to form the new Czechoslovakia. Transylvania went to Roumania, and Croatia and other southern provinces to Yugoslavia. Even Austria—one of the defeated powers—was allotted a small slice of Hungary, in the province of Burgenland. Altogether Hungary lost three-quarters of her territory and one-half of her population.

For the first years after the war the position was unwillingly accepted. The troubles for Hungary were overwhelming. The disorders of successive 'Red' and 'White' terrors left the country weak, and the plunge of the currency impoverished the land. Trade was impossible, for the old provinces were now incorporated in new states whose first act was to erect insuperable tariff barriers. Further, while the agricultural plains remained to Hungary, a large proportion of other natural resources had been lost—a considerable part of the wealth in timber, iron and coal went to the new or enlarged states: an equally important loss was that of labour supply. Natural and economic resources are delicately balanced: some of the consequences could scarcely have been foreseen by the most calculating of the peace-makers. Many of the Hungarian rivers, for example, rise in the Slovak and Ruthene highlands. Lack of control there—or excessive felling of the mountain forests—impelled automatically disastrous spring floods on the Hungarian plains.

Economic distress combined with national pride to prompt the growing demand that the Treaty of Trianon must be drastically revised. It needed no propaganda in Hungary: as soon as men had recovered from the shock of internecine war, they rubbed their eyes as they beheld the disintegration of their ancient frontiers. The humblest peasant backed the propagandists of Budapest when they sought foreign recognition of Hungary's claims to justice. This is only natural: if we had lost the war and the British Empire had been taken from us, we too would have longed for its return. Our task is not to consider Hungary's sentimental aspirations, but the justice of her claims and their importance to the peace of the world.

It was, of course, quite legitimate for Hungary to embark upon a campaign of propaganda towards the revision of the treaties: indeed, her method was greatly to be preferred to those of other powers depending largely upon force. The campaign was cleverly conducted, but in my opinion its sponsors made one vital error. As any publicity expert will confirm, there comes a point when propaganda recoils upon itself. The Hungarian propaganda was overdone. Whereas ten years ago sympathy for Hungary was very pronounced in Great Britain—over two hundred members of Parliament signed a memorial favouring treaty revision—it is probable that this sympathy had begun to recede even before Hungary inclined to the Axis. The directors of propaganda failed to perceive the moment when the character of the publicity should have been changed.

The Hungarian claim did not lack for capable sponsors. One of the most influential was Lord Rothermere, who at one time was almost idolised in Hungary—there was even a popular suggestion that he might be invited to become its king! His powerful newspapers flung themselves into the Hungarian cause. Unfortunately for Hungary, his intervention revealed another of the principles of publicity: his newspapers naturally presented only one side of the case, and the British public is not so easily beguiled. Further, every extravagant presentation of the revisionist argument provoked equally extravagant opposition.

More powerful than official propaganda, maybe, was the influence of the Magyars themselves. It was a wise decision to persuade people to come to Hungary: tours were organised at low cost, and in one year the number of British visitors to Hungary increased from 400 to 3000. They were given a royal welcome, with official receptions. Nevertheless, the real influential propaganda came from the people—friendly, intelligent and hospitable, with a wavelength of thought akin to our own, with a high opinion of England which was very gratifying. There can be few visitors to Hungary who have not come away with amicable impressions.

No one could fail to be impressed, too, by the unanimity of the people on the subject of treaty revision. The Hungarian you met might be a Fascist or a Communist, but his outlook on frontiers was the same. Everywhere was seen the eternal slogan 'Nem, nem, soha!'—'No, no, never!' 'No, no, never will I consent to the degradation of my country.' The children were taught in school that they must work for the recovery of the lost provinces of Hungary—the most common feature of a schoolroom was a map showing Hungary before and after the war. The dismembered map was everywhere: in Budapest you found it even in a public square, worked out in flowers.

I remember once dining with a Hungarian family. The grace, when translated, startled me:

"I believe in one God, I believe in one Fatherland;
I believe in one divine hour coming.
I believe in the resurrection of Hungary. Amen."

Such a feeling was quite natural, and was particularly appreciated by British visitors, who always esteem loyalty. But because you like a people, it does not follow that they are right. The warmth of Hungarian hospitality impelled friendly ideas but warped detached judgment. Too many public men from England went to Hungary, were royally entertained, and seriously adopted the Hungarian viewpoint—without taking the trouble to stray over the frontier and appreciate that of Hungary's neighbours. This is fatal. Hungary definitely has a case for treaty revision, but the surrounding states equally definitely have a counter-claim. We have seen by now that there are two sides to every one of these danger problems of Europe: that is why they are dangerous.

Nor was America neglected. There had never been any cause for enmity between the two countries, and Hungarian propaganda astutely played on this and on isolationist themes. The romantic appeal of the Magyars had its effects. For every American who went to the Czechoslovak, Roumanian, or Yugoslav borderlands, a hundred went to Budapest.

Let us consider the Hungarian case. It is claimed that Hungary has had an undisturbed history of a thousand years. This is not quite true: there has been a Hungary for a thousand years, but it has had many vicissitudes, and for long periods has been a subject state. Further, historical argument is not always logical: even if the Hungarians had held their subject races under their sway for a thousand years, it does not follow that it is right to continue. Moral ideas have changed considerably in the last century, and the principle of self-determination is generally held by enlightened people.

The next argument is more forcible—that the pre-war Hungary was a geographic and economic unit, that its break-up has caused ruin to thousands, and that the simple trading system has become impossibly complicated. There is a strong basis of fact behind this argument. The Hungarian railway system naturally converged on Budapest. Not only were the outlying lines quite inadequate for the new states, but communications in Hungary proper were hopelessly confused by the new frontiers. There were Hungarian towns twenty or thirty miles apart; yet if a man wished to travel by rail, to avoid crossing foreign frontiers he must go to Budapest and come back on another line, a total distance of two or three hundred miles.

Details of the frontier demarcation have certainly led to incessant trouble. In some cases a town was in one country, its railway station in another. The waterworks of one Hungarian town were in Czechoslovakia. At one point there were mines on one side of the frontier, but the workers' cottages were on the other. There were innumerable instances where the frontier cut a farm in two, and theoretically the farmer had to carry his passport every time he went to milk his cows. These were petty things, but dangerous irritants, and those who have studied propaganda will know that they lost nothing in the telling as they were passed from lip to lip across the countryside.

Far more serious was the dislocation of trade. Instead of the economic unit of Austria-Hungary, we saw five independent states, all tariff-ridden. Hungary had agricultural products and Czechoslovakia had manufactures, but the two countries for years preferred to stare at each other rather than to exchange their surpluses. It is quite true that thousands of people have suffered privation and ruin because of the Treaty of Trianon. Yet this must have been foreseen, and an accept-

ance of the Fourteen Points automatically involved an acceptance of the inevitable dislocation of commerce. The real solution of this difficulty, however, does not lie in the re-creation
of the Austro-Hungarian Empire, but in the removal of the
artificial barriers to trade which abound on every hand.

We now approach the most serious of the Hungarian complaints—that the populations were transferred without a
plebiscite, against their will, and that they would willingly return to Hungarian rule today. Here at once it is necessary to
make a very definite distinction between subject races and
Magyars. It is quite certain that most of the exiled Magyars
would welcome reunion with Hungary. It is equally certain
that the ex-subject races would *not*. The Czechs had their
difficulties in Slovakia and Ruthenia—but no one could truth-
fully present the Slovaks or Ruthenes as pining for return to
Hungary!

It is not generally appreciated that the subject races of the
old Austro-Hungarian Empire had themselves decided on
autonomy long before the powers met at Paris to consider
terms of peace. The councils were necessarily improvised;
and, as they were convened by subject races, had no 'legal'
standing. But the fight for freedom can only be won by
rebels: the greatest patriots in the world's history were often
illegal.

At the very moment when Austria-Hungary was submit-
ting to the Allies, but while Germany was still at war, a
Slovak National Council had been convened in Bratislava; it
voted its independence, proceeded to take over the administration of the province, and joined with Bohemia to form the
new Czechoslovak Republic. A day later—October 29th,
1918—another National Council met at Zagreb: delegates
represented Croatia-Slavonia, Slovenia, Dalmatia, Bosnia,
Voyvodina *and Istria* (the Julian March). The delegates were
naturally hurriedly elected, and not all districts were represented because of the confusion of traffic, but it is merely futile
to argue that the union of these provinces with Yugoslavia

was not by the will of the people. At the same time the Roumanians of Transylvania had invited the Roumanian army to occupy their territory.

It is playing with the question to imagine for one moment that these people wish to return to Hungarian rule: for, unfortunately, their pre-1918 experience was not quite so happy as it ought to have been. I must confess that my own first impressions entirely favoured Hungary—until I passed beyond its borders. The Hungarian is a gentleman of the old school: you can't help liking him. Yet, even allowing for the exaggerations of propaganda, you cannot avoid feelings of concern when you travel the lands which once were Hungary.

We have seen that it was Hungary's policy to Magyarise her subject populations. For that matter the Hungarians today are of mixed ancestry, for in the seventeenth century their land was occupied by a medley of races, all of whom were successfully Magyarised, and whose descendants today would be highly indignant if told that they were not true Hungarians. (There are several aristocratic Hungarian families of Irish descent!) A mixed population lends itself to such settlement, but a compact national race is another matter. A handful of Slovaks scattered over Hungary would find it more convenient to speak Hungarian and to adopt Hungarian customs, but this did not apply to the Slovaks of Slovakia.

Long before the World War this policy of Magyarisation was pursued. There was nothing brutal about it—none of the petty atrocities which have disfigured some of the post-war states. A young man who wanted to get on had to adopt Hungarian conditions, for practically all higher education was given only in the Magyar tongue. Even in elementary schools education was often given only in Magyar; sometimes in a generation a district would apparently pass from Slovak to Magyar. Actually, of course, it had only altered its language. Today there are dozens of remarkably interesting cases where districts are changing back again: the younger generation speaks Slovak exclusively; the people over thirty speak

Magyar, and usually Slovak as well. In their youth they were classed as Magyars; today they call themselves Slovaks.

Much as I esteem the Hungarian, I cannot claim that he is a born ruler of subject races. The Czechs and Slovaks are own cousins, yet there is a vast difference between their intellect, education, energy and capacity: unhappily, as we have seen, much of the gulf can be traced to the fact that the Czechs spent the years of rapid modern development under Austria, the Slovaks under Hungary. Yet my most serious misgivings were aroused as I journeyed about Ruthenia. Here was a pitiful story—a peasant people deprived of almost all which comes under the general term 'civilisation.' Here is a race which was almost completely illiterate; which for dozens of generations lived and worked under conditions akin to feudal serfdom; which never strayed beyond poverty and often verged on starvation—I should class their standard of life as the lowest in peasant Europe. The Czechoslovak government worked hard in laying the foundations of a new Ruthenia, but would have been the first to admit that this is one of the most backward peoples in Europe. It is not that the Ruthenes are naturally unintelligent, for their brothers in Galicia and Ukraine are bright enough. Ruthene dullness can only be ascribed to centuries of neglect and repression, and the best friend of Hungary could not hold up Ruthenia as a monument to Magyar rule.

You must picture pre-1918 Hungary as a land of big estates, governed in semi-feudal style by their seigneurs. To a considerable extent this applies to Hungary today, although many thousands of peasants have now been settled in small-holdings. It is a common argument from the Anti-Revisionist Powers that whereas they have expropriated the great estates and have parcelled them out among the peasants, in Hungary the old system is still predominant. The potentialities of the argument should be accepted with reserve.

No one who has visited peasant Europe can be unaware of the peasant hunger for land. Just a few acres of land to call his own—such is the ambition of every peasant. Consequently the decisions of the Czechoslovak, Roumanian and Yugoslav governments were hailed with delight by their peoples; all the great estates were to be expropriated—no man might own more than 750 acres; compensation was to be paid, and the land was to be divided among the peasants who had worked it.

In Czechoslovakia the scheme worked very fairly. Naturally the landlords protested vehemently: had you and I been land-lords, we also would have protested. It was claimed that the compensation was inadequate, and in any case the loss was accentuated by the slump in the value of the crown. The re-division of the land, however, was scientifically arranged, and any mistakes were those due to undue hurry. It is very impor-tant to note that Magyar peasants as well as Slovaks received allocations of land. The grumbling came from the unlucky ones, for there was not enough land to go round—half a million peasants in Czechoslovakia were still landless.

In Roumania the grievances of the landlords were even more emphatic. Most of the great estates in Transylvania, taken from Hungary, were owned by Magyars or Germans. They were duly expropriated, and very inadequate compensa-tion paid. At the same time Roumanian currency did not merely slump in value—it collapsed. Consequently the sums received by the landlords were of trifling value. One of them remarked to me: 'If any man got the value of a pair of shoes from the "sale" of his estate, then he was lucky!' This is naturally exaggerated, but comparisons of figures in many corners of Roumania convinced me that the average payment to the landowners was about 5 per cent of the actual value of their land. I ought to make it quite clear that Roumanian land-owners were just as unlucky as Magyars or Germans.

Our traditional sympathy for the little man ought not to blind us to a realisation of the landlord's case. One of these—a Roumanian—put it to me simply and fairly: 'If Roumania became a Communist country, then I understand that this would be no place for me. I would throw up my hands and

hand over all my worldly goods without squealing. But Roumania is a capitalist country, supposed to be governed by the
laws and customs of a capitalist state. Why, then, should the
greater part of my land be stolen from me for distribution in
Communistic fashion?'

His last phrase was not quite correct. In fact, here is the
surprising feature of the business. While the Succession States
have been dividing up the large estate into peasant strips,
Soviet Russia has been abolishing peasant strips, combining
hundreds of them into large estates! The fact that they are
communally owned and worked does not alter the principle of
the change; it is simply an economic question—Is it better to
work land in tiny fragments or in large self-contained areas?
In these days of fierce competition the answer seems obvious.

Before I wandered extensively over the Balkans, my sympathies were entirely with the peasant proprietor. My sympathies
are still with the peasant, but I am not now convinced that he
was wise in becoming his own proprietor. I have lived with
peasants in most countries of South-Western Europe. Most of
them farmed their own tiny fields, but some still worked on
the 'rump' estates of 750 acres still in the hands of the feudal
landlords. I would not like to claim that the 'free' peasants
were happier than those who worked for a master, and their
standard of living was certainly lower.

I must not be misunderstood as advocating feudalism. There
may be something in Pope's dictum that the best forms of
government are those which are best administered. Feudalism
survived in Spain, with appalling results. There most of the
great landlords looked upon their estates as sources of wealth.
They seldom visited them, but left them in charge of an agent,
whose job was to get as much out of the estate as he possibly
could. Not in all cases did the agent consider the welfare of
the peasants, and revolution was inevitable. But in South-
Eastern Europe the fashion is for landowners to live on their
estates: there are exceptions of the worst Spanish type, of
course, but Magyars are country folk, and are content with

only an occasional visit to town. Thus, although a landlord may employ five hundred peasants, there is a personal relation between them. Many of them belong to families which have worked on the estate for generations. They are not tied to the estate in any way; the 'feudalism' consists of a peculiar interest in the estate, and assumption from birth that they will work for the same family, and some form of communal estate life. It is quite common, for example, for the landlord to be responsible for the feeding of his peasants.

It is a remarkable sight, a flash-back to mediaeval days, to see a concourse of workers being fed communally. I recall the amazement of a Magyar magnate when he found me eating with his peasants. I passed to neighbouring villages, where peasants owned their own fields, and found sparser and more spartan fare—a lower standard of life even than in Balkan villages.

One peasant explained the two systems to me: 'I was happy when I worked for a master, for he was my friend. I am very happy now, for I am my own master, owning my own ground. It makes me feel proud, to walk across my own field, and know that it is mine, and will be my son's after me. My family is able to live, though my fields are not large, and we are proud when we eat our own corn. But I know that there are disadvantages. If bad times come, if I am unable to sell my grain, then I shall be ruined. My old master, if there was no market for the grain, would store it until the market was open again. But I cannot wait—we live on the edge of poverty, and have no reserves. If I do not sell my crop at once, then I cannot pay my debts, and the moneylender will seize my land. Or if I am sick, and cannot till my lands? In the old days my master would look after me until I was well. Today I would be dependent upon charity —and in our poor country not much charity is possible. Nor do I want charity—I am proud because I own my fields.'

It is inadvisable to make sweeping statements about landlords and peasants. Everything depends on their quality. I have met in Hungary landlords who were the protectors of their people: there are others who are only concerned with financial yields, and will turn an estate over to grazing if the price of corn is poor, thereby throwing dozens of men out of work.

Peasant agricultural methods are necessarily primitive. A man owning ten acres of land cannot afford modern machinery; most of the labour is performed by hand, not machines. True, not all the great landlords have proved themselves receptive to new ideas! Yet there is something in the idea of paternal feudalism which is not unattractive. I remember arguing with a Hungarian magnate who still owned a large estate, and looked after it himself. In his broad fields a dozen men were ploughing, each plough pulled by a pair of steady, sturdy oxen.

'But why not a tractor?' I asked. 'These flat fields were made for tractors. One man with a tractor could do the work of a dozen with oxen.'

'I quite agree,' he replied. 'And I could afford a tractor. But in Hungary we are very old-fashioned. In England you prefer to use a machine which one man can drive, and to throw the other eleven out of work. In Hungary we do not use many machines, but there is work for all.'

The fact that his remark would have been eagerly accepted by the Luddites, and that it evokes vague sympathetic response today, is no more than an indication of the vastness of the economic problems of the modern world.

In Czechoslovakia the problems of the peasant proprietor were tackled energetically. Agrarian banks relieved the peasant of his most forbidding menace—the shadow of the moneylender. For it is not enough to break up a big estate and divide the land among the peasants—they must be financed for some years until they have found their feet. Even then, as my friend said, they have no reserves. In Roumania the position is not so happy. Poverty, inefficiency and corruption have restricted government action, and many of the peasant proprietors are hopelessly in debt, their lands heavily mortgaged. In Yugoslavia the prospect is a little brighter, but both in Roumania and Yugoslavia governments have had a habit of passing most beneficent legislation which was never put into effect.

It can be taken as certain that agrarian reform will be a very live issue in Hungary immediately after the war. World economic disturbances occasioned deep distress in Hungary, as in other lands. There, however, it was possible to divert the misery of a proud people by blaming everything on the Treaty of Trianon. This halcyon period of the propagandist has passed. Peasant discontent can no longer be repressed. Whether the readjustment of Hungarian agriculture takes the form of the establishment of communal farms or peasant plots is a matter for discussion: economically the large farm unit is an advantage, but economics cannot compete with the pride of ownership. The point is that the present system, with its strong legacies of feudal privilege, is doomed. Today, 36 Magyar magnates own a million acres of land. The 1,200,000 peasants who are settled on their own farms own a total of 950,000 acres. 36 men own more more than 1,200,000! You do not need to be a Socialist to admit the injustice of this. Further, the large landowner paid only 10 pengoes in tax per acre; the peasant paid 16 pengoes. Wages on the large estates had become depressed to the lowest possible limits. This cannot be blamed for all time on the Treaty of Trianon, or on the peace treaty which will follow the present war.

II

Before outlining the events which led to Hungary's adherence to the Axis, the violent revision of her frontiers and her subsequent active participation in the war, it would be as well to consider the frontier problems of Hungary as they existed prior to Munich in 1938. We can take it as an axiom that anything which happened then and subsequently will be quashed by the terms of the new peace, and that any reconsideration of Hungary's case will begin from the frontiers allocated to her at Trianon. It can also be asserted as axiomatic that Hungarian dreams of empire or sentimental aspiration for the recovery of her lost provinces will be decisively ended.

The real kernel of the Hungarian problem is the very practical question of the 3 million Hungarians living outside the frontiers of Hungary. The actual number of exiled Hungarians was in dispute. The records of Czechoslovakia, Roumania and Yugoslavia gave a total a little under 2 ½ millions, but Hungary claimed that there were 3 ½ millions. The explanation may lie in the process of de-Magyarisation to which I have referred. In any case, we are concerned with the principle rather than the details, so can take 3 millions as the basis of our argument. Of these, about a half lived near the 1938 frontiers, to some extent in compact masses, while over half a million formed a Magyar 'island' in the middle of Roumanian Transylvania. It is essential to consider the problem of the two groups separately.

The first one appears simple enough. Round about the frontiers of Hungary (*i.e.* the pre-Munich frontiers—this is understood in all references in this and the following section) was a fringe of territory, varying in depth and housing a population of hundreds of thousands of Hungarians. At first sight it seemed quite obvious that the frontiers of Hungary should be extended so as to include all compact masses of Magyars contiguous to the present borders. While agreeing that the peace conference at Paris, through its experts, had no venomous designs on Hungary, it is obvious that many decisions must have been influenced by the victor-vanquished motive. The Succession States vigorously claimed more than they expected to get: Hungary was too weak and broken to protest. In the event of dispute, what more natural than that victors should favour their own side? In their determination to leave no subject races under Hungary, did they not plunder too freely? There were cases of towns housing 10,000 Magyars and 1000 Roumanians being awarded to Roumania.

Quite definitely Hungary had a grievance here. Those of us who can recall the confusion and extravagant hatred of those days—when respectable statesmen were clamouring to hang the Kaiser—will agree that justice in such an atmosphere was difficult if not impossible. It is offering no undue criticism of the men who mapped the new states to suggest that atmosphere and stress combined to rob Hungary of the ethnic frontier which the Fourteen Points had suggested. The proof of the pudding is proverbially in the digestion, and it is a fact that if the frontiers of Hungary had been pushed outwards by ten

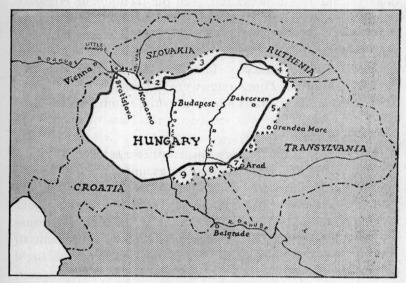

HUNGARIAN FRONTIER REVISION

or twenty miles, some hundreds of thousands of Hungarians would again be included in Hungary.

(Let us insist again at this point that a perfect ethnic frontier between Hungary and her neighbours is quite impossible. Any line drawn must leave hundreds of thousands of Hungarians outside Hungary, and include thousands of other nationalities within Hungary. Even today 10 per cent of the population of the present Hungary is non-Magyar.)

The Hungarians complain that no plebiscites were held—

although, so far as I can see, none were promised. They point to the examples in Schleswig-Holstein and Silesia. The first is not a true type, for it was far removed from the scene of strife, and a plebiscite in an atmosphere of comparative calm was possible and achieved. In Silesia it was not, and the result was not especially satisfactory, as we have seen. Nevertheless, it might have been more satisfactory to have held plebiscites in the disputed areas along the Hungarian frontiers; had this been done and the results honoured, then the frontiers of Hungary would have been wider than they were. Indeed, it would be possible to give a reasonable idea of how the line would have run. For—and this is rather important—it was quite well known when the Treaty of Trianon was drawn up, that two or three millions of Hungarians were left outside of Hungary, many of them in districts adjacent to the frontier. That is to say, the frontier line was settled on the basis of other than ethnic considerations.

For this reason, and because this frontier can serve as typical of others in Europe, I propose to examine the Hungarian boundaries in more detail than hitherto. We will go round the frontier district by district, to see where the Hungarian blocks of population existed and what would be the effect of transferring their territory to Hungary. (It is perhaps advisable to recall that this examination refers to the conditions of 1938, before the first partition of Czechoslovakia.)

We need not halt at the Burgenland, the small strip of Hungary ceded to Austria—numbered 1 in my sketch map. The population is overwhelmingly German, and it is quite certain that the question of its return will never be raised by Hungary.

In Czechoslovakia, however, we strike one of the thorniest points of our problem. There were something like 800,000 Magyars in Czechoslovakia, of whom nearly seven-eighths were found in Slovakia. About half of these lived in districts contiguous to the Hungarian frontier, the remainder being scattered further 'inland.'

The southern frontier of Slovakia was determined quite

frankly by geographical rather than ethnic considerations.
The Danube suggested a 'natural' frontier, and the line continued eastwards on a basis of easy communications—for
Slovakia. Beginning from the west, we find a district about
Bratislava predominantly Slovak. It is true that Bratislava—
the old Pozsony—has played a great part in Hungarian history.
It was at one time the capital of the country, when the Turks
were in Budapest, and more than one king of Hungary was
crowned in its cathedral. It was here that Maria Theresa called
the ranks of Hungary to her aid: the Magyars rallied loyally,
but the idea of a woman ruler was obnoxious to them. Consequently, Maria Theresa was proclaimed *king* of Hungary at
Pozsony—you may still see her signature there, *Maria Rex*.
Thus the sentimental affection of the Hungarians for the city
can be well understood. Nevertheless, even the Hungarians
admit that Bratislava and its district has no Magyar majority—
there are plenty of Magyars there, but they are hopelessly outnumbered by Slovaks. In this district you will find plenty of
examples of the process I quoted—of Magyarised Slovaks who
have now become Slovaks again.

A little to the east of Bratislava, however, lies a region which
is more than predominantly Magyar—it is almost entirely
Magyar. It is interesting to note that part of this district (numbered 2 on the sketch map) was left in Hungary in the original
draft of the peace treaty. Then it was argued that it was a
purely agricultural district, dependent upon Bratislava for its
prosperity, and was thus allocated to Czechoslovakia. At this
point, I think, the detached British reader has his first misgivings.

Even if the district were originally dependent economically
on Bratislava, it is not so certain that Bratislava depended upon
the district. Is there any reason why its economic structure
should not have been rebuilt around another town—Komarno,
for example? Komarno is a purely Magyar town—also of
sentimental interest to Hungary, for it was the birthplace of
Maurus Jokai. It was awarded, with its hinterland, to Slovakia

because there the Vah enters the Danube—the Vah being the principal river of Slovakia. Certainly the importance of Komarno to its Slovakian background must not be underestimated: the river port has been developed, and now carries a considerable traffic.

Economics are *very* important, argued the statesmen at Paris, and can override ethnic claims. Yet at least they are scarcely consistent, for Poland's claims to Danzig are considerably stronger than the Slovak claims to Komarno. In district 2 the ruling was given in favour of economics. If the Hungarian frontier had been pushed to the north an average of twenty miles, some 300,000 Magyars would have been restored to Hungary, carrying with them only about 20,000 Slovaks. Yet if this had been done, Slovakian trade would have received a serious blow, for access to the Danube would have been confined to ten or fifteen miles about Bratislava. I leave the reader to decide the just action, warning him that this is the simplest cast around the Hungarian frontiers.

After a short interval where the Slovaks definitely occupy territory right up to the original frontier, we approach another area housing a large Magyar population—district 3. Here, except in certain districts, the proportion of Slovaks is somewhat higher. Nevertheless, the real problem here is again one of communications. Except for the extreme south, Slovakia is almost entirely mountainous. Consequently some of its principal lines of communication lie along the southern plain, from west to east. Thus if the frontier were pushed north even an average of twenty miles, the principal railways and roads would be cut, and the mountainous country further north would make it extremely difficult to replace them. The reader must decide whether this is an adequate reason for detaching Magyars from their homeland, but he will at least agree that it was understandable that the Slovaks should try to hold on to the territory allocated to them. A rectification of the frontier on purely ethnic lines would restore some 120,000 Magyars to their homeland, but there was justice in the Slovak claim that in doing so the economic communications of Southern Slovakia would be paralysed.

District 4 presents the same problem. We are now in Ruthenia, a primitive country we have already met. The predominant race in this province is Ruthenian, a Ukrainian tribe. They are a simple mountain folk, shepherds and foresters. Their valleys run from north to south, and in many cases the sole communication between valleys is via the narrow plain, the valley of the Tisa. This valley is predominantly inhabited by Magyars. Again a move north of the frontier is quite possible on ethnic grounds, another 80,000 Magyars rejoining Hungary. The objections are (a) the economic life of Ruthenia would be completely paralysed—a people already living in deadly poverty would find life even more difficult, with their market towns and only railways in foreign lands. (There are nearly 600,000 Ruthenes, and their economic welfare must not be overlooked in argument. If I own the only road to a station, am I justified in closing it, and preventing seven other people from reaching it with their trade?); (b) the second reason is perhaps more forcible. Ruthenia was allocated to Czechoslovakia on grounds of strategy as well as of kinship. It was realised in Paris that the newly created or enlarged states would have to face their problems together, and it was decided that there must be direct communication between Czechoslovakia and Roumania.

Summing up, then, a frontier move of an average of twenty miles to the north would have brought something like 500,000 Magyars back into Hungary, while 'sacrificing' only some 50,-000 Slovaks. (There are also German and Jewish minorities, but these are negligible proportionately to the problem.) The remaining 300,000[1] Magyars are hopelessly scattered in enclosures surrounded by Slovaks, or in districts where Slovaks are predominant.

[1] These figures, of course, are approximate. It might prove that only 400,000 Magyars could rejoin Hungary, while 400,000 still remained in Czechoslovakia. Details could only be ascertained by district plebiscites: enough is known to indicate the broad outlines of the probable outcome.

Here, then, was a pretty problem, a quarrel between ethnic and economic considerations. Justice to Hungary meant serious hardship to Czechoslovakia. If conditions were perfect, and customs barriers did not exist, then many of the arguments would lose their force. But if conditions were perfect, then it would not matter very much whether a Magyar lived in Hungary or Czechoslovakia. Yet we have to consider realities, not dreams. The Hungarians clamoured for treaty revision, the Czechoslovaks refused it. Here was a question vastly more complicated than any Alsace-Lorraine.

III

It is argued that, since revision could not in any case solve the whole of the Magyar problem, it was unacceptable as a method. With the best will in the world, and sacrificing all economic, defensive and strategic considerations, only about one-half of the exiled Hungarians in Czechoslovakia could be restored to their homeland. The redisposition of the frontier of district 2 only—the communications of Slovakia and Ruthenia being considered paramount in the other cases—would certainly have appeased the local population, but—so it was argued—would inevitably have provoked implacable irritation among the other Magyar minorities. And would Hungary have been satisfied? Having achieved a partial success, she would have clamoured for more—would never rest until all her co-nationals were reunited. These arguments were potent, and, until the rape of Czechoslovakia, prevented even minor revisions of the frontier—for, by manipulation, at least 100,000 Magyars could have rejoined Hungary *without* cutting the natural lines of communication of Czechoslovakia. It is claimed that this would never have satisfied Hungary.

For myself, I should have been tempted to try. It would at least have 'shown willing,' and Czechoslovakia would have gained the respect of the world. Just as important, if Hungary did not respond to such a gesture, she would have alienated world sympathy.

Recognising the real and serious difficulties of revision in districts 3 and 4, I would like to have seen the Czechs make a tentative offer of part of district 2. Near Bratislava an arm of the Danube branches off, and pursues a course ten or twelve miles to the north, eventually rejoining the parent river via the Vah at Komarno. This island between the Danube and the Little Danube is almost entirely populated by Magyars. It was originally allocated to Hungary by the peace conference, and it was the only revision along the Czechoslovak frontier which could be effected without serious economic effects.

From every other point of view except that of reunion with their own countrymen, Hungarian grievances in Czechoslovakia were grossly exaggerated. Magyars in Czechoslovakia were persuaded by propaganda that their state was much worse than it was. Actually, except for racial bias, there was no reason in the world why a Magyar should not live happily in Czechoslovakia. It was a well-governed, democratic land, and if I could not live in Britain or Scandinavia, I would have chosen Czechoslovakia as my home from all the other European countries. I cannot expect the Magyar to take so detached an outlook; he cannot forget that twenty years ago he was ruling Slovakia, regarding the Slovaks as a somewhat inferior race. I have the greatest tolerance for India, for example; I can live quite happily beside Indians: but if the Indians turned on us, beat us, annexed my land and ruled me, then I might not be so happy.

One feature must be insistently recorded—that in Czechoslovakia there was no nauseating record of the petty persecution of Magyar minorities which has disfigured other countries. True, it is probable that Hungary regarded Czechoslovakia as Enemy Number One among the Succession States. This outlook was perhaps impelled by jealousy at Czechoslovakia's progress, or realisation that with every bound of prosperity the prospect of revision became more remote. I have wandered often and extensively among the Magyar population of Czechoslovakia. There were complaints, but of the petty and inevitable kind. I did indeed wonder in 1937 whether the problem was about to solve itself. Ten years earlier the Magyars had formed one political party, and had voted as such. In 1937 they had split up, and were to be found in the ranks of local Conservative, Liberal, Labour and Communist parties. In Kosice—Kassa, a town of Magyar traditions —I heard a Magyar nationalist orator vigorously heckled by Magyar Communists. These men were emphatically against any revision in favour of ultra-Conservative Hungary. I do not pretend that they are large in numbers or influence, but ten years ago they could scarcely have existed. In another ten years the outlook on the whole question might have changed, particularly if Europe could have been guided into economic paths of sanity—and if there had been no Nazi Germany next door. A year later the first stage of Hungarian frontier revision was accomplished—at a bitter cost.

IV

It is ironical that, having advocated for many years the revision of peace treaties, I was very unhappy when revision came—by force. Had the Sudetens been transferred to Germany years ago, as a move towards the appeasement of Europe, I would have welcomed the move. Had the Hungarian frontiers been rectified, I would have been glad. But it was difficult to believe that a revision by force was likely to make any real contribution to European peace. That of October 1938 certainly did not.

It was natural that Hungary should advance her claim at the time of the Czechoslovak crisis—and, as we have seen, Hungary's claims to slices of Czechoslovak territory were ten times stronger than those of Germany. Unlike Germany, however, Hungary was unable to back her demands by sufficient force. The real character of the problem was then revealed— the old game of power politics was resumed. Unable to reach a settlement with Czechoslovakia, the Hungarian claim to

Ruthenia was referred to Hitler and Mussolini. The only people not consulted, in fact, were the Ruthenes themselves!

The 'compromise' worked out was disastrous to Czechoslovakia. The 1910 census was used as a basis, and if it was misleading in the old Austria it was fantastic in Hungary. We have observed the process of Magyarisation in the pre-war decades; we have seen that anybody who wished to get on had to speak Magyar, and was classed as Hungarian, and that Hungarian officials and troops helped to swell the Magyar total. Consequently towns which today have only 20 per cent of Hungarian population were torn from Czechoslovakia. With them went a countryside with an almost 100 per cent Slovak or Ruthene population.

The difficulties of communication were entirely ignored— the frontier was pushed to the very fringe of the mountains. Roads and railways were cut in haphazard fashion. Indeed, the railway system of the dismembered Czechoslovakia was a nightmare, for main lines were cut by foreign territory in a dozen places—it was almost impossible to travel for a hundred miles in any direction without crossing German, Hungarian or Polish territory.

The first solution of the Ruthene problem was a masterpiece of inanity. Here the wills of Hitler and Mussolini clashed. Hitler wished Ruthenia to remain part of Czechoslovakia, so that it could still serve as a corridor to Roumania. Mussolini wished to see a common frontier between Poland and Hungary—a barrier, if a friendly barrier, against German expansion to the south-east. Neither, of course, considered the unfortunate inhabitants; Ruthenia afforded an example of power politics at their best—or worst.

Morally the claim of the Ruthenes to remain within Czechoslovakia could not be disputed. Economically it was possible to state a case for the return of the province to Hungary. In the result, Ruthenia was carved in two, and its political and economic situations were alike impossible. The valley of the Tisa, with the plain as far as Uzhorod, the capital, went to

Hungary. Ruthenia became a detached rump of mountain land.[1]

Strategically the victory went to Mussolini. The only communications from rump Czechoslovakia to Roumania lay along the valley of the Tisa—now in Hungarian hands. Yet the settlement satisfied nobody. Czechs and Slovaks were disgusted in that large Slovak and Ruthene areas have been handed over to Hungary against the wishes of their inhabitants. The Hungarians were disappointed because they have not obtained the whole of Ruthenia. The Germans saw that their much-desired corridor to Roumania was cut. The Poles were angry because there was still an autonomous Ruthenia within Czechoslovakia—an absurd example which encouraged autonomist demands within the Polish Ukraine! The feelings of the Ruthenes themselves may be imagined—the configuration of their valleys was such that they were never prosperous, and now they must face the sheerest poverty; they had been treated with less consideration than a herd of cattle. Alas for the second of President Wilson's principles, twenty years after!

This episode supplied an excellent example of how treaty revision should *not* be carried out. The effect of the aftermath of the Czech crisis was that minority problems remained—but the minorities were placed on the other side of the frontier. There were now 800,000 Czechs in Germany and Poland, and over 600,000 Slovaks and Ruthenes in Hungary. It is significant that for years I have received literature from Hungarian revisionist sources: in November 1938 I received a bulky parcel of maps, facts, figures and comments from Moravia— the *Czechoslovak* campaign for treaty revision had begun!

It was quite certain that the 1938 solution was not final: it lasted less than six months. While German troops invaded Bohemia, Moravia and Slovakia, Hungary moved again. This time Germany could scarcely say nay; she wanted Hungary as

[1] For a map showing the successive stages of Hungarian frontier revision, see page 267.

an ally, so could not grumble at imitative action. So Hungarian troops marched into the rump Ruthenia.

It was an unfortunate moment for Ruthenia. The tiny, uneconomic autonomous state had not yet found its feet. Immediately before the days of crisis there had been grave governmental difficulties—we have seen that foreign influence was not lacking. Suspecting treachery, the Czechs arrested Ruthene leaders and disarmed Ruthene troops. A few days later the Hungarian army crossed the frontier.

According to the Hungarian press, it received a warm welcome. Certainly it did—from two sources: naturally, from the scattered Magyar population, and also from renegade Ruthenes on the lookout for positions under the new authority. Otherwise serious resistance was offered—by irregular bands of ill-armed patriots; and, it is interesting to note, by Ukrainian nationalists from Poland. The end was inevitable, however, and Ruthenia was overrun. Months later there was still guerrilla fighting among the northern mountains. And although Ruthenia was promised autonomy by the Hungarians, there is still no sign of the form this will take, if any.

So Hungary rules Ruthenia again. It is not every country which has a second chance, after a thousand years of neglect.

v

In another section we have considered the problem of the Magyar 'island' in Transylvania: in addition to the isolated settlements, there is a fringe of Magyar population on the Roumanian side of the 1919 frontier. The features of this problem are akin to those of the Magyars in Czechoslovakia.

The Roumanians in 1918 first claimed the frontier line of the Tisa, considerably west of the present line. This would have been the grossest injustice, and the Roumanian demand was refused. The final frontier represented the inevitable compromise. Once again economic considerations prevailed over ethnic claims, however, and some 400,000 Magyars were to be found immediately contiguous to the Hungarian frontier.

In the north and centre, for example, were the towns of Satu Mare and Oradea Mare (these are their Roumanian names). They are both important railway junctions, considered vital to the communications of Roumania.

The 'ribbon' of Magyars was not continuous. From the north it ran as far as Oradea Mare, to a depth of twenty to thirty miles. In this district (No. 5) lived some 250,000 Magyars, 30,000 Germans and 120,000 Roumanians.

The considerable ethnic majority of the Magyars cannot be doubted, however misleading rival statistics may prove. The problem presented to the peacemakers was a modified version of that of Slovakia—that important north-to-south communications ran through the disputed areas, which were therefore awarded to Roumania. Speaking generally, the Magyars end where the hills begin. Roumania was awarded a stretch of plain for her communications, and a strategic strip to safeguard them. Passing the validity of this argument, nevertheless, it is not so strong as in the case of Slovakia. There the communications are the only ones possible, so forbidding are the mountains to the north. In Roumania it would be expensive, but quite possible, to run new railways east of a revised frontier.

It was argued, too, that revision would sever districts from their natural market towns. This is quite true, but the principle had little influence on the actual demarcation of the frontier from the Hungarian point of view. There were plenty of examples of Hungarian towns cut off from their natural countryside. Incidentally, it is surprising how quickly districts and towns can sometimes recover from economic earthquakes of separation, and how rapidly new relations are made.

District 6 was a small one, and quite unimportant except that it cut a railway line. It housed 30,000 Magyars and 10,000 Roumanians.

District 7, about Arad, would form an unwieldy salient into Roumanian territory if it were added to Hungary, but Europe knows many geographical shapes far more grotesque. The population consisted of about 80,000 Magyars and 20,000 Roumanians. In all cases there are small minorities of Germans and Jews as well.

Thus a revision of the Hungarian-Roumanian frontiers of 1919 could have restored about 350,000 Magyars to Hungary at the expense of 150,000 Roumanians. The Roumanian case was: (a) the ethnic frontier would cut communications vital to our prosperity, and we have no money to build new ones; (b) why should we hand over 150,000 of our own people to the rule of the Magyars? We saw quite enough of their methods before the war.

The quarrel between Hungary and Roumania was a bitter one. That between Hungary and Czechoslovakia was like strife between two intellectuals, with sarcastic wit predominating. Hungary and Roumania were more primitive in the fashion of their quarrel, and the reason is to be found in history. There has always been a tendency in the Balkans to confuse patriotism with hatred of the other country.

The 'solution' of Roumanian-Hungarian difficulties at Vienna in August 1940 gave the northern half of Transylvania to Hungary. It satisfied neither side. It merely made a re-hash of the ethnic muddle, handing over more Roumanians than Magyars to Hungarian rule; and it completely ignored the other factor in the situation, for the north-south railway was cut completely in two! This specimen of treaty revision is scarcely likely to survive. I have suggested that Roumania and Hungary will be fighting between themselves the moment the war is over—unless we are very prompt in our police procedure.

VI

Just outside the south-eastern corner of Hungary lies one of the most remarkable provinces in Europe—the Banat. The name means 'frontier province,' and it is. All other ethnic complications pale beside the social tangle of the Banat. I recall one incredible morning when I rode through a succession of

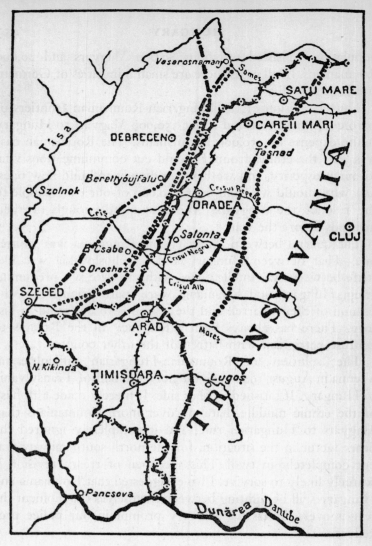

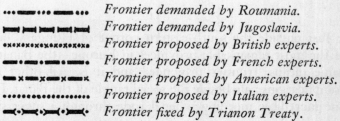

••• ▬ •••   *Frontier demanded by Roumania.*
▬▬▬▬▬   *Frontier demanded by Jugoslavia.*
⊗×⊗×⊗×⊗×⊗×   *Frontier proposed by British experts.*
▬ • ▬ • ▬ •   *Frontier proposed by French experts.*
▬×▬×▬×▬×   *Frontier proposed by American experts.*
•••••••••••••   *Frontier proposed by Italian experts.*
▬‹•›▬‹•›▬‹•›   *Frontier fixed by Trianon Treaty.*

The difficulties of the Roumanian-Hungarian frontiers are illustrated by this map, which shows the demands and suggestions considered by the Peace Conference in 1919.

seven villages; they were inhabited by Magyars, Germans, Czechs, Serbs, Roumanians, Slovaks—and French! The Tower of Babel was a comparative holiday.

The Banat was settled by the Magyars in the tenth century, but most of them were driven off by Tartar raiders. Four hundred years later, after the Turkish conquest of Serbia, Serbian refugees appeared, but in 1552 the Banat was itself captured by the Turks. Not until 1718 did it recover its freedom, to be attached to the Austrian crown. The desolation of the Turkish régime was appalling. From being one of the most fertile provinces in Europe, it was now almost a desert. Most of its inhabitants had been murdered, starved or driven into exile.

Maria Theresa, who was responsible for many remarkable schemes of colonisation in the Balkans, took in hand the reclamation of the province. From all corners of the Austrian Empire settlers were invited, with special privileges; they came also from Bavaria, the Rhine provinces and Alsace. Added to the surviving remnants of the original populations, they made up an ethnic medley of a complexity unknown even in the Balkans. The seven nationalities I have mentioned by no means exhaust the races of the Banat; there are sprinklings of Croats, Slovenes, Italians, Spaniards, Gypsies and others, and plenty of Jews.

Even this is not the end, for the nationalities themselves are divisible. In the eighteenth century the German kingdoms were not united, and a Bavarian differed considerably from a Prussian. (He does today, but will not do so within a few more generations of National Socialism.) The Germans of the Banat have preserved the characteristics of their ancient kingdoms, and it is not difficult for an ethnic student to distinguish, by their dialect, customs and culture, Bavarians, Saxons, Westphalians and Alsatians. There are French-speaking Alsatians as well, and I have scarcely recovered from my surprise at being hailed in fluent if archaic French as I rode a bicycle through this racial curiosity. Even the Serbian minority has a sub-minority, for some districts are inhabited by Bunyevaks, who are Catholic Serbs.

After the war both Roumania and Yugoslavia claimed the Banat—half the nations of Europe *could* have claimed it. Indeed, there was very nearly serious trouble over its allocation, for it is now a fertile province again, one of the most

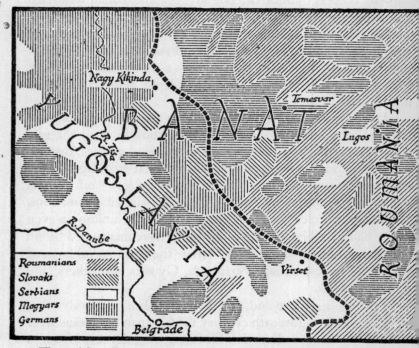

The racial medley in the Banat. The shadings merely show racial *majorities* in each area—every district contains important minorities of several other races.

prosperous corners of the Balkans. The standard of life of its people is certainly the highest in Roumania. Its grain, wine and tobacco are famous; it is lavishly supplied with timber, and its hills shelter deposits of coal and metals. By the peace treaties eventually two-thirds of the Banat went to Roumania, one-third to Yugoslavia.

Now the outstanding feature of Maria Theresa's settlers—
we have met them in Transylvania—has been their remarkable loyalty to the régime of the day. They were workers, and
were not politically-minded. If they were handed over to
another rule, they made no demands for treaty revision—they
went on working, and prospered while their neighbours
starved. The last change of government hit them hardest of all,
for they had gravitated to the market of Budapest, and all
their extensive trade was in the Hungarian direction. After
1918 most of their trade passed artificially into Transylvania,
and there have been many difficulties and not a little hardship.
Nevertheless the peasants of the Banat kept on working, and
even if not so prosperous as in pre-1914 days, at least they
were better off than their neighbours.

I can imagine the lifted eyebrows of the statesmen at Paris
who had to allocate the Banat. Here was a Hungarian province, claimed by Roumania and Yugoslavia. Yet its population
figures for its northern section ran:

Germans (assorted)	220,000	Roumanians	130,000
Hungarians	140,000	Serbs	130,000

together with oddments of the other races I have mentioned
(some of them by this time partially or wholly Magyarised).

Nor do these peoples live in self-contained districts, but are
hopelessly scattered. It is quite a common thing to find four
races *and four religions* in a single village. It is interesting to
note by the way, the populations of the Banat have always
lived at peace with one another. It appears to be easy for small
numbers of people to live in peace, but masses make for war.

Actually, purely political considerations led to the division
of the Banat, but any other decision would have been equally
right or wrong.

It has been argued that a plebiscite would reveal a majority
for Hungary—that the Germans would opt for Hungary in
a body. Loyal as they then were to Roumania and Yugoslavia,
I did on my first visit remark a general feeling among the

Germans that their trade would be bettered if they could return to the rule of Budapest, and that given a perfectly free choice they would vote in its favour. But it is only fair to say that I found no popular demand among the Germans as there was, of course, among the Magyars.

On the rise of Hitler, the situation changed. The Germans of the Banat were 'organised' from Berlin. They were ordered to buy up land wherever they could; they became very assertive, and local Roumanians complained that they were boycotted—in their own country.

The position in 1939 was, therefore, that the Banat was divided between Roumania and Yugoslavia, and that its population was still a hopeless medley of races—though the proportion of Roumanians and Yugoslavs in their own areas had naturally increased. The Roumanians retained their share of the Banat after the Vienna award, but must be very anxious when they view events over the Yugoslav border.

After the defeat of Yugoslavia, the country was divided into a series of puppet 'kingdoms' and subject provinces. The Yugoslav portion of the Banat was kept firmly under German rule—it is significant that while German settlers have been withdrawn from other corners of Europe, the opposite policy has been pursued here.

At one period there was a suggestion that a portion of Transylvania was to be carved out to form a new German state, all the settlers in adjoining districts being gathered within its borders. There are now ominous signs that the Banat is to have the honour of becoming the new German province, presumably because (a) it is potentially rich, (b) the proportion of Germans is already high, due to the mixed settlements following the retirement of the Turks. The figures for the whole province in 1919 were:

Germans	330,000	Roumanians	270,000
Hungarians	230,000	Serbs	270,000

Today the proportion of Roumanians and Serbs is higher.

It is quite possible that the Germans intend to found a new state here. Apart from its economic wealth, the strategic position of the Banat is important: with strong German garrisons it could dominate the Balkans: the Banat would become, in effect, a Balkan East Prussia.

Thus Roumania watches anxiously, awaiting the summons to surrender her share of the Banat—perhaps in return for 'compensation' in the form of territory seized from Russia. The Hungarians await events moodily, knowing that if the Banat becomes German, its chances of returning to Hungary are appreciably lessened—and Hungary itself becomes a German corridor. The local peasant farmers are apprehensive, for they would lose their land. The only people happy are the local Germans—and not all of them. Nevertheless Hitler is not likely to consider their feelings, or those of the other Balkan Germans who must be brought in to populate the new state. It is reported that he has already chosen its name: Donaustaat —Danube State.

VII

One further zone adjoining the 1938 Hungarian frontiers demands consideration. Just to the west of the Banat is a district called the Backa—numbered 9. It will be seen as a Magyar triangle pushing into Northern Yugoslavia. The district was awarded to Yugoslavia because on its northern edge lies the town and neighbourhood of Subotica, which is predominantly Yugoslav. In this area there are about 100,000 Yugoslavs, whereas the Backa houses some 300,000 Magyars— together, of course, with German and other minorities. A further consideration was strategic—with Hungarians occupying the Backa, it was argued, the position of Belgrade was indefensible. Here no serious economic difficulty is involved— it is simply the question that if the Backa were handed to Hungary, 100,000 Yugoslavs would go with it.

Just before the German attack on Yugoslavia in April 1941, Hungary had signed a pact of 'eternal friendship' with her.

Immediately she was called upon to allow her territory to be used as the base for the onslaught on her neighbour—though Count Paul Teleki, the Hungarian Prime Minister, recognising the disgrace to the honour of his country, committed suicide. With Yugoslavia overpowered, Hungarian nationalism could not be restrained by mere pacts of eternal friendship. With German backing, Hungarian troops seized the whole of the Backa, together with the smaller district of Boranja, immediately to the west. Later, Hitler permitted the Hungarians to advance their frontiers further west, at the expense of Croatia and Slovenia: the occupied districts were Prekomurje and Medjumurje. This frontier is likely to endure—until the defeat of the Axis Powers.

VIII

The condition and shape of Hungary after the war are likely to depend to no small extent on internal conditions. My own impression is that the present authoritarian government is unlikely to survive defeat, and will be replaced by some form of democratic régime, anxious to work in friendly fashion with its neighbours. If so, then the problem immediately becomes easier of solution. At the same time, it must not be forgotten that Hungarian demands for treaty revision were not party questions, but were universally held. A democratic Hungary would drop sentimental claims for the restoration of the old empire frontiers, but not for the amendment of boundaries so as to bring all Magyars under Hungarian rule. As this conforms with the Spirit of the Atlantic Charter, we must examine the problem from that angle.

(*a*) The frontiers seized by Hungary at the expense of Slovakia must be canceled as quite unfair. (At the moment of writing, most Hungarians seem to be convinced that they will be allowed to keep their Slovak and Ruthenian gains even if Germany loses!) Returning to the 1938 boundaries, revision could be made to Hungary's advantage without strangling the internal communications of Slovakia. The new frontier might follow the Little Danube—the island between it and the Danube proper reverting to Hungary. To the east of Komarno two other small stretches of territory (in districts 2 and 3) with predominant Magyar population could be added to Hungary—in all, a total of from 250,000 to 300,000 Magyars. Admittedly there would be many thousands of Magyars north of the new frontiers. Some of these, however, are Magyarised Slovaks—this district was the scene of one of the most intense campaigns of Magyarisation. The others could return to Hungary at their option: in exchange, the 150,000 Slovaks in Northern Hungary, and a smaller number in the newly ceded districts, would return to their own land.

(b) The problem of Ruthenia is far more difficult. If the same procedure were adopted, the Hungarian frontier could be pushed to the north at the expense of economic communications, except that a strip of plain must be left for valley-to-valley communication. By this method another 60,000 or 70,000 Magyars would return to Hungary. This would leave no more than 400,000 Magyars in Czechoslovakia, to be returned by organised transfer.

There is a strong case, however, for considering the problem of Ruthenia as a whole. It will be immensely difficult to discover the wishes of the Ruthenes themselves, so low has been their level of cultural and political education. In view of the prospective Polish-Czechoslovak federation, the Ruthenes may prefer to join their brothers on the Polish side of the mountains—which, again, do not act as a barrier but as a binder, for branches of the Hucul tribe live in adjacent valleys in Poland and Ruthenia.

(c) I have outlined in the Roumanian section a suggestion for the settlement of the Hungarian frontier problem in the east. With the Magyars of Transylvania re-settled in the north-east of that province, the frontier further south could follow the ethnic line more closely than it does. It would be possible, if required, to reconstruct the railway twenty miles further east. In any case, the communications of the whole of this area must be vastly improved: new railways are already much overdue.

Plebiscites would have to be held to decide local wishes— the best frontier would have to be determined literally village by village. Quite apart from Transylvania, an adjustment of the frontier about Satu Mare, Oradea and Arad would restore about 300,000 Magyars to Hungary.

(*d*) The question of the Germans in the Banat is difficult. If they could be returned to Germany—it would be much against their will—the resultant situation would be easier. An adjustment of the frontier in favour of Hungary would then provide space for the absorption of large numbers of Magyars at present scattered over Transylvania. Roumania would object to giving up any share of this fertile land, but she cannot have all the land and no minorities.

(*e*) Yugoslavia might be prepared to cede the northern portion of the Backa triangle to Hungary, the Yugoslavs around Subotica being exchanged for Magyars further south.[1] This possibility depends entirely on the character of post-war Hungary. At the moment, of course, the Yugoslavs bitterly resent the treacherous action of the Hungarian government, and are in no mood for any concessions.

By a series of such minor modifications of frontier, a total of at least a million Magyars would be returned to their fatherland. If the Transylvanian solution were also adopted, there would be from half to three-quarters of a million Magyars in Czechoslovakia, Roumania or Yugoslavia in isolated settlements: these could be returned to Hungary. With the anticipated programme of agrarian reform, and with the emigration of minorities from Hungary, such a number of immigrants could be absorbed without undue difficulty, over a reasonable period and with suitable financial backing.

I repeat that much depends upon the character of the post-war Hungary. An authoritarian state, brooding over misfor-

---

[1] The possibility of such a solution has, however, been complicated by the atrocities of war: thousands of Yugoslavs at Subotica have been massacred.

tunes of its own creation, pondering the moment for revenge
—such a state could expect little generosity from the neighbours she had treated so scurvily. A democratic Hungary, in
close economic and political federation with her neighbours
—that would be a different situation: and one which would
ease considerably the difficulties of Hungarian frontier revision.

CHAPTER TWELVE

FRANCE

I

I HAVE emphasised that judgments which are intended to have permanent results should not be allowed to depend upon the hazards of war: or upon sentiment. There are people today who have but scant sympathy for France because they consider that she 'let us down.' Some of these people may reverse just as violently if the Free French forces achieve especial military distinction, or if the French nation eventually revolts against its oppressors.

It is true that France bears no small share of responsibility —not for the war, but for the character of the Germany which made the war possible. Many French would deny this indignantly: in 1919, they argue, they wanted to hold Germany down indefinitely, and the British and Americans refused to let them. It is equally true that our own policy, or lack of policy, contributed to the unhappy *dénouement*. Our indecision was as disastrous as France's decision: not only because of the effect it had on Germany, but because of the effect it had on France.

The demand of France for security in 1919 was elementary and quite understandable. Twice her territory had been ravaged within half a century. Millions of her men had been killed or maimed. Her economy was severely hit; she banked on reparations for the repair of the immense damage of the war: when these failed—by German trickery, most French believed—her currency slid rapidly towards inflation.

Largely by French insistence, the Treaty of Versailles was dictated, not negotiated. This had one unfortunate result. The men who drew up the original draft naturally allowed a small margin for negotiation: when the Treaty was imposed, it was slightly more severe than it need have been. This applied largely, however, to the economic clauses, which in time cancelled themselves, and not to the territorial provisions.

(The French do not carry the whole share of the blame. There were long disputes between the Allies before main issues could be settled—while a weary world waited in exhaustion for real peace instead of an armistice. The universal and popular cry for demobilisation affected politicians, impelling haste where serious and prolonged study was essential.)

From one point of view, it was a mistake when President Wilson insisted on placing the covenant of the League of Nations as part of the Treaty. (On the other hand, Wilson's instinct was right when he recognised that the very principle of self-determination on which the states created by the treaties were based depended for their existence on international co-operation.) It was only natural that Germans should hate the Treaty of Versailles, product of their defeat. Therefore, they hated the League of Nations—to which, at the time, they were not admitted. They regard it suspiciously as an instrument of power politics to be used by the victors: and it must be confessed that more than one French government so used it.

The real tragedy of 1919, especially for France, was the withdrawal of the United States. Foch had demanded the Rhine frontier to guarantee French security. Britain and America demurred—it would mean placing millions of Germans under French rule: the antithesis of the doctrine of self-determination which we had preached. Nevertheless, recognising that France's apprehension was reasonable enough, both countries offered in place to give a guarantee of her frontiers. France was satisfied: with Britain and the United States behind her, no Germany would ever dare to attack.

Then the United States refused to ratify the guarantees their President had given. There was a saving clause in the agreement, by which Britain in turn might withdraw from the guarantee if the United States declined ratification. This she did—and made another mistake. It was as essential that Britain and France should be as close together in peace as in war. Yet by 1920 there was serious friction between them, and by 1923 they were almost on opposite sides.

In her disappointment, France reverted to older forms of security—straightforward alliances. A second front was essential: Russia was in the throes of revolutionary war, but Poland offered an obvious alternative. Next, France built up the Little Entente—Czechoslovakia, Roumania and Yugoslavia —ostensibly directed against Hungary, but capable of extension.

Yet these alliances were eventually wrecked—by France. Her internal political condition became chaotic: a wide range of parties haggled and disputed: to many the party was more important than the community. On the extreme right and left powerful Fascist and Communist sections exerted their opposing influences. For some years France hovered on the verge of civil war; her social services were behind those of Western Europe, but she came near to revolutionary methods in her efforts to make progress, so strong was the opposition in certain controlling sections. With internal affairs the subject of such passions, her outlook abroad became weak and uncertain.

The construction of the Maginot Line affected traditional French outlook. France had no territorial ambitions—merely wanted to hold what she held—to keep Germany out of France. This had been the basis of her alliances. Now her frontier was secure, why should France help Poles and Czechs? The idea was dangerous to France, not to say treacherous to the Poles and Czechs.

We have noted their reactions. Poland, with French support now lukewarm, promptly made an accommodation with

Germany. Many Frenchmen were uneasy. German rearmament was already a reality: some method must be found of keeping the battle from France.

Thus in May 1935 the Franco-Soviet Pact was signed. Had it been firmly based, it might have prevented the war. Too many politicians in France were fundamentally opposed to the new alliance, however; they disliked the Nazis, but liked the Communists even less. The pact was seldom worth more than a scrap of paper; its phrases could scarcely be read through the fog of suspicion which enveloped it. Here was sheer tragedy: such an alliance, beneficial to both parties, might have done more than to prevent war; it might have brought Russia into European affairs, to the benefit of all, including Russia.

This is no place to discuss the collapse of France at the first blow when real war came. There were political parties of the right and left which must bear a big share of responsibility. The French Communists, who turned about with alacrity in August 1939, must now be bitterly disillusioned men.

With industrial strife, political dissension and moral apathy pervading France, all the weak vacillations of the pre-war years are easily explained. French foreign policy usually followed that of Britain, with fatal results; it could do no other, for French leaders at least knew the weakness of their country: a moral as well as a material weakness—from which we barely escaped ourselves. The downfall of France can be traced directly to that short-sighted selfishness which is one of the principal failings of our own generation. We preferred a life of ease to that eternal vigilance which alone can preserve freedom, the dopish wishful thinking of astrologers in Sunday newspapers to a square facing of the realities of the situation. Thanks to the English Channel and their natural resilience and stolidity, the British had a chance to recover from the disaster which overcame France: they took it, but they must allocate blame to France with reserve.

In this and the Italian chapter our task is to examine the
frontiers of France, as they were drawn in 1919 and as they
may be fixed after victory in 194—? It may be that we shall
notice little if any change.

II

When Alsace and Lorraine were rejoined to France by the
Treaty of Versailles, the popular impression was that of a
final curtain to a drama. It was quite wrong. Since then a
highly interesting act has been played, and the *dénouement*
is still to come.

Certainly the drama has been lengthly. Alsace and Lorraine
were duchies in the Middle Ages, when populations changed
their allegiance at the behest of their overlords. Lorraine was
always strongly populated by people of French stock. After
the vicissitudes of the period, the Duchy was formally purchased by Louis XV in 1735 for his father-in-law, Stanislas
of Poland. France had ruled over the greater part of the territory for generations previously. (It is important to correct the
impression of the conjoint name: almost the whole of Alsace
but only one-fifth of the province of Lorraine, were annexed
by Germany in 1871.)

In the meantime Alsace had long been a German duchy; its
boundaries seldom coincided with those of today—for a considerable period Mulhouse was Swiss! During the Middle Ages
Alsace was the cradle of German culture. Then it formed part
of the spoils of Richelieu—his reward for assisting the German
princes during the Thirty Years' War against Austria. This
was in 1681. Alsace accepted the change philosophically: in
those days a change of overlord was common and meant comparatively little. The Alsatian way of life continued unper-
turbed: nor did the French government attempt to alter it.
Indeed, Louis XIV was wiser than men of our own day; he
accepted the advice of Colbert to make Alsace so happy that
the province would never want to change masters again.

The Revolution made Alsace French in spirit if not in
speech. Ideas in the province had always been progressive,

and liberty, equality and fraternity appealed strongly to the Alsatian mind. Nowhere in France was there a more fervent revolutionary spirit. There was more than usual significance in the fact that Rouget de l'Isle first sang the Marseillaise in a house in Strasbourg—where the host spoke German! So strong was local feeling that, at the Congress of Vienna in 1815, when Austria claimed Alsace, the Allies refused to admit the claim on the grounds that the province was an integral part of France.

Her rapid defeats in 1870 laid France at the mercy of the new Germany. Alsace was an obvious demand—less the small territory of Belfort, which as a reward for its gallant defence was allowed to remain in France. The seizure of Eastern Lorraine was strategic: Bismarck was over-persuaded by his generals that it was essential to the defence of Germany. He himself had strong qualms about taking over Metz, which, he said, had 'too many foreigners.'

(Not only French: in the district are large numbers of Poles, brought in to exploit the local coalfields. Germans formed only a small minority.)

The historical claims were thus mixed. The principal foundation of the German demand for Alsace was on the basis of language. It is true that French was little spoken—but in older days nobody bothered about trifles like this. Countries like Belgium and Switzerland could not exist if the German argument held. Not until the surge of nationalism in the middle of the nineteenth century did French begin to gain at the expense of German. In the south, about Mulhouse, French influence and language had always been predominant: it seems that French ideas were halted by the Vosges, but passed easily through the Belfort Gap between the Vosges and the Juras. Sometimes, further north, the language division was remarkably abrupt. I recall one village where all the people down one side of the street spoke French, those on the other side German. But they had lived on friendly terms for many generations.

In 1871 democratic ideas like plebiscites were not considered proper—especially by Imperial Germany! There is little doubt that the result in Alsace-Lorraine would have been a considerable majority for retention by France.

It has often been represented that Alsace-Lorraine formed one of the causes of the war. This is scarcely true. After 1871 French resentment was strong—naturally, at the loss of provinces which had been French for the last two hundred years, to say nothing of the blow to national pride. Gradually passions cooled. The statue of Strasbourg in the Place de la Concorde was still veiled, but by 1914 the position was this—that no French government could have dared to make war to recover Alsace-Lorraine. Once war was declared, of course, their recovery became a major war aim. They did not provoke war, but they might have prolonged it.

The first impulse in Alsace-Lorraine after 1871 was a vigorous resistance to all German efforts. Until 1887 all deputies to the Reichstag from the seized provinces were 'protesters.' Naturally this could not be sustained, and after twenty years of struggle the local patriots dropped the idea of reunion with France, and substituted instead the vision of an autonomous state within the German Empire. Had the war been delayed another twenty years, this might indeed have come to pass. But the abortive sweep of the French army into Alsace in 1914 raised hopes which had long been buried. Not that opinion was united—for the position was gravely complicated by the presence of 300,000 German immigrants who had settled in the provinces, and by an intense process of Germanisation of the original inhabitants. Nor did the progress of the war tend to make either France or Germany more popular, torn as was Alsace into two parts by the broad line of devastation and death. Yet November 1918 brought high hopes—visions, indeed, too romantic for a practical world.

Although the German attempt to assimilate Alsace-Lorraine between 1871 and 1914 had met with some success, it is significant that when German troops crossed the Rhine they were warned that they were entering 'hostile territory.' Hundreds of Alsatians and Lorrainers were imprisoned for the duration of the war as suspects, and thousands were exiled to 'safer' parts of Germany.

It is significant, too, to note the change of the wording on war memorials. In France the inscription reads: 'To the sons of ——, who died for France in the World War.' The Alsatians fought on both sides; nor were their civilians exempt from its destruction. I noted that a common war memorial epitaph read: 'To the sons and daughters of ——, victims of the World War.'

No plebiscite was held in 1918. The difficulties would have been immense. Tens of thousands of French left the provinces in 1871: 300,000 Germans had been settled there since; these, with their descendants, now numbered half a million. For a fair plebiscite, the conditions of 1871 would have to be reproduced, and this was almost impossible. In any case, Alsace-Lorraine was covered by the Fourteen Points, claimed by Germany as the promised basis of peace.

Some of the German immigrants, and all the soldiers and officials, returned to Germany in 1919, so that the proportion of French considerably increased. In Lorraine the French language was predominant, but Alsace remained largely German-speaking. Nevertheless, there was no mistaking the warmth of their greeting to the advancing French armies in the last days of the war. I saw this for myself.

From the first moment of reunion it was obvious that the path of Alsace-Lorraine was to be no arterial road, but a rough and precipitous track. The currency was in a state of chaos: the value of the German marks in the provinces dropped almost to zero, and financial ruin threatened. The legal system was in the utmost confusion. The older people knew something of the French laws existing in 1870; for nearly fifty years they had lived under an entirely different set of German regulations: now they were suddenly flung back to the French code, with the innumerable additions of the Third Republic —a code in many respects inferior to that of the German Empire. Social services in Alsace, in particular, were considerably in advance of those of France. The immediate removal of the German administrators of the provinces, though natural, did not assist in the restoration of stability.

With a great courage and a good deal of generosity the French government tackled these problems. It shouldered the burden of the depreciated marks until such time as Germany could be compelled to make reparation. The legal chaos was straightened out: the best of France's administrators were seconded to the needs of the recovered departments. Germanic ideas were treated with the utmost tolerance. Energetic action was taken to heal the war scars, and the Alsatian villages were among the first to be rebuilt. Certainly, since the war, France deserved well of Alsace-Lorraine.

The real Alsatians—that is to say, not the German immigrants—on the whole welcomed return to France as they had strongly protested when they were seized by Germany. There were many difficulties, however. In France all connection between Church and State had been severed: in Alsace the hold of the Church is strong and 'atheist' France was suspect. The French attitude was very conciliatory, if not in the true spirit of French logic—the Church in Alsace retained its old powers. Alsace had been organised federally, and looked to Strasbourg rather than to Berlin: the sudden change to Paris was not appreciated. The French wisely declined to hurry history, and Alsace-Lorraine was administered separately from France. The educational difficulty was intense. The French have been free from those petty oppressions which have disfigured the Italian record. While Germany forbade the teaching of French, France permitted the teaching of German.

It is to be understood that there would be large numbers of Alsatians who would oppose French rule. An autonomous movement was founded. It was backed generally by Germans who had not opted to return to Germany, by most of the priests, and by people to whom religion meant more than democracy or who felt the Germanic strain within them. At first the demand was for an autonomous Alsace-Lorraine within the French Republic, but later the programme became frankly separatist. In 1928 some of the leaders of the movement were tried and condemned for sedition, and popular passion was inflamed.

One interesting argument was advanced by the autonomists. With Alsace-Lorraine independent, and linking up with Switzerland, Luxembourg and Belgium, France and Germany would be separated by a chain of neutral states. This, it was argued, would be a great benefit to the peace of the world. With these states guaranteed, it would be quite impossible ever for France and Germany to go to war!

The emergence of Hitler altered the atmosphere in Alsace. There was a strong Communist element in the province, which has always held advanced political views. These Communists took part in the general opposition to the approaching Nazi menace. The priests too, however suspicious they might be of France, had no wish to fall into the hands of Hitler. The rise of the Nazis at least helped France in one respect, for ten years ago the situation in Alsace was serious. Now the autonomous movement divided: part of it was even dissolved: another portion still demanded local autonomy, but went back to the once-discarded suggestion that Alsace should remain within France. A third section, consisting largely of people of German stock, not true Alsatians, became an open or underground organisation for the return of Alsace to the Reich.

This section proved its nuisance value even before the war. The greater part of the Maginot Line covered the boundaries of Alsace-Lorraine, and its construction offered unlimited opportunities for espionage and sabotage, which were freely accepted. The movement became frankly subversive, and in the early months of the war many of its members were arrested and some of the leaders executed.

(I found that the construction of the Maginot Line had another effect. Many Alsatians, who had hesitated to decide on French or German loyalty, made their decision in favour of France—because they were convinced that the Maginot Line was so strong that Alsace-Lorraine could never again be taken by Germany!)

In the early days of the war the frontier areas were evacuated. If the campaign had been normal, the area would have
been the scene of violent battle: it was wise to clear civilians
out of the potential battle area—it would have been wise if
the policy had been continued further north. From the security point of view, too, the move was admirable, for among the
autonomists were to be found an admirable basis for a local
'Fifth Column.'

Alsace was a strange land when I visited it last in May 1940.
Strasbourg was a dead city. Most of the shops were closed;
many bore the signs of hurried departure the previous September. Through their windows I saw mildewed bread and rotted
vegetables: abandoned cats prowled the streets, reverting to
primitive hunting instincts. The only traffic was that of the
Army services. The atmosphere was all wrong: Strasbourg
was built for commerce and culture, not as a battlefield.

The strange character of the first winter of war upset some
of the Alsatian evacuees—among whom there had been many
protests. Why were they kept away from their homes when
nothing was happening? they demanded.

The evacuation of German-speaking Alsatians to the interior of France led to many difficulties. In most respects the
Alsatian standard of life was considerably higher than that
of the Midi, where many evacuees were quartered: ideas of
cooking, cleanliness and culture differed considerably. Had it
been sufficiently prolonged, however, the enforced mix-up
might have done a good deal of service to France. Provincial-
ism has been a source both of strength and of weakness. Her
liberal ideas have sometimes been abused. For France is of
course a medley of races as confused as any in Europe, and her
efforts to unify them have been largely those of the spirit.
There is a large gap between the outlook of the Breton and
Norman in the north and the Basque and Catalan in the south.
In normal times France could draw on the virtues of her outlying provinces—which have, indeed, supplied her with leading men out of all proportion to their populations. It was

amazing how closely French races were bound by ideas which
Germans would class as merely sentimental.

Yet there were serious autonomist movements in some of
the historic provinces. That in Brittany was the most marked.
The usual demand was not for complete independence, but
for local self-government. This was held by the highly-
centralised French system to be dangerous. Hence came one
of the bases of opposition to any idea of an autonomous Alsace
—a scheme which is bound to be revived after victory. If
Alsace, why not Brittany? If Brittany, why not the Basque
countries or the Catalan region? France might find herself no
more than a small regional federal state, in no condition to
protect herself against a powerful neighbour, and in poor
shape to progress economically. It is significant, the French
point out, that autonomous movements in Brittany and elsewhere were encouraged and in some cases subsidised by Germany, as a potential weakness to France.

(Incidentally, it is worth while keeping an eye on the
French Basques and Catalans. Many of them are the most
loyal of the citizens of France. At the same time, of course,
they have strong cultural and racial ties with their brothers
over the Spanish border. Spanish Basques and Catalans have
long demanded autonomy, and will certainly demand it again.
Their French relatives have shown no desire to pass under
Spanish rule: on the contrary. Circumstances might arise
wherein Hitler might offer the French Basque and Catalan
countries as a bribe to Spain, or discover a 'spontaneous' demand for union with their brother races. This situation seems
unlikely to arise, but it is not impossible.)

At the moment of writing, Alsace-Lorraine is administered
as a German province. Formal annexation has not yet been
announced, but the farcical customs frontiers of occupied
France have already been removed to those of 1914.

The annexation has been accomplished in fact, however.
Alsatians and Lorrainers of French origin or sympathies have
been expelled to France—under conditions only slightly better

than those of the expulsions from Western Poland. Often they were turned out on a few hours' notice, and deprived of all their possessions. In their place Germans are again being settled, especially in Alsace, so as to emphasise the German character of the province at the time for final reckoning.

The position of Alsace-Lorraine after victory ought to be settled without undue difficulty. Naturally, the German 'solution' cannot be accepted for a moment. The Germans planted there since the French collapse must be expelled and the original inhabitants returned. This will take time, but before the final solution is fixed we must obviously return to the conditions prevailing at the time of the German seizure of the provinces: there can be no condonation of aggression.

Not until this is done can there be a real attempt to appraise the wishes of the inhabitants. My own impression is that they would wish to remain with France. Those who did not should be given the option of moving into Germany. We may even see a considerable diminution of autonomist claims. Responsible people must have seen by now how the internal weakness of France not merely led to her downfall, but was actually an invitation to war. They may have learned their lesson.

I hope so: no one who has visited Alsace ever failed to react to the beauty of its mountains or the charm of its people. Although racially akin, there is a great gap between the Alsatians and any other German race: and nearly all comparisons favour the Alsatian. If you want to know what the Germans were like before they were Prussianised, go to Alsace.

III

The Germans have annexed Alsace-Lorraine in all but form —have made it quite plain that they stay there if they win. At the same time, they hold another threat over France, that of annexing her rich departments of the north-east.

Here, of course, the Germans have no ethnic claims whatsoever. The Flamands and the Picards may differ in dialect

from the Provençals or the Normans, but they are 100 per
cent French, have never been subjected to Germany and have
never wanted to be. The German move in this case is part of
the economic 'New Order.' By this Germany is to be the
factory of Europe, with Germans as the skilled and highly-
paid workers—and with satellite states to supply food and
cheap ordinary labour. A clear objective is to seize industrial
areas; if the industries compete with existing German manufactures, then they are closed down: this happened in the
Sudetenland, to the great distress of tens of thousands of people who had yearned to 'return' to the fatherland. In conquered Poland the frontiers of the Reich were immediately
pushed to the east so as to include not only the resources of
Silesia, but far beyond the boundaries of 1918 to cover the
industrial district of Lodz.

Similarly the Germans propose to incorporate Belgium in
the Reich, either directly or as a satellite state, so that its industries can be totally controlled by Germany. The Belgian
Fascist party has given open and covert assistance to this plan,
a fact which will doubtless be remembered at the right
moment.

Adjoining Belgium lies the rich industrial area about Lille:
a small but important coalfield as a basis for huge textile production. This the Germans wish to control. The departments
of Nord and Pas de Calais, probably the Somme as well, are
to be added to the Belgian administration.

The advantages to Germany of such an annexation would
be twofold: not only the gain of richly developed industries,
but a very strong strategic position—against Britain.

At the moment this section of the German plan has only
been put tentatively into operation. Its consummation is held
over the heads of the French. If they co-operate 'loyally'
with Germany, then they may be allowed to retain their
provinces. If not—

Fortunately, this problem should only prove of temporary
and academic interest.

IV

Although a part of Belgium, not France, the small districts of Eupen and Malmedy should be considered alongside the problem of Alsace-Lorraine. The basis of the allocation of these two small districts to Belgium in 1919 was strategic. 1914 had revealed that Liége was at the mercy of a German army. The frontier was moved east at Eupen to occupy an essential part of the German railway system, and at Malmedy to the watershed of the Ardennes, to put a wider strip of difficult country between Liége and Germany. The two districts are very small—the total population is only 60,000. It is undisputed that the population is largely German-speaking, but it is claimed that most of the people are really Walloons in origin, and have been Germanised since 1815. It is indeed certain that they were French-speaking before that date. Many of the family names of the people are still French.

Small though they were, Eupen and Malmedy were not neglected by the German propaganda machine, and the local Nazi party flourished—for the rise of Hitler robbed Belgium of any chance of assimilating the German portion of the people. Nevertheless, the Nazis were never able to command a majority vote in the two districts. In the attack of May 10th, 1940, part of the population proved loyal; the other part gave the usual long-prepared 'Fifth Column' assistance to the invaders. There were even small local units, well armed in advance, to attack the Belgian outposts in the rear. The two districts were promptly reincorporated in the Reich.

I do not know Belgium's ideas about Eupen and Malmedy after the war is over. Her anxiety to secure her frontier can be appreciated most readily, but the course of events has already proved that the inclusion of a potentially hostile population is not the best way of safeguarding a frontier. A local plebiscite seems to be indicated, with exchanges of population if necessary.

V

It is not within the scope of this book to consider the state of France after the war. It is her good fortune that so many tens of thousands of her sons are gallantly continuing the fight: for, as has been stressed, there is one type of mind which would seek to direct the clauses of the peace treaties according to the military valour of the country affected rather than to the justice of its cause.

(Practically every country overrun or enslaved by Germany has its 'free' movement in Britain or elsewhere. These range from complete legitimate governments to small committees of diplomats and others who defied their country's decision to submit, and who try to keep alive the spirit of their countries in spite of the meagre resources at their disposal. Almost without exception these committees are composed of men loyally determined to help us to rid Europe of the Nazi menace.

It is only proper to record, however, that in some quarters they are regarded as a form of reinsurance, even inspired by their own governments. Thus, it is argued, when Ruritania decides to submit to Hitler, it instructs its Minister in London to resign his appointment and to form a Free Ruritanian movement. Then it wins either way. If Hitler comes out on top, the recalcitrant Ruritanians can be forgiven; if Britain wins, then the Ruritanian government might go under, but the Free Ruritanians would have saved their country by their lip-service to the Allied cause. I think that this argument is untrue, unsound and potentially dangerous. I know many of the 'free' men of the submissive countries, and am convinced that the idea I have outlined is a sheer travesty. We ought to do all we can to encourage these men who have put principle before race; we shall need their co-operation very badly and urgently as soon as victory is won.)

The present Fascist régime in France is of course alien to all French traditions and ideas. Nothing is more certain than that it will disappear with the collapse of Germany. Already France has recovered to some extent from the sudden, shocked surprise which turned her military defeat into a major disaster. She followed Pétain because of the great personal esteem in which he was held: here was a man who had proved himself time and time again a servant of France; he could be trusted—he was not one of those corrupt politicians. (It is easier in France than in Britain for a soldier to win popular support: indeed, in peace-time Britain the names of our leading soldiers are almost unknown to the ordinary man. At the moment we have no military man who can compare with the stature of Pétain in France: the best comparison is with Kitchener in 1914. This was one of our few examples of putting a soldier in political control—and it was not successful. Wellington provided another case of a great soldier who failed to repeat his prowess as a politician. In France the procedure has been quite common. Napoleon pursued it with apparent advantages.)

There were, of course, Fascist or near-Fascist parties in France before the war; they supply the main driving force of the Laval régime. Working with them are many honourable Frenchmen who believe that unity is essential to the very life of France today, and who have agreed to programmes alien to them and their race lest by a show of disunity they should invite further German aggression. The situation has been complicated by what many people consider to be a mistake in the Free French propaganda. After the first shock had passed, few Frenchmen had a word to say for the Vichy government: but nearly all were loyal to Pétain. It was a mistake to make personal attacks on the aged marshal instead of concentrating on his unpopular assistants.

Further, we must realise that up to the battles of 1940 General de Gaulle was only known to a limited portion of the French population, and even to them only as a very clever soldier, a specialist in tank warfare. To most, his qualifications for the leadership of France could not compare with those of

Pétain. Further, his political views incline towards the Right
—and there are still thousands of Frenchmen to whom Communism is more important than country. Nevertheless, there is
evidence that de Gaulle is continually gaining ground. His
own personal utterances have been most statesmanlike. (Indeed, when he appears on French platforms he may even
cause a sensation, for he must be classed already among the
orators of his day.) Most important of all, his courage and
achievements have impressed tens of thousands of Frenchmen
who see him as he should be seen, personifying the traditional
gallantry of the French race.

It is far too early to estimate the time and character of victory, yet much may depend on the way in which it comes. If
it involves fighting in France, and if a large part of the French
population rallies to our cause—as I believe it would—then
even those doubters who can only despise the France which
'let us down,' or who base their decisions on military prowess, will swing again to the French side. (These people are
more numerous and influential than they should be.)

The situation in France altered radically in November,
1942, after the Allied landing in North Africa. With no
further prospect of 'collaboration,' the Germans occupied the
rump of France, making a typically dishonest attempt to
secure the French fleet at Toulon.

In North Africa the political situation was confused. General Giraud was a respected fighting soldier, but Admiral
Darlan appeared unexpectedly on the scene at the critical
moment. He had some backing in the United States—which
had never broken off diplomatic relations with Vichy—but
was completely distrusted in every European country as one
of the leading collaborationists with the Nazis. The temper
and trials of Europe are scarcely calculated to understand
compromise with people who have worked with Hitler—
stricken people make a clear cut between those who are for
them and those who are against them.

Even after Darlan's assassination, the situation in North

Africa was disquieting. It revealed that the chasms which had divided France in 1940 were not yet bridged; that there were still a number of leading men with Fascist leanings; and that many still considered political advantages as more urgent than the salvation of their country.

From the military point of view, however, the outlook was brighter. Giraud's men might not accept the designation of Fighting French, but they fought. We are entitled to hope—indeed, to expect—that Frenchmen will seek the earliest opportunities to resolve their differences—and to proclaim firmly the intention to restore a democratic France.

It is certain that a French force must be available to return to France immediately Germany is defeated or driven from French soil: otherwise there might be something like civil war in France. Revolt against Vichy would follow almost automatically on German defeat. In the battle of force the Germans hold all the advantages, but in warfare of the mind the French are much more subtle. They surround the German army of occupation with hatred: and the German, with his inferiority complex, hates being hated.

Our first objective after victory must be to restore peace to France. General de Gaulle has made his position quite clear; he is a soldier, seeking only to deliver his country from the German invader. That done, he proposes to re-establish democratic France. There are plenty of statesmen available to help; they are of proved courage—they are not alone in the fact that they made serious mistakes. Maybe it will be a man like Herriot or Blum who will ease the differences between the leaders of the French factions.

I am certain that it will be a criterion of peace that we assist in the recovery of France. The character of that assistance may depend upon the conduct of France during the remaining period of the war—as it will depend, of course, on the resources available to Britain and the United States after a sustained combat. At the best, it will take France long to recover, but she is resilient. The material devastation cannot be compared with that of the last war, but her economic system is in ruins, part of her machinery stolen in Germany, and her country flooded with worthless paper money. For the French there is indicated a long period of persistent labour and high courage against tremendous difficulties: yet I am confident that she will win through.

So far as her frontier problems are concerned, we have already discussed her north-eastern boundaries at length: others are mentioned in the chapter on Italy. An immediate return to the *status quo* of 1939 is obviously indicated as a basis of any discussion. Then Alsace-Lorraine may require more serious consideration than some people imagine: how serious may depend as much upon the character of the new Germany as that of the new France. German claims to areas of North-Eastern France will, of course, vanish in a night.

Not all Frenchmen will be chastened by the experience of defeat: more will be exhilarated by eventual victory. In some quarters we are bound to witness a demand for the Rhine frontier.

It is not new; indeed, it was one of the ideas for which Richelieu projected his series of wars: an objective ultimately attained, lost again, and regained by Napoleon. In 1919 the project was revived by Foch, who claimed that the Rhine was the strategic frontier of France, and that only by holding it could her security be maintained. His scheme was dismissed, to be replaced by the abortive Anglo-American guarantee of the French frontiers.

Nevertheless, under the terms of the Armistice and the Treaty of Versailles, French forces did occupy a considerable Rhineland area. In this district they encouraged local separatist movements. (Almost every locality in Europe has its autonomist malcontents: even Scotland.) Some of the French machinations at this time were not very creditable, but they achieved only minute results. The very fact that the autonomist organisations were backed by France was enough to damn them in German eyes: this even in a Germany facing the appalling aftermath of defeat.

If the outcry for the Rhine frontier is raised again in France,

I think it should be resisted. The people who live in the Rhine valley are Germans—we have seen that a river is no natural frontier. Economically, the middle Rhine has developed in the German system. (The only major difficulty is that the iron-fields of Lorraine are supplied by the coal-fields of the Saar, with a frontier between: this difficulty can be dissolved almost instantly by an infusion of common sense.) Nothing would be more likely to keep the German ultra-nationalist spirit alive than the seizure of her western provinces. A military occupation of the Rhineland is one thing, its annexation another—it would be contrary in deed and spirit to the Atlantic Charter.

After considering briefly the position on the French-Italian borders, we must return to this point again.

CHAPTER THIRTEEN

ITALY

I

THE tragedy of the Italian people transcends even that of the Germans. Few who have visited Italy failed to esteem the hard-working peaceable Italian peasants, far happier in their simple rural pursuits than in preparation for war. Few doubt that the majority of Italians would finish the war tomorrow if they could, flinging over the Fascist régime: this is not true of the Germans.

The Italians are as mixed a race as any in Europe; they were the last of the major nations to emerge from long years of subjection and division. Not until 1870 did a united Italy appear on the map: even then Italian provinces lay without the new frontiers: these were the *terre irredente*—the unredeemed lands—which formed the key to Italian policy for two generations.

It was obvious that Italy by herself was helpless. She had a large population, but few natural riches. Yet many of her leaders dreamed of strength and empire. They won some backing, for the soil of Italy could not support the rapidly increasing population. Yet she was too late in the day: the plums had been seized by earlier colonising powers.

Italy had formed in 1882 an alliance with Germany and Austria. It seemed unnatural, for Italian provinces were under Austrian domination, and these were the first objective of the new state. At the outbreak of war in 1914 she withdrew, and remained neutral until May 1915, when she entered the war on the Allied side. In the Yugoslav section we have seen how the Treaty of London, with its wide promises, inclined Italy to change sides—a perfectly legitimate change, for her vital interests were almost coincident with the British.

Her war record was not marked by successes so much as by the courage of the Italian soldiers, who fought bloody campaigns in almost impossible conditions. In 1917 there occurred the German-Austrian break-through at Caporetto—on the Italian side, a moral as well as a military collapse. Thereafter, with Allied assistance, Italy pulled herself together: but her success of Vittorio Venetia, of which the Fascists make so

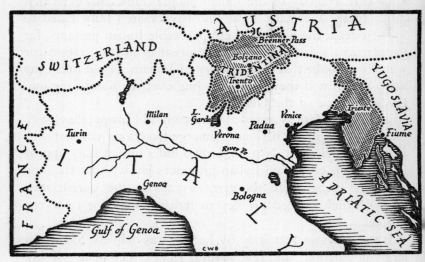

ITALIAN GAINS, 1919

much, was only won when the war was nearly over and the Austrians already demoralised.

Nevertheless, it is important to correct one common error. Because the Italians have surrendered so frequently in Africa to much inferior numbers, there has arisen a legend that they are natural cowards. This is quite wrong: during the last war I was attached for a while to an Italian division; its men fought magnificently—their hearts were in the battle. Their hearts are not in the present battle: that is the difference.

Italian difficulties and disappointments after the World War were directly responsible for the rise of Fascism. Economic distress was heightened by the cessation of emigration to the United States, which in previous years had relieved Italy of a large share of her surplus population. Italian democracy was not old enough to deal with its vigorous adversaries—a free Italy had existed for less than fifty years.

It is at moments of discontent that extreme opinions flourish and have their chance. The Italians were disillusioned over their war gains—they had been promised so much for their huge sacrifices. They discovered that accessions of territory did not necessarily bring increase of wealth. They were treated as junior partners at the peace conferences, and resented the inferiority imposed upon them. Economically Italy made the poorest recovery from the turmoil of war. There existed dozens of political parties: some with able and conscientious leaders, others with selfish opportunists. The latter often submerged the former.

The Fascist party, like most non-democratic movements, was started by disgruntled Socialists. Although a capable journalist named Benito Mussolini was its leader, he lacked the instinct to power. Some of his fellows saw an opportunity of benefiting from the confusion in Italy, and planned the so-called 'march on Rome.' Mussolini did not go with them; his restraint was not caused by cowardice—that was never one of his failings—but by lack of faith. One of his women, Gemma Daniani, emphasised the reports that the 'march' had been successful, and almost forced Mussolini to follow his friends to Rome.

The story was new then, but has become familiar since by constant imitation elsewhere. Men of authority in Italy were very apprehensive about a Communist menace: nor, indeed, was their apprehension unfounded. The democratic government seemed unwilling to intimidate or forcibly restrain its dangerous opponents. Here was the Fascist party offering its services. To the big industrialists it appeared that only the

Fascists knew how to deal with the Communists: their 'realist' methods of castor oil and the big stick promised suitable results. Yet the primary cause of the Fascist success was not the backing they enjoyed, but the indecision of their opponents. The democratic parties in Italy can plead that they were up against something new—that, even though they quarrelled among themselves, they never imagined that an opponent would openly overthrow all semblance of legality and seize power by force. Other countries should have learned the lesson, but did not. Five minutes of decisive action at the time of the 'march on Rome,' and the rising power of Fascism would have faded. But there were too many people who were so afraid of one bogy that they could not see the other: so apprehensive of Communism that they were willing to go to any length to combat it. They had to pay a bitter price.

The rise of Fascism scarcely altered the basis of Italian foreign policy; it merely stated it with greater force. Disappointed in the meagre rewards allocated to them—only a portion of the promises contained in the Treaty of London—the Italians had immediately planned to gain more. Their first contacts were with the revisionist group of small powers—Austria, Hungary and Bulgaria: one might have gathered from the spate of propaganda that Italy had been treated as one of the losers instead of a victor! At the same time there was constant suspicion of Germany, prostrate then, but obviously destined to rise again. Italy was perhaps the first country to anticipate the German seizure of Austria—and knew full well how her own security would be menaced by such a step.

The three small revisionist powers were almost useless as allies: France was regarded with jealous suspicion and Germany with legitimate alarm. Despite his rise as an opponent of Communism, Mussolini's first move was towards Russia! From 1924 to 1933 he forgot all about ideologies and pursued a policy of friendship with the Soviet government. In 1935 he forgot his differences with France and joined the Stresa front against Germany. Then followed the Abyssinian campaign.

To the average British citizen here was a perfectly clear case of aggression, and public opinion was remarkably united against Italy. Mussolini, however, bitterly denounced British perfidy, and he had at least a basis for his fury. More than one British statesman had agreed that Italian claims to Abyssinia should not be opposed: now, when he proposed to move, the British objected strongly. The French had been even more conciliatory: Laval in particular was quite willing to allow Italy to take Abyssinia—anything to keep her in the anti-German front! Hence the farce of partial and hesitant sanctions, wrecked by divisions, indecision and weakness. The unhappy episode did more than to arouse Mussolini's resentment; it convinced him that France and Britain were decadent and that a big-stick policy would pay.

At first it seemed that he was right. He intervened openly if not gloriously in the Spanish Civil War and received no more than minor reproaches. He was certain that Britain and France were in full retreat and could be bullied into surrender of principles and property—they would face anything rather than war. The tragedy was that all this time we had the answer to hand. In 1937 British and French ships were sunk off Spain: nobody would admit the ownership of the submarines which sank them. A conference at Nyon acted promptly: since nobody owned the submarines, they were pirates: naval patrols were organised, with orders to sink all submarines at sight. The sinkings of merchantmen ceased abruptly!

It was in Spain that the Axis was forged. The German and Italian leaders had the same aim—expansion. The weapon adopted was the Anti-Comintern Pact, an 'ideological' campaign against Communism. This side of the weapon was farcical from the beginning; it was merely a move to upset the *status quo* in Europe. In the ensuing disorder Germany could advance to the east, and there would doubtless be some pickings for Italy.

All this time the Italian peasant was strangely indifferent to glory. He had been roused to some resentment by sanctions which could always be represented as unfair. Apart from the prestige of victory, there was little gain: much was promised, but it was soon established that for some time to come Abyssinia was likely to be an economic liability rather than an asset. There was considerable discontent in Italy: pressure of population had been greatly increased during the last twenty years, following the violent reduction in emigration: the standard of life was low. In times of difficulty, dictators throughout the ages have sought diversion abroad.

The Munich settlement made Mussolini quite certain that he had only to ask loudly, and with a show of force, and he would get what he wanted. Within three months he had tabled his next demands.

II

'Savoy! Nice! Corsica! Tunis!' shouted the well-drilled Italian deputies in November 1938, thereby adding new zones to the overloaded danger-map of Europe. The best reply to the new claim was made by the students of Paris, who paraded the streets bearing placards, 'We want Vesuvius!'

The county of Savoy was part of the Burgundian kingdom. Later, its counts acquired the neighbouring territory of Piedmont, and their interests tended to stray to the other side of the Alps. The people, however, were of mixed stock, French predominating. In the interminable series of wars and treaties of the seventeenth and eighteenth centuries French frontiers were gradually extended at the expense of Savoy, but the eastern part of the county did not become French until 1860.

It was the result of a 'deal'—and the man who gave the province away was Cavour. At that time Italy was disintegrated, struggling for liberty. In return for French help Cavour promised Savoy and possibly Nice. The French help was small, but the Italians won their war of liberation and handed over the payment without protest—indeed, without demand.

An arrangement of this kind might be considered immoral

today, but it was common enough then. And it was made between realists who knew perfectly well what they were doing. Today there is no question about the character of the two counties; they house many thousands of Italian stock, but they are overwhelmingly French. In culture this is especially noticeable. Indeed, it could be claimed that, even on the other side of the Alps, the people of Piedmont have been more affected by French culture than by Italian. The general sentiment of the north-east corner of Italy has always been Francophile in its tendencies.

Nice, like most Mediterranean cities, had a more varied history. Its first recorded conquest was by the Greeks, who overcame the native Ligurians and established the settlement of Nike. The colony flourished until the coming of the Romans: then its decline began. Harassed by barbarians, it was destroyed in the sixth century. Local nobles took control, but the country was too small to enjoy complete independence; it was a feudal shuttlecock between the princes of Savoy and the kings of France, changing hands a dozen times.

Mussolini's propagandists make great play with the fact that in 1814 Nice threw herself into the arms of the new kingdom of Sardinia. They fail to mention the cause: the Niçois are a people of peace, and had not appreciated conscription into Napoleon's army. What Mussolini does not explain is that, as a result of the bargain with France for assistance in the wars of liberation in 1860, another plebiscite was held. Over 26,000 people voted for return to France, and only 159 against! Since that time the story of Nice has been one of expanding prosperity. There is a strain of Italian blood in most Niçois veins— this is a border area, where races mingled: but of the sympathies of the people, not even an Italian apologist could have any doubts.

The story of Corsica is far more complicated. Ligurians, Phœnicians, Etruscans, Carthaginians, Romans, Vandals, Goths, Franks, Moors, Tuscans—all these had controlled Corsica before A.D. 828. Then the island became a benefice of the popes. One gave it to Pisa, another to Spanish Aragon. In the fourteenth century it fell into the hands of the Genoese. Neither they nor any of the previous overlords cared anything for Corsica except as a source of supply of timber and taxes. The Genoese hold, in fact, was only substantive in the coastal area. For a considerable period Corsica was actually owned by a bank—the Bank of San Georgio, in Genoa.

The wretched inhabitants of the island, of a weird medley of blood, lived but little above starvation level; they were freely pirated, to lead unspeakable lives in galleys and brothels. Small wonder that Corsican thought even today is suspicious of governments! Corsican ideals were founded on the family; any other unit was too big to be trusted: a village was usually one large family. Above all, rulers were people to be hated, not revered. Law was oppression, not justice. So the people made their own wild justice, the vendetta. It persisted until our own day, and in 1931 I was in Corsica when the French government sent a military expedition to round up the Corsican bandits. The action was overdue: most of the men wanted were not those who had killed an enemy in a feud, but bandits who had turned gangster.[1]

The vendetta grew directly from the anarchy of Corsica during the period of Genoese rule. Eventually the republic sold the island to France.

Always the Corsicans had chafed under the harsh Genoese rule—for generations the island was in a state of constant insurrection. They objected just as strongly to France. Patriots fought for independence—or for autonomy under the *British* flag. For two years, from 1794, British troops did actually occupy Corsica, until they retired before an expedition sent against the island by a Corsican—Napoleon Bonaparte. His rise to the Emperor's throne was enough to make Corsica French.

More than that: Napoleon was only one of the first emigrants to the mainland. Many of his marshals were Corsicans.

[1] See my *Savoy! Corsica! Tunis!*

Since that time Corsica has supplied a surprisingly large proportion of officers and non-commissioned officers to the regular army of France: you would find its men in police forces all over France. Continuous emigration from the island is imperative. There are 800,000 Corsicans in the world, but only 280,000 of them live in Corsica: the island cannot support a larger population. On the other hand, France has a constant need for more labour.

Apart from sentiment, which is very strong, here is the best argument against Mussolini's claim. The Corsican can go to France to get work—he *must* go; he cannot do this in Italy, which is already over-populated and needs fields for emigration herself.

No one could doubt the spirit of Corsica today. M. Daladier visited the island as a reply to the 'spontaneous' demonstration in the Italian Parliament and had a monarch's reception. The Corsicans outdo the French in patriotic ardour; they are the backbone of France's professional army. Great Britain during the war lost 750,000 dead out of a population of 42 millions—say one in fifty. But Corsica lost 40,000 of her sons out of a total population of 280,000—one in seven. Before Italy could realise her ambition, she would have to conquer Corsica: even if there were no France, the Corsicans would resist to the last—and Napoleon was no fluke. They may speak the bastard dialect of an ancient tribe in Northern Italy, but they class themselves very emphatically as French.

A few months before the war began I returned to Corsica to observe the reactions to the Italian demands. In Bastia a procession marched down the street: I joined in. I always do join in processions—an awkward habit, for sometimes I have tagged myself on to the tail-end of a funeral. This *was* a funeral, of sorts. The crowd marched to the seashore. There they erected a gibbet from the top of which dangled a dummy figure representing Mussolini. Below, the people jibed and jeered: all of their remarks were uncomplimentary, and most of them were unprintable.

Corsica is one of the few places where a plebiscite could be held immediately, decisively and fairly. There are a few thousand Italians on the island: most of these are poverty-stricken charcoal-burners, uninterested in power politics; some of them were withdrawn by Mussolini in 1939. The Corsican population is overwhelmingly French in its sentiment: the ties are very close—for every Corsican in Corsica there are three on the mainland. There has scarcely been formed a demand for autonomy, as in Brittany. Economically, France gives far more to the unfertile island than she receives.

The Italian view is that the cession of Corsica would tidy up the map. Historical arguments are stressed—the Ligurian origin of the first Corsican people, the long rule of Genoa. The real Italian objective is strategic: I have said that Corsica is of small economic importance, but French aeroplanes based on Ajaccio can command the whole of Central Italy. This was the real reason behind the stimulated outcry.

Today Corsica is of little account with us, but has been the subject of wordy warfare between France and Italy. Hitler, having inveigled his partner into the war with wide promises, found it inconvenient to fulfil them. Italy had not proved quite the asset he anticipated: France might be more useful. So he promised France that he would keep the Italians out of Corsica in return for French assistance! He kept his promise until November, 1942, when he marched into Vichy France. Then, as a sop to his partner, he allowed the Italians to occupy Corsica. They encountered a stormy reception. Then the Corsicans accepted the situation, hiding their rifles in the mountains until the day comes when they can be used to better effect than in a forlorn hope. I would not care to be a member of the Italian garrison at that time. The Corsicans are among the finest fighters in the world. And they hold very decided ideas about the future of Corsica.

Actually, by far the most serious of the Italian demands was that for Tunis. Its problems do not come within the scope of this book, but nevertheless they dominate relations between France and Italy. Tunis today is a French protectorate. Its population (by the census figures of 1936) is assorted:

French	108,068
Italians	94,289
Other Europeans (mostly Maltese, with some Spaniards and Greeks)	10,849
Jews	59,222
Tunisians (of very mixed Arab and Berber stock)	2,265,750
Other Moslems (Algerians and Tripolitans)	64,623

Since 1936 the proportion of French has increased. I noted that the Italians were by no means all Fascists. Indeed, they had retained that regionalism which Mussolini has tried to stamp out. Meeting a European, I would ask his race. 'A Sicilian!' he would reply: not an Italian.

France occupied Tunis only in 1878. Italy was very annoyed—she was just going to take such a step herself. Since then Tunis has been a serious subject of contention between the two countries. In 1896 a convention guaranteed the Italian citizenship of local residents, who were to have their own schools and other racial rights. A new agreement was negotiated in 1935 by Laval and Mussolini. For the next twenty years the Tunisian Italians were to remain Italian: children born after that time should be French citizens. As compensation, Laval agreed to the extension of Italian influence in Abyssinia: and Mussolini never ratified the pact he had made. The question at issue was not the status of Italian colonists but the possession of Tunis itself.

I was near the Tunis-Libyan frontier at the outbreak of the war. I found the Arabs fuming with hatred against the Italians and their claims. Next door, in Libya, Mussolini had settled 20,000 Italian families. He did it by banishing 80,000 Arabs to the semi-starvation of the desert, with many attendant cruelties. The story of these lost nothing in the telling as it passed from lip to lip across the desert. In Tunis it helped the

French: among the Arabs—who of course form the over-whelming numerical majority of the population—there is already a strong nationalist autonomist movement, akin to that in Syria. But the most fervent nationalist would rather see the French in Tunis than the Italians.

Mussolini must be one of the most disappointed men in Europe. He thought he saw a very easy way ahead when his satellites made their parrot cry, 'Savoy! Nice! Corsica! Tunis!' Some even added 'Djibuti' as well, but Italian aspirations in East Africa are today pitched in a lower key! Nor does it seem that Italy is destined to become the master of Tunis.

III

To Mussolini's chagrin, his threatening bluff failed. France might have a sense of inferiority beside Germany, but none beside Italy. The Duce glowered in his resentment while Hitler went from one prize to another—Memel and Czecho-slovakia. But by this time Italy was already cast for a sub-servient and minor part. At the outbreak of war, Hitler did not even call on his partner to join him: Italy would be more useful as a neutral—as a leak in the blockade. The plan was assisted by British and French policy, which still hoped to wean Italy away from Germany, as it had done in 1915. But history did not repeat itself.

Certainly Italy was not ready for war: the administration was corrupt, and there were serious deficiencies in supplies. But the rapid German victories in the spring of 1940 made Mussolini think that he was about to miss the boat. Here was a heaven-sent chance of getting booty without fighting. When France was already beaten, Italy entered the war. Ten days later France was suing for an armistice.

Alas for Mussolini, he had made two miscalculations. He had imagined that his partner would allow him to occupy large slices of French territory—that he would secure pos-session of Savoy, Nice, Corsica and Tunis. But Hitler was playing a deeper game—thinking ahead against the days when he would use France on his side. While German armies swept over France, the Italians were allowed to occupy a few frontier posts only!

The second miscalculation was far more serious. Mussolini had never imagined that Britain would carry on the fight alone once France had fallen. If he could have foreseen his military disasters in Tripoli, Libya and East Africa, he would have thought more than twice before plunging into the war. Today the state of his country is parlous. Mussolini has done more than to lose his empire; he has lost Italy, which is now little more than a German colony.

IV

At first, however, it seemed that he had made an appreciable gain in joining hands with Germany. After the wars of liberation fought in the middle of the last century, Italy recovered from Austria practically all the Italian-speaking provinces. The exceptions were the districts adjoining the north-east frontier, and the Trentino—then the Southern Tyrol. The strategic frontier in the Trentino was most unfavourable. The Austrians held all the passes and their military roads threatened some of the richest districts of Italy. Further, some 400,000 Italians were still under Austrian rule. Consequently the annexation of the Trentino was one of Italy's war aims, suitably agreed in the pact with Britain and France, which brought Italy into the war in 1915.

Apart from the valuable reinforcement, there was every sympathy in this country for Italy's aspirations. Nowhere in the world had there been such interest in her fight for freedom against her ancient enemy, and she fully appreciated the moral and material support she drew from Britain. I doubt if we realised that the allocation of the Trentino to Italy meant that over 200,000 Austrians would now pass under Italian rule. In 1919 we did not trouble very much about the feelings of our enemies—they had asked for what was coming to them.

Italy argued that strategy overruled any ethnic claims. It

was essential that her frontiers should march with the high mountains—that it should be quite impossible for Austria again to threaten Italy by her possession of the passes. Such argument was perfectly legitimate, and was held to be valid. The new Italian frontier repatriated the 400,000 Italians, and brought in 225,000 Austrians with them, as it advanced to the Brenner Pass.

The Brenner is the lowest of the Alpine passes—a mere 4500 feet above sea-level. A dozen times Teutonic raiders have swarmed over it to attack Italy. Its gradients are so moderate that both road and railway pass over it. The neighbouring mountains are stern and forbidding, a natural defence. The Italians set themselves to fortify the Brenner so that no enemy might pass.

The greatest problem was that of the Austrian population —which forms a homogeneous mass immediately adjacent to the frontier. An intense process of Italianisation began, of the type I have described in the Julian March section. German schools and newspapers were all closed down; place and street names were altered, and it was unsafe to speak German in a public place. I was once arrested myself for asking a policeman the way to a village, and referring to it by its old Austrian name. (I was released as soon as the policeman found that I was English; he had thought that I was German.)

But the German race is stubborn, and the Austrians of the northern Trentino are just as German as ever they were. I never met one of them who showed any signs of turning into an Italian: you did not need to be an ethnic expert to see where the Germans end and the Italians begin. Even in the darkest days there was always a feeling that the final frontier between Germans and Italians had not yet been drawn.

The defence of the Brenner frontier has legitimately formed a major issue of Italian policy. So long as a weak Austria squatted on the other side, there could be no danger to Italy. The emergence of Hitler changed the situation in a night. Italy succeeded France as the champion of Austria, and

Hitler was told quite plainly to keep out; that is one advantage of the dictators—they are accustomed to plain speaking.

The testing time came when Chancellor Dolfuss of Austria was murdered by the Nazis in 1934. For the moment it seemed that Hitler was about to invade Austria. Mussolini acted promptly, and an army encamped below the Brenner. The results seem to have justified the argument that Germany might have halted in 1914 had she been warned quite clearly of the consequences of invading Belgium—and that it would have paid to have warned her in 1939 of the consequences of invading Czechoslovakia. In 1934 it was made perfectly plain to Hitler that if he marched into Austria he must fight Mussolini: he was not prepared to fight Mussolini, so he did not march into Austria.

When Hitler did march into Austria in March 1938, Mussolini's army was not at the Brenner. Abyssinia had intervened. Mussolini, with almost all the world against him, desperately needed friends. Hitler was prepared to be his friend—at a price. The price was paid in March 1938, and within twenty-four hours German troops were on the Brenner.

'Mussolini, I shall never forget what you have done for me this day,' Hitler telegraphed. With no less than justice, for that day saw one of the keystones of Italian security violently swept away. The neutrality of Austria was just as vital to Italy as that of Belgium to England. When the news of the occupation of Austria came through, a well-known Italian journalist said to me (with great courage, since he used a name which is *tabu* in Italy): 'This is our biggest defeat since Caporetto.' Mussolini is a realist, and no fool. He could have held the Brenner for ever against a weak Austria, but with the might of Germany on the other side of the pass, its strategic value is worth about fourpence. Mussolini also is not likely to forget what he did for Hitler that day.

Sometimes the least publicised danger spot provides the biggest surprise. In the summer of 1939 a strange campaign opened in Trentino. Germans who had retained their nationality were given marching orders. Within a period, apparently, the district was to become purely Italian.

We have argued that an exchange of populations could often assist in the pacification of Europe. As we anticipated, the Germans of the Trentino were not so happy about this method of making the racial and strategic frontiers concurrent. They complained bitterly, indeed, about the leaders who had 'sold' them. A year earlier Nazi newspapers were publishing atrocity stories about Germans in the Trentino who were 'unable to secure fundamental human rights.' Now the down-trodden people found that the dictators had made a bargain over their heads. Three-quarters of them have been moved into Germany—another useful precedent for our post-war settlement.

Today the Trentino is Italian. Yet not even Mussolini can be happy at the situation. He is virtually a local *gauleiter*, acting for Hitler: Germans control the essential Italian services to an increasing extent. An Axis victory could only increase the Italian subserviency. The Trentino may be peopled with Italians, but it lies on the way to an ancient German ambition —the port of Trieste.

V

The problems of Italian frontiers can be decided fairly easily.

(*a*) The Italian claims for Savoy, Nice, Corsica and Tunis can be dismissed.

(*b*) The removal of the German population from the Trentino is a useful piece of clearing-up, so that Italy's northern frontier will stand.

(*c*) As we have seen in the Yugoslav chapter, there is a strong case for moderate frontier revision in the north-east, in accordance with economic requirements and the wishes of the inhabitants.

Should any form of Danubian federation be formed after the war, there may be a demand that it should be allocated its natural port, Trieste. Despite the mixed ethnic character of its hinterland, Trieste is largely Italian in population. A suitable basis of operation could probably be agreed by the allocation of special zones within the port: it is to the great advantage of Trieste to be in close economic touch with the middle Danube basin.

(*d*) Italy's claims in the eastern Adriatic are discussed in other chapters. She will, of course, have to give up the part of Dalmatia which she has seized, and her puppet kingdoms in Yugoslavia will take their place among the tragic humours of history. She will probably also lose Zara, the one enclave in Dalmatia she possessed. Its allocation was merely a concession to pride; economically it belongs to its hinterland. Any Italians who do not wish to become Yugoslav subjects can be evacuated to the home country: the number involved will be a few thousands only.

(*e*) Italy will withdraw from Albania. Her claims against Greece were always fantastic, and the campaign from Albania the least glorious in her history.

In spite of acts of treachery, the general attitude towards the Italian people is not of stern animosity, but of an almost amused tolerance. There seems to be a general assumption that Italy's African possessions will be returned to her—with the exception, of course, of Abyssinia.

Nevertheless, this tolerant outlook on Italy may harden as the war progresses, bringing increasing hardship in its train. The Atlantic Charter stated that we have no ambitions for Italian territory: this will hold good. It does not follow automatically that Italy is to be allowed to maintain or develop strategic bases which could always be a menace to the Suez Canal.

I have mentioned one idea which is being discussed—that Libya, or part of Libya, should be allocated as a settlement for Jews. In spite of intense efforts at colonisation, the European population is small. (In 1927 it was 33,000, but more settlers have been planted since then.) The native population is about

800,000—but this includes about 200,000 Jews, whose ancestors established themselves here three thousand years ago. Though Libya is now largely a desert, it was a thriving country centuries ago. By the folly of man large areas were allowed to go out of cultivation, but could again be reclaimed by a vigorous race.

The idea of a Jewish settlement in Libya would be vigorously opposed by the Arabs, who have visions of an independent Arab federation in North Africa. Italy would naturally protest at either scheme.

Her post-war position in Europe will be determined largely by the character of the new Italy—for it seems certain that the Fascist régime will disappear in the moment of defeat. In Germany we are going to have great difficulty in persuading the Germans to drop their warrior-complex: this presents no problem at all in Italy, where the average man has no pining for glory, but merely wants to be left to get on with his job.

CHAPTER FOURTEEN

GERMANY

I

THE importance of the various problems outlined in this book is not proportionate to the space I have allocated to them. Some are of minor import, but complex; others are interesting and representative examples, demanding lengthy exposition: the less we know about a problem in Great Britain, the greater our need for a detailed explanation.

Though this chapter is one of my shortest, it is perhaps the most important of all. After hundreds of my lectures I have been asked: 'What are we going to do with Germany after the war?' I do not pretend that my answers have satisfied either my questioners or myself.

Yet this is the most vital problem of all. The solving of all others depends so largely on the solution to this. I could perhaps avoid it, claiming weakly that I have undertaken no more than a superficial examination only of Europe's frontier problems. Yet, because these depend so largely upon the character of the new Germany, I must at least offer a few ideas as a basis for discussion: I cannot undertake to do more.

We can begin, I think, with one firm premise: that this war shall be the last, so far as human ingenuity can ensure. Five times in eighty years Germany has disturbed the peace of Europe: this must never happen again. This involves a firm application of the Eighth Point of the Atlantic Charter—the disarmament of Germany. I have suggested that the British outlook is likely to be as firm as any—for the first few years; then we may weaken or, more probably, lose interest. Fortunately, this attitude is not likely to be adopted by our allies, who have suffered more than ourselves and would suffer more again if a militaristic Germany revived.

Since we have to ensure *at all costs* against a repetition of the present tragedy, it follows that we have to be stern with Germany. This does not mean a wild revenge, much less the picture of massacre painted by Dr. Goebbels; it does mean that

GERMANY'S WAR LOSSES IN EUROPE

the inconvenience of a million Germans is of small account compared with the peace of Europe.

II

Before making up our minds on the problem of Germany's frontiers, it is perhaps necessary to clarify our minds in respect of the significance of Point Eight of the Atlantic Charter—the one which proclaims the unilateral disarmament of Germany.

First, it is necessary to insist that we are not merely fighting Hitler and the Nazis: we are fighting Germany. There is no need to enter into the argument whether all Germans are bad, or whether there are plenty of good among them; it is certain that 90 per cent are solidly ranged behind Hitler today. The fact that a fair proportion of these would desert him tomorrow if he failed is no consolation to us: weathercocks are of little use in statecraft—they only show which way the wind is blowing; they cannot divert it into a required direction.

We are, of course, fighting against the German War Machine we faced in 1914. In that year we talked a lot about German militarism and the Junkers. Maybe some of us did not appreciate very clearly what the terms meant, but surely we do now. Germany is like no other power in Europe: normally the State controls the Army, but in Germany the Army controls the State.

The Junkers, the German officer class, mostly scions of Prussian patrician families, heirs to the militarism of Frederick the Great, never pretended to accept the Treaty of Versailles. To them a peace was but an armistice, giving them time to prepare for the next battle. After guiding Germany's internal and external affairs for generations, they withdrew skilfully so that others might ensure the odium of peace terms which were bound to be onerous and unpopular.

They used their token army of 100,000 men as a cadre, ready to officer the vast force they contemplated. They loaned hundreds of officers to Russia, which country had lost most of her own in the World or Revolutionary wars. The Germans trained the Russians, as they were engaged to do—and also got constant practice in the handling of large bodies of men and of weapons forbidden in Germany. Their technicians and scientists prepared blue-prints for new and improved instruments of war: plants and jigs were assembled. At length, in view of the lethargic interest in France and Britain, these even made the prototypes of their new offensive weapons. Tanks were forbidden by the peace conditions, but I saw them in Germany *long before Hitler became Chancellor.* And, when I reported this fact, I found that I had brought no news.

Hitler seemed to the Junkers a useful instrument. He preached that the Germans had not really lost the war—a very comforting doctrine for militarists. They intended only to use him. After his rise to power, the German army was still a state within a state. Even the power of the Gestapo ceased at the barrack gates. I remember a German friend of mine who didn't like Hitler. What was more, Hitler didn't like him. He said to me: 'For safety, I must do one of two things: either I must emigrate, or else I must join the German army.'

When Hitler had firmly established himself in power, the German General Staff did not find him quite so pliable as they had expected. A succession of major and minor purges was necessary before the Nazis discovered men who would work intimately with them. But when a general was dismissed, another man was appointed—still a Junker, brought up as a part of the German War Machine. Hitler gained his first victory over the Junkers at the time of the march into the Rhineland. Of course they wanted to march as much as he did, but did not think that the time was ripe. He was confident that France and Britain would not move. So the Junkers marched: if France had mobilised, they were all ready to throw Hitler overboard.

There was no mobilisation. Indeed, in Britain there was not great interest. Hitler chose his time well. He marched in at a week-end, which was not playing the game. Besides, there was something much more exciting just then, a Cup Final or a Grand National, I have forgotten which.

After that the militarisation of Germany continued apace. The training of the raw conscript masses was very thorough. It is worth while pointing out that the Germans seldom invent things. They pick the brains of other people and develop their ideas. The only war weapon the Germans ever introduced was —poison gas. And even this was known in China three thousand years ago.

In their policy of rearmament the German General Staff used the plan Hitler adopted so successfully later—'little by little.' After this war they will try to do the same again. When defeat appears inevitable, they are quite capable of flinging Hitler over and appealing for a negotiated peace. If they got it, they would immediately commence their preparations for the next war.

They will do this even if their defeat is absolute. They really believe that the British in particular are degenerate, which is certainly not true; they also believe that both British and Americans are carelessly uninterested in European affairs, that we shall soon forget our stern outlook and relapse into an easy-going tolerance. This *has* been true in the past: it is not certain that the attitude of mind which engendered our weakness has yet disappeared. Indeed, there are still many thousands of sincere people who believe that if only Hitler would die, we could make peace with the kindly Germans they met in the Bavarian Alps or saw so dramatically in the Passion Play in Oberammergau.

The concentrated thought and teaching of generations will not disappear in a night. Hitler's *herrenvolk* ideas are only propagandist developments of older German culture. Long before Hitler was born, the Prussian Junkers had appropriated the Jewish idea of a chosen race and had adapted it to their own ends. Nietzsche developed the idea in his *Superman*. It would be as well if we reiterated daily that this is not merely a war against Hitlerite Germany.

Let us envisage the moment of victory and apply the lessons of past failures. First, Hitler, Goering, *and Keitel*, Chief of the General Staff and master of the German War Machine, must sign the surrender, so that any subsequent ignominy shall not be piled on the government which seeks to build up a new Germany. All the resources of publicity should be used to make it clear to the Germans what is happening.

Then the war criminals should be dealt with firmly *and rapidly*. The only real warning to gangsters is the fate of other gangsters.

Next, it must be brought home to the Germans that they

have lost, and *why* they have lost. It was argued after the last war that the Germans never realised their defeat: this is not true, for the miseries of the post-war years carried eternal reminders. But few Germans knew why and how they had been defeated, and long before Hitler the blame was freely laid upon Jews and democrats. The General Staff escaped criticism: indeed, Hindenburg was a legendary figure. 'Hindenburg is divine' screamed the publicists of the day. Later, Hitler merely had the mantle of divinity transferred to his own shoulders.

Defeat must be paraded throughout Germany. The smallest towns must see detachments of Allied troops, and hear Allied aeroplanes overhead. German victory marches should be copied in Berlin and the principal provincial cities. Actually I do not foresee any difficulty in persuading the Germans that they have really lost the war! For the first time in modern war, the battle has come home to Germany. At first a bombardment from the skies, effective morally as well as materially, the war may not conclude without a campaign across Germany. This would probably have a salutary effect.

The greatest efforts must be made to ensure a sense of *personal* responsibility in the Germans. All peoples try to shelter behind their governments: after the overthrow of Hitler, the Germans will certainly parade some form of real or pseudo-democracy. Responsibility should not be evaded so easily. It is generally agreed that the folly of extravagant demands for reparations shall not be repeated. (Though there seems to be no reason why the Germans should not be forced to honour the printed currency they have scattered about Europe. Further, in recent years the Nazis have been making huge investments abroad, especially in the Balkans, with a view to obtaining complete economic control of smaller states. These investments can be confiscated and can be set off against the huge cost of German ravages in the same countries.) There will, of course, be acute distress in Germany, even at the best, but this can be blamed on the Allies, not on themselves. What is necessary is a personal retribution. This was singularly lacking after the last war, *when no responsible German ever uttered a word of regret for all the devastation their armies had caused*: there was no contrition even for wilful damage and misery—not even from the Churches. All responsibility was collective—and could readily be transferred to the other side. Even a collective fine arouses only resentment, and seldom any consciousness of retribution.

Their individual measure of guilt can be brought home to the German people simply and effectively. The occupied countries have been systematically looted: it goes without saying that all machinery, art treasures, etc., which can be traced shall be returned. Further, individual contributions should be made. Devastating German armies have caused an acute shortage of household goods, bedding and similar equipment in Europe. Immediately after victory, the needs of the unhappy countries should be met from Germany. Every German house should give up part of its furniture, bedding and kitchen equipment, to be dispatched to Poland, Russia, Yugoslavia or one of the other outraged countries. The receipt should state clearly *why* it has been necessary to requisition the goods.

The first essential is to break the power of the German General Staff forever. This objective requires more careful planning than any of the others: it is vital. As a beginning, we might consider the following:

(*a*) There should be no German army of any size, not even a token force. The protection of German frontiers can be covered by international guarantee, backed by the Allied army of occupation. Nor should Germans be allowed to join foreign armies. Uniforms should be reduced to a minimum, and licence to use them be issued by an Allied authority. The prestige of the German General Staff depended to no small extent on the German passion for uniforms—itself an instinctive reaction to the German sense of inferiority, springing directly from their lack of education in political freedom. Only policemen should be allowed uniforms—even postmen should depend upon badges and armlets. Allied officers should be installed as observers in all police headquarters: the police would carry arms, for immediate internal conditions are likely to be stormy, but our observers must ensure that the force is not made an experimental military cadre.

We must face up to the fact that the German General Staff will try to get round any regulations we may make. They will bide their time, waiting for us to slip back into our old easy-going habits, short-sighted selfishness and mental laziness. Then they will form all kinds of apparently innocuous societies: 'The Organisation of German Foresters and Hunters,' for example. Our attitude should be made absolutely clear from the start, and exemplary methods should be used to deal with the first infringements. There will be Germans who will help to give us warning—though most of them will still be on the other side.

(*b*) Members of the German General Staff should share in the punishment meted out to war criminals. They are equally responsible with the Nazis for the opening of the war, and even more directly responsible for its innumerable breaches of international law. They, not the Nazis, first considered treaties as scraps of paper.

In deciding upon punishment for war criminals, the greatest care must be taken not to make martyrs of them. Hitler *could* be more dangerous dead than alive.

(*c*) No armaments should be manufactured in Germany. This applies to aircraft of all kinds. Civil aviation in Germany should be developed by an international company, using only aircraft manufactured abroad. (For that matter, an international European Airways Corporation, in charge of the entire civil aviation of the Continent, is already overdue.)

It should be proclaimed periodically—and especially when a new British or American government took office—that the policy stood indefinitely, and that the first sign of a tank, gun or aeroplane in Germany meant war.

(*d*) Germany should be allowed no navy. For any necessary protection of fishing rights or other purposes in local waters, small craft should be loaned to her by Britain or any other nominated power. Commander and crew would be British, but German fishery protection or coastguard officers would be on board to carry on their jobs. German shipyards would not be allowed to build warships for foreign powers.

(e) Bridgeheads on the Rhine should be established *without time limit*. The Siegfried fortifications should be destroyed or occupied by Allied troops. In the difficult period immediately after a German defeat, the armies of occupation would of course need to be spread over Germany, including Berlin and Munich. The garrisons on the Rhine should be permanent.

An Allied force of naval, military and air arms should also be established on the Kiel Canal, or within easy striking distance of it. We have envisaged a small movement of the Danish frontier south in Schleswig: it might be more convenient to establish our control force in this territory. Heligoland and other strategic islands may also be occupied for a lengthy period.

Perhaps more important, bridgeheads on the Oder should be established, to be held by Polish and Russian troops. The importance of this step lies in the fact that the eastern powers are not likely to forget so quickly as those in the west.

(f) On the other hand, our terms should be definite. They should be clearly stated—enforced to the uttermost limit, but never exceeded. The Germans must be given no second opportunity of saying that at the moment of victory they were inveigled into defeat under false pretences. Moreover, it is a fine characteristic of our people to feel sympathy for a beaten enemy, for the underdog. The Germans must not be allowed to take advantage of this generous trait; most of them do not understand it, and some of them would seek to abuse it.

These terms are designed to smash the power of the German General Staff—*not* as a punishment on the German people: indeed, the relief from the armaments burden could be considered a great advantage. The conditions are negative, to blot out the evil: from them we and the German people can begin to build the good.

III

On the whole, the population of Germany is very homogenous, except in the border regions, where there occurs the inevitable medley of populations. By the census of 1925—*i.e.* in the Versailles Reich, before Hitler's additions—the total population was 62,410,619: of these, little more than 2 per cent were non-Germans. This, it should be emphasised, is the German figure. Neighbouring states would place it as at least 50 per cent higher. It often happens that a man of mixed parentage speaks both languages with almost equal fluency; he is claimed as a national by both sides to the argument—and could easily be assimilated by either. The Germans have certainly classed as their nationals many people of foreign racial stock: often in records anyone who could speak German at all was counted as one.

Some of these minorities we have already met. The largest consists of the Poles. According to German figures, they numbered 721,000 in 1925: the Poles say that this figure is absurdly understated, and place it at 1,200,000. It is certainly far too low, for—apart from the fallacy of the language test as a basis of race—Germans have consistently included the Mazurians of East Prussia as Germans. This is quite wrong. The Mazurians are Slavs; they may not be purely Polish, but they are definitely not German.

For our purposes, if we agreed that there are approximately a million Poles in Germany, we should not stray far from accuracy. Of these, about two-thirds live in Upper Silesia, where they have retained their racial characteristics and language to a remarkable degree. Every form of Germanisation has been employed for many generations. Of the 300,000 Polish children in Germany, only 2000 were able to attend Polish schools. There was only one secondary school—and even this would have been closed down but for a Polish counter-threat to close the German schools in Poland. The Polish press was held down firmly even before the rise of Hitler: cultural institutions were scarcely allowed to exist. The policy of Germanisation was carried forcibly into religion—important to Poles. Of the Catholic priests to minister to the large Polish population, only six were Poles. There was not a single Polish Protestant pastor in Germany. In such circumstances it is remarkable that Polish racial consciousness has survived at all: actually it is stronger now than for many generations.

Of the remaining Poles, nearly 100,000 are to be found in East Prussia, a similar number scattered on the German side of the frontier between Silesia and the Baltic, while there are many thousands of Poles employed as miners in the Ruhr. We have already envisaged that the entire Polish minority will be incorporated within Poland, either as a result of modification of frontiers, or, more generally, by exchange of populations.

About Glatz, just north of the north-eastern frontier of Bohemia, is a small conclave of Czechs. By German statistics they number 12,000, but my own estimate would at least double that figure. Other observers go as high as 40,000. These should obviously be withdrawn into Czechoslovakia as Germans are expelled.

Actually, next in importance to the Polish minority is that which consists of the Lusatian Serbs. Few people in Britain have ever heard of them, but some astute tourists—and especially artists—have visited them in the Spreewald: it needs no ethnic knowledge to recognise that they are no Germans. Their costumes, language and customs are those of a milder culture.

The Lusatian Serbs are the sole descendants of the Slav tribes which once occupied the whole of the Elbe valley. Their ancestors were brutally massacred by those Teutonic Knights who later marched along the Baltic coasts. Traces of the Slav occupation can be found all over Eastern Germany. As far west as the Baltic island of Rügen there are frequent Slavonic place-names, and even more numerous archaeological reminders of the early Slav occupation.[1]

Actually the Lusatian Serbs are not Serbs at all: the present

[1] See map page 58.

name is a corruption of Sorbs, their tribal designation. They are also known as Wends. There is no dispute about their racial origin; they are Slavs, speaking a Slavonic language akin to Polish and Czech, and for centuries lived under Czech rule. They live in a district straddling the borders of Prussia and Saxony. According to official figures, they number no more than 81,000. A century ago, however, German official sources admitted that there were more than 150,000 of them, and it is unlikely that their numbers have decreased. Lusatian Serbs today claim a total of 160,000 for their tribe, pointing out with truth that they have been subjected to intense Germanisation. Nor had they the advantage of the Poles of a mother race from which they could draw cultural inspiration. They were a Slavonic island completely surrounded by a Teuton sea, and it is indeed remarkable that their race has survived at all. In the Prussian part of the Wendish area all children attend German schools; in Saxony, about one-third attend mixed schools.

The Lusatian Serbs are very much attached to their home-land and would require considerable inducements to move. They have not taken kindly to German militarism, however, and must hate to see generations of their young men decimated in wars which mean nothing to them. They might welcome the opportunity of colonising areas vacated by German set-tlers—in the Banat or East Prussia, for example.

IV

We can now pass to an examination of the post-war fron-tiers of Germany.

In the west, we have argued, there is likely to be little if any change in the country's boundaries. In the north-west the only question likely to be raised is that of the Danish frontier.

What should have been a successful example of the method of local plebiscites was carried out in 1919 in Schleswig. In 1864 Prussia seized the Danish provinces of Schleswig-Hol-stein after one of Bismarck's 'made' wars. In 1919 it was proposed to hand them back to Denmark, and a plebiscite was held. The southern section voted heavily for Germany, the middle portion was about half-and-half, and the northern half of Schleswig was preponderantly Danish. Denmark, very wisely, accepted this northern section only, so as to have no cause for future quarrel with Germany. It included a small German minority which on the rise of Hitler became very vociferous. The agitation served as a constant reminder of German power, and was a contribution to the surrender of Denmark almost without a blow to German aggression in April 1940. Actually, there were more Danes in Germany than there were Germans in Denmark: both minorities were negligible. Here is one case where exchange of population could be carried out without harm to individuals and with permanent gain to both states.

There are about 15,000 Danes in Germany. We have seen that Denmark refused to recover them because it involved taking over a German minority as well. This sensible gesture was evidently not appreciated by the Nazis. It may be considered policy to push the Danish frontier south for strategic purposes: in a previous section we have mentioned the prospects of an Allied occupation of the Kiel Canal zone, or at least of an area from which it could be commanded.

v

This brings us to a very important point: consideration of the eastern frontiers of Germany. As in the case of the Fourteen Points, some of the clauses of the Atlantic Charter seem to clash, in spirit if not in words. Clause 2 suggests that any territorial changes should agree with the wishes of the populations involved. Point Eight insists upon the effective disarmament of Germany, so that it shall never again be possible for her to inflict war upon Europe. We now have to decide which of these two principles is the more important.

We must expect other people's views to be more emphatic than our own. Despite our losses, we have only felt the fringe of the war. Countries like Poland, Russia and Yugoslavia have felt its full force, accompanied by atrocities unparalleled since the Middle Ages—not the excesses of hot blood, but outrages deliberately planned and violently executed. To these people there is no argument. In all circumstances the English Channel gives the British some measure of security. They have none and they are determined that this time there shall be no half-measures—that *never* again shall Germany be placed in a position whence she can ravage Europe.

Hence the firm demand that she shall be so weakened industrially and territorially that revenge is impossible. With Upper Silesia given to the Polish-Czech federation, and with East Prussia added to Poland, Germany would be so weakened and her neighbours so strengthened that military resurgence would be difficult if not impossible even if there were hesitation in the west. It is certain that we shall have to face a demand for the cession of East Prussia on strategic grounds. Less than two million Germans are involved: perhaps only half of them would have to be moved. Why should we consider the feelings of a million Germans, when they have littered the fields of Europe with millions of our dead? A bold stroke like the seizure of East Prussia might ensure the peace of Europe as nothing else could.

Why should we concern ourselves over German pride? Rather, why should we not strike hard at the very root of that Prussianism which is admittedly our real enemy? Turn the Junkers from their lands, source of their power; then they will lose half their influence at a blow. At the same time, tell the Germans continuously *why* it was done—don't wait for apologists to invent excuses to prove that Germany never made the war, and that she never lost it. Let there be no possible doubt: and let it be reiterated continuously that the move is permanent and final. The effect would be salutary.

Such are the arguments we shall have to face, and they are strong. If we are convinced that the disarmament of Germany is the first essential of the peace, then the move is not illogical.

Is there any problem of peace and war in Europe once the German menace is banished for ever? Britain and Russia alone, by their influence, could secure the small nations or the new federations against war—always providing that the German menace *is* removed for ever.

Probably the consensus of opinion in Britain today is in favour of the complete demilitarism of Germany. What will it be in ten or twenty years' time? If we are determined to pursue a European policy, then we can sit back and consider the arguments on both sides with due deliberation. If it appears likely that we propose to slip back into our island shell, then we can scarcely blame the Poles and others if they seize points of future vantage, for they will certainly need them.

VI

While the German western frontiers need scarcely be changed, therefore, we shall have to give very serious attention to those in the east. We must face up to the fact that the loss of East Prussia would be bitterly resented by all Germans— even the 'good' Germans so prominently displayed in the arguments of some propagandists. Most of these Germans hold similar opinions about the 'Corridor'. The opinion of Otto Strasser, leader of one of the anti-Nazi parties, is interesting. Though generally he is most moderate, even offering to pay substantial reparations to Poland to rebuild her devastated towns and in acknowledgement of the bitter wrong of the German attack, he declares that no German government, whatever its 'colour' or creed, would ever accept the loss of East Prussia. Further, he apparently envisages taking the Corridor area from Poland, compensating her with the Baltic states or Russian territory! If this is the view of a moderate German, that of the extremists can be guessed. However, we are planning a peace for the benefit of Europe, not for the solace of Germany.

At the same time, such a move would contradict directly our other proviso—that for the peace to be truly permanent, it must ultimately be accepted by Germany. A great deal would depend on the mental presentation of the case, and on the subsequent treatment of the German people.

A problem much discussed is the internal shape of Germany after the war. Much will depend on this new form. Had we supported the Weimar government, which showed at least the first signs of democracy, then a different situation might have arisen. Our problem is difficult: to ensure peace, and at the same time to support a sound Germany, without which Europe is incomplete.

There are in all countries jingoes who talk airily about the 'extermination' of Germany. The idea is immoral and absurd. The Romans killed or enslaved the men of Carthage, and carried off the women: but that is no example for us. In any case, there were 100,000 Carthaginians: there are over 80 million Germans. Europe hates them now, but one day will need them.

In the early days of the war, before serious fighting developed, one idea was widely canvassed. It was alleged in France to emanate from the Vatican, but I was never able to obtain the slightest confirmation of this. After defeat, Germany would be divided into two: in the south, there would be a Catholic Germany to which we should be kind; in the north, a Protestant Germany to which we should not.

Such a scheme would merely cry out for a new unifying Hitler. At least it touches on one essential—the necessity for repressing the power of Prussia. An artificial division of Germany into two portions would merely irritate everybody. Instead, we should use the provincial patriotism which still exists in many parts of Germany. It is not nearly so strong as it was a generation ago—the Nazis made a violent onslaught upon it—but it does still exist, and should be encouraged. Its appeal should be the basis of our radio propaganda: the Prussians are not popular in other parts of Germany: Hitler would not have had such an easy rise to power had he been a Prussian instead of an Austrian.

Our aim should be the re-establishment—by Germans, not by exterior force—of the old German states of Bavaria, Saxony, Württemberg and so on. Prussia should be deprived of

THE STATES OF GERMANY

her more recent acquisitions: without Hanover and the Rhine provinces (which should form separate states) her domination would lose more of its force. These states would all be united in a German Federation, of course, and foreign and economic affairs would be controlled by a German Parliament. Local government would be entirely in local hands—with Saxon officials in Saxony. It is difficult for an Englishman or an American to realise the power of local officials in a firmly regulated state. The dismissal of Prussians from provincial posts would be in itself a revolution in Germany.

The development of the new Germany should be left to the fullest possible extent to Germans. Our main purpose is to ensure that a militant state never again threatens the peace of Europe. What happens inside Germany is primarily (but not exclusively) the affair of Germans. There is nothing to prevent the federated provinces from taking different forms—republics, monarchies or cantonal commonwealths, of different political lines: totalitarian states are scarcely likely to arise without uniforms and without arms!

Berlin would revert to the capitalship of Brandenburg only: a new capital for the German Federation would be necessary. Ratisbon (Regensburg) is an obvious candidate: so, in certain circumstances is Vienna.

The case of Austria has been much debated. Obviously her future depends very largely on the wishes of the Austrians. Her old place in the world is gone; she was the centre of an empire—a political rather than an ethnic organisation. When she failed to control the medley of provinces, refusing to realise that peoples of varying races can be ruled by democratic methods but not by force, then her empire broke up, and the *raison d'être* of Austria had gone; she became a German province with no specific reason for independent existence. An entirely independent Austria is an anachronism, if only from the economic point of view. The Austria of 1919–38 can scarcely be revived: or, if she were revived, could not exist.

There are two possibilities. Austria, joining a Polish-Czech-Hungarian Federation, might restore the economic unity of the middle Danube basin. Or she might prefer to continue as a state within the German Federation. Austrian friends of mine, sincere anti-Nazis, men who have suffered for their faith, confess with sorrow that they believe that Austria today or in the immediate future would choose the latter course. They may be wrong—they hope they are. Our first task is going to be to find out, and it is not going to be easy.

Plebiscites are suggested as panaceas for all frontier evils. We have argued that a plebiscite is only effective when it is held under conditions which are not merely fair, but which are recognised as fair by all contesting parties. This is a condition most difficult to realise.

It is almost impossible to hold a satisfactory plebiscite in the turmoil of the immediate post-war months, when tempers are still strained and hot blood forbids calm judgment. I have argued, too, that the character of the local authority affects the voting, particularly so far as the less secure sections of the population are concerned, since they are especially liable to direct or indirect pressure from employers or local officials. Thus, a plebiscite held in any German frontier province with German police in the offing and with German employers and 'patriotic' societies threatening voters with dire consequences, is always likely to favour Germany. It is not enough to send in Allied troops merely to control the mechanism of the plebiscite and to guard voters on the day of election. For a really free choice, we should have to occupy *and police* the area for a considerable period, probably years, before taking a final vote. In the meantime, the people of the province have to live.

The plebiscite recommends itself as a method when no other principle is involved. It could be used freely in Balkan territorial disputes, for example, since these generally affect only the two countries directly interested. Where Germany is concerned, the overriding consideration is that of security. A large majority of the people of East Prussia would most certainly vote *against* secession from Germany. We have, however, accepted the democratic principle that the few shall not be allowed to dominate the welfare of the many.

The advantages of the German Federation I have suggested are that (*a*) it would add to the security of Europe by limiting the power of Prussia, primarily responsible for the militarisation of Germany; (*b*) it would not cripple the economic, social or cultural development of Germany; (c) while it would arouse considerable opposition, it would be supported by a considerable section of German opinion. It is the only scheme, indeed, which could command a reasonable German backing. This point is very important.

We may, therefore, see on the map of Europe a German Federation composed of such historic states as Prussia, Bavaria, Austria, Saxony, Mecklenburg, Hanover, Schleswig-Holstein, Oldenburg, Westphalia, Thuringia, Württemberg, Hesse and the Rhenish Provinces. This list is not final. One or two others of the historic states may be deemed by their people to be sufficiently important for local autonomy. On the other hand, there should be no return to the maze of pigmy states and free cities which once comprised Germany.

Since Prussia and all it stands for are the major objectives of all our precautions, it might be advisable to let the name disappear entirely from the map of Germany. We have already detached Hanover and the Rhine; the remainder could be split up into the old provinces of Brandenburg, Pomerania and Silesia. This would be a mortal blow to Prussian power.

Although ideas in Germany have tended strongly towards unification in the last half-century, and especially in the last ten years, there still exist ample traits of the provincial tendencies which helped to make German culture and social life strong, but which weakened her military strength. The feudal, aggressive, warlike spirit of the Prussians was countered—ineffectively, in the long run—by the artistic, philosophic dreams of the Bavarians and Rhinelanders. In between came the materialists of the industrial districts of Saxony and the Ruhr. They were not so dangerous to European peace except as part of a lopsided economic system. They accepted the ideas of the French Revolution and then those of Napoleon: Herr Krupp wore a *tricolore* sash!

In the federated scheme local ideals would grow in force: local patriotisms would re-emerge. The separation of Germany into its component states would be a considerable advance towards the security for which we plan. We must face up to the fact, however, that although this plan is more acceptable to many Germans than any other, it would be violently opposed. Merely because its decentralisation came about as a result of defeat in war, the re-unification of Germany would become a solemn patriotic duty. Immediately the palsy of defeat had been shaken off, there would be serious movements to that end. This would be our testing time—not immediately after victory, when our power would be absolute. We ought not to consider the division of Germany unless we are prepared to maintain that division.

It will not be easy. The danger may not arise from new Hitlers—these at least we ought to be able to recognise when we see them—but from statesmen, honourable in their own lights, who will try to persuade us that their ideas are for the good of Europe. Stresemann was such a leader. He was able to persuade many of his honesty: yet he was no European, but purely German. He was ready to accept many of the imposed conditions in the west (though he never abandoned hope of recovering Alsace-Lorraine) if he could gain a free hand in the east. In the next twenty years we are likely to meet few Hitlers but many Stresemanns. The fundamental principles of our policy should be decided *now*. We in Britain have already lost much moral ground because of our inconsistency. We ought not to have agreed to the formation of Czechoslovakia, for example, unless we were determined to maintain it. Fortunately, Europe's faith in our good word has been regained to some extent by our courage in battle, but we cannot afford to lose it again: and battle is an elementary and expensive method of recovering trust. We have to convince our friends, when we make the new peace treaty, that we mean what we say: above all, we have to convince the Germans.

I have emphasised that many among us will be weary at the moment of victory. In Britain as in America, there is bound to be some clamour for return to isolationism. If we retire from Europe after victory we shall betray our friends: by the Atlantic Charter we have already agreed not to do this.

VII

One of our first tasks after victory will be to rewrite the German history books. Perhaps our second task will be to rewrite our own. History will have to be taught on a world rather than a national basis.[1]

Much has been written, and more debated, about the re-education of Germany after the war. Except among thoughtful men, there is a tendency to regard this as absolutely necessary and relatively easy: the first premise is right, the second wrong.

Indeed, it is going to be intensely difficult. An entire generation of twelve million German children has been educated on a Nazi basis. It is much easier to learn than to unlearn.

Yet we must not be discouraged by the immensity of the task. History and other textbooks can be rewritten, but our crisis will be in the shortage of teachers to use them. Yet not all the German teachers of today are Nazis—though they are Germans: our re-writing of German history must be fair or they will not teach it. We must not expect them to teach a perverted history, any more than we would expect our own teachers to do it at home.

There are potential teachers among the thousands of *émigrés*. While we are training others, we may have to loan German-speaking teachers from Britain and the United States: especially the latter, for there is not such a prejudice against Americans as against British—not at present, at any rate. Perhaps some clever man can write a history book which can be universally used.

(The regionalism of the new Germany should not be overlooked in planning the education of its children. The approach to history, for example, might very usefully differ in Hanover and Bavaria.)

---

[1] It was significant that H. G. Wells' *Outline of History* was translated into German and widely sold in pre-Hitler days, but was promptly banned by the Nazis on their accession to power.

In spite of all difficulties, it is possible to foresee a new angle to the education of the present generation of German children. But the young men and women in the twenties to thirties of today? These present our biggest problem. After defeat, they will not be convinced that Nazism is an evil creed, but they will merely feel that they have been defeated by superior force. Their immediate reaction will be to plan ahead the accumulation of a force yet stronger. (The first move of a disarmed Germany must necessarily be towards powerful alliances. It is almost certain that the defeated state will make attractive approaches to either Britain or Russia, or both, either after defeat or immediately before it.)

It will be useless to impose on these people the dictum that Germany was solely responsible for the war. They can only be persuaded—and that will take a long time. Our attitude meanwhile will be clear: inside their own country Germans can do pretty much as they please; but they shall never be allowed again to move beyond their own frontiers. Indeed, it should always be made clear that we march at the first sign of a recurrence of military power.

We must adopt Hitler's principle, and repeat this until we are sick of it. Of all the peoples in Europe, the Germans are most susceptible to propaganda. They have never known political freedom; are unaccustomed to the habit of individualistic thought. I doubt if even Hitler, or Stalin, could ever cultivate the mass mind in Britain, even if he had military control of our islands. The fact that the Germans are so susceptible to mass persuasion lightens our task; but does not make it easy—for, like the Russians, the Germans tend to adopt a patriotic creed almost as a religion.

We shall be aided to some considerable extent by the fact that the Nazi régime has identified itself so closely with the war. This argument may not appeal to fervent Nazis, but it certainly will to millions of Germans who follow Hitler today but might desert him tomorrow. He has staked everything on victory—has left himself no line of retreat: his doctrine of *herrenvolk* simply does not envisage a quiet decent German getting on with his job—at home; it is built on conquest. Most Germans share his dream today; but when he fails, it will be possible to persuade some of them that the dream was evil. They will see the other side of the 'master race' ideal when some other race are the masters and not themselves!

Much will obviously depend on the conditions prevailing at the moment of defeat. Germany will be utterly exhausted —only an exhausted state would ever surrender: Dr. Goebbels is right when he preys on the minds of his people as to their fate if they lose. All the fiery speeches of our 'exterminators' are duly quoted; coupled with the knowledge of atrocities and hatred in the occupied countries, they help to breed the courage of despair: a very dangerous courage.

Many Germans remember vividly the appalling weeks and months which followed their collapse in 1918. They are likely to struggle to the last to avoid a repetition: unless we can persuade them that our ideas have changed. We have already announced that our policy does not include starvation—that immediately after victory we shall send food into Germany. This is very wise; it gives us a first-class propaganda weapon which should be firmly exploited in the last months of the campaign; but it will not influence the outlook of post-war Germany to any great extent. No single act will relieve the hatred born of resentment and despair. We must depend upon a combination of deeds and words in a single policy.

Perhaps Nazi Germany will be decisively defeated in the field. This would be better for our purpose than a slow economic strangulation. Military defeat leaves a smaller legacy of hate than a prolonged blockade, and is more readily recognised as defeat. Further, the prestige of the Nazi régime is inextricably bound up in military victory.

Some people pin their hopes on a German rising against the Nazi leaders. This is only likely *after* a military defeat. History has shown that revolutions need long and careful preparation; they may appear on the surface as spontaneous outbursts, but they are not. There has never been a revolution in Germany—this is one of the causes of the political backwardness of the country—and there is no immediate sign of one ahead. We cannot depend on the German people to win the war for us: until they face defeat, they are wholeheartedly our enemies.

Whatever the form of the German defeat, we must use to the full the hours of disillusion which will immediately follow, and during which ideas can be implanted.

I have suggested that the military party in Germany is likely to throw over the Nazis in a last effort to save the situation; they themselves would retire into the background when all was irretrievably lost, so that they could pass on to others the odium of surrender. Probably one of them would stay on to play the Hindenburg. They may stage some temporary government of 'moderates' in an effort to secure more lenient terms.

We are then faced with the difficulty of finding responsible people with whom we can negotiate. This in itself is going to be difficult. When Napoleon was defeated, there were always the Bourbons—Europe could go back to the old days. The Bourbons had roots; they were far too deep, but they were known. When we had dethroned the Kaiser, there was no ready-made alternative in Germany: the Weimar Republic had no roots—no traditions: that in Germany meant no authority. It was never understood or appreciated; its only associations were with defeat.

With whom shall we negotiate? Not the military clique, for they are our real opponents, the baneful influence which must be extirpated. The 'moderate' leaders who may be formed into a government at the moment of despair? Most of these are to be counted among the men who followed Hitler when he was winning. They will endeavour to prove to us that they have really been in opposition all the time—and of some of them this may be true; it is seldom possible to make a demonstrative opposition in a dictator state. Some of these opposition Germans will be worthy of trust, but shall we find ourselves able to trust them?

Many people favour a government formed by *émigrés* from Nazi persecution. Many of these are likely to be invaluable to us and to Germany in the desperate post-war days. At the same time they can scarcely take over the government of Germany. Most of them are quite unknown there and carry no authority. By the nature of the persecution, a large proportion are Jews—and if we installed a Jewish government in Germany it would make all Hitler's predictions come true.

It is probable that the first post-war government of Germany will be provisional, under Allied control; it may even include members of parties we do not like, for the first essential is the preservation of order. Otherwise it is easy to foresee complete chaos. Hitler has already nominated *gauleiters* to rule over districts of conquered Britain—there are even Welsh- and Gaelic-speaking men among them for the appropriate areas. I suggest that we should now decide on the men who should take over the temporary control of Germany; they should be relieved of all other duties to study the problems of their respective districts: not all of them would be British, by any means—among our allies we have ample fields of choice. As Germany settled into order, they could be gradually withdrawn.

The preliminaries for this course of action have already been arranged. The Schools of Military Government at Oxford and Charlottesville have given a wide training to many first-class men.

I believe that these men, with their attendant forces for police purposes, would be welcomed by many Germans. There is a real fear throughout the land that defeat can only be followed by massacre and civil war and famine. We should make the alternatives clear: the firmest control will be preferred to massacre and famine.

Above all, even if Hitler and his friends have been relegated to the background as a measure of ingratiation, they should be hauled to the fore again to sign the terms of surrender.

CHAPTER FIFTEEN

THE NEW EUROPE

I

TERRITORIALLY, we have argued, the changes in the European scene imposed by peace treaties are likely to be far less violent than they were in 1919. Summarising briefly, we can say:

(*a*) Changes of frontier in the west, if any, will be very small.

(*b*) The eastern boundaries of Germany, particularly East Prussia and Silesia, provide one of our major problems, but one which should be considered firmly.

(*c*) The once-difficult problem of Russian-Polish relations is likely to be smoothed out by common sense and comradeship in arms.

(*d*) On the other hand, the future standing of the Baltic states may occasion some difficulty.

(*e*) In the Balkans, Bessarabia hangs in suspense. Few people after victory will be especially interested in Roumania, but her claim should not be hopelessly prejudiced by the conduct of her government.

(*f*) Bulgaria will keep the Southern Dobrudja, but otherwise will retire immediately to her frontiers of 1938.

(*g*) Italy may have to face Yugoslav demands for a portion of Istria, or the Julian Marsh, and will also retire from Albania.

(*h*) Transylvania will be divided between Hungary and Roumania approximately in the proportion of the respective populations, but with the Magyars transplanted to districts adjacent to the 1938 Hungarian frontier.

(*i*) Czechoslovakia will be restored and the agreement of Munich cancelled.

Many of the moves are likely to take place spontaneously in the moment of victory—as in 1918, when the peace treaties often did little more than to confirm an existing state of affairs.

We have argued in favour of an organised transfer of minority populations, since no land frontier can ever be totally satisfactory to both parties, and since nationalism is likely to be a powerful force in all countries—especially the occupied lands, where it has been stimulated rather than subdued by Nazi oppression. This migration should be internationally organised and financed over a period of years. Minorities who prefer to remain behind must be prepared to lose their nationality. An English emigrant to America, after a period of probation, ceases to hold any British rights and becomes an American. A German who elects to live in Poland will similarly be classed and treated as a Pole.

All this should be planned *now*, at least in general terms. It may be foolish to count your chickens before they are hatched, but it is only prudent to make arrangements for gathering the harvest once you have planted the seed.

The proposed transfer of populations will be unpopular in the regions affected. The more advanced the standard of life, the more repugnant the prospects of a move. In Eastern Europe the problem is less complex.

Yet, in spite of the nationalist fervour which will be abroad in Europe, we have to provide something better. It will not be easy. The little countries which have struggled so desperately to retain their national identity are not going to surrender it for an impractical ideal.

We must, therefore, move a sure step at a time, and each step must be impelled by community of interests. Perhaps our best example is the Pan-American Congress rather than the British Empire. Indeed, the commonwealth of British nations is in some respects less close than it was a quarter of a century ago; there is no suggestion that the dominions will ever be content to merge their identities or even their major interests in a purely British structure. This does not mean that the Empire is unsound in its foundations. On the contrary: the fact that decisions like peace and war have been unanimously approved (except by Eire) is a sign of community of interests which is more forceful than sentiment.

Nor can we expect all progress to be rapid. The war, like most evils, has produced some good. Relations between Russia and Britain, and between Russia and Poland, have been clarified to such an extent that the event may have a major influence on European affairs. Yet the progress of peace has had set-backs. One of the obviously desirable things in Europe is a strong Balkan combination. Today Yugoslavia and Greece are closer together than they were in 1938, due to common misfortunes and common interests. On the other hand, they are much further away from Bulgaria and Roumania than they were; the conduct of their neighbours has occasioned bitter feelings which will not be easily assuaged by a change in the character of their governments.

It is important to recall constantly that the New Europe sketched in this book is only a beginning, not an end: a firm foundation on which a bigger edifice can eventually be erected as man's outlook broadens.

In the first chapter we considered some aspects of the next step after justice is done. In the light of our rapid review of some of Europe's problems, we must return to this point again.

II

I have confessed that I look upon a World Federation as a distant ideal. When I argue with Federalists I cannot disprove their many contentions—indeed, I agree with most of them—yet I find that many of them fail to consider the difficulties of the details involved. More than one ideal has never been attained because its backers overlooked the small intricacies in their view of their goal. The man who imagines, for example, that Poles and Germans in our lifetime will dwell side by side in peace and friendship is either a fool or shockingly uninformed.

A World Federation, too, would have to be real: the League of Nations lost a considerable part of its potential force because the United States refused to join it. A World Federation would lose practically the whole of its force if the United States stayed outside.

American friends assure us that opinion in the United States on such projects is not even as advanced as our own—which itself is limited enough: we have been brought up as Nationalists, and under the present circumstances few of us are prepared to underwrite all-risk policies with which we have no direct concern. A federation is like an alliance—it must be impelled by some definite purpose. For example, a federation between Belgium and Bulgaria would be meaningless: who could expect a Belgian to risk his life and liberty for a Bulgarian danger? Or to admit Bulgarian workmen, with their lower standards of living, to Belgium where the inevitable result would be Belgians ousted from work by cheap labour? There would be no vital purpose behind such a strained partnership. But a close alliance between Belgium and Holland, or between Bulgaria and Yugoslavia, would be intrinsically sound.

In June 1940 Mr. Churchill made a last attempt to keep France in the war by offering a solemn bond of union, going considerably beyond the usual limits of federation. The incident is almost forgotten today. How long is it since you heard it mentioned? I have said that it was generally looked upon merely as a desperate effort to keep France in the war. It aroused no enthusiasm either at the time or when sober reflection was possible. Yet Britain and France are two advanced countries with many vital communal interests: if federation is to be our watchword, then Britain and France ought to be the first two countries involved. But can we claim that we are even now mentally prepared for such a step?

The representation of the countries of the world in the

suggested Federated Parliament is another matter of grave concern. It is normally argued that representation would be based on democratic principles—say, one member for every million inhabitants. Unfortunately, it so happens that the most progressive nations of the world are heavily outnumbered by others not so advanced; for example, China would have 450 members, India 350, Russia 160, Japan 90, Britain 45 and Australia 6. This means that China, India and Japan could at any time out-vote the rest of the world put together! Thus, if these three countries decided that all the cotton mills in Lancashire should be closed down and the manufacture of cotton transferred to Japan, India or China, then there would be nothing to be said—in theory, at any rate. Or if the Asiatic countries decided that their peoples should be entitled to emigrate in unlimited numbers to Australia, there could be no combating their right to do so. By this time, it will be remembered, under a World Federation there could be no question of the defence of Australia by force.

I suggest that the people of Great Britain are not yet in the state of mind when they are prepared to witness such happenings. I am quite certain that the peoples of most other countries are not. Impelled by the miseries they have suffered by the war, and by the fear of their recurrence, some of the smaller peoples may be prepared to give up some portion of their national privileges in association with their neighbours or with some strong power. This is perhaps the practical way in which federalism may come. It differs from the old system of alliances in that, once sovereign powers are surrendered, it will be difficult to reclaim them. Further, one successful federation, however limited, may prove an example to be widely followed.

I have emphasised that, once victory is assured, we may see another surge of Nationalism akin to that of 1919. Nations will only make alliances which favour their security; only for that purpose are they likely to surrender any of their sovereign powers. Can you see Belgium giving up any of her sovereign powers to Bulgaria, or Australia to Japan? Can you see the United States giving up any of her sovereign powers to anybody?

This last is perhaps the strongest objection to the proposed union of the English-speaking peoples. In the long run I believe it would be of immense benefit to mankind, but the immediate and economic difficulties are so intense that any attempt to force the scheme would be fatal. It seems certain that American opinion is by no means prepared for such a fusion of interests; it is equally certain that millions of British people believe that since the United States is today of such vital strength, any such amalgamation would mean inevitably that the United States would be the predominating and thus the ruling partner. These considerations do not rule out the closest possible co-operation between Britain and the United States. Indeed, this is essential if civilisation is to survive, much less to advance. Intrinsic federation would follow more firmly from years of practical and single-aimed association than from months of talk. Conclusive argument is not enough: often the mind defies mere reason.

Even a European Federation is decidedly ambitious in view of the present immaturity of public opinion. It involves automatically the admission of Germany—it would be meaningless without Germany. Again, the limited outlook of the European peoples is the greatest difficulty to the culmination of such an ideal; nevertheless even a Federation of Europe is an easier objective than that of a world. Not many people can think in terms of hemispheres.

III

I suggest that nothing we have seen in our perambulations about Europe promises more satisfying immediate and distant results than a series of regional federations. I emphasise again that these will not abolish war, but they will make the path to war much more difficult. If Europe survives the next fifty years in peace, then war may be banished for ever.

Some of the suggested regional federations have already

been considered—one or two are already in the first stages
of construction. Poland and Czechoslovakia have made the
first move. Their union might be joined by Lithuania (and
possibly Estonia and Latvia) and Hungary (and possibly Austria). There has been some talk of the federation being extended to cover the Balkans as well. My own opinion is that a
separate Balkan federation is advisable, joined to the Central
European block by the closest ties. If a customs union between
all countries involved in both federations could be organised,
then we should have made a first-class advance.

Denmark, Norway, Sweden and Finland form another
obvious combination; they have the prime essentials to a successful union—communal interests and approximately equal
standards of life. Estonia and Latvia may have a choice to
make between association with the Scandinavian group, the
Central European bloc or Russia.

Germany, we have suggested, is a federation in herself: so,
obviously, is Russia. There is no natural partner for Italy,
unless she joined with Spain and Portugal in a Latin federation. It is not essential by any means, however, that every
country in Europe should be included in a federation. There
is no reason on earth, for example, why Switzerland should
not pursue her old course of honoured independence. Or she
might feel attracted by the protective and economic power of
the Western European Federation composed of Britain,
France, Holland and Belgium.

Not all these groupings are likely to be made immediately
after the war: this is indeed improbable. They require the
most careful preparation, not merely in economic or political
fields, but in the minds of men. This mental preparation can
only be accomplished in times of peace—a real peace, not the
excited aftermath of war. The issues are large. If federation is
to be the key to world peace, it must be irrevocable: the
Dutchman has to learn to appreciate that when he surrenders
his national rights to the Western European Federation, he
surrenders them for ever.

Further, means must be studied for the closest co-operation between the different federations, both in the economical and political spheres. The abolition of customs dues between the Balkan states would be a considerable advance—which would be nullified if the Balkan Federation set up high tariffs against the rest of Europe. There are signs that this mistake will not be made. The Scandinavian states are likely to remain within the 'sterling bloc' and to work in collaboration with us. It seems certain, too, that the Polish-Czech Federation will also be in close agreement with us on the major affairs: may even be associated in the 'sterling bloc.' This feature of post-war development will be important: customs barriers can be as great a disturbant of peace as political frontiers. Shrinking distances impel closer economic relationships.

After the last war the economy of Europe was gravely disturbed by the sudden creation of dozens of new currencies. It would be a great advantage if many of these could be abolished. The countries associated with us in the 'sterling bloc' might adopt the pound as their basis of currency: for the British part, we should have to agree to a decimal system—by no means difficult. The basic unit would be five pounds and the shilling: the only coin to alter in value would be the penny, which would be counted ten to the shilling. It will be rather surprising if some development of this kind does not mature.

If Anglo-American collaboration became as vital a thing as many of us hope, a sterling-dollar bloc would revolutionise the economic life of the world. Not many countries would want to stay outside it!

The frontiers we have suggested are a beginning, not an end. Regional federations may be the next stage, and these will not necessarily develop immediately. Even these are ultimately not enough.

Continental federation might perhaps best be approached by a European Senate, including representatives of all federations and nations. To this should be submitted all proposed major legislation affecting foreign affairs, international economics and defence. In the first instance the power of the Senate might be only advisory—its function would be to ensure that no nation took action which would harm others. If it declared to this end, the moral effect would be great.

The complete disarmament of Germany and the other aggressive powers means that the rest of the states of Europe will be able to reduce their own armaments to a serious degree. It should be possible to secure against further aggression by air power alone. The international control of a European air force may not come in our lifetime; but, when it does, the outlook for peace will be bright.

In the past there has been a natural tendency to judge the strength of a nation by its expenditure on arms. The time may come when a country is judged by the amount it spends on education and culture.

IV

Some at least of the difficulties once envisaged have been removed. The German attack on Russia, for example, solved many problems. Others will disappear or decline in importance as the war progresses: on the other hand, new ones may arise.

There was at one time a fear that the Germans would succeed in Nazifying the occupied countries. This is now improbable, to say the least. Instead, Europe is a maze of resistance and sabotage, and at the first sign of weakness the Germans will find their subject people actively against them. Even in Holland, where bribes, threats and advantages have been freely employed, the Germans have been unable to increase the local Nazi party beyond 100,000. (In deploring this, the German apologist gave away the secret of Nazi strength; he explained that pre-war Holland was so prosperous that the Nazi movement could make but little headway!)

Another group of thoughtful men wondered if the peoples of Europe would be too exhausted to reap the harvest of victory—Britain by her world-wide exertions, Russia by her heavy fighting, the subject peoples by the effort of resistance under conditions of unparalleled harshness.

I do not share this apprehension. My fear is not of the exhaustion of body or mind, but of selfish loss of enthusiasm. Fortunately we have allies who have more to forget than we have: and although too many British and Americans will want to relapse too quickly into easier ways, there should remain enough alert minds to ensure that we do not lose what we have gained. Once the disarmament of Germany has been accomplished, the practical effort required to maintain it is comparatively small. Even in a democracy, the actual thinking is done by a comparatively small number of people: this is unfortunate but true. Our happiness and security may depend upon how far these people are able to persuade others to their will. If the most urgent question of the hour after victory should prove to be an additional 2 per cent on profits or an extra five cents an hour on wages, then the outlook is gloomy. It may be that our misfortunes will drive us towards a longer view; or, better still, we may be so convinced by sheer reason; in that case the outlook is very promising.

A third danger is very real in the minds of thousands of people today. A fair proportion among us was brought up on suspicion of Russia. Many folks, inspired by Russia's gallant fight, have now veered to the opposite tack. Others have not. Their view is quite clear. They appreciate Russian gallantry and tenacity as much as anybody; they are all-out in favour of maximum aid to Russia, recognising that her cause is ours. But afterwards? Here the fog of suspicion has still left some misty patches.

These honest doubters are prompted by one of Stalin's phrases: he constantly affirms that Russia is fighting against 'Hitlerite Germany,' whereas most of us in Europe are convinced that the issue is much deeper than that. Does not the phrase shed a light on Russia's post-war policy? it is argued. Is Stalin's real objective a Communist Germany?

Further consideration increases the apprehension. A German-Russian combination would be immensely powerful, and would certainly dominate Europe. The disarmament of Germany—the keystone of European security—would be impossible to maintain or even effect. Any future director of such a tremendous force, should he be impelled by thoughts of further domination, could plunge the world into war again.

This is a prospect which is anxiously apprehended by some of our own people: we must face it seriously. Yet on examination it loses many of its possibilities and dangers.

(*a*) It is contrary to all Stalin's pronouncements. He has agreed without reservation to the Atlantic Charter, including the disarmament of Germany: indeed, he has emphasised this latter point even more forcibly than Churchill himself.

(*b*) In a partnership between Germany and Russia, the industrial power would almost inevitably become the stronger, staffed as it was by a race of hard-working and efficient organisers and exploiters. Russia would certainly become the junior partner in the combination.

(*c*) According to some observers, there are no signs that Stalin is yet anxious to establish over-close contact with western powers. His propaganda has hitherto been based, naturally enough in his circumstances, on the glories of life under the Soviet compared with the misery and squalor in other lands. Potential trouble was recognised when Russian troops marched into the cities of Eastern Poland; so far from misery and squalor, they found a standard of life higher than their own. (This is no criticism of the Soviet's efforts to raise the standard of life in Russia. It is obvious that if a man has been persuaded to a view, and finds that it is wrong, he is more liable to discontent. Time is required for reorientation of the mind in Russia as well as in Britain.)

My own opinion is that the argument of Russian isolation has been exaggerated, and that in any case the outlook is likely to be clear after victory.

(*d*) The conduct of the Germans in occupied Russia has

been harsh beyond description. Neither Stalin nor his people are likely to forget in a hurry.

Almost every sign since Russia was attacked points to co-operation with Britain and the United States in the future world. Every appeal has been made to Russians, not Communists. Further, Russia has been cruelly ravaged by war. Certainly she will be in no mood for dramatic adventures. Instead, she has a great task of recovery in which she will need external help. Her post-war attitude is likely to be realist, and may prove a useful antidote to British sentimentality. Stalin knows as well as we do that a militarist Germany, even if it is labelled Communist, is a danger to Europe—and Russia. The Soviet régime will emerge from a victorious war firmly established: then some of its earlier ideas may be abandoned.

A second form of apprehension is that Communism will sweep all over Europe. This depends largely on how we face up to our post-war problems. Communism thrives on discontent. Further, it can present an almost religious appeal to men and women desperately anxious to see a better world. For Communism does not necessarily mean the present Russian system, with its police control and severe limitation of personal liberty. We *may* see a spread of Communism—unless its opponents have something better to offer.

v

I wish that some clever economist, or group of economists, would propound a plan for the post-war world which would implement the promises of 'equal access to raw materials,' and so on. Theoretically, this happy state has existed for a long time. Germany, for example, has always been able to buy raw materials in British colonies as easily as we did ourselves— always provided she had the necessary supplies of foreign currency. I wish that I knew enough about currencies to be as confident of a solution to commercial problems as I am of the possibility of settling the frontiers of Europe.

Obviously some form of material and international control

is essential. Production must be planned. Occasionally we read of the wilful destruction of hundreds of tons of coffee, and hold up our hands in horror at such waste. We are right, for there are hundreds of thousands of homes where an extra pound of coffee would be very welcome. Yet the time might come when everybody had enough coffee: there is a limit to the amount a man can or wants to drink. If, after this limit, producing countries still kept expanding their production, then obviously it would be necessary to destroy the surplus quantities. The more sensible method would be to restrict the plantation of coffee to the required area to meet consumption. The world *can* produce too much—even too much food.

Emergency planning will be necessary most of all immediately after victory. All over Europe, perhaps all over the world, there will be a serious shortage of many commodities. If competition were uncontrolled, all the nations would be outbidding one another for supplies, and the richest would win. It is obvious that war-time controls must be preserved for a long period: however little this may be welcomed by that section of the industrial community which thinks in terms of immediate advantages, it is ultimately to the benefit of all.

Although my object has been to present an outline of the new frontiers, economic problems are ineradicably intermingled. I have suggested, for example, that some millions of Germans shall be returned to their fatherland: at the same time German frontiers are likely to be restricted rather than expanded. This means a more intense industrialisation of Germany, to support a larger population on the same or smaller territory. The short-term, nationalist, revengeful argument is: 'Let the Germans go short: lower their standard of living—let the food which supplied 70 millions now suffice for 80 millions.' But any lowering of the standard of living in Germany involves almost automatically a reduction in the price of German goods—which would then undersell our own in foreign markets.

Our general economic aim should be to raise living standards all over the world. We cannot solve the problem of making worse conditions better by making better conditions worse.

I have suggested that a partial solution to some of our economic difficulties could be found in the raising of consumption power in Eastern Europe. I do not pretend that it is easy: indeed, many of the states involved are themselves on the verge or even in the early stages of industrialisation. This is a natural development: industry cannot be kept as the special preserve of a few countries.

Europe is too crowded. Many of our problems date back directly to the serious limitation of emigration. The agricultural population of most of the lands of Eastern Europe is already larger than the land can support. In Poland and all the Balkan states there are hundreds of thousands of surplus agricultural workers: peasant farms have been reduced to an uneconomic size. This means that the farmer ekes out a mere existence—he has no money to spare for foreign products.

There are only two solutions: emigration or industrialisation. In Russia the latter method was applied—the surplus agricultural labourers were diverted into industry. Such was the backward state of the country that to date Russia's problem has been that of shortage of labour rather than that of surplus; her problems are postponed until the day when all requirements are satiated. But industrialisation meant that hundreds of thousands of German and British workmen, who used to supply manufactured products to Russia, were thrown out of work.

In Poland the same process of industrialisation has begun: in the Balkan states it is contemplated. (In 1938 only 5 per cent of Balkan populations were employed in factories.) Work *must* be found for their men: the countries are poor: unemployment insurance benefit does not exist, and social services are of trivial extent. Unless we can rapidly raise the standard of life, we run the risk once again of being undersold by cheaper foreign labour: we should already have learned our lesson from Japan. The time has gone when economy was a matter of catch phrases: there exists such confusion as to deny a straight and easy road to prosperity. Even that popular phrase 'abolition of all customs barriers' has its dangers; if it were immediately applied, we might find Manchester cotton goods ousted from London shops by cheaper Polish cotton goods from Lodz. The one cliché which still retains its original force, and more, is that planning must replace indiscriminate competition.

Our primary problem is to increase consumption. How can it be done? By a European or a World Lease and Lend Act? Or a vast hire-purchase scheme? Or, in the first instance, by giving things away?

The standard of life can only be raised by persuading people that what they regarded as luxuries are really necessities. 'The world owes me a car' was an American slogan: so every man strove to raise his standard of life to include the ownership of a car—and an immense car-manufacturing industry developed in the United States.

There is a traditional story of American enterprise. Once, over a great area of China, people lived in hovels: by night, if there was illumination at all, it was provided by rushes; usually there was none. For years American oil companies strove to 'sell' the idea of oil lighting, but few Chinese were interested. Then one company made a present of an oil lamp to thousands of Chinese families. The effect was instantaneous: once they saw the advantages, they were determined to buy the necessary oil.

There is a tremendous demand for agricultural machinery in the Balkans, for example. The peasant farmers cannot afford to buy; they might, however, respond to a system of hire-purchase; they would certainly respond to a system of payment in kind. Our principal difficulties are not of production but of distribution. The economists have to work out some scheme of a more even spread: it may be that the richer countries will have to give a good deal to the poorer.

Foreign investment in the Balkans must be of a new character. Hitherto it has been so hazardous that financiers would only advance money if the chances of gain were very high. Returns of 30 or 40 per cent were not unknown: on the other hand, few Balkan countries ever repaid their debts in full. There has too often been a political issue behind the loans— British, French, German, Italian and American financiers competing in offering money, with ulterior motives suggested or condoned by their governments.

This method assisted the lamentable state of corruption in many Balkan states: half the loans were never expended on the objects for which they were advanced. Sometimes they helped to balance budgets: in most cases a considerable proportion went into the pockets of ministers and their officials. Drastic reform is essential in Balkan administration—and there are signs that it may come. The civil service of most southeastern states is not merely corrupt—it is ridiculously cumbersome in size. The tribal spirit so persists that any politician considers it a point of honour to provide jobs for his friends and relations: these in turn make what they can while their patrons are in office.

This pernicious system must end. It has led to abnormally high taxation in countries where incomes are ridiculously low. A Balkan peasant will grow enough grain to feed his family on the eternal *mamaliga*: his average income in spending money is sixty dollars *a year*. And out of this taxes must be paid!

The process of industrialisation in the Balkans is still in its infancy, but so far it has scarcely relieved the labour problem while at the same time making life more difficult for the agricultural workers. I have referred to the peasant longing for an iron plough—to us this is one of the simplest and most essential agricultural implements, but in the Balkans there are still over half a million wooden ploughs in current use. In Yugoslavia a firm started to manufacture iron ploughs: the government, imitating the methods of more 'advanced' countries, duly imposed a protective tariff. Thus the enterprising peasant who bought a British or German iron plough had to pay $10 duty on it—one-seventh of his annual income on duty alone —while the Yugoslav firm manufactured only fifty ploughs a year! Not all the troubles of the Balkans are due to misdrawn frontiers and jealous neighbours: these young countries have a lot to learn.

In the rural areas of Eastern Europe the main quarrel has never been that of capital and labour, but of town and country. The towns contribute only 20 per cent of the country's assets, but take 50 per cent of the national income. The peasant, almost illiterate, purely parochial in his outlook, exploited, over-patient, unorganised, carries the heavier weight of life. There are signs that he is awakening. The peasant parties of the Balkans are more than political organisations. They are spreading education and culture among their people: through their co-operative societies they will, if encouraged, revolutionise the economic condition of the village. If we could solve the problem of the poor peasant, Europe would be well set on the way towards industrial recovery. We shall have to try—not only the people of the Balkans, but ourselves.

I have anticipated great economic difficulties: yet they ought not to be insoluble. If we keep our heads, and if the states of the world co-operate in peace as the allies did in war, then the prospect may be bright.

We shall need courage and ideas. Even a person as little versed in economics as myself can see the anomalies in our present financial system, which keep the Balkan peasant short of clothing while our mills stand idle, and keep our unemployed short of food when the wheat of the Balkans rots on the ground or the fields lie untilled. Similarly, it needs no economist to see the fallacy of the notion that the war need be followed by a period of poverty. Thanks to our war effort, the soil of our island is cultivated more intensively than ever before; our productive system is in full operation, and could be switched from the needs of war to those of peace as easily as the shadow factories were switched from peace to war; our mineral supplies are far from exhaustion; we shall have a host of skilled men and women seeking work. If anything keeps us from supplying what our people need it must be some fault in our financial organisation.

I hold no brief for the noisy purveyors of economic nostrums so voluble on our street corners. But among the chaff they scatter so freely there may be grains of corn. We must not refuse consideration of ideas merely because they are novel.

VI

It has often been argued that the greatest obstacle to a United States of Europe is the lack of a common language. Our babel of tongues has more than once been blamed for our over-frequent wars. The argument is fallacious. In mediaeval days there *was* a universal language for educated men—Latin: but its use did not prevent the most vicious spate of wars in history. In our own time states of South America have fought freely, despite their common use of the Spanish tongue.

In spite of this, obviously a common language would be an enormous advantage to international understanding—it is perhaps no accident that Esperanto was banned in the totalitarian countries. More than one of the artificial languages (Esperanto, Ido, Ino) has many advantages—ease of learning, simplicity of grammar, logic, adaptability and melodious sound. Yet the fact remains that after fifty years of vigorous propaganda and intense idealism, none of them has made serious headway.

The alternative to an artificial international language is the extension of some national language for internationl use. The objections are many and obvious—intricate grammar, over-rich vocabularies and, above all, racial prejudice. For some time French was the language of culture and diplomacy, but its use is scarcely likely to be extended: nor is that of German, widespread as is its use in Central and South-Eastern Europe. Russian is too complicated, and has little use outside the Soviet territories.

We can suggest, without being accused of Chauvinism, that English is best suited to international use. It is already the language of the British Commonwealth and the United States of America, and it is taught as a secondary language in many lands. It is expressive, comparatively simple, adaptable, in an advanced state of evolution (shown in its shedding of inflexions); it is the key to a mighty literature and a multitude of scientific and technical works.

Its greatest disadvantage is its abominable system of spelling —despair of many an Englishman, to say nothing of foreigners! With this difficulty removed by the adoption of phonetic spelling, English has important claims for use as a world language. In China there are of course dozens of races and tongues: members of the different tribes often converse with one another—in pidgin English.

There is no need to descend to the expressions which sound like cross-talk comedy. Yet the wide use of pidgin English does show that a vocabulary far narrower than our own will suffice for the necessities of intercourse. The vocabulary of many a Balkan peasant is limited to six hundred words, and with them he manages to say everything he needs to say. Obviously, a simplified English would meet the case of international necessity, and the necessary work of preparation has already been done. The vocabulary and grammar of our language have already been stripped to their bare bones as Basic English.

By this scheme, apart from technical terms already in international use, English is reduced to a thousand fundamental words! The language thus formed sounds somewhat stilted to ears accustomed to the cadences of literary English, but it is capable of expressing the most complex ideas, and is very simple to learn. (For examination, study the New Testament recently produced in Basic English.)

Of course, Basic English would only be an *auxiliary* tongue for international intercourse—there is no suggestion that it should supplant any language, and certainly not literary English. It would be taught to all children, even in elementary schools. Its universal use in international intercourse, over a period, might have profound effects. It could never solve the problems of Europe by itself, but it might prove of great service in the maintenance of peace once attained.

VII

Since I wrote this book, the United States has entered the war. I was always confident that she would, but of course could not foresee the mode of entry. It gives me new hope and immense encouragement—not merely for victory in war, but for collaboration in peace. It is not correct to say that American isolationism has been killed by the treacherous Japanese attack, but it has been deprived of most of its force. The isolationism which revives after the war will be only a shadow of what it might have been.

In the early days of the war there was some irritation in this country about the United States. The Americans had perceived the character of the Nazi menace before we did, had proclaimed it clearly to the world, and now apparently proposed to do nothing about it. Indeed, their neutrality legislation in some respects favoured our opponents.

Europe has taken small trouble to examine the state of mind of the American citizen. He is primarily and entirely an American: the British have fought and ventured all over the world; he has confined himself to his own continent. His country for a long time has been able to progress independent of foreign powers. Only the development of modern communications—and the growing naval force of Japan—brought the United States into the world. The very nature of the American population, with its sentimental links with most countries in Europe, forbade over-intimate contact with European problems—lest the squabbles of Europe might transfer themselves to the United States.

Foreign policy was dominated by the sentiment in Washington's farewell address: 'The great rule of conduct for us, in regard to foreign nations, is in extending our commercial relations, to have with them as little political connection as possible.' The theme was developed by a subsequent president, Jefferson, who warned his fellow countrymen against 'entangling alliances.' The policy was admirable in its day, when the United States could stand aside from the rest of the world: today she cannot.

Europeans experienced the same exasperation in the first years of the last war. From enlightened Americans we received spiritual support, for the flame of freedom always burned fiercely among them: so strongly, indeed, that an event which played an important part in bringing the United States into the war was not only the sinking of American ships, but the fall of the Tsardom, prime opponent of liberty.

With their sentimental and crusading spirit—considerably more marked than with us—the United States flung herself into the war, and ensured victory considerably earlier than it might have come. Then came disillusion. The crusaders had imagined an immediate democratic Europe: instead, the great war was succeeded by a period of minor wars; nor did Europe appear to be very grateful for American aid. Isolationism had always been strong: after victory it gained tremendously in influence. The President had lost most of his backing, and it was a disillusioned nation which agreed to a separate peace with Germany. The failure to 'make the world safe for democracy' was preached by the isolationists as an argument for their creed; they overlooked or ignored the fact that the United States had contributed very effectively to its failure by refusing to enter the League of Nations—which had to be universal to achieve real results. Failure in due course of countries to keep up their instalments of war debts convinced many more Americans that they had been wrong to enter Europe: again, they did not perceive that they had contributed largely to the economic crisis which made further payments impossible. We have already noted how the stoppage of immigration aggravated many of Europe's problems:

the establishment of a system of high tariffs set a fashion which helped to bring calamity.

Understanding between Britain and the United States suffered a set-back through the abdication of King Edward VIII. To us the marital status of Mrs. Simpson was the determining factor—we simply could not imagine a *divorcée* being consecrated in Westminster Abbey or sitting on Britain's throne. To the Americans, accustomed as they are to easy divorce, her status seemed of no importance whatever. They therefore looked for our virtual rejection of her in other directions, in a snobbish contempt for 'commoners' or a patriotic prejudice against 'foreigners'—suggestions both wide of the mark. This misunderstanding might easily have had serious consequences for the welfare of the world, but it was fortunately overcome by the popularity which our present King and Queen earned when they visited the United States.

American public opinion is rather like our own in its movements impelled by sentiment. Often it is better informed, however: regular readers of the leading American papers could gain a very accurate picture of what was going on in Europe, for the quality of foreign reporting was high. Because they saw the character of the Nazi régime before we did, they were irritated. They had helped us to outlaw militant Germany in 1918: why were we allowing her to become militaristic again? The failure of the British and the French to act early lost us many friends: the policy of appeasement was anathema to men who saw the true state of affairs in Germany more clearly than did our leaders, and it played into the hands of the isolationists. If we were not prepared to move, why should they?

Munich convinced millions of Americans that we never should move. President Roosevelt, in spite of all his prestige, was unable to secure a repeal of the legislation enforcing an embargo on the shipment of munitions to belligerents—legislation passed so that no American should make financial gain out of war. Not until after the actual outbreak of war was it possible to secure the most moderate amendment. As the months passed, isolationists made great play with the term 'a phoney war.'

Then came the collapse of France—and, with it, a real prospect of a Nazi Europe. At the same time it became plain, in dramatic fashion, that there was nothing 'phoney' about Britain's determination to fight on until the end, whatever it might cost. (The Americans knew better than we did how dangerous was the situation in the summer of 1940.) The United States was aroused: conscription was introduced—and at the presidential election both candidates pledged their determination to aid Britain to the utmost.

President Roosevelt is more than one of the great figures of our day. History will acclaim him as a leader almost without rival. His own thoughts and opinions were perfectly clear, but he had to carry a diversified nation of 130 million people with him. This he did with consummate skill and statesmanship. If to us his progress seemed slow, it was very sure.

From the moment of his re-election, if not from the beginning of the war, I considered American entry into the war as inevitable. There were millions of Americans who did not share the vision of their leader: some of these would never have been convinced by argument, for there is no complaint so deliberate as short sight.

The Japanese attack solved many problems. I had pictured the majority of Americans, irritated beyond sufferance by Nazi brutality, following their president into war; they would be opposed by an important minority—who would object to the brutality just as forcibly, but who would claim that Europe's troubles were her own—that, even if the United States intervened, Europe would be just as unruly afterwards. On entry into war, these people would have dropped their opposition as good patriots should; but immediately victory was won they would certainly have revived it.

Intervention might have followed from one of two sources. When the President ordered the Navy to shoot, there was an obvious risk of grave incidents. Even these might not have aroused the necessary degree of unity essential for modern total war. But Japan was quite a different proposition. In the autumn of 1941 it was estimated that 30 per cent of Americans were still isolationist so far as Europe was concerned. Not 3 per cent were isolationist as regards Japan! For two generations there has been serious rivalry between the United States and Japan, always with the prospect of a serious clash. Hence the humiliation recorded by observers in America at the treacherous Japanese attack while carrying on negotiations—humiliation that the United States should have been caught by the same trick against which she had so often warned others.

It will prove a very dangerous humiliation—for Japan! The capture of a number of Pacific islands will never win the war. It will take time to mobilise the immense resources of the United States, but then they will be irresistible: nor can the industrial life of America be seriously disturbed by enemy action. No one will envy the Japanese when the hour of retribution comes: and no one will pity them.

The character of the attack is said to have killed isolationism in a night. I doubt this: it was far too firmly rooted. There is a remarkable degree of unity in the United States today—the feeling we experienced after Dunkirk, when a democracy shows itself in its grandest mood. But after victory there will still be Americans who want to keep clear of Europe.

The close Anglo-American co-operation and comradeship which will develop as the war progresses has revived dreams of an English-speaking federation. The idea is excellent, subject to two essential conditions: (a) that its implications are fully understood, and wholeheartedly accepted by a substantial majority in both countries. There is no indication that such is the case today; the idea is only lightly held in most British circles—where, however, active and practical co-operation with the United States to the utmost limit is favoured, so that more drastic thoughts might follow; (b) that it does not involve the retirement of Britain from Europe. There are some people who would use an Anglo-American Federation to this end. It would not only be impossible, but immoral. The two countries between them control a large proportion of the world's goods; it would be criminal if they declined to share these with less favoured nations.

For my own part, I believe that the United States will play an increasingly important part in world affairs; and that isolationism will gradually die—killed by cold logic, not the sentimental shock of battle. The promise for future peace is far stronger than it was in 1918. With Britain, the United States and Russia carrying on their war-time collaboration into peace, there is every prospect of a fair and firm settlement of European problems.

The Japanese onslaught affects another of our considerations. In some quarters it is held that Japan will surrender the day after Hitler's collapse. This is doubtful: the Japanese leaders are desperate and may fight to the last. Thus, after we have beaten Germany, we may have to gather our forces for a final onslaught on Japan. That is to say, we should still have a powerful army in being while the preliminary resettlement of Europe was being made.

VIII

Also since this book was written and published in Britain, I have made my first journey to the United States. I came home encouraged by what I saw in the factories and the shipyards, where the instruments of victory are being forged: thrilled at my experiences in camps and airfields, mingling with the men who will stand side by side with ours on the battlefield: invigorated by the contacts I made, from president to taxi-driver.

Yet my greatest thrill came not from material things, but from matters of the mind. I had to correct some erroneous impressions—like most Englishmen, I had under-estimated the isolationist influences. But I was addressing audiences across the United States, from coast to coast; they had a choice of subjects—I could tell them exciting spy stories, or they could grill me with questions about that good old chopping block, the shortcomings of Britain. The majority of audiences, however, chose Post-War Europe. Of universities and young peoples' clubs, *all* without exception wanted to discuss the re-settlement of Europe. The keenness and atmosphere were most stimulating.

In Europe no one has ever doubted that the United States will play a worthy part in the winning of victory. One question only is asked; it comes especially from the smaller nations. 'Will it be the same as in 1919? Will America help us to win the war, and then slide off and leave us to lose the peace?'

No one can answer that question for certain. My own opinion is that the answer will be no. When victory is assured, or at critical moments of the war, isolationists will re-emerge (in Britain as well as in America) preaching their easy and selfish creed, which appears to offer immediate advantages, but which leads to ultimate disaster. On the other hand, there is a very firm feeling among all ranks of Americans that this sort of thing must never be allowed to happen again—and a realisation that peace can only be secured by universal and long-term guarantees. I found an intense eagerness to know more of the problems of Europe which had to be solved; nor were my audiences frightened by their complexity.

I noted one small difficulty. Only a minority of Americans appear to appreciate the intense nationalism which still pervades Europe—this in spite of the intense nationalism which pervades America. Too many people argued, 'The Greeks must do this,' or 'The Poles must give up that,' not appreciating that Greeks and Poles are fighting for freedom to live as Greeks and Poles. It is a good criterion of any settlement that you should not ask other people to do what you would not be prepared to do yourself.

Too often the solution suggested was purely economic— our old friend, the Brazilian coffee which had to be burned, was trotted out regularly. I do not deny the importance of economic solutions; on the contrary, I rate them very highly, but by themselves they will do little or nothing. Let us be certain of this—no Pole would be satisfied by a cup of Brazilian coffee while he could not live as a Pole in a free Poland; he would rather be without coffee at all.

Often, too, I heard the old comparison between Europe and the United States. It is more than strained; the basis of comparison does not exist. Poles and Greeks came to America to become Americans; in Europe they remain Poles and Greeks, since there is no such thing as a European. One day there will be, if we are wise, but that day has scarcely yet dawned.

The appeasement and rehabilitation of Europe will depend as largely on American opinion and action as on any other factor. If the isolationists were to gain control, then we can only begin to prepare for World War III. The sincere and intense interest convinced me that America is more likely to be dominated by different views.

Some of the isolationists are already deeply disturbed by the trend of events. If the close Anglo-American collaboration impelled by the war were to be continued into the peace, then future prospects for the world would be very bright— but the influence of the isolationists would recede. A red herring is being drawn across the path, therefore, in the form of intense criticism of British colonial policy. This criticism is often based on information years or even generations out of date, and is usually voiced by men belonging to business circles which would gain substantially if the United States could gain control of British (or Dutch) colonies, especially in the Pacific. Yet, even this campaign, which scarcely helps the progress of the United Nations to victory, is having one effect unforeseen by its sponsors. In 1919 the United States refused to accept any mandates or colonial responsibilities; ideas may be different when this war is through. But a country which is being fed on stories of natives being exploited by British big business is not likely to undertake new responsibilities in order that natives can be exploited by American big business.

It is unfortunate that Dr. Goebbels has so many unwitting

assistants in both countries. If ever we needed an argument in favour of close Anglo-American collaboration, we have it in the desperate German efforts to divide us. If Britain and America stand firmly together, then the German leaders know not only that they cannot win World War II, but that they will never be able to prepare for World War III.

IX

Every word I have written depends upon absolute victory over the Axis Powers. Sometimes foreign visitors are amazed at the universal and unshakable British confidence. It is a source of weakness—it tends to a slackening of effort in quieter times; and of strength, for our confidence is so firm that we do not know when we are beaten, so recover from an impossible situation. It seems that only an emergency can raise the best out of us; but that best is very good. Yet the situation is sometimes tragic, for if we produced our best earlier, the emergency might never arise.

No one can prophesy to what extent we shall learn the lesson of our past failures. There will probably always be a majority of people only interested in parochial matters; but I believe that the size of the more important minority is rapidly increasing. Classes on world affairs are a feature at British secondary and public schools: in the services, the proportion of men interested is very high. During 1941 over a quarter of a million people attended lectures I gave on topical subjects; their keenness and the quality of the subsequent questions was very encouraging.

'Eternal vigilance is the price of liberty'; and of peace. When victory is achieved, there is much to be done: the reshaping of Europe is only our first task. Every effort of our thought and imagination will be demanded—even now, every moment which can be spared from the essential organisation for victory. A military triumph would be an empty success if we did not know how to use it. Surely it is not too much to hope that men and women who have given so much in war will sustain their efforts to preserve the peace which was their goal!

A great obligation lies on those who believe that the peace of the world is our main objective, that at all costs our present catastrophe must never be allowed to happen again. They will have to convince the lukewarm and the uninterested. It needs a vast amount of hard work. (In many countries the Communists have been able to secure an influence out of all proportion to their numbers by their capacity for action. If secretaries or committee workers are wanted, they are forthcoming: the rest of us sit back, glad that somebody else will do all the spade-work—and then we grumble because Communists are found in so many key positions.)

Our task is far more difficult than that Hitler faced. He told the Germans what they wanted to believe; our doctrine is not so comforting—we have to turn the British into Europeans, and both British and Americans into world citizens. We have to make them realise that Transylvania and the Polish Corridor mean more to *them* than Hollywood and football; that we have to pay dearly in cash and comforts, today and tomorrow, for our failure to be interested in Europe during the inter-war years; and that we shall have to pay a substantial share towards the rehabilitation of Europe.

I am optimistic; if our many ideas, some incoherent and some unexpressed, can be concentrated into a practical policy, supported by a large majority of thinking people, then the future is bright. The word 'practical' is most important: I have tried to follow it in the suggestions made in this book: suggestions which plan to lay the foundations of the new Europe, no more. From the point where I leave off, a vast amount of planning, thought, sympathy, goodwill and good faith is demanded. The leadership of Europe is likely to devolve to no small extent upon the British; they must be prepared for unusual activity—practical work, not sentimental dreams. Peace will never be secured by resolutions condemning war.

I am cheered not only by the changing attitude of an influential section of the British people, but by the character and outlook of some of our leaders. A few hours before writing these final words, I called in turn on two of the Foreign Ministers of Allied governments at present in this country. Both were men of long and intimate experience; both represented countries overrun by the enemy and teeming with problems. And both, spontaneously and unprompted, remarked that they were exceedingly pleased with Mr. Churchill—not merely because he was a dynamic war leader, but because of his wide knowledge, realistic appreciation and far-sighted outlook on Europeon affairs. In the last ten years I have interviewed dozens of Foreign Ministers, but this is the first time that any of them have ever admired the knowledge, realism and far sight of a British Prime Minister!

We shall need all these things. The task of rebuilding Europe is colossal, yet it is well within our powers; nor do we face it alone. A greater task is the maintenance of the edifice we build. On Armistice Day we used to renew a vow that we would not break faith with those who slept in Flanders fields. We did break faith; not wilfully, but carelessly. This, too, must not happen again. Today our dead are scattered in every corner of the world; we owe it to them, to ourselves and to our children; the spirit which is prepared to sacrifice life and limb at the call of war is surely prepared to give of the fruits of mind and energy at the call of peace.

The greatest incentive is the consideration of our ethical war aims; sometimes it is easier to visualise the horror of the alternatives following defeat. It is worth while sitting down occasionally to think over the deeper promptings of our cause. They have been admirably expressed in President Roosevelt's 'Four Freedoms'—freedom of speech, freedom of religion, freedom from want, and freedom from fear. If we can attain these, we shall not merely have achieved a new Europe, but a new world.

INDEX